Victoria Finlay

Victoria Finlay studied social anthropology at St Andrew's University and William & Mary College, Virginia, before working for Reuters in London and Scandinavia. She spent twelve years as a journalist in Hong Kong, five of them as arts editor of *The South China Morning Post*, when she also presented a weekly radio programme. She now lives in England, and divides her time between researching her next book and working for an international environmental charity, www.arcworld.org. Her first book *Colour, Travels through the Paintbox*, was published by Hodder & Stoughton in 2002. *Jewels: A Secret History* is her third book.

Victoria Finlay

Jewels

A Secret History

SCEPTRE

First published in Great Britain in 2005 by Hodder & Stoughton
A division of Hodder Headline

A Sceptre paperback

1

A CIP catalogue record for this title is available from the British Library

ISBN: 978 0 340 83014 7
ISBN: 0 340 83014 X

Typeset in Monotype Sabon by
Rowland Phototypesetting Ltd,
Bury St Edmunds, Suffolk

Printed and bound by
Clays Ltd, St Ives plc

Hodder Headline's policy is to use papers that are natural,
renewable and recyclable products and made from wood grown
in sustainable forests. The logging and manufacturing processes are expected
to conform to the environmental regulations of the country of origin.

Hodder & Stoughton Ltd
A division of Hodder Headline
338 Euston Road
London NW1 3BH

For Martin.

And for Patrick, my father.
Please stay with us a little longer.

Contents

Isle of Lewis
R. Oykel
R. Ythan
Grampian Mts
R. Tay
Perth
THE FIT COAST
JUTLAND
Hadrian's Wall
Whitby
North Sea
Catterick
York
Ba
R. Oa
Bristol
London
Amsterdam
SAXONY
Cheddar Gorge
Portsmouth
Antwerp
R. Elbe
Bruges
Cologne
Habachtal
Isle of Wight
Idar-Oberstein
Prague
Paris
Versailles
Linz
Vie
BURGUNDY
R. Rhine
Zurich
Atlantic Ocean
Geneva
Venice
Trieste
Marseilles
Santiago de Compostela
Rome
Madrid
Naples
Toledo
Sardinia
R. Achates
Sicil
Mediter

A EUROPEAN
TREASURE MAP

0   m
0   kilon

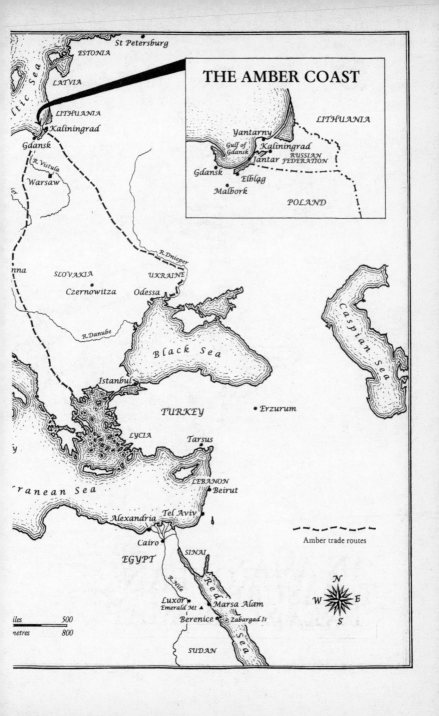

THE AMBER COAST

St Petersburg
ESTONIA
Baltic Sea
LATVIA
LITHUANIA
Kaliningrad
Gdansk
R.Vistula
Warsaw

LITHUANIA
Yantarny
Gulf of Gdansk
Kaliningrad
Jantar
RUSSIAN FEDERATION
Gdansk
Elblag
Malbork
POLAND

Vienna
SLOVAKIA
Czernowitza
R.Dnieper
UKRAINE
Odessa

R.Danube

Black Sea

Caspian Sea

Istanbul

TURKEY
• Erzurum

LYCIA
Tarsus

LEBANON
Beirut

Mediterranean Sea
Alexandria
Tel Aviv
Cairo
SINAI
EGYPT
R.Nile
Red Sea
Luxor
Emerald Mt ▲
Marsa Alam
Berenice
Zabargad Is

Amber trade routes

N
W E
S

SUDAN

miles   500
netres   800

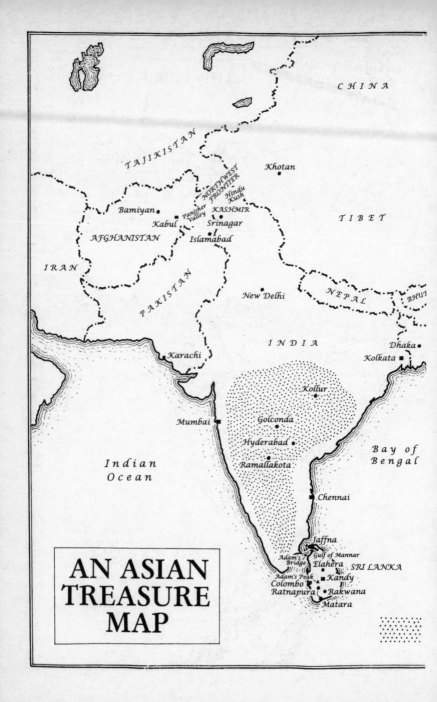

AN ASIAN TREASURE MAP

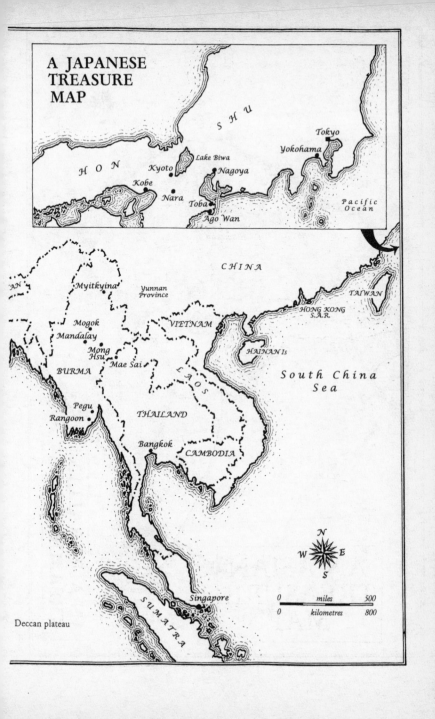

A JAPANESE TREASURE MAP

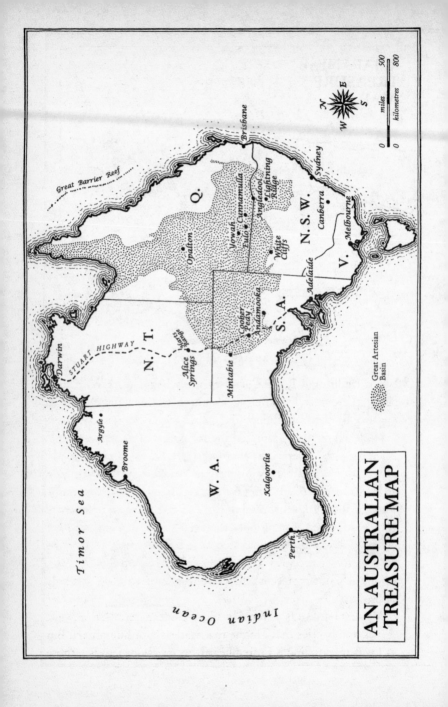

AN AUSTRALIAN
TREASURE MAP

Beginning the Search

'I seem to have been only like a boy playing on the sea shore,
and diverting myself in now and then finding a smoother
pebble or a prettier shell than ordinary, whilst the great
ocean of truth lay all undiscovered before me.'

SIR ISAAC NEWTON

'I'm not suggesting we stop analysing stones, but am just
proposing a better balance. The heart of our product is its
beauty and the romance surrounding it. Today's gemmology
is too often a heartless shell. We are selling illusion.
We need to become conjurors.'

RICHARD HUGHES[1]

When traditional Russian icon painters begin work on a new
piece, they start by covering a simple wooden panel with a
mixture of chalk and glue. The whiteness will shine out from
the finished painting, representing the purity of the human soul.
Then they give their saints shape and colour, using paints made
of traditional materials – bright blue from Afghan mines, pale
green from corroded copper, deep red from Spanish mercury.
Then, if the icon is a special one, they cover most of the picture
with gold, often leaving only the saint's face to peer out of a
little window. And the final step, if it is a very special icon indeed, is to set precious stones around it. They do this because,
while the paint represents the earth, the jewels are the symbols
of heaven.[2]

My first book was inspired by those paint materials: the twigs,
stones and beetles that are the raw materials of human art. But
as I was researching it I often heard stories about jewels – those

other, more famous, sources of colour. I heard of how people were once hanged for picking up amber pebbles from the beaches of northern Europe; how the deepest colour for black was named after a rare jewel formed by the same process as coal; how Christopher Columbus was thrown into prison for not admitting to his royal sponsors that he had found pearls; and, perhaps most extraordinary of all, I heard how, with recent discoveries of how to make gem-quality diamonds in laboratories, the market for the most precious stones is tottering on the edge of change.

And then I was given a ring. It is an engagement ring, and its three small square stones – one pale green, like chewing gum, one dark green, like a sea-worn bottle, and one deep red, like a smooth brick – are made of glass. They don't have a carat value like most jewels but they do have a wonderful story. They are eight hundred years old, and they were scraped from a wall almost eighty years ago, by a boy who later became a bishop, in a place whose sacred beauty had affected the lives of entire empires.

Perhaps the greatest church in Christendom is the Hagia Sophia[3] in Istanbul – which was once Constantinople, the capital of Byzantine Christianity for many centuries. But in 1453 the Muslims captured the city, and the Hagia Sophia became a mosque. This was greatly resented by many people over the centuries, including one Christian boy who grew up there in the 1920s. He and his friends sometimes pretended to be Muslim boys and went up to the women's section in the gallery, put their hands behind their backs and pretended to pray while they prised out the mosaic stones from the wall to sell to tourists in the marketplace. When this boy grew up he became a priest, then a metropolitan, or Orthodox bishop, and he forgot his childish mischief. But one day, some years ago when he was very old, he found his three last stones and gave them to my fiancé. Later, when we decided to make them into an engagement ring, they became jewels in their own right – and a reminder to me of how the most precious thing about stones in a jewellery box is not always their rarity, their size or their perfection. It is their stories.

So, with my new ring on my finger, I set off on journeys to find them – not so much the gems as the stories behind them. The search took me to the greatest gem fair in the world; to the ancient City of Jewels in Sri Lanka; to Burma to visit the fabled ruby mines of Mogok; to the Japanese village where a young noodle-seller dreamed of growing pearls in oysters; to Antwerp's busy diamond district; and to California, to meet a man whose father 'invented' emeralds, and who himself has found a way to make perfect yellow diamonds.

This book is, mostly, written in praise of small things. There are a few boulders in its pages, but they are really just for show. Even the biggest jewels are mostly rather small: the word in English comes from the Old French for 'little joys' and in gem terms the phrase 'hen's egg' usually means gigantic. The book is also, largely, a celebration of mineral things. Only jet, coral and the creatures that reluctantly make up the insides of some rare pearls have ever been alive, while other prized 'stones', including amber, and plant-opals and ordinary pearls, have exuded and/or been extruded from living things. But most gems are crystals that have formed in the depths of the earth and emerged millions – or in one case hundreds – of years later, with a beauty for which men and women have, on occasion, been prepared to commit theft, treason, torture and murder.

I had expected to find good anecdotes but what I had not expected to find was an industry in crisis. There has always been some fakery in the business of stones – it is its nature – but never before have so many good fakes and improvement treatments been available, as well as a whole new technology producing synthetic stones, which are made up of the same constituents as natural ones and are often so good that even the experts struggle to tell the difference. 'I'm a jewellery appraiser,' said a woman I met at a major gems conference, 'and I'm very scared.'

In the course of my research I found that although, of course, some rare stones have amazing and frightening dynastic tales, every jewel, however small or flawed, has its story: about the earth that was excavated to retrieve it, the families who depended on it, the people who designed the cutting method, the others who bought or were given it, and the meanings and properties attributed to it. Whole human, geological and cultural histories are wrapped up in every stone we wear or desire, even if it is only an imitation. So while in one way it is the stones and jewels themselves, found in mines and oceans, and occasionally in tombs, wrecks and secret hoards, that are the 'buried treasure' of the title, the other hidden treasures are the cultural layers of meaning and fascination that can always be found wrapped around them.

Even my decision to write this book has a strange story. In the spring of 2002 I was in Hong Kong, where I lived, finishing writing *Colour* and at the same time preparing a proposal for this follow-up book about gems. One night I received a phone call from my partner: his father had died suddenly of a heart-attack. We went to join his family in England and stayed for several weeks, through the condolences, funeral arrangements and grief. Derek had been an Anglican clergyman, and the stories that emerged of how his enthusiasm and belief, stubbornness and love had changed so many people's lives were deeply affecting. In the middle of this my partner and I went for a walk by the Thames near Oxford. Writing a book didn't seem terribly important any more, I said. Stories about buried treasure seemed so frivolous. It didn't have to be that, my partner pointed out, reminding me of my earlier excitement that the stories of gems – with their striving and greed, beauty and marvels – had so many levels. On one level, they were stories of human nature, on another the story of the earth and its formations, and on yet another they were a marvellous spiritual metaphor. He also reminded me of how supportive his father had been of the idea. 'If he could, I'm sure he'd tell you that you must do it,' he said. At that moment, as we stood looking at the river, a small canal boat called *Little Gem* went by.

I learned later that it was rare for *Little Gem* to be on that stretch of the Thames: she is a weekend hire barge based near Rugby, and only very occasionally finds herself so far south.[4] But even at the time it seemed too nice a coincidence to ignore: next to his family and his church, Derek's greatest passion had been canals and canal boats. Not many books have been written because of the random passing of a barge on a river, but this is one. I hope you enjoy it.

Author's Note

In 1802 the wealthy Viennese banker Jacob Friedrich van der Null bought up eleven of Europe's top mineral collections, and decided he wanted them to be catalogued and classified. He selected a young German mineralogist called Friedrich Mohs, whose only serious work experience to date had been as a pit foreman in the Neudorf silver mines. Mohs wrote ample notes on the different stones' brittleness, specific gravity, magnetism, electricity, taste, odour and hardness. The most difficult one to measure was hardness. He puzzled for a long time about how he could quantify how much harder a lump of topaz is than a nugget of gold, or how much harder a diamond is than everything else.

Mohs' genius lay in realising that he had been approaching the problem from the wrong direction. Instead of finding a way of determining the absolute hardness of minerals, he decided to develop a comparative scale instead. So he chose ten minerals 'of which every preceding one is scratched by that which follows it', and gave them each a number according to his new scratching order. The softest was talc, which scored one, while the hardest was diamond, which therefore got ten. Everything else came somewhere in the middle. Glass turned out to have a value of just over five, and Mohs soon discovered that so-called 'organic' gemstones, including jet, pearl and amber, were always softer than glass, while most mineral gems were harder. He acknowledged that the values were arbitrary, diamond at ten being several times harder than rubies at nine, but the system was at least easy to use. You can do it at home: anything that can be scratched by a fingernail is below two; anything that takes a mark from a pocket-knife blade is below five; anything that can scratch quartz is above seven. Even today Mohs' scale is an important element in gem classification. It is the logic behind the organisation of this book, and it is also a useful thing to know before choosing a gemstone. Diamonds, rubies and sapphires are extremely durable and therefore good for rings; emeralds at eight are a little softer, while amber at around 2.5 will easily lose its polish and is usually better worn as earrings, or a necklace.

I

Amber

2–2.5

'In the sea of the changeable winds, his merchants fished
for pearls. In the sea where the North Star culminates, they
fished for yellow amber.'
Inscription on an obelisk erected by a KING OF NINEVEH

'If the insect could speak it would certainly have modified all
the knowledge about the history of the distant past.'
IMMANUEL KANT, *on seeing a fly trapped in amber.*[1]

In the ancient Cheddar Gorge of Somerset in England, there is
a huge cavern. Since it was first discovered more than a century
ago it has yielded many rare artefacts and bones from the
ancient past, including even a complete seated skeleton, nine
thousand years old. But in 1950 this place, named 'Gough's
Cave' after the Victorian sea-captain who found it, also yielded
what is perhaps the oldest piece of traded gem-type material
ever discovered. It is dark red and rather dirty, like a scuffed
piece of translucent toffee, and it is almost the size of a dozen
credit cards stacked together.[2] It is a piece of amber and it was
traded at least twelve and a half thousand years ago. It looks
an unlikely treasure, but treasure it is because it is possibly the
first indication we have today of a human fascination with
amber that has lasted since prehistoric times.[3]

At the time of its discovery there was no way to ascertain
where the amber in Gough's Cave had come from – whether
from Britain (some rare pieces of native amber had been found
on the Isle of Wight)[4] or further afield. However, fourteen years

later a professor at Vassar College in New York came up with the answer. Using dental equipment designed for tooth fillings, he ground up a tiny fragment of the amber, and then observed how it absorbed infrared light. He determined that it was of Baltic origin[5] and was therefore around forty million years old.[6]

This was no huge surprise: most of the world's amber is from the Baltic area of northern Europe. But how could the amber have got into Gough's Cave so long ago? Today a small amount of amber is washed up every year on eastern English beaches, but when the Gough's Cave piece arrived, Britain was still linked to the rest of Europe by a vast land-bridge, which only disappeared around eight and a half thousand years ago. Similarly the Baltic was not a sea but a huge freshwater lake, and it remained enclosed by land until the North Sea crashed through Denmark around 5500 BC. So, for that little piece of amber to travel the hundreds of kilometres from its place of origin to Somerset, it must have been carried there: by human hands.

Perhaps it was a one-off piece, kept in a pouch by a single long-distance migrant, but it is more likely, given the distance involved, that it got there in a complicated series of trades.[7] The amber would have been handed from one early merchant to another, swapped for food, weapons, flints or furs, and its presence in the Somerset cave was the earliest evidence of what would become an extensive trading network across Europe: the Amber Route.

To follow it back, we will travel east, across what are now the southern English counties, covered then with balmier forests and plains, and over the ancient land-bridge into what is now northern France or the Netherlands, which were then on higher ground. We will continue into northern Germany, then further north towards Denmark or perhaps east, to the extended flatlands of the Vistula delta in Poland, which for thousands of years has been the most productive source of amber in the world.[8] Amber trading happened here in such a frenzy that it has been said to have hastened the arrival of the Bronze Age in Baltic Europe. And in addition to the piece found in Gough's Cave there is evidence in ancient tombs and caves all over Europe, and even in North Africa and the Middle East, that Baltic amber travelled for many kilometres, from Stone Age times to now. The height of its mystery was the time of the Ancient Greeks, who said that King Menelaus' palace was lined with it, and it was almost equal in its magnificence to the Kingdom of Heaven.[9]

But why? Nowadays amber is often seen as a poor cousin to the other treasures of the jewellery box. It tends to be light, soft, cheap and not very rare at all. But accident, history and some remarkable physical qualities have meant that it has some-times been valued more highly than gold. It so intrigued early physicists that they named one of the most extraordinary natu-ral phenomena in the universe after it; and in its time it has inspired treasure-seekers, dictators, thieves, crusaders, scientists, madmen and film-makers. For some it has been a proof of God's existence; for others it has confirmed the reverse.

Mysterious Origins

The only thing the Ancient Greeks knew about amber was that it came from very far away, from a place, as a king of Nineveh had inscribed on an obelisk, 'where the North Star culminates'. Their taciturn suppliers did not enlighten them. The Phoenicians dealt in amber throughout the Mediterranean and as far away as modern Iraq. They were a nation of traders and inventors, based in what is now Lebanon, and like many gem dealers today, would not reveal their sources. The captain of one Phoenician ship was so determined to keep secret the origin of his tin that when a rival tried to follow him, he scuttled his own vessel on a sandbank, then lured his pursuers to a similar fate.[10] The buyers of the ancient world therefore relied on myth and rumour to tell them where their amber came from[11] and for a while their main clue came from a Greek legend about a boy racer, whose failure to control his vehicle almost led to the total destruction of the world.

According to legend, Phaeton was the son of the sun god. Every day he watched his father driving his chariot across the heavens, and every day he begged to have a go. One day he had his chance. His seven sisters helped to harness the horses and he set out with all the confidence of a pampered teenager. But tragedy struck, as it always does in ancient myths. The joy-rider soon lost control and the chariot veered off-course. It seemed that the world would be destroyed, but Zeus, the king of the gods, sent a thunderbolt to kill the boy and stop the damage. Phaeton's body came to earth beside a north-flowing river, which the barbarian tribes called the Eridanus. As punishment for helping him, his sisters were turned into black poplars. As they wept over the fate of their beautiful, arrogant brother, their tears fell into the river and became amber.[12]

The fifth century BC writer Herodotus thought this story was rubbish. It wasn't the girls who changed into trees that worried him, or even the magic chariot, but the river that flowed north-wards out of Europe that really aroused his suspicions. It was an extraordinary concept for the Greeks, for whom almost every known river flowed into the Mediterranean. 'I do not admit there is a river that the barbarians call Eridanus, which flows into the sea towards the north, and from which amber is said to come,' he stated firmly, in his *Histories*. First, he argued, Eridanus was a Greek name, and so it had probably been coined by a Greek rather than by 'barbarians'. But the most important problem was lack of evidence: 'Though I have diligently en-quired, I have never been able to hear from any man who has himself seen a sea on that side of Europe.'

These were reasonable objections for a historian of that time, especially one who had only a vague idea of countries north of the Black Sea and anyway believed they were 'so densely filled by swarms of bees that it was impossible to penetrate'. But perhaps Herodotus should have analysed the story more carefully before he dismissed it altogether. After all, it involved weeping trees, lightning strikes, metamorphosis, death, the heat of the sun, and the unlikely river that flowed north, all of which feature in the real story of the gem. The Greeks called amber *elektron*, meaning 'the sun', because it comes in all the colours of the sun, bright yellow to sunset red; and because when it is rubbed, it attracts lint and dried grass to it, and creates sparks of light. Later the English physician William Gilbert noticed that amber shared this quality of attraction with several other substances, including tourmaline, glass, jet, sealing wax, sulphur and resin, and in 1600 he named the phenomenon 'electricity', after the Greek name for amber.

Amber really is the tears of trees – not of black poplars, although they do produce a thick resin, but of conifers that grew in great forests millions of years ago. Many evergreens ooze resin as a self-healing mechanism, but for a normal forest with a modest drizzle of resin to be transformed into an amber forest with a flood of it, something special had to happen. One theory is that it was global warming – a time in prehistory when the earth was acting like a reckless Phaeton and the sun appeared to get too close. Another suggests it was a matter of evolution and that some trees were programmed to weep plenty of tears. Or perhaps trees had been weakened by unidentified disease, and were just trying to save themselves.

Whatever the reason, at some point in prehistory a species of conifer went into medical overdrive. Judging from the massive lumps of amber that are sometimes found today, some of which can weigh four kilos[13] or more, it must have been quite a sight. There would have been resin hanging from the branches like great toffee apples, spilling on to the forest floor in honeyed

'Amber really is the tears of trees'

pools and even oozing under the bark of the trees like coagulated butter. As well as being very sticky, the whole place must have smelled intoxicatingly of incense.

Over the years most of the resin dripped into the soil and was absorbed. But – and this is where the metamorphosis element of the myth comes in – some solidified, and the long process of fossilisation began. Much of the fossilised amber is still buried hundreds of metres underground, hidden for ever in the tucks and folds of the earth. But around fifteen million years ago some of it was washed from the rocks and transported by rivers and glaciers to be dropped near what became a vast seabed. Herodotus was mistaken in his main objection to the story of Phaeton: as we know, there is a rather impressive sea hundreds of miles north of Greece which has supplied the world with amber for at least thirteen thousand years. And although this great classical historian clearly did not interview the right people for his research into amber, a century or so later there was a man who did.

Around 330 BC the Greek explorer and writer Pytheas left his home in the South of France to find the mysterious northern lands; the first Greek writer to do so. First he visited Britain – known as the 'Tin Islands', despite the Phoenicians' efforts to keep their tin source quiet. He then turned north to Iceland[14] before heading south again for the third part of his extraordinary journey. He had found tin; he had found icebergs; and he had got particularly excited about the existence of tides. It was now time to find amber. According to Pliny,[15] Pytheas described an estuary on the ocean 'called Mentonomon', occupied by Germanic people and a day away from an island called Abalus or Basilia. It was a place, he recounted, where amber 'is thrown up by the waves in spring'. The inhabitants used it as fuel for their fires, and sold it to their neighbours, the Teutons.

Today it is not clear which island Pytheas might have seen, but the estuary he mentioned was most likely either in Jutland or the Baltic, where the local people really did burn amber. Nine in ten pieces of amber are not of export quality, and on an open fire it makes a lovely scented blaze. Today the Germans call amber '*Bernstein*', which means 'burning stone'. The Poles have the same word: *bursztyn*.

When Pytheas travelled there, the coastline had already been the centre of amber trading for many thousands of years. And when I went there, some 2300 years later, there was still activity, albeit of a rather more touristic kind.

Amber-washing Champion

I had timed my trip to the 'northern sea' in August, to coincide with the so-called 'Amber-washing Championships' at Jantar, a coastal settlement about thirty kilometres east of the Polish port of Gdansk. Photographs of previous years' championships showed participants in the sea, holding nets to scoop up chunks of amber floating among the seaweed. I imagined myself joining in, wading in the waves with a borrowed net, learning the techniques and secrets of the 'amber washers' of northern Poland. I believed then that most of Poland's amber was still thrown up by the sea, although I was later to discover that this is not quite the case.

I arrived on the beach in Jantar just as four children, in school uniforms, were singing the Polish version of 'Long Haired Lover From Liverpool' from a temporary outdoor stage.[16] The audience whistled and clapped – I was less enthusiastic, but then again I didn't know that this would be the highlight of my day. Down by the seashore a dozen people were crouched on the sand apparently searching for lost contact lenses. I went to help and then realised I had stumbled on the amber competition itself. Each competitor had five minutes to pick up as many fragments of amber as they could from among the seaweed and twigs that the organisers had planted on the beach. The amber pieces were no bigger than shirt buttons and the whole thing was as exhilarating as a grape-peeling competition. 'What happened to the amber-washing and -gathering that I saw in the photographs?' I asked.

'Changed,' a man said. Too much amber had been lost in the sea. 'That's the trouble with amber,' he went on. 'It floats – except when you need it to.'

Amber is lighter than seawater, but only just. On a stormy winter's night the Baltic scoops it off the seabed and sends it bobbing to the surface like yellow warning buoys. In the morning it can be seen floating round the rocks along the coast or lying on the beach. Local people, in life-jackets, do still fish it out of the water with huge nets in a way that explains amber's ancient English nickname, 'scoopstone'. Usually the pieces are small but occasionally large bricks are cast up, as if there were a great building underwater, in desperate need of restoration. The ancient Lithuanians told their children that amber came from the palace of a mermaid, called Jurate, who was punished for falling in love with a handsome fisherman: she lost him

Seventeenth-century amber fisherman

in the same storm that smashed her home into pieces. The Lithuanians believed that the large blocks of amber were from the palace walls, while the chips were her tears, of which there were many, because love lasts longer than any material object. In 1914 an autumn storm cast almost a tonne of Jurate's castle on to a Baltic beach;[17] in 1862, local legend says, there were more than two tonnes. Such great hauls of amber treasure happened throughout history; no wonder people thought it was magical.

As the stormclouds rushed in, I walked up the beach under my umbrella, hoping to find pieces of amber left by waves rather than the contest organisers. I saw a few grains dotted in the sand, but nothing worth bringing home: winter is the best time for collecting amber, when the waves are high, and this was still summer. When I turned back, the competition had ended and holidaymakers surrounded the little piles of debris, picking at the wood and weed, searching for amber souvenirs. Behind them, children queued in the rain for a go on a bouncy castle. A few men were wearing crusader uniforms, in an attempt to give a medieval 'authenticity' to the event: over

Amber fishermen in the Baltic

their armour they wore loose white robes emblazoned with a red cross and sword. One young 'knight' had his arm round a young woman and they were deep in conversation. And I realised that, in a quirky way, this whole scene contained some of the main ingredients of amber's medieval history: castles that would later be flattened to the ground; knights keeping a careful watch on activities at the beach; a rainstorm with its potential for a valuable harvest and the hasty, almost surreptitious, search for amber on the seashore. In fact, only the boy in knight's costume walking with his girlfriend was acting completely out of time.

The Amber Gallows

The Teutonic Knights pose a problem for historians. Were they 'caped crusaders' or ruthless traders? Missionaries or mercenaries? In Polish museums they are usually portrayed romantically, as monks in flowing white robes fighting for their beliefs, but the truth is more complicated. And certainly in the rather cloudy history of amber in Europe they are some of the less attractive inclusions.

Most crusaders in the Middle Ages were volunteers: they fought under the banner of Christ's cross – from which they took the name crusader – and, in return, the Pope promised them a ticket to heaven. However, the Knights Templar, the Hospitallers and the Teutonic Knights were all military orders, whose members took lifelong monastic vows of poverty, chastity and obedience, and also pledged to fight Christ's enemies. Most crusades took them to the Holy Land, but in 1204, six years after the formation of the Teutonic Knights, Pope Innocent III heard that Orthodox monks were venturing west from Russia to bring their eastern brand of Christianity to the pagans of the Baltic. He sent a band of Teutonic Knights to investigate. The German adventurers, 'not always free from a shadow of a criminal past . . . looking for fortune and easy life'[18] did not leave the area for more than three hundred years.

They conquered Prussia, then moved on to modern Estonia, Lithuania and Latvia, using scorched-earth tactics to win territory

Teutonic Knights' Stronghold at Marienberg, or Malbork

but not hearts. Crops were burned, cattle slaughtered and families murdered. The people crumbled and they agreed to worship the Teutons' God. At the height of their power the Knights controlled around a hundred and twenty massive red-brick castles that dominated Teutonic Prussia and the neighbouring states, and all around them the people lived in fear. In *The Teutonic Knights in Latvia*,[19] Peter Olins describes the hopelessness of the situation for the Baltic peoples: Russian priests baptised them in the Orthodox tradition, Teutonic Knights rebaptised them as Catholics, and the Russians reappeared to return them to the Orthodox Church. 'Then arrived the Danes and the Swedes and they baptised in their dominions all those who were already baptised by the Germans, and as the latter did not like the Danish and Swedish baptism they sent their priests again. The Danes hanged sometimes the ones who had accepted the Germans.' The Latvians, especially, were terrified. The next priests who arrived on their shores were met by a frightened delegation. 'We are already baptised,' they said. 'What more do you expect us to do?'

When they were not enforcing baptisms the knights were plagued by boredom. They were not permitted to hunt in the forests for pleasure or to win the hearts of ladies – two traditional pursuits of medieval knights. Indeed, any knight found breaking his vow of chastity with a woman was demoted to 'brother-servant' for a year; the penalty for breaking his vow with a man was execution.[20] These knight-monks were not allowed to drink much or to joust, although they could watch jousting. So they put their energies into other pursuits: a few chose a life of prayer, but many preferred internal politics, tax collection and international trade – in all of which their Order engaged with enthusiasm. It set up a special commerce department, which ensured that by the fourteenth century the Teutonic state was the only one in Europe without debts.[21] Such priorities did not meet with much approval outside monkish circles. In

1299 the people of Riga wrote to Pope Boniface VIII to complain that 'Whereas they are Knights and wish to be treated as such, they deal in every trade unbecoming to knighthood, and even in its meanest kinds, like market-men; they are selling fruit, cabbage, radish, onion and other such commodities . . .'[22]

More important than the vegetables, though, was the amber. By the fifteenth century the routes established by Stone Age traders to carry amber were among the most important trading routes in Europe. There were three main Amber Roads from the Polish Baltic.[23] The first two started from the Teutonic castle of Marienberg, then crossed Bohemia and Moravia to the Danube. From there the roads forked: one branch went to Greece while the second crossed the Alps to northern Italy. The third route ran overland to the river Dnieper, then to the Black Sea and Constantinople to meet caravans from central Asia and the Muslim empires of the East.

We know from surviving documents and diaries that amber made a substantial impact on some who saw it. In the sixth century BC, an exiled priest sitting by a river near Babylon had a vision: 'I looked,' he wrote, and 'a stormy wind blew from the north, a great cloud with flashing fire and brilliant light round it.' It was the fire of God, he said, and at the centre of it there was 'a brilliance. Like that of amber.'[24] For his listeners it would have been a vivid image. Amber was the colour of sunlight. It was exotic and mysterious, and it came from far away. In fact there cannot have been many better earthly similes that the Israelite prophet Ezekiel could have used, if he wanted to describe the very epicentre of spiritual power.

Ezekiel looked into amber and saw God, but the Teutonic Knights saw something less noble: gold. They kept amber prices high by holding a monopoly, and defending it with threats and terror. Only they were allowed to own amber, and the penalty for those who disregarded this rule was death. Many ancient cultures believed that amber attracted luck as it did dried grass, but it brought only sadness to the medieval Baltic peoples. As late as the winter of 1519 a Dominican monk called Simonis Grunovii arrived on the Prussian coast from Rome to buy an amber icon for the Pope. He described[25] how the peasants were made to run with nets into the sea to fish for amber: they were roped together, and when the waves became too high they climbed the high poles they carried to avoid drowning. They 'become frozen in icy waters and have to be thawed before they can be taken to their huts', Grunovii wrote, 'and for this reason big fires are kept upon the shore.' Although amber was expensive and the people were poor, few dared to pick it up from the beaches. If they were caught, they were hanged 'on the nearest tree', '*ohne Berhörung und Frage*' – without hearing or questioning. This was not idle rumour. Grunovii had seen several bodies swinging from branches.

Grunovii probably did not realise it, but when he turned for home with his own (permitted) piece of amber, the Teutonic Knights' reign of terror was near its end. A dissident group led by the German monk Martin Luther[26] was emerging in northern

Amber hook and net

Europe, protesting about what it called the Roman Catholic Church's abuses of faith. 'Take a wife', Luther told the Knights' Grand Master Albrecht in 1523; the military orders were outdated, he said, and had no part in the modern world. Albrecht agreed: two years later he dissolved the Knights and their amber monopoly, appointed himself 'Duke of Prussia', and proposed marriage to a Danish princess. The people welcomed the change: craftsmen in the city of Danzig (today's Gdansk) were allowed to work with amber – which the Knights had forbidden – and the next two centuries were a time of comparative free-

dom and creativity, in amber-carving and in almost everything
else.

As the era of the Teutonic Knights ended,[27] so did their medieval world-view. Gradually people came to realise that the world
was older than had once been thought and that Creation had
taken longer than the six days described in Genesis. Amber,
with its ability to preserve physical evidence from the past,
would later help to undermine the medieval understanding of
historical time. It would show that there had been an era before
humans had set foot in the world, and would allow people to
see part of it for themselves.

Trapped in Amber

Forty million years ago, when the soft Baltic resin lay in pools
on the forest floor or dripped from the branches, the rest of the
life of the forest was going on. Bees were buzzing, spiders spinning, petals dropping, lizards stalking, and flies resting. And
some of that life was suffocating in the resin, giving us today
an astonishing three-dimensional view of what the amber forest
looked like. With many gemstones, it is their origin in faraway
places that gives them extra value, but with amber the element
of 'far away' is usually measured in time, not distance. Now the
magic of amber – the reason that some rare samples are worth
huge sums – lies in the evidence of another world that is trapped
inside it, like a story.

The Museum of Amber Inclusions at the University of Gdansk
consists of just a few display cases in a small corridor. But as
the curator Elżbieta Sontag pointed out (standing surrounded
by cages of pet chinchillas and stick insects left for her to look
after during the university holidays): 'The important thing about
museums is the collection, not how big the exhibition area is.'
She had hated amber when she was a child, she said casually, as
she rummaged through the collection. 'My cousins used to come

from Warsaw and buy big necklaces and I thought, How ugly.'
I agreed. When I was eight I had an amber bracelet with faceted
beads and tried to like it, but it was too orange, and weighed
too little, and I didn't like the way you could see the string
through the beads. 'What changed your mind?' I asked. In reply
she put a honey-coloured sample under a microscope and
beckoned me to take a look.

I found myself gazing at a forty-million-year-old spider, looking exactly as it must have in the final seconds of its life. Every
hair was immaculate; one leg was raised for ever in a state of
potential motion. The resin must have been very liquid as there
was no sign of the smearing you might see when a creature had
been trapped against its will in a sticky substance. 'They didn't
all go down without a struggle,' said Dr Sontag, and replaced
it with another spider that had evidently tried desperately to
clamber out of the pool into which it had fallen. It was astonishing to see these ancient creatures; like looking into the heart of
creation with an amber spyglass.

In 1993 the popularity of amber suddenly soared for two unexpected reasons. First, United Parcel Service started delivering
to and from Poland: transforming the ancient 'Amber Road'
into an international postal network, and meaning that people
from beyond the Baltic were able to receive deliveries of amber.[28]
Second, the Hollywood movie *Jurassic Park* put forward the
theory that scientists could reconstruct dinosaurs from DNA
preserved in blood-sucking insects found in amber mined in the
Dominican Republic. The thesis is tricky for several reasons,
one of the most obvious being that Dominican amber, like the
succinite amber from the Baltic, is between thirty and forty-
five million years old[29] while dinosaurs died out some sixty-five
million years ago. But it is not impossible. If dinosaur DNA
could conceivably be held in insect blood (and there are several
scientists today, including one at the Natural History Museum
in London, who are researching the theory) a few rare types of

amber might contain it. They include amber from the Isle of Wight, and some Lebanese pieces that formed 135 million years ago, with prehistoric mosquitoes entombed inside them. 'But even if it were possible, the film would have to be called *Lower Cretaceous Park*,' said Dr Sontag. 'The Jurassic era ended about 144 million years ago.'

Looking through her forty-million-year-old Baltic collection (which, we agreed, might be used to re-create 'Eocene Park'[30]) was like viewing a selection of video stills from the past. In one, two mites were eating a caddis fly, its wings partly torn apart. Another showed a mite in the process of laying eggs. Other samples contained filmy spiders' webs, and others had little bubbles that had come from the insects as they died. Visually the last samples were nothing special, but for some palaeontologists they are the most exciting of all, since the tiny bubbles hold clues to the air and bacteria of the prehistoric forest. 'Fossil flatulence', American amber expert David Grimaldi[31] once called them.

The pieces in the collection were a time detective's dream. Yet oddly, although we now know so much about the insects, plants and even the atmosphere of this long-extinct forest, we are still ignorant of the trees that produced the amber resin. Some argue that they were the ancestors of cedars, others that they were great weeping larches or pines, or the long-extinct agathis. 'But really,' said Dr Sontag, 'we simply don't know.'

Everything we were seeing was very small: amber is sizeist about what it includes. Out of the live creatures in Dr Sontag's laboratory, a stick insect might easily have got stuck in the resin, but even if chinchillas had existed forty million years ago we would not have known it from amber. They would simply have hopped out of the sticky puddle, washed their feet and gone about their business. There are no signs, sadly, of the earliest known horses, which we know from fossil evidence lived in the Eocene period and measured just thirty centimetres (about three hands) to the shoulder. The largest preserved creatures ever

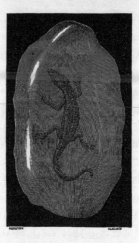

Lizard in amber

found in Baltic amber are lizards, 'And they have only ever found three complete examples of those,' said Dr Sontag. The university has seen many fakes, sometimes called Piltdown Lizards.[32] The major clue is that if the species in the amber is still living today, it is without doubt a forgery. Species only last about five million years, so true amber fossils are at least nine generations of evolution from what we know today.

Although to scientists the differences are huge, the spiders and insects in the amber looked much like those we know today. Then Dr Sontag put an unfamiliar insect under the microscope. 'What's that?' I asked.

'What do you think it is?'

It looked like a very long fly. It had ten or twelve legs, and several wings. 'An early cousin of the dragon-fly?'

I heard muffled laughter and looked up. 'It's two flies copulating,' she said.

I looked again and realised it was true. They were caught for ever *in flagrante delicto*. and if I didn't know better I would say that the one behind had an expression of amazement on his face.

Colours and Fakery

The other interesting thing about Dr Sontag's pieces was the range of colours, like cream swirling in lemon mousse, or the last shafts of light in a clouded sunset sky. The amber came in everything from ivory to ebony with all the colours of the rainbow in between. Most were in an autumn range, of yellow, orange, red and brown, but some were wintry: blue, black and, most precious of all, white. It looks like froth on beer and is created by a similar process. Millions of years ago these little drops of resin were shaken into a pale cloud, and eventually, very slowly, they will return to resin colour – the colour we refer to when we talk about 'amber' traffic-lights. Blue amber is rare and rather disconcerting, an ethereal ultramarine aura on something darker. Black is even rarer – when you find it today it has usually been artificially coloured – and although pine-green is popular in jewellery it is usually an indication that the piece has spent time in an oven – especially when it contains sparkles.

Treatments are an increasing problem in the amber trade. If you pick up amber from the beach you can be sure that it has not been doctored, but for everything else, 'Buyer, beware'.[33] One test is to paint a small amount of nail-polish remover on it: real amber is so ancient that it will not be affected by the acetone; but if the material is younger – like copal, which is less than a million years old – or plastic, it will disintegrate and feel tacky. A more radical test is to try to burn it: amber smells subtly of a pine forest in the morning; copal is like pine-scented lavatory freshener, and plastic fills the air with noxious fumes.

Today, unfortunately, the tests are not entirely reliable. In Russia apparently,[34] a whole institute is dedicated to devising tests to recognise imitation amber – the knowledge is applied to develop better fakes. Several factories in Russia and China raise scorpions, frogs and ant colonies. When these hapless

creatures reach maturity they are placed in moulds and smoth-
ered, gently, in a warm soup of melted amber to be sold as
key-rings in Hong Kong. The first examples of these fakes were
easy to spot, but as the technology improves even experts find
it difficult. Many less reputable dealers do not even feel the need
to declare the processes, protesting when challenged, that they
had 'never claimed it was *real* amber'. The only solution, according to amber expert Gabriela Gierłowska, is to use your eyes
and judgement, and always demand a certificate. 'If a piece of
amber seems cheap, there is always a reason,' she said, 'and it
is probably not a good reason.'

Buying amber in Poland does not mean that it comes from
there, despite what some shops might claim. Most of the amber
on sale in Gdansk does not come from Poland at all, and was
not washed up on a beach. Instead it comes from a mine in
what is sometimes called the 'Wild West' of Russia. It is the
biggest amber mine in the world and, as with amber itself, some
of the history preserved in it is both extraordinary and violent.

A Place Like Brazil

The amber mine is in a part of Russia I had never noticed on
maps. And, like Herodotus, before I had proof I was not entirely
sure that it existed. It is a fairly small state, the size of Connecticut or Northern Ireland, squashed between Poland to the south
and Lithuania to the north, separated from the rest of Russia
by at least five hundred kilometres. Known as the Kaliningrad
Oblast, or Region, for forty-five years it was one of the hardest
places in the Soviet Union for anyone to get to – and that
included Soviet passport-holders.

The night before I was due to go I stayed in a town called
Elblag on the border. I went out for a beer and, after I had
explained my mission, the barman introduced me to another
customer, who had once been an amber salesman in America.

'Many Polish people have been amber salesmen in America. You should not attach too much importance to it,' he said self-effacingly. When I told him about my plan to visit the mine, he raised his eyebrows. 'You must be careful,' he said. 'Kaliningrad is like Brazil.'

'What do you mean?' I asked.

'I mean this part of Russia is not like Europe. In fact, this part of Russia is not even like Russia. It is a dangerous place. I am not saying you will definitely be hurt or killed,' he added, 'I am just saying you must be careful.'

The next morning I passed through passport control, then a metal detector. I beeped loudly but none of the guards looked up. They were too busy sifting for interesting items in my luggage. Out came cameras, books and British newspapers. I was assigned a tough-looking female guard, who rattled English at me like a machine-gun.

'What is your profession?'

'Why do you have two cameras?'

'Why three notebooks?'

She was terrifying. But the next question was unexpected: 'What do you think about her?' She was pointing at a picture of the late Princess of Wales in one of the papers. 'I really admired her,' she said. 'I wanted to be like her.' I gave her the paper as a present and she waved me on smiling, wishing me luck in my amber search. Perhaps this bit of Russia would not be quite as horrible as everyone had said.

Two hours later, Kaliningrad bus station was even bleaker than I had expected. A woman with bright pink lipstick, a tight brown skirt and a missing tooth berated me drunkenly. As I struggled to find a taxi driver, her place was taken by an old man in a torn jacket. He jostled me and picked my coat pocket – which fortunately contained only my map of Kaliningrad. I felt briefly as if I was in hell – or, perhaps, the slums of Brazil.

This little bit of Europe was not always Russian. Before the

Second World War it was part of East Prussia, populated by German speakers: a legacy of the Teutonic Knights. In 1945 the Russians captured the city of Königsberg, and when Europe was divided after the war Joseph Stalin decreed that it should become Russian. He renamed it Kaliningrad, made it into a military zone, closed it to foreigners, and ruled that Soviet citizens from other states had to have a special visa to travel there. The reason it was so special to the Soviet government was found, like amber, in the Baltic Sea. Even today, Kaliningrad is the only port in Russia that does not freeze in winter. The city might be stuck in the middle of foreign territory, but all those years after the fall of the Teutonic Knights it is still vital for defence.

When the ancient city of Königsberg became the new city of Kaliningrad, two things happened. First, the Germans were sent away, and second, the vacuum left by their departure sucked in new inhabitants. They came from all over the Soviet Union – Siberia, Georgia, the Ukraine and the Volga, so many different places that the region became a model for dysfunction. Nothing symbolised this better than its new name: the city was named after Mikhail Ivanovich Kalinin, president of the USSR from 1922[35] and one of Stalin's strongest supporters. It was a city he had never visited and had never cared for.

The new inhabitants found a city in ruins: ninety per cent of it was gone. In the Kaliningrad History Museum there is a 1930s photograph of an island in the city centre. It shows a typical northern European scene, with brick houses, a tall cathedral, cobbled streets and a pretty waterway. Today it is a bleak, empty park, full of drunks: a blank testament to how the whole city was rebuilt by officials who cared more for quotas than for aesthetics.

The Beginning of the Amber Road

The amber mine is an hour east of the city, along a straight, military road that leads to the coastline of the Samland peninsula. As we drove there early the next morning, my translator Olga explained how until the end of the war the town near the mine was called Palmnicken, but when the Communists arrived, with their emphasis on utilitarianism, they had changed it to Yantarny, which simply means 'Amber'.

My first stop was at the mine. In the past there had been several, but today only one is operating, and special permission is needed to visit. Two kilometres out of the town we came to a desolate yellow brick building in the middle of scrubland, surrounded by barbed wire. Olga went in and eventually returned with a young man in khaki combats whom she had found asleep at a desk. He agreed to take us to the mine for a few dollars, jumped into the front seat and directed us on to a muddy, pot-holed track. Buckthorn and elder grew beside it: during the Cold War, when the amber trade was bad, people had collected the berries to supplement their diet.

We stopped in front of what looked like a ruin. It was made of grey breezeblocks, falling down: the headquarters of the mine operations. We were not allowed in. The young guard beckoned us up a grassy ridge that stood behind it. We followed him, and there it was – the greatest amber mine in the world. It was a shallow brown crater, about the size of a small town, fringed with ridges like the one we were standing on, the trees covered with a patina of dust. It should have been full of bulldozers and people with hard hats, but it looked deserted. Eventually, as my eyes adjusted to the distance, I saw two all-terrain walking excavators digging elegantly into the ground. They were so far away that they looked tiny, although they weigh eight tonnes and are usually hard to miss.

They were excavating 'blue earth'. This is the layer of grey clay in which lumps of amber sit like raisins in rye bread. Blue earth stuffed with amber can be found all over the Baltic, but the reason the mines are here and nowhere else is that the blue earth on the Samland peninsula is just fifteen metres below the surface; in many parts of Poland and the Baltic States it is forty metres down or more, making mining uneconomical. It is becoming uneconomical at Yantarny: prices have dropped, the ageing equipment has not been replaced and many workers have been laid off. The world's amber markets are exploring alternative areas, like the Ukraine. 'It is terrible for the town,' the young guard said.

The only people who make an easy profit now are the amateur diggers.[36] Some months before, when Olga had visited, none of the diggers were working. There was just one man, digging an illegal pit. 'I was worried for him: there could have been a mud-slide, and who would have known?' The local government tries half-heartedly to take precautions. All the security guards come from other parts of Russia – our guide was from St Petersburg – so theoretically they would be less susceptible to local corruption. In truth, millions of dollars' worth of amber go missing every year, smuggled across the border in suitcases and bags.

As we drove back along that unmade track, past the elder and buckthorn, and the tumbledown brick building with two yellow dogs asleep outside, I realised that *this* was now the beginning of the fabled Amber Road. It is a humble beginning for something that was once great.

Evil Preserved

Before I had come to Russia I had searched for information on Yantarny and found precious little – some environmental assessments (it has apparently spewed more than a hundred million tonnes of waste into the sea over fifty years),[37] and a vivid account of the 'Wild West' atmosphere that prevailed there a few years ago when locals, beset by job losses, spent their days standing at the wastepipes of a disused mine on the beach, waiting to fish out amber from the grey effluent. But I found an intriguing footnote in an academic journal, which suggested that for several years the exploitation of amber at Yantarny was controlled by the secret police and carried out by prisoners in a gulag. I was determined to find out more.

Gulags were labour camps, set up in 1919 to deal with the dispossessed landowners and intelligentsia after the Revolution, and were expanded when Stalin found out how cheap it was to build canals or operate mines with slave labour. As his domestic ambitions increased, so did the number of people brought into the gulags on increasingly spurious charges – indeed, many prisoners were never told why they were there. Most of the four hundred and fifty or so gulags were in Siberia or Kazakhstan, but they could be found anywhere that needed free labour – including, perhaps, an amber mine on the edge of Europe.

Olga had not heard of a gulag in Kaliningrad. 'This will be a difficult question to ask even now,' she warned me, 'but we will try.' Our first stop would be the local museum where, if there had been a prison camp, somebody was sure to know about it.

Imprisoned in Amber

Yantarny Museum was full of the flotsam and jetsam of history: in one room, gramophones and tattered photos testified to a time when the people of Palmnicken liked to dance; another room, filled with red badges and Communist flags, recorded a period after the rules had changed. The guide, Mischa Permjakov, was showing round a primary-school group. He was explaining why so few amber artefacts dated from the ancient Prussian era, before the Teutonic Knights had appeared. 'Why do you think the ancient Prussians didn't value amber?' he asked

Amber mine on the Baltic sea

the children. When they said they didn't know, he asked them what their favourite toy was.

'A teddy-bear,' several squealed.

'But if you had thousands of teddy-bears would you still be interested in them? Well, the Prussians had thousands and thousands of pieces of amber,' he said. 'They weren't interested in them at all. It was only the people from outside who liked them and wanted to trade.'

Later he told us that the mine had been developed for the same reason – outside interest. In the 1850s Moritz Becker, a German businessman, had been on holiday in Palmnicken. When he saw amber artefacts on sale and found out that the material was collected at the whim of winter storms he wondered whether there might be a more sure way of retrieving it. He and business partner Wilhelm Stantien raised some money and hired machinery to dredge the sea. They found tonnes of amber. By the late 1860s they had already excavated two shaft mines – one was called Anna, the other Henrietta. Henrietta yielded very few jewels and was soon closed, but Anna operated until just before the Second World War.

Drawings from those years show amber mining to be unpleasant work. A cartoon from a German magazine depicts two men with pickaxes standing in groundwater up to their knees while a third adjusts some precarious tunnel supports. Their faces look strained: apparently it stank of sulphur down there.

Searching the miners at the end of a shift

A second drawing shows miners being body-searched at the end of their shift: their boots have been removed, their knapsacks are open for inspection and they look nervous. Although no one has since matched the Teutonic Knights for amber-related brutality, there were heavy penalties for pilferers. 'They would sometimes be beaten,' Mischa said. 'Or they would go to prison.'

The Nurturing Effects of Amber

Only one piece of amber in ten is worth stealing: the other nine are too flawed to be made into jewellery. However, they still have their uses. 'Some of the amber is melted down,' Mischa said, 'and it is made into these . . .' He showed us a large cabinet full of small orange teddy-bears. They looked plastic and they might as well have been. It is cheap and easy to reconstitute amber like this: it is crushed to powder, then pushed into moulds under high temperature and pressure. The final product has the colour of amber and its chemical formula, but it does not have its history or true nature. If the prophet Ezekiel had seen this stuff, he would not have thought it marvellous, he probably would not even have commented on it. It was a curious echo of the earlier example of the Prussians and the teddy-bears: there were hundreds of figurines in that cabinet and I wouldn't have paid anything for them at all.

There are other uses for low-quality amber. During Becker and Stantien's early days, something curious was observed among the workers at the mine and factory. People who worked on ordinary manual jobs had the same rate of respiratory infections as the rest of the population, but those who polished the amber had fewer. This seemed to confirm an old superstition, and the company studied the ancient use of amber as a remedy. They realised that the sailors who had smoked pipes with amber mouthpieces because it was 'good for their lungs' might have had a point.

In ancient Lithuania people called amber '*gintaras*', meaning 'protector' – the Russian word янтарно, *yantarno*, has the same origin – and took it as a cure for rheumatism. First-century Roman doctors gave amber to tonsillitis patients,[38] and in the twelfth century Albertus Magnus named it one of the six great cures of all time. In the mid-twentieth century some Soviet doctors prescribed 'succinic acid' from Baltic amber as a health supplement for athletes.[39] It has the advantage of not showing up in Olympic drug tests because it is formed naturally in the human body. In around 1886 the future Nobel Prize winner Robert Koch proved the efficacy of this substance by living on butter for a month: his body produced excess succinic acid, but he suffered no ill effects.[40] Flagman Vodka, official purveyor to the Kremlin, apparently includes one per cent amber extract to stave off hangovers. The healing property of amber is not proven but it makes sense: whenever trees are hurt they send out resin to heal their wounds, much as human bodies send out red corpuscles. So it is not surprising if resin has some benefits to human health.

The Gulag

We had almost reached the end of the museum tour. I glanced at Olga, who nodded, so I asked Mischa about the gulag. He froze. 'There was a camp . . .' he said – and stopped as a colleague walked past. Later we asked him again but he said he knew no more. I asked why it wasn't mentioned in the museum display. 'People prefer to see the good things, and this is not good history. It's like what happened at the Anna mine,' he said. 'We thought at one point we would mention that in the museum, but local people protested. They thought it was too upsetting.'

Later, when we drove to the Anna mine I learned about what had happened there. The disused shaft is dramatic, built high into the cliff above a stunning white beach. We were the only people there, apart from a man who was sunbathing beside a multicoloured umbrella. It was a quiet, beautiful place and, on a sunny summer's day, it seemed impossible that anything terrible could have happened there.

But on 30 January 1945, it did. Seven thousand Jews arrived at gunpoint in the middle of the night. As the Allied armies broke through the German defences and approached northern

Poland, the order had come in from Berlin to close the concentration camps and destroy all evidence. The commander of the Stutthoff camp on the Samland peninsula decided to fulfil his orders cheaply and quickly: he would throw the prisoners into the amber mine and seal it. He ordered them to be marched many kilometres in their thin clothing to what would become their grave. But the mine manager refused, saying he didn't want his mine involved. Instead the prisoners – shivering with cold and fear – were ordered on to the beach. There, they were divided into columns of fifty and made to run into the water where they were mown down by machine-guns. Twelve of the seven thousand escaped somehow, from all those bullets and the icy sea.

At the base of the mine there is a monument to those who died; just a few stones stuck together with concrete, and a simple plaque nailed to one side. It looks as if it was put up with no forethought and no budget and this is probably the case. In the town there is debate about whether the area should become a spa or a monument. So far, the spa is winning. They are people who have made their livelihoods out of a material that preserves history better than almost anything else, but the tendency of the inhabitants of Yantarny is to hide history away, and to try and forget it.

The museum had given us no useful information about the camp, so our next stop was the local library, in the middle of a 1950s housing estate. The metal girders that made up the skeleton of the building had rusted, so the walls were decorated with a brown grid design. Meanwhile the grass around them had grown so tall that it threatened to take over the children's swings: it was only on the upswing that you could see the entire child. Gulag or no gulag, the amber community was a desolate place in which to grow up.

We went into the library up some broken concrete steps – the entrance was dominated by three industrial-sized sinks, which stank of carbolic soap. Inside, behind the desk, a plump young woman with long fingernails was flicking sulkily through a hairstyles magazine. She knew nothing about local history, she said: 'I'm new here.' She suggested we come back in an hour when the head librarian would be available. When we returned we found an even plumper woman, with even less of a smile for us, who pointed out the clippings library. Olga looked carefully through the files. At the end, she found a short article that mentioned, in passing, two camps, which operated from 1948 to 1953. We asked the librarian for more details but she shrugged and said she came from the Ukraine and knew nothing about it. If you want to forget history, I thought, ducking under rusty bars and over thick nettles to get back to the car, you bring in most of your population from outside. Communism was about encouraging people to forget history, I said to Olga. 'Not exactly,' she answered. 'Communists liked history very much. It just had to be the right history. They liked to remember it selectively.'

Amber is about selective history as well. The insects preserved in it are those that lived around the resin pines; the lizards found in it are only those small enough to be trapped in it; the pollen and leaves come from the plants that grew in the marshy ground where the conifers thrived. We can make up a narrative about the prehistoric forest from the evidence but – like any biographers, archaeologists or detectives – we must bear in mind that what remains is only a fraction of the story.

However, with just a small clue you can sometimes uncover a large truth. As the article that mentioned the camps had been written only a few years before, we decided to go to the newspaper office. Like almost everything else in Yantarny, it was based on Soviet Street, a tree-lined avenue of mansion houses built for wealthy Prussians, but now decaying. The building was open, but the door to the newspaper offices was locked. A notice claimed they were open until six o'clock – an hour away – but no one was there. I stood in the dark corridor feeling frustrated and perplexed. I could not believe the mystery of the Amber Gulag would end like that for me – with a closed door and no answers.

Just then a man walked downstairs, jingling car keys. What were we looking for? The newspaper people? 'They're always going off early,' he said cheerfully. And then he led us to a small office we had not noticed. Olga had told him nothing of our search, and why he should have been inspired to send two strangers to the Social Welfare I don't know. But I'm glad he did, because there we met Valentina Alekseyevna, the senior social-welfare officer. She sat us down in her small room – with striped pink wallpaper and a vase of summer daisies – and told us what happened when a small town was faced with the closure of its main industry. 'It is a crisis,' she said. 'Today there are a thousand people employed in the Yantarny mine and the factory and most are about to lose their jobs. If the amber goes there will be nothing for anyone to do. This town is just about amber.' Official figures showed six hundred people unemployed in Yantarny, 'Although I think there are more,' she said. At the end of the conversation we asked her about the camps. 'I'm from elsewhere in Russia,' came the familiar refrain. But this time her lack of knowledge did not cut the conversation short. She knew of an old lady who had lived there since the 1940s.

Which was why, at six o'clock on a summer's evening, we found ourselves standing on Soviet Street, ringing the bell outside the apartment of Nina Melnikova, eighty years old last birthday.

Nina

A small, slim woman, with short grey hair and a nice smile, opened the door. She was wearing a lime green T-shirt with 'country life: summer breeze' across the front in English. She seemed unperturbed by our arrival, and took us through the kitchen and into her sitting room.

'Do you remember the camps?' I asked her, getting straight to the point. 'Oh, yes,' she said, proudly, as she poured us little cups of strong tea. 'I was a guard there for five years.'

Until that point I had been intrigued by the chase. If it was really true that, in twentieth-century Europe, gems had been systematically mined by slaves, then it would be a fascinating chapter in the history of gemstones. But now it was confirmed, I felt sad. And sadder still that a smiling old lady with a kind face and pride in her story should be the one to tell me. The Jewish historian Hannah Arendt, in her book about the trial of the Nazi administrator Adolf Eichmann, observes that in many cases the Nazi camps were run by ordinary people who participated in the system with the energy of effective bureaucrats: the evil was astonishing in its banality.[41] And sitting in that nice, clean room eating homemade blueberry jam and discussing an example of one of the most feared institutions of the twentieth century with a woman who had once worked there, I wondered what I would have done in those times.

Nina had come to Kaliningrad in 1948. She and her husband Alexander had been involved in reconstruction projects for the army. They spent one of their leave periods at Yantarny with friends who were working at the camp. Staff were needed, and they were offered jobs. 'Of course we said yes. I came from the Steppes, which were bare. Here, there were so many trees. I thought it was beautiful.' There were two gulags: one for men working in the mine, the other for women, employed in the factory. Most were political prisoners; others were there for small crimes, like stealing fish. 'Things that nobody would even go to court for nowadays,' Nina said. Had she read *A Day in the Life of Ivan Denisovich*?[42] I asked. 'It wasn't like that,' she said. 'It was quite nice, really.' The prisoners had porridge every morning and meat or fish most days: 'Nobody died of starvation. They ate almost as well as we did.' She even said there were no harsh punishments, although that seemed hard to believe.

Nina's job was surprising: she had been in charge of organising the camp's social programme. 'It was made easy for me,' she said. 'A whole jazz band was in residence.' The men had played under duress for the Nazis during their occupation; Stalin considered it a crime to have encouraged the enemy to dance, and after the war the musicians were sentenced to hard labour – although they were allowed to keep their instruments. 'They were very good,' Nina said. 'They often played in town.' The poor souls in Solzhenitsyn's books did not enjoy weekend dances, so perhaps Nina was right, and Yantarny was softer than the other gulags. But forced labour is still forced labour, and for five years from 1948, most of the amber in the world was processed under those conditions. Stalin died in 1953 and the prisoners were given an amnesty. They were offered jobs and houses in Yantarny but, hardly surprisingly, almost no one took up the offer. They had been bugs trapped in amber[43] and when they had the chance to go, they went. Only the guards stayed on.

Nina became personnel manager at the factory and stayed there until she retired. Did she have any amber jewellery? 'Just a little,' she said. 'When we were younger the important thing was getting enough food for our family. We didn't think about pretty things.' She showed us the three pieces she owned: two necklaces with oval beads as big as quails' eggs and a pretty 1950s brooch with a peach-coloured leaf from which hung three amber berries. She had been given the first necklace by the head of production, who had told her that since she was the only manager who had never asked for a piece of jewellery, they had made one for her without being asked. He had given her the second in the 1960s: the then Soviet premier, Nikita Khrushchev, had ordered diplomatic gifts to take to India and they had made

Nina Melnikova with her amber necklaces

an extra one, in case it might be needed. But it was not, and it was offered to Nina. At first she said no but her boss insisted: 'Why not take it, Nina? Think about it. This necklace is almost unique. Nobody else has one like it – only you and Indira Gandhi.' And was there a story about the brooch? I asked. She smiled. 'For you!' she said, and gave it to me.

I didn't know what to say but Olga smiled. 'You must take it. You can't say no. It is Russian hospitality.'

The Most Expensive Amber Gift of All

When Nina pinned the brooch to my shirt – and, indeed, when Khrushchev took necklaces to Indira Gandhi – they were following a long tradition of giving amber as diplomatic gifts. In the sixth century the Aestii – predecessors of the Estonians – sent amber[44] to King Theodoric of the Ostrogoths, who had just conquered Italy. It was chosen deliberately, to remind Theodoric that, like the Aestii, his people had come from the Baltic.[45] Throughout the seventeenth century wealthy Poles had collected amber artefacts but as Maria Gonzaga, the lady-in-waiting to Queen Ludwika, noted in 1646, it was not just for their own enjoyment: 'There are a number of rooms adorned with unusually rare works of art ... made with gold, silver, amber and gems,' she wrote, describing a royal visit to an aristocrat's home in Warsaw. 'But that nobleman does not display them in order to boast of his wealth. Instead he uses them to create a convenient opportunity for presenting those of noble birth with gifts.'[46] She herself had received a lovely amber casket.

But the most famous example of amber as a tool of diplomacy was a present given in 1716 by Frederick William I of Prussia to Peter the Great of Russia. At the time it did not create much of a stir, but two centuries later when it disappeared it became one of the most famous pieces of gem material in history. And the curious thing is that it was not jewellery at all but a smart alternative to wallpaper: the so-called Amber Room.

The first years of the room give few clues as to how precious it would later become, although they do provide indications of trouble to come. In 1699 the Prussian Elector Frederick III learned that his palace cellars contained tonnes of amber left by the Teutonic Knights and decided to commission a chamber whose walls would be lined entirely with 'Baltic gold', as amber was known. He employed a Prussian architect and a master craftsman from Denmark who knew the secrets of amber furniture-making. This man knew how to soften the raw lumps into smooth mosaics; how to mix them with cognac, honey and linseed oil to give them luminescence and colour; and having cut them, how to glue them on to a wooden frame – although, as the room's later owners discovered, he had not quite worked out how to make them stay. Ten years later – with the architect fired and the Danish craftsman imprisoned because he had not wanted to give up the mosaic panels he had created – part of the Amber Chamber was installed as a study in which Frederick apparently liked to play noughts and crosses amid its subtle glow. But it was never finished. And in 1713 when Frederick died it seemed that it never would be.

His son, Frederick William, was the opposite of his father – he despised court life, preferring his own two hobbies of making war and collecting giants. He disliked his father's delicate, French-inspired Amber Chamber so intensely that it was packed up and put into storage. Three years later, however, he had a clever idea. The Russians had just defeated the Swedes at the battle of Poltava, and Prussia needed them as allies. So Frederick Wilhelm gave his jewelled panels to Peter the Great. Not only was amber expensive – being worth twelve times the price of gold – but the gift also contained a hidden message, a tacit reminder that Prussia still controlled the Baltic region, which Russia coveted. 'Nice gift,'[47] said the Tsar approvingly – and in return sent Frederick William the one thing guaranteed to give him pleasure: fifty-five Russians, each of whom was more than seven feet tall, to serve in his Prussian army.

Peter's original intention was to turn the chamber into one of the 'Wonder Rooms' he admired in the houses of rich western Europeans. However, when it arrived it was in an appalling condition: the amber tiles were dropping off their frames, and there were no reassembly instructions. He packed it up in disgust and never looked at it again. Forty years later his daughter, the Empress Elizabeth, remembered that her father had once been given an 'Amber Chamber' and that it was somewhere in storage. It took many years, many roubles, dozens of craftsmen in Italy, Russia and Prussia and a great deal of determination, but when the panels were finally installed in the Tsar's Summer Palace near St Petersburg the little chamber had been transformed into a magnificent hall with great pilasters beside the doors, new panels and gilded mirrors – a baroque version of King Menelaus' palace in Ancient Greece. It was no longer the modest 'Amber Chamber' but the spectacular 'Amber Room', and it became famous as one of the most complicated, high-maintenance and expensively appointed rooms in the world.

It was stunning in candlelight. The poet Théophile Gautier saw it in 1866 and left a vivid description: 'The eye ∴ . . is amazed and blinded by the wealth and warmth of tints, representing all colours of the spectrum of yellow – from smoky topaz to a light lemon . . . The gold of carvings seems dim and false in comparison, especially where the sun falls on the walls and runs through transparent veins of amber.'[48] He devoted several pages in his memoirs to describing Russian interiors, and concluded that the unusually bright decorations resulted from the eye's need 'to console itself from the implacable whiteness of winter'.[49] What greater relief from that monochrome of snow than the Amber Room, which traps the sunshine all night long?

Although the Nazis never totally conquered Leningrad during the Second World War, they occupied the surrounding areas, including the Summer Palace, which had become a museum. The curators tried to hide the amber under temporary panels, but the Germans found and dismantled it, then despatched it to Königsberg Castle in today's Kaliningrad, where they reinstalled it. Some time between August 1944, when it was crated up to protect it from Allied air-raids, and April 1945, when the castle fell to the Red Army, the Amber Room went missing. Ever since, many people, including the East German Stasi and the KGB, have searched for it, in quarries, shipwrecks, churches, slate mines and subterranean labyrinths. Some people even appeared to have been tortured and murdered for it. In 1987 George Stein, a West German fruit farmer and a persistent seeker of the Amber Room, was discovered dead in a Bavarian forest, covered with cuts, his belly sliced open with a scalpel. No wonder the Amber Room kept hitting the headlines.

Perhaps they were all looking in the wrong direction. Recently two British investigative reporters, Catherine Scott-Clark and Adrian Levy, spent three years as Amber Room detectives, following up leads in Russia, Poland, Germany and elsewhere. In their book *The Amber Room* they concluded that it no longer existed: it had probably been accidentally destroyed in 1945 by fire at Königsberg Castle. It must have made an astonishing scented blaze. And the mystery, they decided, was a spectacular hoax. The Russians had spread the rumour that the Nazis had stolen it as a justification for keeping the millions of pounds' worth of artworks taken from Germany after the war. If the Germans still had the Russian Amber Room, the argument went, then why should the Russians not keep German war treasures?[50] Even George Stein's death had an alternative explanation: evidence from a Hamburg psychiatric hospital suggested that he had been in the habit of making sado-masochistic cuts on his own stomach. They concluded that his death was likely to have been a ritual suicide and that his hunt for buried treasure had been literally led by madness.

Why was it so important to find the room? Even if it had been recovered, it would probably have been in a terrible state of disrepair after fifty years in a damp tunnel, far worse than it had been when Empress Elizabeth took it over.[51] Some reports suggest it was already in poor condition when it disappeared. As early as 1913 the Russian authorities had backed out of a conservation contract for the Amber Room with the Moritz Stumpf Company of Gdansk. Experts had called for 'rescue conservation', but even then it was considered too expensive. The Amber Room was an unusual, fragile and expensive piece of baroque interior design – a style that is not much valued nowadays. But its value today comes less from what it is, than from the stories connected to it. It was once owned by kings, tsars and empresses, and now it is lost under mysterious circumstances involving two totalitarian regimes and several apparent murders. And that is enough of a detective story to make even wall panels into a legend long after their own lifetime.

In 1978 the Soviets conceded that their room would not be coming home and commissioned a replacement. Fifty years before, a Communist government would have had nothing to do with anything that celebrated so blatantly the dazzling but oppressive years of the tsars. But times were changing: the Russian people wanted colourful things; the Soviet Union was opening up; and, most importantly, foreign sponsors were willing to pay the eight million dollars the new Amber Room cost. It took twenty-five years and six tonnes of amber, and it was finally opened in May 2003 by President Vladimir Putin, in front of more than forty world leaders. Many said it was beautiful, but there was quiet criticism as well: most of the amber had been pressed and treated like the teddy-bears on show at the Yantarny Museum. Was it art or Disney?

Perhaps it was both: the Amber Room had never been a simple celebration of beauty. Frederick commissioned it when he wanted to prove his authority as king; his son Frederick William used it to prove who was in charge of the Baltic. When the Russians started to rebuild it during the Cold War they intended it to be a sign of Soviet power, but when Putin opened it in 2003 it had been skilfully transformed into a PR display for the New Russia.

The story of the Amber Room embodies the history of amber itself. It was rarely a simple commodity. It was for show, used to prove something and make something happen. So, the Phoenicians, the Aestii, the Teutonic Knights, the Prussians, the Soviets, the Germans and the Russians used amber to boost their political standing. Yet as I travelled through the lands of amber I hoped to find something more redeeming about this fossil gemstone. I kept wondering whether it might reflect another kind of power – the kind that Ezekiel had seen in it, or that Queen Elizabeth I's physician, William Gilbert, had wondered at when he coined the word 'electricity'.

Return from Kaliningrad

I don't know what I would have expected if someone had suggested I'd share the ride back to Poland with professional smugglers, but it would not have been the nineteen women who clanked on to the 6.30 a.m. bus to Gdansk loaded with plastic bags. They were all in their fifties, with high-heeled shoes and immaculately coiffed blonde hair. The bus smelt of hairspray. 'They are vodka smugglers,' the man next to me explained. 'They do this every day.' The border is riddled with smuggling rings. Sometimes it is money, sometimes alcohol, sometimes petrol – and, of course, many kilos of amber come over the border without papers or provenance every day. At my request, he asked one of the smugglers if she ever took amber across, but she refused to answer. 'She thinks I'm the police,' he said. She had good reason to think so. The Polish Customs Office claim to have confiscated eighty kilos of amber in the first three months of 2005, including a single haul of twenty-one kilos,[52] but the fines are so small that it is worth the risk.

When we reached the border there was a flurry, and the chief smuggler went off, handbag swinging, to check which customs officers were on duty. They called one 'Hitler' and if it was his shift they would turn back, bottle bags clanking. But Hitler was otherwise occupied, and an hour later another officer appeared. 'Does anyone have anything to declare?' he asked, from the front of the bus.

'Oh, no,' said the ladies, wide-eyed.

'Does anyone have any alcohol?'

'Oh, no,' they fluttered.

If anyone had been watching from outside the officer would

have looked very efficient, marching up and down the aisle, interrogating the passengers. But he only searched two Russian weekend tourists, with little backpacks, and a businessman with a briefcase; neither was carrying amber or alcohol.

'Someone's paid him off,' my neighbour whispered.

As soon as the officer had left, the woman in front of me began to gossip about him. 'Sssh you fool,' hissed another from a few rows up. 'He might come back.' What a contrast it was to smuggling in the time of the Teutonic Knights, when the penalty was death.

The Amber Altar

Back in Gdansk the city was celebrating the sunshine: the streets were full of people eating impossibly tall ice-creams as they strolled past old façades and statues. As I stood in the medieval precinct of Long Market, listening to a string quartet playing in the open air, it felt a universe away from Kaliningrad, where everything was grey, dull and disconnected. However, sixty years before, the two cities had been almost the same: Gdansk, too, had been mostly rubble. But while the Russians had rebuilt their city without regard to the past, the Poles had rebuilt theirs with pride. If their people were poor, then they were going to make sure their buildings were rich. If they had lost everything, then they were going to build it again, just the same. Although most elements of the 'seventeenth-century' houses lining Long Market were barely fifty years old, they looked wonderful. It was a good simile for the new Amber Room. Much as a rebuilt Gdansk is better than a Kaliningrad, so perhaps it is also better to have a non-authentic Amber Room made with pressed and treated amber, if the other choice is to have nothing at all. The new one might not be made of amber harvested by oppressed labour under the Teutonic Knights, but at least visitors have a chance to walk through a room whose décor makes gold seem dim by comparison; and begin to understand what amber might once have signified, even if it doesn't signify it now.

A few streets away from Long Market something is slowly taking shape that might prove to be more extraordinary than the Amber Room. It is an altar, and when it is finished it will be the largest and perhaps most beautiful amber construction in the world. The medieval St Bridget's Church was as damaged as the rest of Gdansk during the war, but because in 1948 the Stalinists who took power recognised the Catholic Church quite justifiably as a threat to their regime,[53] it was left for decades as a ruin. In the mid-1970s St Bridget's was given a copy of a painting called *Our Lady of Częstochowa*[54] in memory of twenty-eight Gdansk shipyard workers killed by the Communist authorities. The church still had no roof, so the priest hung the painting outside, as a statement of support for the Solidarity movement. It was there in all weathers, rain and snow, but was apparently undamaged.[55] It was like a miracle, the shipyard workers said. It became a sacred symbol for them and St Bridget's became a centre for anti-communist activity.

In 1999, with Communist rule ended in Poland, and *Our Lady of Częstochowa* hanging above the altar of the now rebuilt church, someone had the idea of making her a dress of amber. Icon-makers have traditionally used the most precious of garments in dressing the Virgin. In medieval paintings, for example, she is usually shown in blue because ultramarine[56] was then the most expensive pigment in the world; in sixteenth-century Holland she was sometimes depicted in red because cochineal was the rarest and most precious dyestuff. So in Gdansk she was clothed in white amber.

The icon's cloak was created by the local artist Mariusz Drapikowski, from material donated by local amber producers from their private collections. When it was finished it was blessed by Pope John Paul II (himself a Pole) and the congregation decided to make an amber altar to surround the icon. It will contain eight tonnes of amber, to the Amber Room's six, and will measure 120 square metres to the room's eighty-six. It will also be made of only natural materials, however long it takes to gather them: and – most important to the Poles – the amber will all be sourced in Poland, dug out of the ground with special permission from the government, and gathered from the beaches in the traditional way. But the biggest difference is that unlike the Amber Room, the altar will celebrate a higher power than that of a king, tsar or empress. 'I want to show how the celestial light shines through it,' said Drapikowski. 'I want to build this altar out of light.'

The design will contain all the elements of amber: the fossilised insects, the rainbow colours, the suffering, the beauty, the electricity and the history. But most of all it will contain the wonder of this electric, eclectic material that was possibly the world's first traded gemstone. And the hope is that it will be a material demonstration of why – when looking for a simile to persuade his listeners that he had really seen the glory of God – the prophet Ezekiel should have picked the image of amber.

Jet

'[England] has much and excellent jet, which is black and
sparkling, glittering at the fire, and, when heated, drives away
serpents; being warmed with rubbing it holds fast whatever is
applied to it, like amber.'

VENERABLE BEDE[1]

'Black was best looking . . . Ebony was the best wood, the
hardest wood; it was black. Virginia ham was the best ham. It
was black on the outside. Tuxedos and tail coats were black
and they were a man's finest, most expensive clothes . . . The
best caviar was black. The rarest jewels were black: black
opals, black pearls.'

ANN PETRY[2]

At first it seemed like an ordinary skeleton – or, at least, the
ordinary sixteen-hundred-year-old skeleton of a wealthy female.
Skeleton 952 was discovered in an excavation near Catterick
Roman fort in north Yorkshire, and had been buried with several
items of jewellery. There were the remains of what once must
have been an impressive necklace, with more than six hundred
jet beads, spread out like hungry black ants between the bones
of the ribs. There was also a shale[3] armband and an expanding
bronze anklet. But as the archaeologists moved the earth away
from the bones, they noticed two unusual things: first, that
there were two pebbles in the skull space where the tongue had
once been; second, that of all the bodies discovered in the
ancient cemetery, this one was at a short distance from the

others and furthest from the Roman road. Such a richly accoutred person should surely be in the best location; not in the worst.

Nearly two millennia after its foundation, Catterick is still a base for Britain's armed forces and the archaeologists had to complete their dig quickly, in the nine months before a roundabout and road were built over the site, linking it with the guarded gates of Catterick's Royal Air Force base. They found the remains of sixteen adults and a baby, all of whom had been buried in the fourth century, towards the end of the Roman occupation of Britain. And although only a few of them wore any kind of adornments, the site still needed to have good security measures. It wasn't only the ancient jewellery the archaeologists were worried about: sometimes souvenir-hunters have been known to take the skulls and bones.

They sent the bones to a laboratory, but it wasn't until some time after the results had come back that Pete Wilson, the archaeologist leading the excavation, noticed a discrepancy. He called the laboratory: 'I said, "You've got Skeleton 952 down as a male." And he said, "Yes, that's because it is male." I asked him if he was absolutely certain, and he said, "Yes."' And later the proof came in. 'She' had been a slender, young man in his early twenties.

Why was he wearing a necklace? Males in Roman Britain were almost never buried with jewellery – and in any case this one could never have been mistaken for the classical equivalent of a chest medallion. It was far too ornate: the jewellery experts at English Heritage have reconstructed an elaborate three-strand necklace that would look overblown even if worn by a countess in an opera box at the height of the nineteenth century. Also, although homosexuality was generally tolerated, and even encouraged, during Roman times, people were evidently less sure about cross-dressing – and nothing like this from Roman Britain had ever been found before, let alone worn by a man.

The jet necklace was being kept in the splendid half-ruined eighteenth-century Fort Cumberland near Portsmouth, where Dr Wilson and his team-members from English Heritage are based. Our meeting coincided with a National Archaeology Open Day, so the conversation was punctuated by the booms (and on one occasion 'oh bugger') of the Civil War being re-enacted outside the window. Dr Wilson passed me some white cotton gloves to put on before I picked up the ornaments that had caused the speculation. They were so light that they felt almost hollow, as black as velvet and beautifully made; some were like cubes with the corners cut off; some like washers; some solid black wiggles; all were less than two centimetres long.

Perhaps more than any other gemstone, ancient jet must be handled with care: it is one of the softest, scoring between 2.5 and 4 on Mohs' scale. Most other minerals will scratch it – a steel blade easily slices a groove into it – so it is usually too soft to be cut in facets like harder gemstones. The most common way to polish jet is either *en cabochon*, which means rounded like a little head ('cabbage' comes from the same Norman French root), or as I was seeing them in Portsmouth – as beads.

What had these objects meant to the man who had worn them and to those who had buried him? Holding the burial beads through the thin cotton felt like a metaphor for experiencing the past. We know it is there, we know what it looks like; we roughly know its weight and colour. But our experience of it is gloved: in the end we can only imagine what it meant.

Archaeology is all about guesswork and speculation: a pinch of facts mixed with a trowel of trust. As Dr Wilson said, 'It's a big jigsaw in which ninety-seven per cent of the pieces are missing, but you have to keep asking, "Why?"' A novelist would have invented the answers to the conundrum of Skeleton 952: perhaps he was a Roman lady-boy, buried by his friends during a spectacular party at dead of night on the edge of the cemetery; or perhaps he had dressed as a woman all his life to avoid conscription into the legion and had died with his secret intact. There were so many possibilities. A mystery was hidden among the white bones and black beads.

What Is Jet?

Jet was once alive. Most other gems have mineral[4] or resin origins, but once upon a time, jet was pure wood. It comes from forests that existed 170 million years ago. They were not ordinary forests, but were composed of just one, very peculiar type of tree, which propagated itself in an aggressive natural form of monoculture. The jet tree was a bizarre species of conifer, with a banded spiky trunk, lower branches sweeping the ground like a Restoration actor's bow, and cones the size of a human head. Its foliage created such darkness on the forest floor that it stifled everything around it. Today the tree's formal family name is 'Araucaria': because although it became extinct in most of the world after the prehistoric period, its descendant, the Chile pine, lived on in the Andes, sharing their home with the Araucara Indians who slept in their shade and made alcohol from their needles. Araucaria is better known in Britain by its nickname given on the day in 1834 when a Sir William Molesworth of Cornwall held a planting party in his garden. He wanted to celebrate the arrival of a South American tree he had bought for twenty-five pounds, then the price of a small house. His friend Charles Austin thought it a very peculiar piece of flora indeed. The spiny foliage would 'puzzle a monkey' to climb it,[5] he said, and the image stuck.

Jet was used in Britain long before the Romans arrived – jet beads have been found in 4500-year-old Bronze Age barrows in Yorkshire, Derbyshire and Scotland. They were scattered on funeral pyres after the flames had died away[6] – we know this because the jet was intact while the body was gone. We also know that the Romans liked jet. Pliny wrote that it came from

Lycia, in what is now south-eastern Turkey, and took its name, *gagates*, from a town or a river called Gagate. For a long time this was something of a mystery: although there was a port once called Gagate there is no known source of jet anywhere near it. However, there was a source in Britain, and the Romans later exported from there, sending it out to the Empire throughout their occupation of Britain. In the late nineteenth century, archaeologists discovered a Roman jet workshop in the foundations of the railway station in York. The find included several pendants in the form of gorgon heads, which were identical in workmanship and material to pendants found in 1846 in two Roman coffins beneath the fourth-century church of St Gereon in Cologne.

The source of those pendants, as well as Skeleton 952's mysterious necklace, was almost certainly the area around Whitby, on the north Yorkshire coast, a place renowned for the best and hardest jet in the world. It is also a place that for nearly two hundred years – perhaps even 4500 – has been connected with the accoutrements of death. So I went there – to learn more about the clues left by Skeleton 952, the strange story of jet and the meaning this ancient and almost forgotten jewel might possibly have today.

Scratchpads for Dinosaurs

When you drive across the bare Yorkshire moors that link Whitby with the rest of England, or when you look at that bleak, treeless landscape from the sea, it is hard to believe that, once, this region was covered by a great, dark forest. However in the Jurassic period, monkey-puzzle ancestors thrived in this area of the vast continent of Pangea. It was the era of the great dinosaurs – and it is easy to imagine a benign diplodocus pausing for a moment to scratch its haunches against the spiky, tall trees at the edge of the forest before continuing on to a nearby waterhole. The forests remained for thousands, perhaps millions of years. Then, over a few centuries, they died by the grove-full – perhaps because of the same kind of dramatic climate changes that later caused the dinosaurs to become extinct. As the huge trees crashed to the ground, massive log-jams built up. Whitby must have been a horrible place then: the entire area would have been a stinking, rotting swamp.

But things looked up for both Whitby and jet's raw ingredients over the next few million years. The rotting logs were covered with glutinous mud, which allowed them to fossilise anaerobically – without air – and shrink to a black layer of jet just a few centimetres thick. Around it there were deposits of ammonites and even pyrite, or fool's gold, which sometimes makes the jet sparkle. Directly above it a layer of limestone formed, which became known as the 'Top Dogger' because it was part of the Dogger Bank geological layer, formed in Jurassic times. Fine alum shales, sands, silts and carbonaceous clays, testifying to millions of years of work by rivers and seas, lay over the limestone – and above all of that was formed the Anglo-Saxon town of Whitby, a town whose fortunes have mostly depended on two things: the price of fish, and how the rest of England has felt about mourning and memory.

Whitby seems to wear its history on its sleeve and its geology on its cliffs. It is full of cobbled streets, ancient steps, fried fish and pretty sweets, and has been attracting tourists ever since the arrival of the York and North Midland Railway in 1846 marked the end of its long isolation from the rest of the country. Before that the main access to the town was from the sea port, which supported one of the country's biggest whaling and fishing fleets.

It is a lovely ramshackle town. In the 1890s the Irish novelist Bram Stoker set part of *Dracula* there – he arranged for his vampire to arrive at Whitby by sea in a coffin – and his character Mina Murray describes the houses of the old town as 'piled up, one over the other anyhow, like the pictures we see of Nuremberg'.[7] On the surface little has changed. The winding alleys in the medieval town are lined with little piled-up shops, their old-fashioned windows full of crochet patterns, liquorice curls, bright sugar mice, home-made chocolate and sherbet lemons – a display of English childhood in jars, as if everything happy has been thrown together in a nostalgic chaos. Nearby are dusty

The houses of Whitby are 'piled up, one over the other'

mineral shops with curled ammonites crowding against chunks of agates and sea-jet. They compete with modern jewellers selling designer pieces, many of which have been imported. That contrast has been evident in Whitby throughout its history: between tradition and innovation, old and new. In 664 the Synod of Whitby debated the dates on which Easter should be celebrated. The meeting was about more than a holiday. It was about going global or staying local, about whether the Church in England should continue in traditional Celtic ways or bring in something new from Rome – indeed it was probably one of the first formal discussions about whether or not England would join the rest of Europe.

Whitby Abbey is now in ruins, a tourist attraction, complete with audio commentaries on the lives of the monks and nuns who lived there after St Hilda founded it in 657. This abbess was one of the great feminist role models of early English Christianity and one of the miraculous stories about her tells how the monastery once suffered a surfeit of snakes. The abbess took the matter in hand: she lopped off their heads and threw them off the cliffs – where they turned into stone on the beach. The story was accepted as an explanation of how the ammonite fossils – found in great numbers in the cliffs below the abbey, and indeed, all along the Yorkshire coast – came into being. But it has a strange echo in the Roman-era jet gorgons, with the snakes on their heads that turned humans to stone, as well as

Ammonites on Kettleness beach, near Whitby

in a popular theory that was current even in Roman times. Jet was said by many early commentators to have the power to banish snakes, although contemporary snake experts are not familiar with this idea.[8] But jet frequently appears close to the ammonite layer, which may explain how the myth arose.

On my first evening in Whitby I climbed the worn stone steps leading to the abbey,[9] and stopped outside St Mary's Church, which Stoker describes as 'another church, the parish one, round which is a big graveyard, all full of tombstones'.[10] Some time during the eighteenth century, William Scoresby, a whaling captain, was daydreaming through a dull sermon there. He imagined the vicar and his three-tier Georgian pulpit transposed onto the mast of one of his ships; when he returned to sea he invented the crow's nest. As I sat in the dark, looking over the lights of Whitby, I heard a scuffle and some giggles. A torch wobbled round a corner and three teenagers emerged behind its light like the cover of a 1950s children's detective story. They looked as if they had seen a ghost. 'What are you doing?' I asked.

'We're looking for Dracula's grave,' one boy said. 'It's supposed to be somewhere here.'

I didn't spoil their fun by pointing out that Dracula was fictitious, but I did suggest that he probably wouldn't have been seen dead in a Christian graveyard – and that if there was a grave it was probably outside the walls, since vampires disliked crucifixes.

As the torch careered drunkenly but cheerfully towards the far side of the graveyard I was reminded of one of the puzzles posed by Skeleton 952: that his coffin was a surprisingly long way from the road.

Today we are usually casual about the geomancy of where we are buried: we don't mind which side of the church or cemetery we occupy, or our ashes can be strewn in any pretty place where we were happy. But in medieval times these things mattered. Nobody would have liked to be interred on the north side of the church: that was where the dark forces came from, so the rich insisted they were laid to rest on the south side. Similarly, the Romans had very strict beliefs about where they ended up. In a culture so fascinated by death that it had built a necropolis or 'city of the dead' on the outskirts of every town and where the supreme post-mortem compliment was to be buried beside[11] a major road, it was surprising that such an apparently wealthy person as Skeleton 952 had been placed in such a lowly position. Clearly he was a man with whom other Romans had a problem. Or perhaps he was not Roman at all.

The Rise and Fall of Jet

In the era of our mysterious jet-wearer Whitby was probably just a small settlement. But the presence of many early-fourth-century coins and the discovery of Whitby jet in Romano-British burials suggest that there might already have been a thriving jet industry in the area. In the 1920s two perfect jet rings were found during an excavation of a Roman signal station at Kettleness, three kilometres north of Whitby. On the same site there were several pieces of rough jet, some that had been partly carved, which suggested that soldiers worked it, perhaps during long night watches. The archaeologists also unearthed a small black fly-wheel from a weaving spindle. It had been crafted on a lathe and indicated that, even in Roman times, professional jet-workers operated in or near the station. Perhaps they were neighbours of those who had made the crafted beads I had held in Portsmouth.

A small international jet trade in Whitby continued over the thousand years after Skeleton 952 was buried: Viking buttons were found in York and Saxon hairpins in Germany; receipts show that the abbey bought black buttons in the fourteenth century, while beads and dice were dug up in a seventh-century Whitby rubbish dump – it was found when space was being cleared for a new jet workshop at Black Horse Yard in the old town.[12] But then there was a long lull, punctuated by brief resurgences of popularity. John Donne's poem 'A Jet Ring Sent' illustrates the gem's ambiguous status in the seventeenth century. In it he likens the fickleness of his lover's heart to the brittleness of a jet ring she had given him.

> 'Marriage rings are not of this stuff;
> Oh, why should aught less precious, or less tough
> Figure our loves? Except in thy name thou have bid it say,
> I am cheap, and naught but fashion, fling me away.'

In the nineteenth century everything changed: British women perfected the fine art of mourning and the old jet-working methods were revived in Whitby.

The Business of Death

In January 1870 a Mr Charles Bryan hosted an annual supper for his employees at the Black Horse Hotel in Whitby. He began the meal with a toast to 'The health of our most gracious Queen.'[13] Everyone drank with enthusiasm. The diners were the jet workers of Whitby and Queen Victoria's taste for their products had kept them in employment for years.

Seventy years before, there had been no jet workers in England, and the techniques used in carving it had been forgotten. Then, around 1800, John Carter, a publican, and his friend Robert Jefferson started whittling it in their spare time.[14] One day a retired sea captain dropped in for a drink at Carter's pub and saw the men engrossed in their roughly carved black beads. The seaman had an amber bracelet in his pocket, picked up on one of his voyages, and pulled it out to show them. The quality of the beads was much better than Jefferson and Carter were achieving and they wondered how they could match it. Eventually they employed a local turner, and were soon receiving orders from London. By 1832 there were two jet shops, and by 1850 seven people in Whitby were calling themselves 'master jet-makers', including Thomas Andrews, who put 'Jet Ornament Maker to Her Majesty the Queen' on the sign above his shop, and Isaac Greenbury, who claimed to make bracelets for the Empress of France.

The nineteenth century was a time of treasure 'rushes', usually inspired by the chance discovery of gold or a gemstone in a foreign riverbed. The Whitby jet rush of the 1860s and 1870s was different – because it began with a loss. On a cold, damp December day in 1861, Prince Albert was buried at St George's Chapel in Windsor. It was a private funeral, although the whole of England soon knew about the grief of his children – 'little Prince Arthur especially sobbing as if his heart were breaking'.[15] The widowed Queen Victoria was distraught, and would grieve publicly until the day she died, nearly forty years later.

Mourning was already a significant part of life in Victorian England. However, when the Queen's beloved consort died, mourning became a national pastime – and after the Queen adopted Whitby jet as her mourning adornment, it became the height of fashion. Even the few lucky women who were not in mourning during those times of cholera and troubled childbirth ordered necklaces made of jet – because it was so light that large beads could be worn comfortably and to great effect over the big, puffy dresses of the time. Victoria was not the first British queen to mourn with jet. In London's National Portrait Gallery[16] there is a sixteenth-century portrait of Mary Queen of Scots, which shows her burdened with mourning: her jet ornaments symbolise her grief at the violent death of Roman Catholic religion.

The colours of grieving vary almost as much as the cultures of those who grieve. In Armenia people mourned in sky blue to express the hope that their loved ones were now in heaven. In Persia it was the pale brown of withered leaves, while white is still worn in many parts of Asia, to celebrate the belief that the deceased has moved into the light. In Brittany some widows even wore yellow for mourning. However, from at least Ancient Greek and Roman times,[17] black – signifying the absence of light and the long night of sorrow – has been *de rigueur* for funerals in Western culture, and jet the perfect accessory. Also, when jet is warmed, it attracts lint to it, like amber, and this inner electricity supports an innate heat, which means it may spontaneously combust. At times over the centuries, Whitby jet-shop owners have arrived at work to find their premises destroyed by their own jewels. But even this was consoling to some bereaved buyers: what better gem to bring comfort in death than one with the capability of warming those who are cold?

During the 1860s and 1870s the streets of Whitby resounded with the noise of trestle wheels turning to make black brooches, crucifixes, elaborate necklaces and cameos – not always for grieving: some of the carvings were of fruit and flowers that were purely to do with fashion. Lockets bore silhouettes of the departed, or contained locks of their hair. People also were sentimental and liked to spell out their feelings in stones: a necklace of fire-opal, opal, ruby, emerald, vermeil beads,[18] essonite[19] and rubellite meant that they would remember their loved one F-O-R-E-V-E-R.[20] When I first found this out I checked my own necklace which was made of silver beads, amber and pearls. I realised I had been wearing the word S-A-P around my neck for years.

There were jet workshops all over Whitby in those days – in attics, basements, tenements, even built into the side of the cliffs, 'in such positions that they would remind you at once of the swallow's nest,' wrote Hugh Kendall, in the 1930s when the jet industry was thought to be finished. He produced *The Story of Whitby Jet*, based on interviews with Matthew Snowdon, who had been an apprentice sixty years before, and was one of the few people who knew anything about the old industry. He estimated that at least fourteen hundred men had been making jet jewellery in the 1870s, while many more collected the raw material from the beach or small mines[21] along the coast. The mining work was dangerous and often involved men and boys dangling from ropes attached to the cliff top looking for seams. Sometimes they came across fossils: an eight-metre-long[22] *Ichthyosaurus crassimanus*, found by jet miners in 1862, was so spectacular that seventy years later Whitby Museum was extended to contain it. (The architect made a mistake with the measurements, and the skeleton had to be split in half.)[23] Ironically, as Victorian England went wild for the fossils found just above the Yorkshire jet layer, no one realised that jet was a fossil too: until 1904,[24] when its true nature was discovered, it was thought to be a sedimentary layer, like shale.

Despite the craze for jet, the work was badly paid in the early years, and the miners had little money. Their homes were slums and infectious diseases spread because so many people had to sleep in the same beds. In May 1862, 60 per cent of all recorded deaths in Whitby were of jet-workers' children.[25] At its height, however, the industry was worth £200,000[26] a year and the jet bosses were the *nouveaux riches* of the Yorkshire coast. Their workers, though, spent most of their bonuses in the pubs and every week jet-men were summoned to explain their drunken behaviour to the local magistrates.

It was usual in those years, Matthew Snowdon remembered, for him and the other workers to gather by the pier rails after dinner for a chat and a 'whiff' of tobacco, then work through the evening. Some orders were from private clients, but increasing numbers were from the *magasins de deuil*, or mourning shops, established on a Parisian model, that had supplied the women of Britain since the 1840s with the paraphernalia of grief. To a new arrival, the scene by the pier as the men took their early-evening break might have looked like a butchers' convention: or perhaps a band of crazed Good Friday flagellators, resting after the procession. Their artisan smocks, faces, hands and hair were

Jet shop, Whitby

Jet-workers on a Victorian shop sign in Whitby

splattered not with black, as might have been expected, but with deep red.

The Red Devils

In the 1990s and 2000s jet was briefly fashionable again, and London jeweller Hal Redvers-Jones was one of those to arrive in Yorkshire and become what was known locally as a 'red devil'. He opened a small shop at the foot of the abbey steps, and soon found that most visitors knew nothing about jet. 'Doesn't it come in any other colours than black?' they would ask. There was one query that he had no answer to, however, which was why the people who worked with black stones should have been nicknamed 'red devils'. When he asked around, some locals thought it might have had something to do with fingers catching in machinery, but no one knew for sure. Like other modern jet-men, Redvers-Jones used the traditional jeweller's polish, called 'rouge', but it was a small part of the process, and he could not understand why the nickname had been applied only to jet-workers rather than other jewellers. Then, by chance, a property developer bought some derelict houses in Burn's Yard in the West Town, and when the builders opened one of the attics they found a complete jet workshop, including all the tools. Redvers-Jones bought it, and reinstalled it all as a small museum beside his workshop.

The museum is an almost perfectly intact display of the old assembly lines, from the desk of the foreman, who would select the best jet for carving, to the dangerous grinding-stone area where the jet was rough-cut, exuding a faint scent of petroleum that betrayed the gemstone's carboniferous origins. Then there were the craftsmen's benches, where the cameos and beads were made, and the polishing sections where the jet was rubbed with walrus skins bought from whalers. It was in this section of the discarded workshop that Redvers-Jones found his clue to the name 'red devils'. 'I found a rusty old Cadbury's Cocoa tin,' he said, 'and I saw it was full of streaks of rouge polish. Then I found a tin jug, nipped in like a cream jug, and realised they had been putting linseed oil in there to mix with it.'

Before he had seen that jug, he had always thought the red polish should be of butter consistency with the rouge mixed with linseed, just like an artist's oil paint. 'But when I saw that jug I suddenly realised it couldn't have been so solid or it wouldn't have poured.' He realised that the jet-workers must have used something like paraffin to dilute it to the correct consistency. When he tried it, he discovered that not only was it much more effective as a polishing agent, but it created a dramatic effect. When he put it on the wheel it sprayed round the workshop like a massacre, and for the first time he was worthy of the name 'red devil'.

'It just shows that evidence doesn't have to be splendid,' he said. 'I learned about the red because of an old tin I nearly threw away with the rubbish.' It put into perspective the detective work of the archaeologists at Catterick: if we do not know how or why things happened a hundred years ago, then how much harder must it be to unravel the mysteries of sixteen centuries past.

A Significant Death

By the 1880s the red devils were feeling rather blue – and probably less eager to toast the health of the Queen than they had been in 1870. For although Victoria still slept with a photograph of her late husband's death mask above her head, she was now wearing 'white jewellery', consisting mostly of pearls and diamonds, and viewed today by the Royal Family as appropriate at any stage of mourning.[27] The popularity of jet was diminishing, and Whitby was praying for a significant death to boost its trade. A few promising orders were still coming in by telegram to the Whitby workshops: whenever an important European royal died there were calls for black. As late as 1889 a maid-of-honour at Buckingham Palace wrote to her mother saying, 'I am in despair about my clothes, no sooner have I rigged myself out with good tweeds than we are plunged into the deepest mourning for the King of Portugal, jet ornaments for six weeks! . . . It is a lesson, *never*, never to buy anything but black!'[28]

Apart from the longevity of the Queen of England there were other reasons for the eclipse of jet: greed, and that old chestnut of Whitby's history – the choice between staying local or going global. Again, global won – and jet-carvers began to bring in the gem from overseas where it was cheaper and softer. Some was Polish, but most came from near Santiago de Compostela in northern Spain where jet had an important place in local symbolic life: until the 1930s most children wore black beads to ward off the evil eye.[29] Even today many of the devout pilgrims arriving at Santiago de Compostela still go to Azabache, or 'Jet' Street, to buy *figas*, carved hands with the index finger extended – 'giving the finger' to the devil and gossip.[30]

But the imported jet was of poor quality: it chipped and the gloss became matt, causing many potential buyers to give the black finger to all 'Whitby' jet. It didn't help that jet substitutes were starting to appear on the market. 'French jet' was a black glass that Whitby men called 'bastard jet', although London buyers liked it better – the word 'French' gave it a certain racy appeal. Then there was black steel jewellery from Germany, invented by women in Berlin who had sold their real jewels to pay for the 1870 Prussian war against Napoleon, but who also needed something with which to grieve for their dead sons and husbands. Glass and steel were too heavy for big necklaces or earrings, so women in England began to buy a primitive form of plastic invented by Goodyear: 'vulcanite', so-called because it was produced in furnaces. It was a decent visual and weight match for the jewel it replaced, although at first it was easy for anyone to distinguish it from real jet, using a time-honoured test that still works.

If you scratch jet against a piece of rough porcelain – like the back of a tile or the bottom of a tea-cup – it leaves a surprising chocolate-coloured streak. Coal makes a black mark because it is softer, glass a white one, and the original vulcanite, a thin trail of grey. However, when manufacturers realised this they added brown dye to the surface of the plastic to deceive the testers. Today the best way to test Victorian 'jet' is to heat a needle and hold it to the back of the piece. If it is jet, nothing will happen, but vulcanite or other plastic will bubble and give off an acrid smell. A more dramatic – if destructive – test is to hold the piece in the flame of a match. Vulcanite will melt immediately, but if the substance burns with a sooty green flame and gives off a tar-like smell, it is almost certainly jet.

I went to the Whitby Archives to find out more about jet alternatives, and unexpectedly solved the mystery of Pliny's Turkish jet. While there is no source of jet anywhere near south-western Turkey, it can be found in western Anatolia near Erzurum, where there are about six hundred family-run mines in the mountains. They call it *oltu-tasi* and it is the material from which Muslim prayer-beads are made. So, for the Romans to call jet *gagate* after a place in the south-west was akin to calling Cheddar cheese 'Bristol' or tartan 'Glasgow' – in other words, by the name of the port from which it was exported.[31] The name 'jet' is a historical mistake.

'If you want to know about jet then you should be here on a Goths' weekend,' said Eileen Bennett, who worked at the Whitby Archives. Every May and October, she said, several thousand people descend on Whitby to celebrate the Victorian Gothic story of Dracula. 'They dress in black and purple and put eye-liner on – and that's just the fellas! They like black jewellery and those who can afford it wear jet. 'It's very good for the town even though when you first see them you think, "Good God!"' Her friend Gill Swales agreed. 'They're lovely, lovely people,' she said, 'even though they do look a bit strange sometimes.'

All Back and No Front

When I went to Whitby most of the men who had worked with jet in the old days and knew its history were dead, but one name came up again and again: Tommy Roe. I was told that he was a secretive man, and hard to find, but at the archives I had learned he lived 'between Aunt Betsy's mint kisses and a knitwear shop'. Armed with those unlikely instructions, I soon found myself in one of Whitby's seventeenth-century yards. Once upon a time it would have been full of the children who lived in the tenements around it, and the jet-workers coming out for a quick smoke. But today it was empty, except for a tiny old man who was putting out his rubbish. Did he know where Tommy Roe was? 'That's me,' he said shyly, and when I explained my mission he invited me into his home. Only later did I realise how much an act of trust this was.

He comes from a long line of jet-men; the Roes were first recorded in 1569. 'We're a Catholic family and we were caught smuggling jet beads [for rosaries] to the Catholics in York Castle,' he said. At the height of the Puritan persecutions of Catholics in England, simply to own a rosary was enough to brand you a heretic, which is something Mary Queen of Scots was certainly referring to when she showed herself wearing jet in her portrait. The Roes were evidently brave to be jet smugglers then, and some paid for it with their lives.

Tommy had an astonishing memory for local history. It was almost as if, for him, the Reformation and the Victorian era had as much bearing on the present as anything that had happened in his lifetime. His grandfather had gone into jet in the 1870s and made a lot of money until the fashion changed. 'By the 1890s people were tired of jet. When Queen Victoria died, there was a brief boom, but not for long.' The horrors of the First World War had not helped jet either – it was as if there was too much grief for organised mourning – but it was briefly in demand among the flappers in the 1920s, the age of art deco black and white.

Tommy had learned the trade from his parents. His father had a jet workshop, while his mother was employed by Collier's, the ironmongery. He remembered a moment in his childhood worthy of any magic realism novel, when the first Spanish pedlar visited Whitby to sell jet from Santiago de Compostela – 'He was almost lynched.' But then he met Miss Collier: they fell in love and to the much-expressed amazement of the neighbourhood gossips, they were married. 'His name was Mr Pagero, and my mother was nanny for them.'

Sometimes Tommy's mother graded the jet beads and threaded them into necklaces and rosaries 'but she couldn't go into the workshop: it was unlucky'. They were a superstitious family, Tommy admitted. His parents believed that it was lucky to keep jet in your pocket, and that its green smoke assisted in childbirth: he and his four siblings were born with the smell of their father's trade in their nostrils. At the front door of their family home there was a mirror: 'If the devil came in he would see his own reflection and leave in disgust.' Beside it was a jet cross, just to make sure he got the message. 'There were jet posts on the moors at Egton with crosses beside them to ward away the evil eye,' he said. 'They called them witches' posts. Everyone believed it in the old days.' There was a black cross on the wall beside Tommy's door.

'Is that one?' I asked.

'No, it's not. And it's not jet, it's glass. My cousin brought it over and I told her, "It's not jet," and she said, "Shut up, you silly fool, just put it on the wall," so I did.' He didn't have much jet of his own: he had given his best pieces to the museum. 'Whitby people don't like it much. My mother refused to wear it, saying it was organised gloom.'

This is the flip side of working with something associated with mourning: when the fashion for it is gone, all that is left is the grief. In the nineteenth century, jet benefited from its association with Queen Victoria but in the twentieth this was exactly what gave it an image problem. In my childhood I remember it as a strange, dry stone owned and worn by old ladies, and associated with the smell of lavender, fustiness and decay. From Queen Victoria to the Victorian ladies still alive in the 1960s, it was as if the gem originally intended to console people had encouraged them to continue grieving, rather than allowing them to move on.

However, jet had given Tommy Roe some joy: it had taken him round the world, to China, Japan ('where what they said was jet was just plastic rubbish') and America, but it had been gloomy for him too in the end. A few years ago he was beaten up when his workshop was burgled, and more attacks followed. He sold the jet shop. 'I don't miss the fear,' he said, although he was sad to have to change the habits of a lifetime. In old Whitby those who had family members at sea never locked their houses because they believed that if they did, their relatives might never come back. Now, after eight smash-and-grab raids, Tommy locks up: 'I don't let anyone in now. I wouldn't have let you in, if I hadn't been outside anyway.' The old Whitby had had different values, he said: 'We were brought up to be all back and no front. Even if we were rich we'd have no posh cars but would live quietly and never show our worth.' Sixty years ago Church Street, the main walkway in the old town, was lined with small cottages and crowded with large families, 'But even though it didn't look like it, there was more money at the top end of Church Street than in the Yorkshire Bank.' In the past Whitby was a community: 'If you hurt one you hurt us all.

We were brought up to fear God and respect the King and Queen . . .' he said, pointing out across the harbour where we could see some bunting left over from the Queen's Golden Jubilee celebrations a few weeks before. 'It used to be all like that. But now jet's gone; everything's gone.'

Did he have a family, I wondered. 'No,' he said. 'My Joan died before we were married.' They had known each other since they were children, and though they were engaged and in love with each other, they had never had the intimacy of a couple. 'We danced together, that's all. We shouldn't have waited really, but in those days you did wait. And then she died of cancer.' It was ironically his grief for his beloved that turned Tommy towards jet, just as the Victorians had been turned. 'Having a shop kept me sane: I had all that jet in stock anyway and I met so many people through it . . .' There had been nobody else, he added after a pause. 'There was only Joan.'

When I went out into the cobbled street I suddenly saw the place as he saw it. All front and no back; the old things gone and dying. And I realised that almost all my jet stories involved death: of a sweetheart, a town, an era, an industry, a mysterious man in Roman times. This stone's lightness was almost unbearable.

Finding Jet

It was of course the stone's lightness that had made it such an easy jewel for the Romans to gather, and my last quest in Whitby was to discover how Skeleton 952's jet had been found, given that there are no signs that the Romans mined it. It is ironic that now all the old Victorian mines have been closed, the only way to collect it legally is by picking it up from the beaches as the Romans did. And today – as it has probably been for thousands of years – it is a rather clandestine operation.

Hal Redvers-Jones had said that seventeen men worked for

him on and off, searching for jet on the beaches. When I had asked to talk to one, he said it was impossible. 'They don't like to talk much. Some of them don't even tell me their surnames.' There were seven and a half miles of cliffs with jet in them, 'but the seams are sometimes just a few millimetres thick. It's like looking for a needle in a haystack.' He warned me that most people want to keep their sources secret: I would be unlikely to find a jet-comber who would take me with him.

However, I was lucky. I found my guide selling jet ornaments from a painted barrow in the middle of old Whitby. Kevin Dixon said he picked up the rough jet from the beach after storms, then polished it into rounded cabochon pieces, which he sold to tourists. He had some small raw pieces for sale for a pound or two. Some had lines of wood in them – you could see what they had once been.

It had been stormy, and Kevin generously said I could go looking for jet with him. So on my final afternoon in Whitby we went to a section of Whitby's beach called the 'scar'. We walked to the top of Church Street along a row of picturesque cottages – not long ago the homes of fishermen but now empty, waiting for holiday lets – 'all front and no back' just as Tommy Roe had said, and then dropped down to the sea past a fish-smokery, which smelt of another century.

The jet was below the level of the beach, Kevin told me, and pointed to the Bell Buoy about a kilometre out to sea, which marked a natural shelf in the seabed. 'That's where the jet ledge is exposed in the water. It's dangerous for boats.' The violence of the sea dislodges the jet and washes it on to the beach. 'It's one of the good things about storms,' he said. I imagined the jet shelf like a Victorian map chest with the maps stored in flat drawers, waiting to be studied by the sea. As the sea pulls the drawers out it smashes their contents angrily into small pieces and sends them – smooth as plastic – on to the beach as a gift from the past.

Kevin Dixon, jet-worker

As we clambered about the cliffs shale scattered around us like a hailstorm. 'That's the seagulls throwing stones,' Kevin said. 'They think we're after their eggs.' At low tide the sandy beach was decorated with debris and we made our way to a large pool. 'First we'll look on the surface and then we'll kick it around to look at what's underneath,' he said, and instantly bent to pick up two tiny fragments of jet, just big enough for stud earrings.

I felt like a child, looking for hidden treasure. 'I've found some,' I said, a few minutes later, picking up a huge concave piece of gleaming blackness. This was easy. Kevin came over to examine my find. 'It's coconut,' he said.

A few minutes later I found a more promising piece. It even had the woody grain Kevin had told me to look for. But he snapped it in half. 'Wood,' he said. At the next rock-pool, I had better luck – or thought I did until Kevin said, 'Coal!' then went off to pick up several genuine pieces of 170-million-year-old monkey-puzzle. Meanwhile I was gathering a coal[32] collection big enough to last the winter. 'It's always like that the first time,' he said kindly.

I was working through a pile of natural jewellery – ruby chains of seaweed entwined with amethyst mussels – when something black caught my eye, the size and shape of a computer keyboard letter. This was jet: I knew before I asked. It was brighter than coal, crisper, like black glass, and looked more fragile, although it was stronger. And it was so old: it could just possibly have been made of wood on which a dinosaur scratched its backside. In the next hour or so I found several more small samples, including one that is now my favourite. It is about a centimetre square and a few millimetres thick. I love its gleaming plastic-ness, like a tuning button on a 1940s radio. But most of all I love its pattern. Preserved on its surface are the clear vein marks of an extinct leaf.

There are two types of jet: 'blue skin', which has what seem to be ice scratches on it, and 'yellow skin', which shows clear impressions of the feathery leaves and ferns of prehistoric plant life.[33] Mine is of the yellow variety, and it is easy to imagine it as a bright proto-ginkgo leaf, one of thousands that fell everywhere in a prehistoric tumble of golden petals.

Kevin was equally pleased: he had found a chunk of jet the size of a paperback book. He said he would put it away in a drawer until someone commissioned a special carving. The rest, the little pieces, would be polished up for earrings, or necklace beads. Skeleton 952 would have loved them.

A Strange Conclusion

I knew where Skeleton 952's jet had come from, how it was gathered, and how it had been formed. But the most important mystery remained unsolved: that of the jet-loving young man's identity. The archaeologists knew that he was likely to have been something of an outcast, yet he had not been entirely excluded from the garrison. They also knew that he was probably a cross-dresser, probably liked to make a ritual statement with his clothes and, from the jet and shale found with him, that he seemed to like black accessories. And they looked again at the two small stones found in his mouth. The evidence pointed to a rather unexpected theory, that this cross-dressing corpse might have been a member of the mystical cult of Cybele, a group that was considered bizarre even in Roman society, which was remarkable for its extremely odd sects.

The Romans called Cybele the Magna Mater, or 'Great Mother'. As well as representing death, vengeance and fertility, she was sometimes considered to be the goddess of matter itself – the words *mater*, mother, matrix and matter all having the same linguistic root.[34] Her origins were mysterious, but the Romans knew she came from the East and was a most demanding deity. She required her priests or *galli* to make the almost ultimate sacrifice: they had to castrate themselves. The operation – performed with ritual clamps – recalled what had happened when Cybele found her lover, Attis, in bed with a mortal woman. He was so ashamed of what he had done that he cut off his sexual organs.

If Skeleton 952 had been a *gallus*, he would have led an extraordinary life. The parades of Cybele were tumultuous affairs with clashing cymbals, drums, self-flagellation, high-pitched screams and cries of long-haired men, who wore dresses and necklaces, and no longer thought of themselves completely as men. Homer's poem about the Great Mother tells us, 'She loves the clatter of rattles, the din of kettle drums and she loves the wailing of flutes.'[35] Public worship of Cybele included the ritual sacrifice of a ram, while the priest stood beneath on a platform to be spattered with its blood. In fact he would have looked a little like a Victorian jet-worker, resting before his evening shift.

The archaeologists' theory explained the two stones found in Skeleton 952's mouth which might have represented his testicles, the theory being that if Cybele was less powerful than her reputation suggested, the priest would arrive in the afterlife symbolically intact.[36] It would also account for Skeleton 952's three-stranded necklace, which is similar to one pictured on a relief in the Capitoline Museum in Rome in which a richly coiffured *gallus* jangles with elaborate beads and jewellery.[37] It is known that Cybele's priests lived and worked in Britain at the time, from an inscription to Attis at an altar near Hadrian's Wall and an ornamental testicle clamp found in the Thames in the 1970s by a treasure hunter. But the major clue was the fact that the corpse's beads were made of jet: because ever since Roman times Cybele was one of the main deities[38] to be associated with black stones in general, and jet in particular.

There are many stories about Cybele, but they all include references to her turbulent relationship with Attis, a half-god often portrayed as a handsome shepherd or a young huntsman who dies in an accident; some versions of the myth depict him as the goddess's son as well, in what must have seemed a confusing domestic relationship even to the ancients, who were used to such stories. Cybele was often portrayed as almost androgynous – the all-powerful grieving mother and wife protected by her state of mourning from the need to be obviously, sexually feminine. Meanwhile Attis came to symbolise death and resurrection. Their two festivals were celebrated in the spring, and both featured noisy processions and much loss of blood; the wilder Good Friday celebrations of today, held in places like the Philippines, are thought to derive from them.

So, it is probably not just coincidence that the stone later used in rosaries by those who venerate the Virgin Mary had also been associated with Cybele. Perhaps jet-wearing was another ancient sacred tradition carried over into Christianity by pagan believers. Cybele's priests around the Mediterranean wore diadems and necklaces, which, before the Romans conquered Britain, were probably made from the *oltu-tasi* jet of Erzurum in Turkey. Because the *galli*, like sixteenth-century Roman Catholics, wore the black stone as a deliberate and sometimes provocative display of their beliefs.

There are several reasons why jet might have been linked with Cybele. First, she is associated with the pine tree, which, being evergreen, often symbolises eternal life,[39] and is the raw material of jet. Second, she has an affinity with snakes: archaeologists believe that the gorgon heads found in the Cologne church might have had some connection with Cybele: many statues show her with snakes curled round her and, of course, jet was supposed to wield power over them. Also, of course, jet is black, and is therefore an easy visual reference to the most famous black stone in the ancient world, which the Sibylline book of prophecies foresaw would save Rome in its hour of greatest need.

Many sacred stones in different religions are black. The Ka'bah in Mecca is a shrine that Muslims believe they should visit at least once in their lifetime, but which predates Islam by many centuries.[40] It is in the shape of a large rectangular cube (the word 'cube' is said to have come from '*ka'bah*'), covered with black curtains. Built into its eastern wall, there is a black stone scarcely bigger than a worshipper's head. Some say it is a meteorite that came to earth with Adam when he fell from another world; others say it is basalt or lava. It is hard to determine the truth because over the centuries it has been worn smooth by hands and kisses, but has also been attacked by unbelievers and fire so many times that it is now in fragments, held together with silver thread and a silver band.[41]

This is not the only holy black stone in ancient history: Diana, Roman goddess of hunting, had one in Ephesus, now in western Turkey, and another was dedicated to the Phoenician goddess Astarte in Byblos, north of Beirut. But of all the ancient goddesses it was Cybele who loved black stones and jet most of all. Indeed, one of her names in Anatolia is Kubaba, which some have said comes from the same root as '*ka'bah*', suggesting that she might have been the deity worshipped at the black stone of Mecca before the Prophet Muhammad.

Cybele's own black stone was called the Magna Mater. For hundreds of years it was worshipped at Pergamon, now Kuşadasi in western Turkey, but in the late third century BC an emergency request came from Rome. The Roman people were calling for Cybele's stone to protect them against the Carthaginian general Hannibal Barca, who had almost brought the Roman empire to its knees. When it arrived at the port, half of Rome came out to meet it. Everyone was curious about the eastern talisman on which so much depended. The lucky ones who could gaze over the shoulders of the crowd would have seen a small, light stone, 'black like soot, irregular in form but most of all conical, and shaped by the caprices of nature into the approximate shape of a woman's face'. It was probably basalt or lava[42] like the black stone of the Ka'bah but it might have been a large piece of jet. The stone itself was not impressive – but the procession that accompanied it to its new home on the Palatine Hill – clashing cymbals, beating drums and the screams of eunuch priests[43] – would have been memorable.

The stone was set in silver as the face of a protective statue, and the magic apparently worked: Hannibal went home soon after it had arrived. But Cybele never sat easily in the Roman pantheon, and the problem was probably her troublesome priests. The senate had already decreed that no Roman was to become a *gallus*, which one commentator[44] ascribes to 'an aberration in terms of the system of ritual categories', although the truth is probably more prosaic. Imagine being a Roman parent told of your son's decision not only to dress as a woman but also to cut off his testicles with a clamp.[45] No wonder there was an official ruling against it.

And no wonder that our *gallus*, Skeleton 952, was buried in the least prestigious part of the graveyard at Catterick fort, the place most suited to non-citizens. Though he had gained some kind of acceptance in the community: he was at least laid inside the graveyard rather than beyond it. It would be nice to think that although the ordinary citizens of Catterick viewed him and his fellows at first with suspicion, they had eventually come to say to each other that they were 'lovely, lovely people, even though they do look a bit strange at first'.

The world's media loved the story of the transvestite eunuch and his buried treasure. The headlines and puns were competingly eye-catching, ranging from 'Catterick Camp' to 'Privates Not On Parade'. Commentators from the north of Britain decided that Skeleton 952 demonstrated the cosmopolitan nature of ancient Yorkshire, that it could accept such alternative characters in its community. Southerners pointed out that the bejewelled male/female corpse challenged today's stereotype of the tough, macho Yorkshireman.

There was a surge of interest in the archaeologists' work and requests for interviews, usually concentrating on the finer points of testicle removal and Roman transgender identity, from news and features programmes as far away as Thailand and New Zealand. Astonishing new theories were generated overnight: 'One of the newspapers even said the castration operation was the cause of his death,' Dr Wilson said. 'I don't know where that came from.'

The Widow

In the Fitzwilliam Museum in Cambridge, there is an altar dedicated to Cybele. It is a small stone trough that at one time would probably have contained some of the objects involved in worshipping her: incense, small rattles and cymbals, ornamental clamps perhaps and sacred jet beads. On the right side of the altar is a carving of her symbolic tree – the pine – and I was startled to see that the cones were as large as human heads, as the cones of the prehistoric jet tree had been described. On the left a relief shows four men weighed down under a funeral bier bearing the body of Attis.

At the front of the altar Cybele is pictured between two priests, a large female figure swathed in heavy clothes and deep, almost tender gloom. She does not appear to be the vengeful angry goddess of myth, nor the literally petrifying proto-gorgon she is sometimes thought to have been. I was reminded of another ruler who, like the mythical Cybele, made the jet stone famous. On this ancient shrine, the eastern goddess bore a startling resemblance to a more recent personification of mourning: Queen Victoria. Perhaps the nineteenth-century passion for jet was more than the desire for a gemstone or for a symbol: perhaps it was the desire for an archetype.

3

Pearl

—— 2.5⁻4 ——

Pearls are called
God's tears. In Toba
It's raining.[1]

Vegetarians should not wear pearls.

As Julius Caesar stood on the coast of France in 55 BC, watching his ships lining up to invade Britain, he must have had mixed feelings. He would have looked over the twenty or so miles of water that lay between him and the next battle, and thought about the sparse[2] reports his spies had brought to him of the ferocity of the island tribes, their habit of fighting naked with blue paint on their bodies, and of the druids, who seemed to have the island under their mistletoe-stained thumbs. But then the very stylish (although slightly balding) consul might have recalled all that he stood to gain. It was not only Britain's mineral resources or her pretty slaves that had persuaded Caesar to make his military move across the Channel that summer: according to his biographer, Gaius Suetonius Tranquillus, it was something quite different. It was her pearls.[3]

Caesar had already drawn up a strict law in Rome that only aristocrats might wear pearls, and that only Caesar could wear an all-purple toga to match them.[4] Now he wanted to make sure his personal supply was guaranteed, and that the prettiest river pearls in Europe were his – to keep for himself, to donate to a temple or to give to any woman who attracted his attention. Pearls were associated with Venus, the goddess of love, and as such they were excellent chat-up material – as Caesar had found to his advantage. Pearls were widely considered to be a Roman girl's best friend, and he had given them to his favourite mistresses. Two thousand years ago few people could afford to own even one pearl, and a string was a sign of unimaginable wealth.

The fortunes of pearls have changed since and I would guess that anyone reading this could afford to buy a pearl necklace if they wanted one. There are still occasional big stories – in 2004 Christie's set a world record for pearls by selling a necklace for $3.1 million – but pearls can be had for pennies and even good examples cost hundreds rather than thousands of pounds.

Nevertheless, pearls have somehow held on to their mythology. They are still seen by many as something that royalty, footballers' wives and Hollywood stars would be proud to own. And they still tend to be viewed as amazing accidents of nature. Few outside the trade are aware that almost every pearl on sale today was born of the planned sexual violation of a small creature, and that considerable suffering hangs on those necklace strings.

One reason why pearls are plentiful is because of a man who was similar to Caesar in his obsession with them, although in other ways he was the Roman's opposite. His name was Kokichi Mikimoto and he dreamed of making pearls affordable to every woman who wanted them, while ensuring that they retained the mystique that made them so desirable. Unlike Caesar, he never conquered any countries, but he had an extraordinary instinct for public relations and, from humble origins, became the Pearl King of the World.

Caesar's British Pearls

Today, when the world's best pearls come from the South Pacific, China, the Americas and Australia, the idea that there might once have been a valuable pearl industry in the British Isles seems astonishing. Yet for many centuries the rose-pink pearls of Scotland, the black pearls of Ennerdale in Cumbria and the white pearls of Ireland were exported all over Europe. It seems that the best were enough to drive a man to war.

The natural river pearls that Caesar wanted so badly are still around,[5] but it is too late to go fishing for them. Unlike sea-pearls, which come from oysters, fresh-water pearls come from mussels. And although farmed mussels are common throughout the world, wild colonies are now so endangered that in 1998 pearling was forbidden in the UK river system. The problem is sex: pearl mussels breed every summer in an extraordinary session of shared sperm and group sex, in which the male mussels spray semen over the females as they all stand in the water. Today, thanks to pearlers, power stations and pollution, most rivers in Scotland support too few mussels for a good orgy, and breeding doesn't take place. Where there were once pearls in almost every river in the Highlands, Scottish National Heritage estimates that there are now fewer than fifty colonies, and they're all at risk.

Retired pearl-fishermen are now rarer than the pearls, and they are even harder to find. The few shops that bought natural pearls rarely recorded the names of those who found them. And as for their permanent addresses, until a few decades ago most of them didn't have any. Pearlers were mostly Highland travelling people: until the 1960s, or later, they slept for most of the year under the curved cloth structures they called 'bow tents' and earned money from making tin saucepans, telling fortunes and finding pearls. Apart from when they were doing business, they didn't talk much to other folk.

But I was lucky. In the cellar of a second-hand bookshop in Buxton I found a book called *The Summer Walkers* by Timothy Neate. It was an oral history of the travelling people of Scotland, and among the accounts of tinsmiths and horse-dealers there were a few interviews with pearl-fishers. I wrote to the author to ask if any were still around, and received a reply immediately. He warned me to move quickly: life on the road is hard, and the old pearl-fishers were in and out of hospital. I took his advice, and made an appointment to meet the seventy-year-old Gaelic storyteller, Alec John Wilkinson, his seventy-two-year-old brother-in-law, Eddie Davies, and his son, Angus, the following week. Eddie was a retired pearl-fisher, while both Angus and Alec had grown up with the tradition.

It is almost universally true that the people who look for gems professionally are poor, and the pearl-fishers of Scotland were no exception. Alec met me at the door of his house: he couldn't invite me in, he said regretfully, as his wife Mary was ill. 'She's a pearl-fisher,' he said, 'but she doesn't remember much of anything any more.' He climbed into my car and directed me down a winding road, through pine forests and following a river valley, until we reached a small village. I had imagined that pearl-fishers lived in Highland crofts or cottages but I was wrong. Just outside the village we came to the council estate where Alec's son, Angus, and Mary's brother, Eddie, lived just a few doors away from each other. Angus had grown up in houses, but Eddie had travelled until the end of the 1990s. 'When the spring comes and the birds start singing, he still says he wants to be out there on the road,' Alec said.

Eddie's housing estate doesn't look a bad place in the sunshine, although I was told later that four of the fifty homes had seen suicides that year. Recently Eddie's next-door neighbour had hanged himself from an oak tree, and another man, who had lived a few doors away, had drowned himself in the river. 'We should have known there was something wrong,' said Angus. 'The night before he died he'd been down the pub and bought a round for the whole village.' All the houses faced a grey car park, rather than looking out at the splendid estuary behind them. The best view in Eddie's home is from the bathroom window – which contains frosted glass, so he cannot look out.

Eddie Davies, pearl-fisher

After we had settled into armchairs, Eddie sat on the floor beside the fire. Granted, it was a carpeted floor and the fire was an old electric one, but as he cleared his throat and lit a hand-made cigarette it really was as if the years had rolled away and we were by a real fire, surrounded by tents, about to listen to some good yarns. 'I've got some stories about pearls . . .' he began promisingly, then paused. I wondered whether this was the right time to take out the crisp notes that were burning a hole in my pocket. 'You'll need to give the money up front,' Timothy Neate had warned. 'Otherwise they might not say much.' But as Angus passed me a mug of tea, the moment passed and I didn't want to break the mood. Eddie had not been waiting for cash, I realised: he had been pausing for effect.

First, he said, did I know anything about how a pearl was

made? The others looked amused. I had a feeling I was going to fail the test, but I was pretty certain I knew the answer. Surely a natural mussel pearl was made in the same way as a natural oyster pearl? When I was a child I was told that pearls were made when a grain of sand was caught accidentally inside the lips of an oyster. I remembered the cartoon illustration in my junior-school textbook because it was supposed to be funny, but I had always thought it sad. It showed a little oyster rolling its eyes in agony, while the irritating sand inside its shell was gradually encased in layers of shiny liquid called nacre. Then, according to my book, the nacre hardened in layers over the sand, until one day a man in a loincloth dived down to pick up the shell. When he opened it he found a gem. I had always looked in jewellery shop windows with renewed attention after that.

'Isn't it made of sand or grit?' I asked tentatively.

'That can do it,' Eddie agreed kindly, 'but it isn't the whole story.' If you're talking about gambling odds, and the fishermen often do, there is only a thousand to one chance of a pearl forming that way, he said. You would have to open a lot of shells to find even one pearl. 'There's another way. The way the pearl-fishers know,' Eddie explained. 'And it's to do with how river pearls form.' What was the other way? I asked. But Eddie, like his brother-in-law Alec, was a born storyteller so he didn't tell me straight away.

The Rivers

An old word for pearls in English is 'unions',[6] which comes from the Latin *unio*, meaning 'unique'. The experience of the pearl-fishers shows this description to be true: each location produces slightly different gems. 'Show me the pearl and I'll tell you the river,' Eddie boasted, and in his sixty years of pearling he had seen almost all of them. Pearls from the Oykel river, north-west of Inverness, for example, are a sweet rose pink, and have always been the most valuable. 'I only got two from the Oykel in all my days,' Eddie said. He had taken them to the Cairncross brothers in Perth, who were the main buyers. 'They said they were priceless . . . so they gave us a hundred pounds apiece for them,' he said. He said the bright colours in river pearls came from the peat in the water, which probably explains why pearls from Lapland, where there is no peat, tend to be grey. 'The same thing that makes good whisky makes good pearls,' said Eddie. He had known and liked both in his time. 'I'm on the wagon now,' he said. 'Mostly.'

The same rivers that make pearls also breed salmon, and this is no coincidence. Salmon and mussels need each other, and it is only when both are living in a river that they can survive. The salmon are like the mussels' nannies, or perhaps their chauffeurs. After a successful orgy, each female mussel produces about two hundred thousand spat, or young, which can only survive if they hitch a ride on the gills of passing salmon. They stay on the fish all winter, growing bigger as their hosts leap against the currents, then drop off in the spring and turn into mini-mussels, settling in a different part of the river from where they had begun. If it happens to be a place with few pearl-fishers or power stations they have a good chance of living for at least eighty years.[7] It is a genetic twist that ensures the breeding pool changes with every generation.

In return for childcare services, the mussels act as house-cleaners and food-shoppers for the salmon. Pearl mussels are the lungs of the river and can filter up to fifty litres of water a day, which is another reason why they are protected. As a by-product of the filtering process, they give out so much natural effluent around their colonies that they attract hordes of insects, which the salmon eat but the pearlers detest: 'You have to tell about the midges,' said Angus. 'They're dreadful.'

It was not only the salmon and mussels that helped each other on the river. In the old days many of the pearl-fishers

'The same rivers that make pearls also breed salmon'

looked after the mussels: they did not fish in August, the breeding season, and if they found small shells they put them back without opening them. Perhaps if the rivers had always been managed like that, Scottish pearls would still be available, but in the 1960s something happened that endangered the industry. Ironically it began as a success story.

One day in 1967 William Abernethy was fishing in the Tay just north of Perth and found an amazing pearl. It weighed 33½ grains,[8] just under two grams, and was, in Angus's words, 'as big as a blackbird's egg'. It caused such a stir that a correspondent from *The Times* went to Perth to interview James Cairncross, one of the famous jewellers. Cairncross was astonished at the find: 'One would have to live as long as Methuselah to find another to match it,' he said, and allegedly paid Abernethy £11,000 for it – then enough to buy a small Scottish estate.

The Abernethy story had the same appeal as a lottery win: it was a fairy-tale about an ordinary man who had found extraordinary riches. The media presented him as someone who had just been lucky, but Abernethy knew his pearls. 'You know what he'd do to test them? He'd put them in his mouth,' Eddie said. 'The naked eye was good enough for me but Abernethy would test them with his teeth. If it was bumpy it was natural but if it was smooth it was paste or plastic and he'd bite it in two, just to show off.' A television station invited him to its London studios and he was the star guest on the quiz show *What's My Line?* in which the panel had to guess what he did for a living. Nobody won that round: the notion of pearl-fishing in Britain was too far-fetched.

It was the beginning of the end for pearls. Rather as the Romans had hoped to do in 55 BC, a legion came up from the south and, as Eddie described it, 'They started slaughtering the river.' The new weekend pearl-fishers were 'mostly middle-aged men driving big cars with beer coolers in the back' and they would spend afternoons pulling hundreds of live mussels out of the rivers, opening them and throwing away the shells, with not a care for conservation or the breeding season. All they cared about was finding another Abernethy pearl. 'They were cowboys,' said Eddie, who throughout the 1970s and 1980s had watched his livelihood flung carelessly on to the banks of Scotland's rivers. When Scottish National Heritage finally banned pearl-fishing, thirty-one years after Abernethy's lucky day, Eddie celebrated: 'I've got grandchildren,' he said. 'I want there to be pearls in the rivers for them and their bairns to find.'

It was not the first time that the Scottish river mussel had been protected by the government or that a big pearl find had pushed them to the edge of extinction. In 1620 a wonderful gem was discovered in the Kellie burn, a tributary of the Ythan river in Aberdeenshire. King James VI of Scotland had it placed in his crown and soon afterwards the Scottish Privy Council decided that pearl-fishers would henceforth need the king's per-mission to search for Scottish pearls – which meant effectively that no one could do it. It was a strategy born of greed, but it protected the species for a while.[9] However, by the 1760s the benefits of the ban had gone: legions of pearl-poachers were at work in the Highlands and the mussels were in danger of extinction. In 1769 Thomas Pennant, a writer and geologist, published a popular travel book called *Tour in Scotland*. In it he made scathing comments about the rapaciousness of Scottish pearl-traders. 'From the year 1761 to 1764, £10,000 worth [of fresh-water pearls] were sent to London,' he wrote. 'But this fishery is at present exhausted from the avarice of the undertakers.'

The sad thing, Eddie said, lighting another cigarette, was that all the destruction was unnecessary. 'You don't have to open thousands of shells at random like that,' he said. 'Pearl-fishers know if a mussel has a pearl in it just by looking at it.' He stood up to find something to illustrate what he was saying, and had trouble in locating it. The room was foggy from the roll-ups that everyone was smoking by now, but that wasn't the problem. I got up to help him. 'I can hardly see,' Eddie admitted. 'It's not curable, the doctor says. An operation won't help.' When I looked more carefully his eyes were filmy, like the frosted windows hiding the marvellous view from the back of his house. In the sixteenth century 'pearl' was another word for 'cataract', and this was how Eddie Davies, the pearl-fisher, sees the world: as though through a thin slice of shell.

The Secret of the Pearl-Fishers

He eventually found what he was looking for: two halves of a mussel shell. This 'mother-of-pearl' was the only souvenir he had of his pearling days: he could never afford to keep any of the gems. This was the shell of the famous *Margaritifera margaritifera*, which simply means 'bearer of pearls' (twice). Some say that the word margarita comes (via Greek) from the Sanskrit '*manjari*', meaning 'bud'; others say it is related to 'marine' because pearls come from the water.[10] But the third theory[11] is the prettiest: that the word comes from the Persian *murwari*, meaning 'child of the light'. In English it lives on in the name 'Margaret', and in its diminutives, Maisie, Peggy, Megan, Greta and Rita. At the end of the nineteenth century Queen Margherita of Italy had so many strings of pearls 'that they started just under her chin and reached down to her knees'.[12] Her devoted husband, King Umberto, gave her a new one for every birthday and evidently she felt duty-bound to wear them all.

The English called pearls 'margaritas' and 'unions' until the eighteenth century. Our relatively new word for them has an odd origin: it comes from the Latin *perna*, meaning 'ham' or 'pig leg'. That derivation was a mystery to me until, in Eddie's front room, I saw the shells the pearls had come from. They were four or five times bigger than those of the mussels you can buy from a fishmonger, and were wide and slightly curved, like a pig's plump back legs. But their size was not the only unexpected thing about them: Eddie's were covered with stripes and striations. They were slightly dented and didn't close properly, as if they had been in an accident. They were not very pretty at all – but that was the secret, Eddie said: it is the battered or 'marked' shells that are most likely to contain pearls.

That legend of the grain of sand was probably put about by jewellery salesmen wanting to preserve an aura of romance about pearls, but the truth is that, whether we are talking about freshwater pearls in a river mussel or seawater pearls in an oyster, the majority of natural pearls form after a small parasite dies inside a shell. With river mussels the process usually begins when the parasite squeezes through a crack between two deformed shells, in the hope of living off the mussel's flesh. 'The mussel realises it's there and tries to get rid of it. The parasite panics and starts working away and rolling back and forth . . .' As he was talking, Eddie rocked the shell backwards and forwards and I imagined something kicking around inside it, like a mischievous child doing somersaults. When the parasite gets tired, the mussel begins to cover it with nacre to smooth its edges and soothe the irritation. 'And it keeps on covering it for the rest of its life, trying to get rid of it.' At the end of the nineteenth century the French natural scientist Raphael Dubois told an audience at the Académie des Sciences that our love of pearls can come only from our lack of knowledge about their origins. 'The most beautiful pearl is nothing more, in fact, than the brilliant sarcophagus of a worm,'[13] he observed.

In river-mussel society, the deformity seems to be the equivalent of leprosy. 'The other mussels can't deal with them,' Eddie said, 'so they have to hide themselves under big rocks.' This makes it easier for the pearl-fishers to find them, but it also presents us with a poignant metaphor. Like dragons, goblins and other creatures of quests and fairy-tales, the dented mussels are ugly, despised and forced to hide away, yet they also have the pain and responsibility of being the guardians of the treasure.

The experience of the pearl mussels has its parallels in those of the Scottish travelling people, who have always been on the outside, pushed away because they were different. 'They called us pearlies,' said Eddie, 'but that wasn't a bad name, unlike some of the others.' In the old days the travellers had their own traditions, of which others were suspicious. They lived in tents, spoke their own language and rarely sent their children to school long enough for them to learn to read. They also entertained a host of superstitions, some of which got in the way of pearling. If anyone mentioned a rat, pig, weasel or anything that creeps or crawls, if they forgot something, kicked a stone on the road, or heard mention of the McPhee family, a rival band of travellers, they turned back from going fishing. 'There was no point. You wouldn't get any pearls.'

In the special language of the travellers, which is a form of Gaelic, pearls are called '*eanach tom sgaoi*' meaning 'big water things', and perhaps named by optimistic fishers who came home with their thumbs and index fingers slightly apart and saying, 'It was *this* big.' Everyone on the river lived in hope of finding another Abernethy, but the biggest pearl any of the Davies family had found was half its size, although perfectly round and white. One of Eddie's uncles had spotted it when his mare walked into a river and from then on they said she was a lucky mare. 'It was worth hundreds of pounds but he sold it for sixty,' Alec remembered. 'That's why none of us is rich.'

I took that as my cue, and bashfully offered them the money I had brought, which they equally bashfully accepted. I made to leave but they looked at me with astonishment and told me to sit down again – they'd scarcely started. Angus made coffee, Eddie turned up the electric fire and the ghost stories began. One was about an incident that had happened by the river Orner[14] many years ago. 'It was near a graveyard, and I was standing in the backwash – the small river off a big river,' Eddie said. 'A breeze was blowing and you could hear the branches of the trees against each other. You could hear the doves. The sun was trying its best to come through.' He was looking for marked shells, searching through a plate of clear glass set into a box he was floating just beneath the surface of the water. He was so absorbed that he didn't realise for some time that something wasn't right: 'There was no sound from the big river, no sound from the branches, no sign of the doves. I thought, Am I going stone deaf? Then I looked to the bank.' A woman was standing there, in laced boots and long black clothes. 'She was young and I was going to say what a nice day it was, but she was very pale and I couldn't get the words out.' Suddenly she turned away. Eddie came out of the water and looked up the path, 'which is the one they used to take the coffins down. It was thick with rhododendrons, and she wasn't there. I lit a roll-up and had a smoke. Suddenly I could hear the river and the branches, the doves cooing, and I said I'd never fish there again. I told my brother Dickie a few years back, but who'd believe a story like that? I never told my wife.'

Outside Eddie's house the streetlights had been on for hours and I realised I had a long way to drive down spooky country roads. I said goodbye to Eddie and Angus and then gave Alec a lift to the shops. He was the only one who could go into the village and get change for his fifty-pound note: Angus and Eddie owed so much to the shopkeepers and the pub landlord that they wouldn't have been given any. As I dropped him off, he thanked me. 'We don't get a chance to talk about the old days very often. There were some stories there I hadn't heard for a very long time.' Then he went into the off-licence, and I saw the owner taking a couple of bottles off the shelves and lining them up on the counter. It was clear that there would be a lot more talking down at Eddie's house that night.

Scotland's Last Natural-pearl Seller

You can still see the Abernethy pearl at Cairncross's shop in Perth. It has never been sold.[15] But neither has it been worn, which is a shame. Curiously, once they have left their shell, pearls need people to remain beautiful: if they are left in a bank vault they turn dry and yellow. Placed next to human skin, they become luminescent. Because of this the palace servants of the Nizam of Hyderabad in India often wore valuable pearls, so that when the Nizam put them on they were warm and luminous. Sometimes English ladies adopted a similar custom and eighteenth-century visitors to a wealthy household might sometimes, when calling in for afternoon tea, have seen the housemaid wearing more elaborate jewels than her mistress. In 'Warming her Pearls', by the poet Carol Ann Duffy, a maid wears her mistress's pearls throughout the day, and in the evening places them – with unspoken longing – round her employer's cool white throat.

The Cairncross brothers sold their business some years ago, but the shop still bears their name. It is the only shop in Britain with a licence to sell natural native pearls, but with no fresh stock coming in, it won't mean much in the future. I called the manager, John Lochtie, to find out how much a natural Scottish pearl necklace might cost. He told me it was impossible to make one: 'Even trying to match two pearls for earrings is a nightmare,' he said. Most of the remaining British river pearls are made up into silver brooches and might cost upwards of £100. In 1985, *National Geographic* interviewed a New York pearl dealer called Maurice Shire and asked him about the future of the natural-pearl industry. 'In the 1920s there were over three hundred natural-pearl dealers in the US,' he said, 'but by the 1950s we were down to six and now none. With no supply and no market, the business is dead.'[16] That was twenty years ago: had the prediction come true? Was Cairncross, with no new supplies, the only specialist natural-pearl dealer in the world, either of river mussels or sea oysters? He laughed. 'We can't be the only one,' he said. 'Definitely not.' But he had no idea where else to buy natural pearls. 'Australia, perhaps? I'm afraid I don't know. I don't know any names.'

It Is Raining in Toba

That the names of a dozen other natural-pearl dealers did not trip off Mr Lochtie's tongue is partly down to Kokichi Mikimoto, who not only invented a way of farming pearls but, most importantly, persuaded the world market to accept them. He is a character who – if he had not really lived – could easily have been invented by a Hollywood script-writer. He is the perfect slightly flawed protagonist – a poor boy made good; a stubborn man who ignored everyone who told him his dream was impossible.

Mikimoto was born in 1858, the year that Japan opened itself to foreign trade for the first time since 1639. When he was ten an emperor took power in Japan in what was called the Meiji Restoration, ending rule by the warrior classes that had lasted for two and a half centuries. In the same year Mikimoto started work. His father had fallen sick, leaving him, as the eldest son, to help his mother make noodles. Every evening when he had finished his homework he would grind wheat and knead dough, then sell the finished product from his father's barrow until after midnight. Toba was a traditional place then – in fact, even today in the main street there are old wooden houses decorated with paper lanterns, and elderly ladies in kimonos stroll along to collect their provisions. Mikimoto could not have imagined, as he gazed at the castle where the samurai lived, that one day the noodle-seller would be richer than all his clients.

But everything was changing. The first years of the Meiji Restoration were riddled with conflict. Taxes had risen, children were being taken out of the fields and made to go to school, and people were not happy. Some serious public-relations work was needed, and the emperor looked abroad for inspiration. He saw the United States introducing worship of the nation's flag in schools as if it were an ancient custom, the Victorians bringing back tartan to Scotland to restore a sense of national identity, and the French celebrating Bastille Day a century after their revolution. He and his advisers decided to establish some traditions. Within a few years Japan had national holidays, imperial pageants, restored shrines, a 'traditional' Shinto wedding ceremony and, like the Scots, a new national identity. It was an exciting era of invention and reinvention, of materialism and trade – the perfect time for an ambitious, democratically minded and inventive man like Mikimoto to create something traditional in an entirely new way.

As a teenager, Mikimoto began to sell vegetables with his noodles. When trade was slow he amused himself by lying on his back and juggling cabbages with his feet. It was a trick that served him well. One day in 1875 the US naval warship *Silver* called in at Toba. Many little boats went out to sell provisions, and the crew was confused by the choice until they saw a young man on his back sending eggs spinning in circles above his boat. They gave him the exclusive contract. The profit he made that day encouraged him to embark on his first adventure: he made the eleven-day journey on foot to Tokyo that changed his life and the history of pearls.

At the port of Yokahama he saw Chinese merchants buying dried sea cucumber and abalone for prices that astonished him. But what most impressed him was the huge mark-up on the pearls from the *akoya* oysters that thrived in the seas around Toba. He asked the Chinese buyers what they would use them for and was surprised to find that most were not for wearing but for grinding and putting into medicine. Throughout Asia and Europe, pearls were traditionally believed to ease a range of conditions, including eye diseases, fever, insomnia, 'female complaints', dysentery, whooping cough, measles, loss of virility and bed-wetting. Pearl powder was also thought to be a stimulant, but you had to be careful with it or it might cause a nosebleed.[17] These uses have a parallel in contemporary medicine: nacre is one of the latest bio-materials for bone implants, and pearls that are too flawed for jewellery are made into face creams and calcium supplements. Though nobody seems to advertise the potential for pearls to cure bed-wetting any more.

The First Cultured Pearls

After Mikimoto returned home from Tokyo, he started to sell the little 'seed' pearls that came from his area. Within ten years he was one of the province's biggest traders, and when the emperor's mother sent him an order his reputation seemed to be sealed. But supplies were drying up: too many people were fishing for pearls, and the oyster beds in Toba and the nearby bay of Ago Wan were no longer self-perpetuating. Was there a way to encourage them?

Cultured pearls were not a new concept. The third-century

Greek writer Philostratus described how the Arabs apparently 'made' pearls by opening oysters, pricking their flesh until liquid flowed out, then pouring it into special moulds where it would harden into beads.[18] Even if they managed it (which seems unlikely), those 'pearls' are better described as 'artificial' than 'cultured', since they did not grow in either a mussel or an oyster. However, we do know that since at least the fifth century Chinese people had learned how to place little lead medallions of the Buddha on the inside surfaces of live fresh-water mussels, then put them back into the water and leave them to be coated with mother-of-pearl. To untutored eyes in Silk Road market-places, the little gleaming sculptures must have seemed natural proof of a divine truth. Even today they are startling. The Buddha buttons give the appearance of shining from within, like tiny embodiments of enlightenment. Similarly, the Chinese also became expert in making *mabe* pearls: they stuck hemispherical buttons to the inside of oysters or mussels and left them in water. Later they would find perfectly formed cultured half-pearls inside the shells.

But the big challenge was to create a perfectly spherical pearl in either mussels or oysters. In 1758 Carl Linnaeus (motto: 'God creates, Linnaeus arranges') had taken a break from expanding his taxonomy of the natural world to cut little holes in mussel shells and try to make pearls form inside them, which he hoped would be a process that 'Linnaeus creates and God admires'. He found the experiments so fascinating that he once expressed the wish that he had been famous for making pearls rather than for classifying nature. He got as far as working out how to introduce a small limestone sphere into the mussel and also found an ingenious way of holding it suspended within the creature's flesh, using a silver clip.[19] His method, however, was not adopted for commercial production and the process was thought to have been lost, until 1901 when his papers were rediscovered in the archives of the Linnean Society in London.

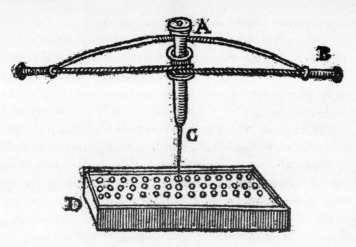

Drilling holes in pearls

By that time technology had moved on: Linnaeus's clip was outdated, and no one took it up.

Mikimoto was not the only person to dream of making pearls at the turn of the twentieth century. As with many inventions, cultured pearls became reality when several people around the world put their minds to solving the problem. In 1884 a Frenchman, Germain Bouchon-Brandely, produced a few pearls from Tahitian black-lipped oysters, but never made money from his discovery. In 1890 William Saville Kent, commissioner of Australian Fisheries, produced a spherical cultured pearl in New South Wales. However, he kept his method secret and after his death, in 1908, no one could carry on. There was also competition from Japan, where two other men besides Mikimoto were working on similar techniques.

However, Mikimoto had other things to worry about. He was having to use his juggling skills for something quite different. He was broke, and trying to stave off financial ruin by borrowing from various lenders. On several occasions his wife Ume wrote to him while he was carrying out his experiments down the coast to say he should stay away: debt-collectors were knocking at the door. He did not need distractions, they agreed, as he had too many experiments to perform. Early on, for example, he had the idea of using mother-of-pearl marbles as the nuclei for his pearls, but he could not persuade the oysters to make jewels with them.

Then in 1892 Toba was hit by 'red tide', a bloom of toxic organisms that makes the sea look as if it is bleeding, while killing most of the fish and all of the oysters. Still he did not give up. Which was just as well because the following year he found a pearl in one of his oysters. He and Ume celebrated, but the trouble was that there was only one pearl from the thousands of oysters. Also, it was only semi-spherical: they had done no better than the Chinese in the fifth century, and far worse than Linnaeus in the eighteenth.

Judging Pearls and the Power of the Baroque

Pearls are usually judged on four standards: size, measured in grains, or twentieths of a gram; colour, ranging from pure white to champagne, apricot, bronze, pink, lavender, grey, black and even, very rarely, green; 'orient', which is how they shimmer and reflect the light into patterns, and is usually dependent on how many layers of nacre there are; and shape. Perfectly round pearls are best, and then, in order of value, drops, ovals, buttons and semi-spheres. The cheapest are usually the uneven pearls: they are called 'baroques' and are covered in bumps and globules, as if the invading parasite did a great deal of panicked jumping around before it was finally enclosed in its calcium-carbonate tomb. Sometimes, though, as with the Scottish pearl mussels, the ugliest pearls are the most valuable of all, especially when they come in a shape that looks vaguely human.

The Canning Jewel lies in the high-security jewellery gallery at London's Victoria and Albert Museum. It is a most curious object, worthy of the pearl-term '*unio*'. When it emerged from its oyster it bore a remarkable resemblance to a man's upper torso. This fact was not lost on its finders, who made it into a muscled Triton, set in gold with dozens of rubies and diamonds. It was acquired by Lord Canning, the first viceroy of India, in the mid-nineteenth century, and for a long time was believed to have been made in Italy in the 1580s. But the sad truth was that Lord Canning bought it new. It was a real pearl, but the setting was a clever Victorian forgery that deceived everyone for years.

The word 'baroque' has another curious offspring. An exuberant new style of architecture became popular in seventeenth-century Europe, and some years later its critics mockingly nicknamed it 'baroque'. They were suggesting that these structures were grotesque, like ugly pearls. But the word caught on, and even became positive. It was as if, after the Prince of Wales famously commented in 1984 that the planned extension to the National Gallery in London was like a 'monstrous carbuncle'[20] – meaning a boil rather than a ruby – the word 'carbuncular' had become a word of praise.[21]

Gems in the form of Teardrops

Four years after the Mikimotos found their first cultured half-pearl in 1893, Ume died. She was thirty-two and her husband was left with four daughters, a baby son and deep grief. Although his quest had, until then, given them both little more than heartache, his wife had encouraged him to the end. 'Since I have seen a pearl produced I can leave without regret,' she told him. And from that time on, Mikimoto sometimes described pearls as teardrops, to reflect a loss from which he never fully recovered.

He threw himself into his work. By the beginning of the century he believed he had the right nucleus. It was a combination of a polished bead made of shell and a tiny two-millimetre square of the frilly mantle of another oyster, which stimulated the flow of nacre. But he still had to determine where best in the oyster to plant it. In 1905 it seemed as if he would never get the chance: there was another red tide and all the oysters died. But instead of giving up, he went down to the beach and opened them all – which must have been an extraordinarily smelly job, particularly after the first few days. But his efforts were rewarded: he found five round pearls. 'The destruction of the oysters is a disaster but these five round pearls have taught me where to place the nucleus,' he wrote. He had at last discovered the secret of how to culture pearls. Within a few years his oysters were producing pearls in thousands, and later in millions.

But, for the oysters at least, it was a painful secret to have revealed. Making cultured pearls involves forcing a piece of polished shell into the oyster's gonads, or reproductive organs. It is ironic that to create the jewel that symbolises purity you have to commit what might be labelled surgical rape in a more sophisticated organism. This is how it works. Professional pearl-grafters relax the two-year-old oysters by placing them in a warm bath. When the shells open they insert a thin, sharp instrument, developed for the purpose by dentists, and use it to make a small cut in the animal's sexual organs. This forms a little pocket, into which the graft and the bead are placed. It takes only a few seconds but the oysters need at least three months to recover from the trauma. Many die. No wonder vegetarian organisations around the world recommend their members not to buy pearls. Mikimoto – who was a kind man – would probably have been astonished if anyone had suggested his industry was cruel.

He always claimed that he was not making pearls simply because he wanted to be rich, and perhaps he was telling the truth. As the tide of Communism swirled round Russia in preparation for revolution, the Pearl King was developing his own vision of promoting the happiness of ordinary people. He believed that everyone, from a poor noodle-seller's wife to the richest person in Japan, should have the right to see beauty, own and wear it, and he would begin the process by democratising pearls. 'I want to live long enough to see the day when we have so many pearls we can sell necklaces for two dollars to every woman who can afford one, and give them away free to every woman who can't,' was one of his favourite statements. Today this does not seem surprising: with a few adjustments for inflation, his wish has almost come true. But in 1905 it was outrageous. Until then pearls were not just the pretty things that, thanks to Mikimoto, we see them as today. Instead they were signifiers – badges, if you like – of extreme wealth and, more importantly, access to power. If a woman had pearls she was influential. Mikimoto was challenging not just the market price of the gem but an entire world of aristocratic assumption. And to understand it, we need to look back to Julius Caesar's Rome to see how Europe's tradition of conspicuous pearl consumption was honed.

Ancient Pearls

Julius Caesar failed to conquer Britain in 55 BC and again the following year. The Romans had to wait nearly a century to invade successfully, and even then the forerunners of the Scots kept them out of the Highlands. But Caesar pursued pearls elsewhere, in line with his extravagant lifestyle. He was a keen collector of carvings, paintings, statues and attractive slaves, sometimes paying so much that he refused to allow the sums to be recorded. He loved luxury – he once boasted that his soldiers fought just as well when they stank of perfume as when they did not – and carried mosaic pavements on war campaigns to beautify his encampments. But his constant delight was pearls. He understood them, loved them, and was known for his ability to weigh them in the palm of his hand to give an accurate appraisal of their value.[22] In his youth he gave a particularly precious pearl to a woman called Servilia whom, it is said, he loved more than any other of his female conquests. He had paid sixty thousand gold pieces for it, and it probably did not pass his notice that this was five times the ransom of twelve thousand gold pieces once demanded by pirates in the Greek seas in exchange for his own life. By this count, Caesar was worth just a fifth of a pearl.[23]

Servilia's gem was not the most expensive pearl recorded that century: shortly after Caesar died, Cleopatra exceeded his record. She and her new lover, Mark Antony, once competed to see who could throw the most lavish dinner party. According to the story,[24] Cleopatra won: she took a pearl from one of her earrings, dissolved it in vinegar and drank it, which meant that the banquet had cost the equivalent of eighty thousand[25] gold pieces, enough to ransom nearly a septet of Caesars.[26] Cleopatra did not share her expensive drink with her guest, although it might have done her more good if she had: many years later the Mughal emperors of India took potions of powdered pearl to improve their virility, which shows at least that money can sometimes be a powerful aphrodisiac. Antony, who was both a heavy drinker and a depressive, might have benefited from it.

This famous story – told by a despairing Pliny to point out the decadence of the empire – suggests a dramatic moment of *plink-fizz* like a headache remedy hitting water, but it probably would not have happened like that. Scholar John Healey has his own theory: 'Cleopatra no doubt swallowed the pearl, undissolved, and subsequently recovered it in the natural course of events,' he suggests.[27] But might it have worked? As an experiment I took a natural river pearl,[28] which had come legally from an American stream, and placed it in a glass of strong wine vinegar. It fell to the bottom and a few bubbles fizzed up promisingly. But when I looked more closely, the bubbles had been air pockets. After two hours, there was still no change in the pearl.

I left it overnight, and when I went back in the morning, some-thing had started to happen. There was debris at the bottom of the glass and the pearl was covered in something grey. It looked like dead skin and came off in my fingers. A day later, the pearl had split in half and on day thirty-two it was floating on the surface of the vinegar. When I took it out, the pearl was soft and when I squashed it in my hand it turned to mush. Perhaps the ancient story had been partially true after all, but it would have been a considerable wager that forced me to sip the sour, greying liquor that had resulted from my experiment.

Pearly Kings and Queens

Cleopatra's famous dissolving pearl would have been a sea pearl, and would probably have come either from the Arabian Gulf or from Sri Lanka. Today neither of these places are pearled commercially, but from antiquity until the 1970s their waters were full of boats and divers. In Sri Lanka experienced divers would weight themselves with stones and stay underwater for up to three minutes, picking up oysters from as deep down as eighteen metres. They would sometimes bleed internally from the pressure although apparently this was seen as lucky.[29] In 1847 Portuguese historian João Ribeiro described watching Sri Lanka pearl-fishing, which at the time was organised almost like a game. Around five thousand boats assembled off the beach, a gun was fired and they raced to get to the oyster beds. At the end of the day they opened the oysters on the sand and some would rot before they were sorted. 'But what beauty was found, eventually, in such a stink.'[30]

Unlike the Sri Lankan fishermen, who could return home to their families at night, the pearlers of the Arabian Gulf were often away for six months at a time. It was lonely work, although at least there was entertainment on board. As recently as the 1970s the pearling captains hired a singer, or *nihâm*, who would lead the crews in special songs. A good *nihâm* could attract a better class of crew who – rather like cruise passengers today – sometimes chose their vessel according to the entertainment on offer. There was a superstition that singing for pearls made men blind, with the chief culprit a song called the *fieri*. Those who performed it said that it began when some fishermen overheard a group of genies singing a song so mesmerising that they begged to learn it. But the genies warned that they would pay a terrible price: if they sang the song they would go blind. The men were determined to learn it anyway because, like the pearls they were singing about, it was simply too beautiful to keep hidden.[31]

Pearls from the Gulf were among the most prestigious gems in Europe and Asia when the Italian adventurer Christopher Columbus was trying to raise interest in his journey west. In fact, it was the vague promise of exotic 'pearls and jewels' (in that order) that was said to have so piqued the interest of the Spanish King Ferdinand and Queen Isabella that they decided to back his risky 1492 expedition.[32] One legend tells that Isabella pawned her earrings and necklaces to raise the funds – forgoing the certainty of a few jewels today for the possibility of a ship-load tomorrow.

Pearls enabled Columbus's initial success, but they were also the cause of his later humiliation. He did not find them during his first or second journeys, but on his third voyage to the New World in 1498 he found what he was looking for. His diaries from that time are full of his excitement at finding villages on the Venezuelan coast where everyone wore pearl bracelets and, even better, where people were willing to trade them for items like buttons, needles, scissors and even broken pottery.[33] However, he omitted to include any of this in the reports he sent back to Ferdinand and Isabella. When they learned about the pearls from their spies in Seville, they were furious and in 1500 Columbus returned to Spain in chains. In 1503 he sent a letter to his sovereigns, complaining at how badly he had been treated:

'When I discovered the Indies,' he wrote, 'I spoke of gold, pearls, precious stones, spices and of the markets and fairs. But because not everything turned up at once, I was vilified.'[34]

From then on in Europe, it was the Age of the Pearl. The gems were shipped back to Spain by the sackload, and the Spanish Royal Family was the envy of the European royal houses. Apparently Queen Elizabeth I gave explicit instructions to her English pirate captains John Hawkins and Francis Drake that they should seize American pearls for her on the Spanish Main as often as they could.

But she never found a pearl as beautiful as the one that was given to her elder sister, Mary Tudor, by Philip II of Spain as an engagement present. The Spanish called it La Peregrina – meaning 'the pilgrim' – and the story was that it had been found by a slave in Panama, who was given his freedom as a reward. The pearl weighed ten grams, was a perfect drop shape and briefly became the wonder of the English court. When Mary died, Philip claimed back his gift and over the next centuries it became true to its name as it moved from country to country, owned at different times by Joseph Bonaparte of Spain, Prince Louis Napoleon of France and the Marquis of Abercorn who bought it for his wife in 1837. It was very heavy and she misplaced it several times – once on a sofa at Windsor Castle, and once during a ball – although fortunately it was rescued from its peregrinations each time. In 1969 the actor Richard Burton bought it for $37,000 at Sotheby's and gave it to his wife, Elizabeth Taylor. It went on accidental pilgrimage in her care too, most famously in a Las Vegas hotel room when her Pekinese puppy picked it up and started to chew it.[35] It was apparently unmarked by this adventure – or, at least, that was what she told the volatile Burton.

Taylor was fortunate because pearls are among the most vulnerable gems. Not only can they easily be scratched (or indeed chewed), being only between 2.5 and 4 on Mohs' scale, but perfume and cosmetics will discolour them, smoke makes them yellow, and water or perspiration rots the string. In 1908 the New York jeweller George Kunz gave a list of occasions when you should not wear pearls. 'If they are worn in the bath, if they are thrown on a dressing-table, dropped on the floor, or otherwise ill-treated, if they are worn on dusty automobile rides, in bicycle riding or during other gymnastic or violent exercise, it is inevitable that their sides will rub together and wear one another away.' If, however, they are kept in a soft bag, occasionally cleaned with a cloth dipped in alcohol and warm water, then dried carefully and wiped regularly to remove perspiration, 'their colour is not likely to be affected for a long period of time'. However, for something so soft pearls are tough. Around 1888 a Dr George Harley[36] made an almost comical attempt to cut a pea-sized pearl into powder. 'We folded it between two plies of note-paper, turned up the corner of the carpet and placing it on the hard, bare floor, stood upon it with all of our weight. Yet notwithstanding that we weigh over twelve stone we failed to make any impression whatever upon the pearl and even stamping on it with the heel of our boot did not suffice so much as to fracture it. It was accordingly given to the servant to break with a hammer, and on his return he informed us that on attempting to break it with the hammer against the pantry table all he succeeded in doing was to make the pearl pierce through the paper and sink into the wooden table, just as if it had been the top part of an iron nail and that it was not until he had given it a hard blow with the hammer against the bottom of a flat-iron that he succeeded in breaking it.'

As well as famous gems like La Peregrina, many ordinary-sized pearls with less amazing stories also arrived in Spanish ports in the sixteenth and early seventeenth centuries. Prices fell swiftly and pearls were no longer only for kings and queens. It was not democratisation to the extent that Mikimoto eventually managed it and nor did it attempt to be, but now even Europe's minor female aristocrats and heiresses could wear pearl chokers above their increasingly low necklines. And they chose to do so in great numbers. In room seven of London's National Portrait Gallery there are several portraits of women who lived in the mid-seventeenth century, including two of Charles II's most famous mistresses – the French spy Louise de Keroualle and the orange-seller Nell Gwyn – as well as his long-suffering wife, Catherine of Braganza, and several other wealthy ladies. All are shown wearing pearl necklaces and earrings. Indeed, it is rare to find a portrait of any woman from that time who is not wearing pearls. This was partly because they wished to demonstrate their modesty by wearing something so pure that the Bible claimed the doors of heaven were made of them.[37] But it was more than that: the public perception of pearls was then that they were exclusive – although with the discovery of the American oyster beds that had changed. Rather like today, when people try to wear the same fashions as film stars, the women of the 1670s and 1680s would have chosen pearls to suggest a certain connection with royalty and exclusivity, even if it was no longer true.

Selling Cultured Pearls

The curious thing is that, however many people wore them, dived for them and drilled holes in them throughout all those centuries, nobody actually knew what pearls were.[38] Or perhaps there were people who knew but did not want to say, as the truth – about parasitic worms and vile stinks on the beaches – was not something that the delicate ladies featured in the National Portrait Gallery would have wanted to know.

The facts were not widely known until the early twentieth century, but before that there were many myths to choose from on the origin of pearls. The fishers of the Persian Gulf used to say pearls were the result of February rain falling into the oysters, citing as proof the 'fact' that if no rain falls at this time the divers find nothing for the rest of the year.[39] Among some tribes in Borneo there was a belief, up to the beginning of the last century, that pearls were the eyes of spirits and consequently every ninth pearl they found was sealed into a bottle with a dead man's finger and offered to the spirits as appeasement. Meanwhile the Chinese told their children that pearls were the tears of sharks, and in Roman times scholars wrote that they were the dew that fell from heaven. In the 1600s the lapidary writer Anselm de Boodt speculated that pearls were produced by the secretion of a 'viscous humour' within oysters, while in England in the 1970s my generation grew up believing they were grains of sand, made beautiful inside an exotic shell.

Pearls being created by the moon's light

As a child in Toba in the 1860s, Mikimoto would have heard yet another story. His mother might have told him that pearls were the tears of their ancestors, shed for the daily troubles of their descendants. Or she might have said that they were created when the moon shone its light into open oyster shells. But perhaps his favourite story – or at least one he certainly told his own children – was about a fisherman who pushed his boat out to sea one afternoon and fell asleep. When he woke up he looked into the water and was surprised to notice little pink pearls playing like children among the oyster shells on the sea-bed. He put his bamboo pole into the sea to catch them and the little pearls ran back to the safety of their mothers-of-pearl. He went back to tell the people of his village and ever since, the story goes, Japanese people have 'known' that pearls are alive.[40]

Despite this pretty mythology, or perhaps because of it, the Japanese never took to pearls or any other jewels before the twentieth century. There wasn't really anywhere for them to wear them. Kimonos were already so highly decorated that a necklace would have confused their lines; earrings would not have been visible, with the elaborate hairstyles of old Japan; and sleeves were so long that no one would ever see a bracelet. Before around 1912 the only women known to wear finger rings were courtesans in Nagasaki,[41] which did not encourage more conventional women to adopt them. So, although Mikimoto sold a large number of pearl hair combs to geishas (and later persuaded Japanese ladies to buy engagement rings made of pearl) he concentrated most of his efforts on trading overseas.

In 1919 he sent his pearls to London, where they caused a sensation. Their shape, colour and lustre were faultless, and they were indistinguishable from natural pearls – except that they were more perfect than most. Jewellers in Europe and America panicked. They had a huge amount to lose: their pearl stocks were worth hundreds of thousands of pounds. After all, it was only three years since the American industrialist Morton Plant and the French jeweller Pierre Cartier had swapped an enormous *beaux-arts* mansion on Fifth Avenue in Manhattan for a 128-pearl necklace, and the deal had sent pearl prices soaring. For the new money-makers in America at the beginning of the twentieth century, ownership of a strand or two of pearls was like having a house in the Hamptons, a smart yacht or a few of the new automobiles that everyone was going mad for.

Everyone in the trade sought a reason to denounce cultured pearls as fakes. They subjected them to numerous tests but, since the centres were made of polished pearl shell and had a similar specific gravity to natural pearls, and since, whether natural or cultured, they were covered with the same substance, they couldn't determine a pearl's origin without cutting it in half. Several eminent scientists were brought in to deliver their verdicts, and without exception they said that Mikimoto's pearls were real. On 4 May 1921, the London *Star* reported that the jewellery market was 'in turmoil', with prices dropping rapidly.

They didn't go the whole way down. Not yet. Pearls still had their devoted fans – and thieves. In the late 1920s a jeweller in Hatton Garden sold a pearl necklace to a client in Paris for £50,000. The jeweller booked himself a seat on the London–Paris express to carry the goods over, but was tipped off that he was being followed by members of an international criminal gang. He cancelled his departure, and telegraphed his apologies. The following afternoon, to almost everyone's surprise, the necklace arrived at its destination. It had been taken over on a different train by a young woman travelling second class. A casual observer would have noticed that she was wearing cheap fur and imitation jewellery bought at a sixpenny store. Only she, her brother and her brother's boss knew that the middle row of her three-strand pearl necklace was worth a fortune.[42] It was, perhaps, the last such story: in 1930 there was a pearl crash. Prices dropped by eighty-five per cent in a single day, and although they rallied a little, there would no longer be ordinary London dealers selling pearl necklaces for two hundred times a clerk's annual salary.[43]

Meanwhile Mikimoto thrived on the attention he was receiving. He was breaking down the old ways of seeing and wearing pearls, and the profits were going straight into his pocket. He became again the showman that at heart he had always been, and in his new uniform of black bowler hat, black coat and small doctor's bag he created the unmistakable costume of an eccentric Pearl King. He never wore pearls, but over the years he handpicked the most perfect specimens from his baskets of oysters and had them strung into a necklace that was called the Taisho-ren or 'boss's string', which he kept in his pocket. Nobody ever wore it, although probably plenty of women wanted to. He lived in the Pearl House near to Ago Bay, south of Toba, where his pearl fisheries were and where he had even set up his own post office – mostly because he liked post offices. He emerged regularly to make spectacular marketing gestures, like a bonfire outside the Kobe Chamber of Commerce in 1932, in which he set fire to 720,000 pearls made by rival oyster-farmers because, he said, they were of poor quality and 'only good for burning'.

By 1938 there were 350 pearl farms in Japan, producing more than ten million pearls annually. But the shadow of war lay over the country and in 1940 the pearl business was ordered to close. Mikimoto, however, refused to join the war effort and he became one of Japan's most public conscientious objectors. Unbelievably he got away with it, although an angry army officer once sent him a sword suggesting he commit *hari kiri* – the daring Japanese method of suicide by disembowelling oneself at a single stroke. Mikimoto said, 'I'm a businessman, not a soldier,' and ignored it. What he did not mention was that he liked America. In 1939 he had sent a model of the Liberty Bell to New York as a peace gift. It included 12,250 pearls and 366 diamonds and was just one of many eccentric scale models that he spent his later years devising.[44] In 1933 he had sent a jewelled model of George Washington's family home in Mount Vernon to be displayed at the Chicago Exposition. The 'lawn' alone was formed of 6459 pearls. It created quite a stir. Nobody in America had ever seen so many perfect pearls in one place before.[45]

Mikimoto not only liked Americans, he also needed them. In all his years of experimenting he had found no better nucleus for his pearls than the pig's toe mussel, which he bought from the traders of the Mississippi river. This is true even today: whether pearls are said to come from Australia, Tahiti, China or Japan, all good ones have an American heart. The pig's toe shell is tough and durable, has a specific gravity similar to that of pearl and, most importantly, doesn't flake after polishing. From the 1910s until today the centre of almost every cultured pearl in the world is found by men and occasionally women swimming through water so muddy they call it black. They don't use scuba equipment because it is too unwieldy; instead they breathe through tubes attached to an air-compressor on a small boat and find the mussels by floating a few centimetres above the riverbed, using a technique that has been described as 'like looking for your spectacles in the dark'.[46] Their main fear is the giant catfish, which can weigh two hundred pounds or more and is said to be able to eat a man alive – although that is probably a rumour circulated to put off the competition. Black-water diving can be lucrative work for poor communities: nuclei for the largest pearls can sell for two hundred dollars apiece.

Two Knits, One Pearl

After all the international controversy about whether cultured pearls were 'real' or 'fake' it was, ironically, the Second World War and the post-war period that secured the newly invented Japanese gems a lustrous international future. The Allied occupation forces arriving in Japan following VJ-Day on 15 August 1945 could immediately see the money-laundering potential of pearls and banned all domestic sales. Mikimoto was only allowed to sell to the occupation forces.[47] It was hardly surprising that the prices were low enough for ordinary American soldiers to afford them, and GIs bought them in huge numbers to take home to their mothers, sisters and sweethearts. In 1945, there was a particularly good harvest because the pearls had been allowed to grow inside the oysters for several more seasons than usual and were especially lustrous.

The arrival of 'pearls for the people' coincided with the reinvention of the 'twin-set'. The combination of a woollen sweater with a cardigan had been created in America in 1934 as a form of thermal underwear. But by the 1950s twin-sets were seen as smart daywear and women, who wouldn't normally have dreamed of being seen in public with their underwear showing, were buying them in vast quantities. When fashion editors on both sides of the Atlantic decided that the pearl necklace reinforced the demure image of the layered woollen look, the future of cultured pearls was assured. After the war, many women in Europe and America had gone out to work for the first time and many used their new buying power to purchase pearls.

Demand was such that expeditions were sent to exotic bays and islands all over the world to test whether cultured pearls could be grown there. Places like Broome in Western Australia (once known for its mother-of-pearl and now for its giant cultured pearls), Tahiti in the South Seas (which has only been producing black pearls commercially since the 1960s, all cultured) and particularly China, would gain a reputation as world suppliers of top pearls, and do it so well that the buyers believed the pearls had always come from those places in large quantities, which they had not. They had always before been overshadowed by the Persian Gulf and Sri Lanka, and later the Americas. For Mikimoto the new market demand meant that when he died in 1954, aged ninety-six, he had far exceeded his childhood dream to be the richest man in Toba: he had also fulfilled his ambition to make pearls the gems of the people, even if the people didn't understand how or why things had changed.

The Case of the Poisoned Pearls

Today the island where Kokichi and Ume Mikimoto had sat for hours patiently opening oyster shells is now a tourist attraction called Pearl Island. It has been built up into a concrete land mass, linked to the Japanese mainland by a covered footbridge. The complex includes a museum, library, shop, gardens, a small café, a statue of the Pearl King in his trademark bowler hat, and several viewing galleries from which, on the hour, you can watch women bobbing in the water in white pyjamas above black wetsuits, pretending to pick up live oysters and put them into floating wooden tubs. These are supposedly the descendants of the famous *ama* divers who, according to popular stories – as well as many lurid woodblocks dating from the eighteenth and nineteenth centuries – have for centuries swum naked to the bottom of the sea. In reality they were looking for abalone rather than pearls, but their presence on Pearl Island is another example of Mikimoto's innate showmanship.

Inside the museum I watched other young women put on a show for visitors. This time they were demonstrating how to graft pearls by inserting the nuclei into the oysters' gonads. 'Does it hurt?' I asked one woman.

'No,' she said, and held up her hands to show that her work did not harm them. I didn't have the heart to tell her I was talking about the oysters.

The place looks successful enough, but behind the show-business the Japanese industry is suffering. Part of the problem is that Japanese pearls are no longer good enough. American gemmologist Richard Wise declined even to include them in his book *Secrets of the Gem Trade*. This is not, he wrote, because the Japanese *akoya* pearls, or the *Pinctada martensii* oysters that produce them, are intrinsically inferior. 'However, assembly line methods currently practiced by the Japanese produce a pearl with such thin layers of nacre, and [so highly processed through bleaching and dyeing] that it more closely resembles a manufac-tured product than it does a true pearl.'[48] The main problem is that pearl-farmers have to decide how long to leave the oysters in the water after grafting the nuclei into them. Today the Japanese tend to allow nine months instead of the two years that Mikimoto recommended, so some of the pearls are really just American-shell beads with a little extra shine from the Japanese seas brushed on top of them.

I wanted to know more about why Japanese pearl-farmers were reducing the growing time of their pearls: with such a difference in quality, it didn't make sense. A few days before, I had sent a formal request, through the Pearl Island Museum, to the Mikimoto Company main office in Tokyo, to visit their Ago Bay farms. This was where Mikimoto had made so many of his experiments and where today's pearl industry can be said to have started. Although I had sent several letters before leaving England, I had received no response. Now I was in Toba I received an answer, but it was negative. There was no expla-nation. When I asked the museum curator he shrugged and looked apologetic. A Japanese-speaking friend had already joined me from Osaka to translate. We had a car and nothing to lose, so late one rainy afternoon we headed uninvited to Ago Bay, about an hour's drive to the south of Toba, to see the area that Kokichi Mikimoto had made his base and where millions of pearls had been born.

The mainland ends in a series of cliffs and coves. A century ago the bay was a wilderness, but its reputation as the source of beautiful Japanese *akoya* pearls has not played in its favour. Modern hotels perch on the cliffs like blemishes on baroque pearls, and the headlands are covered with golf courses and new roads. We had planned to stay at a simple *ryokan* inn on an island at the other side of the bay. When we arrived at the little village of Ago Wan – which was full of restaurants, jewellery shops and little else – we called the inn. Within a few minutes

Ama *divers off Pearl Island*

Toba Bay, Japan, the site of the world's first pearl farm

Kokichi Mikimoto, the 'Pearl King of the World'

an old man had appeared out of the rain and darkness, driving a small motorised dinghy. When we got there his wife had prepared a meal for us of fried and raw fish with rice, and they both seemed friendly until we asked about the pearl farms. Then they pressed their lips together, shook their heads and looked afraid. They had nothing to tell us about the pearl-fisheries of Ago Wan, they said firmly, and turned away, as if they had already said too much.

The next morning the inn-owner reluctantly took us on a detour back to the village, driving us in his boat past the pearl farms we were not allowed to visit. From the surface all we could see were irregular lines of black buoys stretching out into the bay. They looked like a swimming-club outing with everyone in black racing caps waiting for the starting gun to fire, but we knew that beneath them there was a kind of calm and that there should have been cats' cradles of ropes, with thousands of oysters suspended from them in baskets, waiting for someone to put them out of their pain. A few dogs barked from the shore and occasional wisps of cooking smoke floated from little cabins, but there was not a person in sight. Either this was the off-season, or nothing was really happening at all.

Crisis in Ago Bay

In daylight, Ago village was strangely deserted too. Most of the shops were shut, and we saw no other foreign visitors and fewer than half a dozen Japanese tourists. It was May, and certainly not the off-season. We took an early lunch at a small restaurant. There was just one other couple, who seemed to be friends of the waiter. I couldn't resist 'pearl-foot udon soup'. The 'foot' is the hardest bit of the oyster flesh, the only decent piece to eat. The Chinese say that it is an aphrodisiac, but that wasn't my experience. They tasted good – almost eggy – and were bright orange. The soup contained more than a dozen and I ate them all. I regretted my greed. Two hours later I was vomiting in a lay-by on the highway, and for the next two days I did nothing but lie on a mattress in a small *ryokan* in the former capital city of Nara, and hallucinate.

There was a positive side to my distress, though: it had confirmed the answer to the mystery. The probable reason that nobody at Mikimoto wanted a writer to go to the pearl farms of Ago, and why nobody in Ago would talk about pearls, was because something terrible was happening in that bay. Since the 1990s pollution has been pouring into the water, partly as a result of careless husbandry but also in untreated sewage from all the hotels that bring people in to enjoy the 'unspoiled wilderness'. No wonder the Japanese farmers were pulling out their oysters after just nine months: any more than that and they risked losing most of their stock to the effluent in the water – it was killing the *akoya* oysters as well as poisoning me. Similar things are happening in Lake Biwa in central Japan, which was a centre for fresh-water cultured pearls for so many years that 'Biwa Pearls' became a byword for all such gems, whatever their origin. Thanks to the pollution in the area, production at Lake Biwa has now declined almost to the point of non-existence.[49]

Mikimoto, who had spent so many years with his oysters, coaxing them to live, watching them die, knew how delicate they are. Like pearls that cannot be sprayed too much with perfume or warmed too much with smoke, left alone too much or touched too much, the mother oysters and mussels must be treated gently – as the Scottish pearl-fishers, too, had learned to their cost. These creatures are a barometer of how we are treating our planet. Sometimes in our greed to make them produce pretty things for our pleasure we forget that they deserve our respect.

The marketplace, so carefully nurtured by Mikimoto, is also in a delicate balance. The skill of the Pearl King was that he created not only human-made pearls but also a steady stream of people wanting to buy them. He allowed pearls to retain their mystique through all the technological changes, as if they were the same astonishing natural objects that Julius Caesar had loved and hadn't all been mass-produced on farms.

But does the rest of the gemstone industry work the same way? If real diamonds and rubies suddenly became so cheap that we could set them into pavements as mosaics or into clothes as decoration, if any working woman could afford to buy them for fun, and if we couldn't easily tell those that had formed by geology from others forged by people, what would happen? Would the market for natural gemstones collapse, as the market for pearls almost did? Or would the power of storytelling hold the prices aloft?

These are important questions, because it is all beginning to happen. And, as we will find in the diamond chapter in particular, some people in the jewellery industry are very, very afraid.

4

Opal

'If my book is somewhat unorthodox in structure, it is but in
keeping with much of the Opal which it describes.'
TULLIE WOLLASTON, opal hunter, 1924[1]

'Australian history is almost always picturesque; indeed, it is
also so curious and strange, that it is itself the chiefest novelty
the country has to offer and so it pushes the other novelties
into second and third place. It does not read like history, but
like the most beautiful lies; and all of a fresh new sort, no
mouldy old stale ones.'
MARK TWAIN, *Following the Equator*[2]

Most historic gemstones have names, given by their owners,
finders, dealers or publicists and we remember them as 'the
Mountain of Light' or 'the Spoonseller's Emerald', 'the Hano-
verian Pearls' or the 'Taylor-Burton Diamond'. But the most
famous opal in history has no name, even though it does have
a deliciously scandalous story. It was owned by a Roman senator called Nonius in 35 BC and it was the talk of republican
Rome. At the time all the opals known in Europe came from
just one place: the mines of Czernowitza, in present-day
Slovakia. It was a tantalising location because Rome never conquered it, although its legions came close, and this meant that
opals had a rarity value in the empire that other gems could not
match. Although this one was only the size of a hazelnut it was
still worth two million sesterces – enough to buy a villa or two
in a nice part of Rome. That was, if its owner had decided to

sell it. But he did not, and that was where the problems started.

Pliny the Elder tells of how the smooth-talking Roman general Mark Antony desperately wanted to buy the opal. When Nonius refused to sell, Antony applied pressure, and the senator fled, choosing exile with his opal rather than Rome without it.[3] Pliny marvelled at the passion and cruelty of Antony, who cared so much for a jewel that he would banish another man for its sake. And he wondered at the obstinacy of Nonius who agreed to be banished. But the most perplexing thing of all, to Pliny, was that although he had to leave behind the rest of his property, he took with him the opal ring that had been the cause of his exile. Surely, Pliny mused, the little jewel would remind the senator for ever of his misfortune.

Today even the best opals don't cost the price of a villa on the Capitoline Hill, and they do not come from Europe at all but are sourced mostly in the outback of Australia.[4] However, in one way similar principles apply: Australian opals are usually found in such isolated places that many of the people who look for them could be said to have given up their homes and homelands for their sake. To find the stones, and those who search for them, I had to visit some of the remotest parts of the remotest inhabited continent. But before I left for Australia, I met an opal exile, with an astonishing story, selling his stones from a stall in the middle of the United States.

The Biggest Gem Fair in the World

Pliny would have loved the Tucson Gem Fair, which has a great deal to offer both the natural historian and the student of human nature, for he was both. For two weeks in February, this medium-sized town in Arizona becomes the gem capital of the world. There are a dozen enormous marquees all over town, and most hotels are booked up several years ahead – mainly because the beds double as showcases: with merchants sleeping in them at night and showing off their goods in the same space by day. There is something almost indecent about walking up and down the corridors of the Days Inn or the Hilton, peering into other people's bedrooms to see what promises they hold. 'Whole Dinosaur', reads one sign and there, as promised, is a full fossilised lizard laid out on the patterned counterpane. Sometimes you have to hold your breath at the stuffiness or smokiness of a stranger's bedroom but sometimes you pause despite it all, captivated by something seriously rare or deliciously underpriced – and you understand why so many thousands of people flock to this desert town each year. They are partly in search of business, but mostly they are in search of treasure. British gem dealer Geoffrey Munn once described such fairs as 'like a huge pond with one or two wonderful goldfish and thousands of rods hanging over it. Just once in a while you have a great catch.'[5]

The jewels don't just flow through bedrooms: they fill entire ballrooms and marquees, which is where the best catches are often found, although the payback is that for endless rows each stall seems to be selling much the same things, bright stones priced at either pennies or annual salaries. When you see them wholesale like this, the entire gem business seems almost silly: a throwback to childhood marble-swapping or those bead-trading days of early colonialism, when people sold their land, heirlooms and, in one famous instance, Manhattan[6] all for a few little gauds. When rubies are spread out like caviar and there are pearls by the bucketful it is easy to wonder, as Pliny did nearly two thousand years ago, why they should merit quite so much fuss and expense.

It was in a hotel ballroom that I caught sight of Uwe Barfuss. He was almost lost in a sea of sapphire-dealers but while nearly everyone else was dressed in uniform dark suits selling uniform cut stones displayed in uniform white boxes, Uwe was in a T-shirt and lined up in front of him on the display counter was what looked like a parade of walnuts. 'Nice spot for a stall,' I said.

'Yeah,' he said. 'But "ballroom" usually means something different where I come from.' I looked quizzical so he explained. 'It's what we call the opal mines when they get so big you could dance in them.' He was an opal-miner from Queensland, Australia, and because business was slow that afternoon he began to tell me his story, a story which involved hard work, determination, mystical revelations and an extraordinary find called the Angel of Yowah.

Nuts

Diamonds might vary in terms of clarity, colour, size and shape but fundamentally they are all the same material (carbon) and the good ones all do the same thing (sparkle). The same uniformity of appeal is found in most other gemstones. But opals are a little different. In precious opals there might be a dash of red here, a seductive swirl of blue there, and in the centre, perhaps, a flirtatious glance of green. But each stone flickers with a unique fire and a good opal is one with an opinion of its own. So, it seems no coincidence that ever since the 1870s most of the world's opals have come from the deserts of Australia, a land that celebrates individualism like no other.

Uwe had arrived in Australia from Germany in the mid-1950s when he was eleven. Before then his name had rhymed with Hoover but, in an attempt to fit in, he changed it to rhyme with 'Dewey'. His father was a coal-miner who had heard that the dirt tracks of Australia were paved with pretty stones, and as soon as he arrived he started to hunt for them. They were living in Melbourne so this was where he and Uwe began their search. Neighbours thought that father and son were crazy to spend their weekends looking for gemstones in the stream beds of outer suburbia, 'But then in 1962, we found sapphires in a creek, and they stopped laughing.' The Barfusses became front-page local news – in the beginning because of the treasures they had uncovered, but later because they were being pushed off their claim.

The issue was one of ownership. Australia has a system whereby farmers who supposedly 'own the land' actually own only the surface. The mineral rights to the ground underneath are owned separately, but can be claimed. This has brought about a complex system of 'pegging', which means putting pegs into the ground, marked with metal tags saying who the claim belongs to. As long as you follow the local rules you are often allowed to investigate the land's potential for hidden treasure. It is quite unlike the UK where mineral rights are allocated according to ancient laws: if someone found a diamond deposit in someone else's field they would have no right to excavate.

Uwe and his father had pegged out the area in which they had discovered sapphires, but the farmers had sent them away with shotguns because they didn't want their land dug up. The local government took the farmers' side because it wanted to build a dam in that area and the Barfusses had to concede defeat. However, the experience taught the then eighteen-year-old Uwe some lessons. He learned that nothing matched the experience of finding jewels in the ground. He learned how important it was to peg your claim. And, as he watched the reservoir flooding over what should have been his father's claim, he vowed that next time he would not give up. Next time, they agreed, they would turn their attention to opals; for which Australia was famous.

But when they looked at the map they realised the country had more than a dozen opal areas. There was Coober Pedy in south Australia, with its pale stones and reputation for rough living; there were the 'boulder opal' towns of Queensland, where the stones were like bright crystals in black frames; and there was Lightning Ridge in New South Wales, where the opals were dark, and looked like the night sky filled with fireworks. Uwe's father asked the wife of the gemstone baron Harry Spencer[7] which of Australia's many kinds of opal she preferred – she had spent years collecting them all over the country. 'I like Yowah nuts,' she said enigmatically, and on that casual pronouncement, their future was decided.

Some people say Yowah nuts are the prettiest of all Australian opals, others that they are the ugliest. Whatever you think of them they are certainly the most easily identifiable, and as they are found in just a few square kilometres of land they are also the rarest. They are called 'nuts' because when they are found they look like the crinkly shells of walnuts, with all the goodness hidden inside them. When they have been sliced and made into jewellery they look more like church windows, or Aboriginal paintings of the Dreamtime, with all the secret stories and traditional maps coded into seemingly abstract forms. When Uwe opened two sides of a Yowah nut in demonstration, it was like gazing into the Australian landscape after a storm, with limpid violet pools of clear water linked to green meadows by chocolate brown ironstone roads and thinly veined blue rivers. Even under the artificial lights of the display case, everything shimmered as if in sunshine.

However, it took some time for Uwe and his father to see anything of that magic when they decided to try for opals. In 1972 when they reached the hamlet of Yowah in Queensland it was nothing but a bumpy landscape of pale tip heaps spreading out into the red desert. There was little to show that almost a century before it had been one of the busiest places in outback Australia – a centre of the vast Cunnamulla opal field, covering more than ten thousand square miles.

In the 1890s, when Queensland became known for opals, the outback area where the gems were found was a male domain: few women chose to live there. But one celebrated exception was a woman whose name was Isobel Robinson,[8] although everyone called her the Eulo Queen, after the name of the town, not far from Yowah, whose economy she dominated. She wore a gold belt, as thick as her arm, studded with opals the size of Victorian pennies and she glittered as she walked. Nobody knew where she had come from – some said England, others Ireland, others said a cattle station a few miles down the track – but all agreed she had the gift of persuasion when it came to buying opals from men just in from their claims who were thirsty for a drink. By 1898 she owned two hotels, a butcher's shop, a general store and a casino[9] where she employed attractive girls in the back rooms. The Queen was admired for her fearlessness. One night in 1899 some men were arguing about who was the best shot. One turned to Mrs Robinson and asked her to hold a tin matchbox above her head. 'She did not hesitate,' remembered a miner who was there.[10] 'Taking the matchbox she stepped back about twenty paces and held the box up, her opal belt glittering in the candlelight. The hunter fired in a flash, spinning the box out of her fingers.' Another man, who had had several glasses of rum, optimistically held up his Winchester and asked to do the same. She declined.

When the Barfusses arrived, all the old mining areas were almost deserted, the stories of daring and bravado almost forgotten, and the empire of the Eulo Queen had vanished long before. Virtually all mining had ended in 1903, after a drought so bad that a government official recorded travelling a hundred kilometres out of Yowah with 'not a blade of grass, nor any herbage to be seen', Uwe said. 'People said the opal was all mined out and there was nothing left. But we were pretty sure this was what we wanted, so we stayed.' And then they got lucky: they found an old-timer who had a trick for locating opals by a very unexpected method.

Opal has the odd chemical formula $SiO_2.n(H_2O)$, which looks alarming but simply means that it is a mixture of silica and a varying amount of water – as if a glass containing water had turned miraculously into stone. The water – which may form five to ten per cent of the stone's volume – is what makes the opal such a beautiful, limpid gem, and it is one of the many ingredients contributing to its astonishing play of colour. Water can make opals look like reflections on a lake in summer or it can make them look like raging red conflagrations.

The water content also means that, astonishingly, opals can be detected by dowsing – the trick the old-timer had used. Uwe and his father were sceptical at first, 'But we thought it was better than throwing our hats up in the air and seeing where they landed, so we might as well try it.' Opal-miners are too macho to use the dainty willow twigs of water dowsers: instead they just rip out a piece of fencing wire and point it at the ground, and this is what Uwe and his father did. For several days, feeling self-conscious, they walked up and down the area of the old claims, each holding two pieces of wire. Then the wires jumped. They tried a second time and it happened again. When they passed over the same ground a third time, the wires crossed over each other. 'So that's where we pegged our first claim,' Uwe said. 'And that was the mine that later gave us the Angel of Yowah.' He was about to continue, but three potential buyers arrived at his stall, and he was caught up in conversation about yields, prices and the quality of his stones. 'Wait a sec,' he said to me, and gave me his business card. 'Come and see us in Australia. I promise I'll tell you the story of the Angel.'

Red Fire in Alice

I met Uwe again three months later in Alice Springs, Australia's central town. There are no opal mines at Alice, but he was branching out into rubies. He and his wife Verena had recently bought, sight unseen, Australia's only commercially viable ruby mine in the Hart Ranges north of the town, and had arrived with their teenage son Ricardo to start prospecting. On their first day the three had driven around for hours looking for the ruby mine. When they got back to where they had started they were trying to ignore a growing fear that they had spent their life-savings on something that wasn't there. It would not have been the first time someone had been sold a fictitious gem mine: in the so-called 'Great Colorado Diamond Hoax' of 1872 two Kentucky con men talked San Francisco investors out of more than half a million dollars for a diamond mine that did not exist. But fortunately the Great Australian Ruby Hoax was not a story ready to be written. 'Just when we were going to give up for the day Ricardo looked down and saw this red stone just sitting on the ground. It was shining like a stop light and we knew we were there.'

I asked if they had found any more. Before he answered, Uwe glanced around the bar where we were sitting. There were a few locals chatting over some beers, a group of tourists from Melbourne, and a man on his own, smoking and nursing a drink, who had looked up when we mentioned rubies. Uwe changed the subject. 'I promised to tell you about the Angel of Yowah,' he said. 'Though I warn you, it sounds like a fairy-tale.'

After he and his father had pegged their first opal claim in Yowah, they started to dig. They dug and dug and got down ten metres and found nothing. 'Dad and I started thinking that maybe the only nuts in that place were us,' he said. They were five months into their adventure, and they had promised Uwe's mother that they would return home after six. Then, just days before their deadline was up, they found what they were looking for: a substantial bunch of Yowah nuts, like eggs left by a dragon thousands of years ago. At last, it seemed, they had struck opal.[11]

One of the larger nuts was about the size of an emu's egg, and Uwe had left it until last. He was about to cut it lengthways, which was usual, when he stopped. 'It was weird,' he said, 'but I thought I heard a voice and it said, "No, don't do it!"' Again he started to cut it and heard the same voice in his head saying,

'No!' So, wondering how he was going to explain it to his father, he cut the nut the wrong way, round the equator rather than lengthwise. When he opened it, 'It looked as if there was an angel and it was descending from a cloud,' he said. 'It had wings, a robe and a belt . . . and the eyes changed colour as you looked at it. It looked like a stained-glass window.' The stone – weighing 256 grams – is locked in a safe now, but he had a picture of it: it showed an angel in flight, its face, muscular wings, even its feet, all traced in celestial blues, greens and pinks. It was exactly the kind of gem for which a man, or a woman, might risk exile.

'I don't consider myself a very religious person but . . . well, it blew me away,' Uwe said. The discovery was in keeping with Yowah's esoteric reputation. 'Some people say it's the Garden of Eden, and the opals are the fruits and nuts from its trees, turned to stone. There's even a theory that Yowah comes from the name for God, Jehovah,[12] though I don't know if I believe that.' Uwe had once been offered a million Australian dollars (about four hundred thousand pounds) in gold bullion for the Angel, but he had decided that the arrangements for the swap were not secure enough. Another time an American collector had asked him to bring it to a certain location in Los Angeles for viewing, but a military friend advised him not to risk it. 'I don't really want to sell it anyway,' he said, echoing Senator Nonius. 'I wouldn't ever be forced into it.'

Opal is the only gemstone for which the answer to the question 'Animal, vegetable or mineral?' is 'Yes'. Animal opal is found in the stingers of female mosquitoes: it keeps the tips sharp enough to make a good injection into skin. Vegetable opal is found in nettles, which lose the power to sting if grown in a soil that does not contain silicon. The stings work by forming tiny 'hypodermic needles', which are so brittle that they break off after piercing the skin, releasing the venom.[13]

One of the most important questions about opals is why

some of them contain flashes and sparkles and others do not. Before the nineteenth century some scientists thought there was oil trapped in precious opal, others that it was made up of tiny internal cracks that diffracted light, and others that water somehow caused the play of colour, although that did not explain why common and precious opal have a similar water content. A German scientist called H. Behrens came quite close in 1871, when he claimed that the colour was caused by tiny, thin, curved plates focusing the light rays.[14] Eventually, in the 1960s, Australian researchers[15] looked at opals under thirty thousand times magnification and discovered they were made up of tiny silicon spheres measuring several hundred nanometers[16] in diameter. This is a critical measurement, as it is the same width as the wavelength of visible light. The scientists[17] realised that the difference between precious and non-precious opal lay not in the materials they were made of, but in how those materials were organised.

In precious opal the glass-like molecules are stacked like billiard balls set out in neat rows, creating regular triangular gaps between them on the surface; ordinary opal is more like a disorganised school games locker, full of basketballs, soccer balls and golf balls thrown into it in no particular order. When the surface of opal is even and ordered and the molecules are a set distance apart, the white light bounces off in wavelengths that give the appearance of bright colours. And just as the sky looks red when there are big molecules in the atmosphere, the red in opal is caused by the presence of larger spheres in the silicon gel; while the more common blue colour appears when the spheres are small. But whatever the size of the silicon, if the surface has no order to it the light just bounces off in all directions, giving no sense of separate colours at all. It means that paradoxically it is order that causes the irregular iridescent flashes of colour in opal; while it is chaos that makes low-quality opal a uniform grey.

'Ratting' and Other Opal Words

After we had finished our drinks Uwe and Ricardo took me up to Anzac Hill, the town's main lookout point. Seeing the friendly winking of some of Alice Spring's 10,000 or so television sets[18] in homes spreading out to the hills, it was hard to contemplate the vastness of the desert the town occupies. It was more than thirteen hundred kilometres to any major city: this was one of the most isolated towns in the world. Now that we were more private, I asked Uwe again whether he had found anything at the ruby mine. He began to answer, then fell silent. A man was standing in the shadows nearby, apparently enjoying the view. He looked like the man from the bar.

We got back into the car and as he and his son dropped me off at my hotel Uwe confirmed that he had found several rubies on his claim. 'But you can't be too careful,' he added. 'A lot of people are very interested in other people's mines in Australia. When it happens with opals we've got a word for it. Ratting. Don't know what the word for stealing from other people's ruby mines is but we'll probably find out.' As he drove away, the other car was still behind him, apparently following.

Apart from 'ratting' there were several useful expressions to learn before a visit to the main opal towns. Some were straight-forward. 'Play of colour' is what you look for in an opal – the fire of it, its capacity to sparkle with different colours when you tilt it. 'Potch' is the opposite; it is opal without any fire, as if nature had thrown a bucket of dirty water on the flames, and left behind a glassy puddle. The 'opal dirt' is the material from the mines, which the miners take out and sort; and the 'tailings' are what is left, after they have sorted. 'Noodling' is sifting through the dumps, looking for treasure that others might have missed. And 'nobbies' are nodules of opal, like the ones at Yowah; the word probably comes from the eighteenth-century slang word 'nab', meaning 'head-shaped object'. But the first word to learn was 'dugout', because the first stop on my opal trail was Coober Pedy, Australia's most famous mining town, where several hundred Australians live in caves they have dug out under the ground.

White Man in a Hole

'There's one way to guarantee you'll become a millionaire from mining opals in Coober Pedy,' a miner said to me on my first day.

'What's that?' I asked.

'Start off a billionaire,' he said, and went on his way laughing.

Coober Pedy prides itself on being an unprepossessing town – and it lives up to its reputation. You know when you're getting close because all around the town there are dozens of giant pink, conical hills ten metres high or more, which make it look as if an army of giants has set up tents across the desert. These are the mullock heaps and it is extraordinary to think that each wheelbarrow- or truckload of rocks that went into creating this huge and oddly silent landscape has been scrutinised several times for treasure.

The first evening I was there, as the sun set over those strange hummocks, I climbed up an old mining ridge in the main town to enjoy Coober Pedy's lack of beauty from a proper vantage-point. On the next hill half a dozen Aboriginal men in checked flannel shirts were doing pretty much the same thing, all facing west, like witnesses to the dying sun; all smoking cigarettes in companionable silence. The word 'opal' comes from the Greek, meaning 'changing colour', but the landscape that produces it seemed unusually monochrome. Just pink, like the colour of a traditional girl's bedroom stretching as far as you can see, alleviated only by the occasional pastel green of a clump of eucalyptus.

At the end of the children's book *The Iron Man*, by Ted Hughes, a space-bat angel is burned so badly by flying into the

Aboriginal men contemplate the sunset at Coober Pedy

sun that its skin turns to gems, which drop off in the desert of Australia. The whole continent is rich with deposits – diamonds, sapphires, emeralds, topazes, jade, rubies and zircons. But perhaps when Hughes conjured up the image of an Australian desert littered with gemstones, it was the desolate opal landscape of Coober Pedy that he was thinking of.

I had heard that in Coober Pedy most people lived underground, and I had imagined a moonlike surface with everything hidden away, as in the cult children's TV show *The Clangers*, where the little pink residents of a distant planet live in holes protected by manhole covers. Apparently it had once been pretty much like that. But today, from the top at least, it looks like an ordinary outback town. There are thin clapperboard houses, disused parking spaces, and shops with corrugated-metal roofs. However, beneath that there is another layer, in which there are homes, shops, churches and hotels. There are also old mining ballrooms that can no longer be worked, in case a bit of residential Coober Pedy collapses on top of them.

*Ivan Radeka, a miner, outside his underground home
at Coober Pedy*

The urban planning in Coober Pedy follows a theme of eccentricity. The main roads meander absent-mindedly through the town along the opal seams rather than towards any particular destination. Everywhere across the visible townscape there are metal cylinders that look like giant batteries, and in a way they are. Because Coober Pedy is a town that is powered by the need for water, and without these cylindrical reservoirs[19] it could not exist. The average annual rainfall is 17.5 centimetres, which compares very aridly with 108 in New York and 122 in Sydney,[20] and it makes Coober Pedy one of the driest, hottest places in Australia – which is quite an achievement, considering how many dry, hot places the country has. But the people who live there have reason to thank the dryness, however inconvenient.

It was the search for something to drink in this dreadful desert that led to the initial discovery of opals.

In early 1915, fourteen-year-old Willie Hutchison, his father Jim and two partners went looking for gold in the Stuart Ranges – named after John McDouall Stuart, the first European to cross Australia from south to north. Not only had they failed to uncover gold, but as they set up camp by the dried-out Carryingallama creek one afternoon, they realised they did not even have an idea of where to find water. Australian history is full of prospectors who ran out of water – few more vivid than an account from Stuart's original expedition, which ran into trouble in the outback half a century before. The heat of the sun was so intense that every screw in their boxes was drawn, and all horn handles and combs split. 'The lead dropped from their pencils ... Their finger-nails became as brittle as glass, and their hair and the wool on their sheep ceased to grow. Scurvy attacked them all, and Mr Poole, the second in command, died.'[21]

The next morning of their own journey Jim and his two partners set out early on camels to look for water, leaving Willie behind. When they returned they had a fright. 'I found the camp deserted and the cold ashes of the fire showed that it was many hours since the last embers had died out,' Jim remembered.[22] 'I was naturally a bit uneasy at his uncalled-for absence and intended to light a fire on the bank of the creek, which could be seen almost anywhere from the ranges.' Then, as his father was gathering firewood, Willie strolled casually into the camp, and asked his father if they had found water. 'I told him none. He replied, "Well, Dad, I have beaten you."' He had not only found water: he had filled a sugar-bag with pale, sparkling stones, which he spilled out on to the ground for his father to see. They sparked an opal rush. Within months, hundreds of men arrived. Later came many who had returned from the Great War in Europe, and who quickly adapted their trench-building skills to dig caves as protection from a different enemy – the sun.

The first name for the area was the unimaginative 'Stuart Range Opal Field'. However, the newly formed Residents' Association came up with a much better name in 1920 when their thriving village was finally gazetted. *Kupa* and *piti* are from two different Aboriginal languages, and originally signified 'the boy's watering-hole', referring to young Willie Hutchison's adventure in 1915. But Willie died in 1920, aged twenty, in a watering-hole where he had gone for a swim and seized up with cramps, so the new name seemed in poor taste. Today 'Coober Pedy' is almost always said to mean 'white man in a hole', an explanation of which many inhabitants are immensely proud.

Potch and Colour

That night as I walked to my underground hotel I heard two gunshots from the road, then male laughter, which changed quickly to male yelling. Coober Pedy was living up to its rough reputation.

The next morning I went to meet an old-timer called Dawn Jones, and her friend Peter Butler. Dawn had been living at Coober Pedy since 1975 when 'the ratio of men to women was about a hundred to one'. She had had her first child before she was twenty, then had five more. The younger ones still live at home, competing for space with dogs, rescued kangaroos, possums and two bearded dragons, or large lizards, called Potch and Colour.

As we went into the bungalow two of her teenage daughters were arguing about who had let a kangaroo leave its droppings in the laundry basket. They were going to a race meeting at the opal field of Mintabie two hundred miles to the north and their lift was about to arrive. As the girls scooped up their clothes from the floor around us, Dawn and Peter talked about Coober Pedy: the collapsing mine shafts; the eerie 'min-min lights' that appeared over the opal hills at night like UFOs and a character called Machine Gun Joe who had shot off his own arm just below the shoulder. Once, Dawn said, a Hungarian miner had 'stood outside my house and he had explosives strapped to him and he was shouting about how someone had stolen his woman.' The man had grown up in a circus near Budapest, and had been famous for a clown show involving fireworks, so everyone thought this was just another act. 'But he slipped and the dynamite went off and he left himself all over my house. I wouldn't let my dogs lick me for a week after that – because I knew what they'd been eating.'

The stories were full of phrases like 'this Hungarian clown' or 'that Latvian crocodile hunter' or 'the crazy Germans'. Many of those who had been drawn to the opal mines were first-generation arrivals from Europe. The mining towns fulfilled the dreams of the immigrant – freedom from rules, the chance to make a fortune, the opportunity to be self-employed – and, in an updated version of the Nonius story, they had all chosen exile with opals rather than staying at home without them. Also, you didn't need much capital to get started in opals. Hundreds had turned up at Coober Pedy with more hopes than money and some had got rich.

But now everything is more serious. Although mining claims are cheap, prospecting is not. The tunnelling machines use around two hundred litres of petrol each day. 'Before 1950, when they first brought in gelignite, most miners just had handpicks and axes and tents and buckets[23] and they gouged it out by hand,' Peter said. 'But today it's an investment. You've got to find a load of cash upfront.' If the first problem is finding the opal, the next is selling it. Since each stone is different, pricing is arguably more subjective than it is with other gems. 'We say an opal's worth nothing until you've got the money in your pocket,' Peter added. The buyers are mostly Hong Kong Chinese, and they are tough negotiators. 'Some of us miners once said that if they didn't put the prices up we wouldn't sell.

And the dealers just smiled and said, "No problem: we've been stockpiling for years."'

By this time a young man in his teens had arrived to pick up Dawn's daughters. He had a beer in his hand as he got into the truck. 'Smack him in the ear if he drinks, Desray,' she shouted encouragingly to one of them. As they drove away she bellowed, 'Seatbelts, girls!' and they just waved. 'If there's a problem, then the girls know how to drive,' she said confidently, and lit another cigarette.

Doublets and Triplets

If the mining families tend to live on the outskirts of town, the dealers tend to live right in the middle. Tony Wong operates from a large house on Hutchison Street, and he has been in Coober Pedy for so long that he doesn't need to go out to the mines: he just waits for the miners to come to him. He started as an opal-cutter in a Kowloon backstreet and has been coming to Australia as a buyer for thirty years. In the 1970s Hong Kong became an important opal centre because labour was cheap. 'Now we have to send opals to mainland China for cutting,' he said. 'Hong Kong's too expensive.' Different opals go to different countries: the Americans and Japanese demand the highest-quality stones, but Americans prefer reds while the Japanese like the blues and greens. 'Perhaps it's because the colour reminds them of jade,' he said. There has never been much of a market in the UK, perhaps partly because in the 1960s thousands of British people – often from poor families – paid almost nothing for a one-way ticket to Australia. Many of the 'ten-pound Poms' sent opals home as gifts, which is why for a long time, and perhaps even today, it was often seen in the UK as a particularly working-class gemstone.

It wasn't always like that. Even after the disappearance of Nonius, opals were sometimes the most prized stones of all.

The central stone on the thirteenth-century crown of the Holy Roman Emperor was an opal said to be the colour of pure white snow, sparkling with splashes of bright red wine: it was called 'the Orphanus', perhaps because there was no other stone like it.[24] And on New Year's Day 1584,[25] Queen Elizabeth I was delighted to receive an opal parure – a full set of matching jewellery – from one of her favourite courtiers, Sir Christopher Hatton. In gratitude for this (and, perhaps, other services) she arranged for the palace of Ely, near Holborn, to be let to him at a peppercorn rent by the bishops of Ely. The area today is known as Hatton Garden although it has only been London's jewellery quarter since the 1870s. Before that it was a slum; Fagin in Charles Dickens' *Oliver Twist* operated out of Saffron Hill, a few minutes away.

Elizabeth I also gave an opal and ruby hatpin to Sir Francis Drake as a token of thanks for the jewels he purloined for her on the Spanish Main. In the 1800s the tradition of giving opals as favours continued, and around 1805, while he was still in love with her, Napoleon gave his wife Josephine a wonderful red opal weighing nearly 140 grams. It was called 'The Burning of Troy' and he chose it, he said, because she was his Helen. He could have been interested in opals for another reason: he modelled himself on the Romans and perhaps wanted to emulate Mark Antony's passion for these stones.

Even Queen Victoria loved opals throughout her life. When she was thirteen she wrote in her diary about a magical Christmas spent at Kensington Palace: 'After dinner . . . we then went into the drawing-room . . . There were two large round tables on which were placed two trees hung with lights and sugar ornaments. All the presents being placed round the trees . . . Mamma gave me a little lovely pink bag which she had worked with a little sachet likewise done by her; a beautiful little opal brooch and earrings, books, some lovely prints, a pink satin dress and a cloak lined with fur.'[26] Many years later she

*The Orphanus, the opal in the Holy
Roman Emperor's crown*

commissioned a grand tiara with opals and 2678 diamonds, and she often gave opals to her daughters. Perhaps it was in memory of the Ancient Greek opal word *paederos* meaning 'favoured child' or perhaps it was simply remembering the joy of that childhood Christmas.

All of these early stones were almost certainly from the ancient mines of Slovakia – the same source as Nonius' precious stone and the Holy Roman Emperor's red and white one. The mines were worked until the late nineteenth century, although it is said that the local landowners opened them only every three years or so to limit their output. The nearby city of Presov is full of expensive mansions and churches that were built almost entirely on the profits from gems.

Of all the Australian opals, the ones from Coober Pedy are said to be the most similar to those found in Europe, because their fire emerges from a pale, snowy base. Pliny said of those stones that they defied description, 'displaying at once the piercing fire of rubies, the purple brilliancy of amethysts and the

sea-green of emeralds, the whole blended together and flashing
with a brightness that is quite incredible . . . while others speak
of it as resembling the flame of burning brimstone'.

Looking at Tony Wong's stones, however, I thought they
seemed less like hell and more like television. One of his favourites
was luminous white with sparkling dots of red, blue and green,
and reminded me of an untuned TV screen with the small,
coloured pixels of light seeming to shift and move against the pale
background. It was a 'pinfire' opal. When the colour comes in
larger splashes or 'flashes' it is a 'harlequin', which is more valuable. His other pieces were smaller but just as bright. Dipped in
water and placed on a black tray under a bright light, they brought
to mind an underwater nature documentary. They were rich turquoises and greens and scintillated with bright flashes of blue
light. The impression was like looking down at a reef while diving.

Most of those opals were worth several thousand dollars.
'But you can get a similar effect much more cheaply if you
want,' Tony said. Pliny had dedicated a section in his *Natural
History* to imitation opals, since 'there is no stone that is imi-
tated by fraudulent dealers with more exactness than this'. You
can tell the difference, he wrote, because when a glass imitation
opal is held between finger and thumb and exposed to sunshine
it presents the same transparent colour throughout, while genuine opal 'reflects now one hue and now another, as it sheds its
luminous brilliancy upon the fingers'. Today synthetic opals are
made in laboratories in France, Japan, America and elsewhere,
although they have not upset the natural-stone market as other
synthetics have. If you look at them carefully you can see that
they sparkle with obedience, rather than the individual sponta-
neity of the naturals.

The cheaper opals that Tony was talking about were neither
fakes nor synthetics, although some contained glass. They are
called doublets and triplets and are effectively ways of making
slivers of precious opal more impressive. Doublets are made of

Tony Wong, opal dealer

thin strips of opal glued to darkened glass or colourless potch to make them thicker and more vivid. Triplets are essentially opal sandwiches, usually with potch at the back and glass at the front.[27] 'Legally people have to be told if they are being sold doublets or triplets,' Tony said, 'but some bad dealers "forget" to mention it.' The price difference is enormous: a doublet can cost around a quarter the amount of a solid stone and a triplet is even cheaper. With loose opals it is easy to tell them apart: if you look at the stone under light from the side you can usually see two or three different bands of transparent material but if the stone is set in jewellery it can be harder to know for certain. Sometimes owners are warned not to get opals wet: this isn't a problem with solid stones, but it is important with doublets and triplets – because the glue can easily dissolve.

That night I joined Tony for dinner at the Opal Inn Cantonese restaurant, where for decades buyers from Hong Kong have discussed business over dim sum. The sign showed the Chinese characters for opal, pronounced '*o-bau*' in Cantonese, which means 'Australia stone'. However there is a more attractive word, '*sing san wan*', meaning 'lightning-mountain-cloud'. With a name like that no wonder the newly rich of southern China are beginning to be interested. Tony had invited four friends to join us. None was officially a miner but all had weekend mines as a hobby.

The conversation turned to how poor the yields had been recently, and whether this meant they should spend more or less time at the claims. At least, as a dealer Tony didn't have to make that decision, I said. 'Oh, but I do,' he said. 'I've got a mine too.' He had not been lucky either but he wasn't surprised: in Coober Pedy one in ten miners finds opal; one in ten of those makes some money; and one in ten of those makes a fortune. It is a thousand to one chance. 'Better than a state lottery,' Tony said, 'but it's a lot harder work.'

The Church in the Opal Mine

Partly because the mining is such a game of chance and partly because the residents come from so many different cultures, Coober Pedy has a wealth of places to pray for divine guidance, including Serbian Orthodox, Roman Catholic, Anglican and Aboriginal Evangelical churches, all of which are underground. I chose the last, even though I was warned that the congregation might be on the small side because 'when there's good noodling there's not many Aboriginal people at church'.

Because the area is so dry not many Aboriginals lived here in the past, preferring to move on to more reliable water-holes. However, Coober Pedy is part of the wider homelands of the Antikirinya and other Western Desert people, and although they do not appear to have prized opals much or told many stories about them before 1915, they have certainly been involved with them ever since. Some have owned mines and many more have spent their days noodling through abandoned wasteheaps. One of the most notable Aboriginal people in Coober Pedy's recent history was a woman called Tottie Bryant, who revived the opal business in 1946 when she stumbled over a large, sparkling stone eight miles out of town, and uncovered a valuable seam. Tottie and her husband Charlie bought a Model T Ford and became a fixture in those parts, driving through town with their dogs and a pet lamb, which all insisted on sharing the front seat with them.[28]

The Kupa Piti Aboriginal Church was on the edge of town and looked from the outside like an abandoned mine. But the rusted machinery piled around it turned out to be the sign of a recent excavation, and the tunnel entrance led down into a newly painted white cave, lit by bare bulbs. The space was just big enough for about fifty metal chairs placed in front of a wall-hanging with the words 'Come Holy Spirit' embroidered on it. Few of the chairs were occupied. But, after a lively singing session by Aboriginal children, who then filed out to go to Sunday school, a large European man stood up to deliver a sermon to the dozen of us who remained.

There might have been few to appreciate it, but hellfire and brimstone sparkled through that whitewashed catacomb in the opal hills that morning. The speaking style of George McCormack, a building contractor from Northern Ireland turned miner and minister, leaped between charismatically gripping and grandfatherly forgetful ('now what was his name again ... oh yes, Saul'). His theme was that if we did not embrace Christ we would find ourselves heading for some hotter underground caves than this one. 'All that money you might get from mining; all the money of Bill Gates, all of it is as nothing in the sight of God if you don't believe in Jesus,' he boomed.

Then his eyes focused on the back of the room. 'You're here,' he said. 'I thought you were lost.'

'I was,' said a young man, quietly.

The church was so new it had not been officially opened and, George said later, 'It was paid for by the space we are standing in. We had no funds, but we started digging and trusted that Jesus would provide the money to continue.' One day they had found a seam of precious opal, right in the middle. 'We sold it for eight thousand dollars. It was exactly the amount we needed – not too much, not too little. It paid for the entire church, including the whitewash.'

Later George invited the congregation back to his underground home. The walls were flecked with what looked like a marbled pink paint, but it was just the natural pattern of the sandstone. It was surreal to sit with evangelical Christians in a cave, eating homemade coconut cake and discussing whether opal was a manifestation of the Lord or a temptation of the devil (it could be either, was the consensus, depending on who found it). We were joined by the lost-and-found young man, for whom we were all invited to pray and whose nickname was Lucky. He was good-looking in a healthy, outdoorsy way, so it was a surprise to hear that he was a recovering drug addict. He had become a Christian when he was thirteen, the same year he had started mining for opals, so for him the two things were entwined: he believed Jesus helped him avoid accidents and he was also sure that divine guidance was involved in finding the gems. 'I wait and I pray and I get some pictures in my head and I know that Jesus will help me find opal,' he said. The others agreed that when there was opal in a mine 'you can almost smell it'. When you take out the references to Jesus, their accounts were uncannily similar to how Uwe Barfuss had said he found opal in Yowah: by sensing it. There are no known experiments to verify this, but perhaps opal does emit something that we can neither hear nor see, but that even humans – when standing quietly – can feel.

The Luck of the Opals

It had been interesting to meet an opal-miner called Lucky, because opal is generally believed not to be. Of all the gems in the world, it is the only one that is widely thought to bring bad luck. Even today engagement rings in Britain are rarely made with opals. It is not an ancient superstition – Pliny did not mention it, even though his opal story included considerable ill-fortune – and it seems that, for many centuries, opal was actually thought lucky. The Goths believed that it was forged from the eyes of heaven, and tenth-century Arabic scholars wrote that people who wore rose opals (which they called thunderstones) would enjoy 'good fortune and good health'.[29]

In medieval times, opals were thought
to cure eye problems

Their reputation for ill-luck seems to have originated in the nineteenth-century ghost novel, *Anne of Geierstein* by Sir Walter Scott. The story concerned a mysterious aristocrat called Hermione who seemed to be mystically linked to an opal she always wore. 'When her eyes sparkled her cheeks reddened and [the ornament] shot forth the little spark or tongue of flame which it always displayed with an increased vivacity,' Scott wrote. Hermione's maids gossiped that when their mistress was agitated, 'they could see dark red sparks flash from the mystical brooch'. When she had a baby, her husband passed her some holy water, and a drop fell on the opal. It 'shot out a brilliant spark like a falling star and became, the instant afterward, lightless and colourless as a common pebble, while the beautiful baroness sank to the floor of the chapel with a deep sigh of pain'. Hermione was left in her room to recover, but when someone went to check on her two hours later no one was there. 'Just a handful of light grey ashes like such as might have been produced by burning fine paper, found on the bed where she had been laid.' Here, Scott was playing with some real attributes of opal. As one of the softer mineral gems, opals need to be looked after, and if you put them too close to fire they will crack and tarnish. He was also referring to the received wisdom that opals changed subtly in contact with the human body – a property which, as one London jeweller claimed quite seriously in 1890, 'brings out the brilliant tints for which the Opal is famed'.[30] But above all Scott had chosen an apt metaphor: what better mineral to mirror human moods than one that was believed to flash and sulk depending on the light, the heat, and perhaps even the ambience?

Some[31] would have it that *Anne of Geierstein* single-handedly caused the opal market to decline, but it is hard to believe that one book could have had such an enormous impact, and perhaps it didn't do it all on its own. When it came out in 1829 there was scarcely any useful source of opals in the world: the Slovakian seams had long been running out. Most of the opals available were of poor quality, so perhaps the slump was as much to do with supply as demand. One British royal who bought into the superstition was Princess Alexandra, wife of

Queen Victoria's oldest son Bertie, who later became Edward VII. When Victoria died in 1901, the new Queen removed what she called 'the unlucky opals' from that diamond and opal tiara her mother-in-law had commissioned and replaced them with rubies from Ceylon, which remain there today.[32]

Queen Alexandra's belief might not have originated entirely with Walter Scott's novel. It could also have come from a quite separate set of folk stories. In northern Europe it was said that opal's inner magic was forged from the eyes of murdered children, and was therefore a sign of the 'evil eye'. But an equally persuasive theory is that the superstition originating in Scott's book was encouraged by the sellers of competing jewels who felt opals might be a threat to their business. When the Australian stones first came to London in the 1890s the jewellers of Hatton Garden had never seen anything like them and pronounced them worthless. Later they changed their minds and started to put in their orders. Opals became popular and, according to several Australian miners, the diamond dealers, robbed of their buyers, revived the myth that opals were unlucky.

The Opals of the Never Never

The man who introduced Australian opals to London was the dealer Tullie Wollaston. In 1888 he had heard a rumour of an exciting new opal find in Queensland. He was neither a geologist, a mineralogist, nor even a jeweller – he hadn't even seen an opal before – but the twenty-five-year-old adventurer left his wife and their six-week-old baby girl in Adelaide on a whim and spent six weeks travelling to find out the truth. A typical diary entry for the seven-hundred-mile journey ran, 'Dec 22nd – Horrible Day. Gibbers flies and Tender-footed camel. 22 miles.' Other days were far more horrible, and on one of them his partner died of thirst. Tullie still continued on. When he arrived he was disappointed: if this was an opal mine, God help the shareholders, he thought. Then, stumbling along the rough floor of the mine, hot grease dripping from the candle on to his thumb, he caught a glint in the debris and 'picked up from the dust a merry little thing, a real live opal twinkling like Sirius in an east wind'. From that moment he dedicated his life to these curious gems.

Later Tullie would buy from almost all of the Australian opal fields, including Coober Pedy, which he visited within twelve months of Willie Hutchison's discovery in 1915.[33] But he was most associated with Lightning Ridge, 850 kilometres north-west of Sydney. It was the home of what Tullie called 'the Black Opal', and it was my next destination. Not only is Lightning Ridge the source of some of the world's most astonishing gems, but I had also heard that there was a retired miner there with a new theory about how opals were formed. To prove it he was growing his own – at home in his garden shed.

Lightning Ridge

In 2005 a British film company made a movie called *Pobby and Dingan*. It was based on a book about a brother and sister growing up among opal-miners, with all the problems of drinking, ratting and gambling that such a community fosters. The writer had set it in the camps around Lightning Ridge but the location scouts recommended filming it in Coober Pedy instead. Coober Pedy was as rough as the Australian outback's reputation suggested; Lightning Ridge seemed simply too genteel.

On the surface the film people were right, because while the south Australian town is red and dusty and chaotic, Lightning Ridge is lined with green lawns and arranged into suburban roads with nice names like Harlequin Street and Butterfly Avenue. But if you stroll out of town towards the old mining claims you pass through most of the town's tougher history, and discover that in its time it has been a very poor, as well as very

Opals for sale, Lightning Ridge

eccentric place indeed. Here are some of the things you pass: an observatory made entirely out of concrete, including the telescopes; a large ironstone castle, complete with moat, built by an Italian recluse; a man in a caravan who is convinced that the aliens have landed; a dummy hanging from a tree to show what happens to ratters; a dusty track called 'Bankrupt Mines Avenue'. But most of all you pass holes, each marked with little silver pegs. They are often close to wild orange trees, which are useful indicators to miners looking for new claims because they tend to grow from the same ground cracks in which opals are found.

Opals were first found at the Ridge in around 1900, but the earliest attempt at selling them was a disaster. In 1902 a miner called Charlie Nettleton sent a parcel of 103 stones to a Sydney

Signpost, Coocoran Field, near Lightning Ridge

jeweller, who destroyed a quarter of them as 'research', then offered ten shillings for the rest. However, Nettleton was determined to make it work, and walked five hundred kilometres to the White Cliffs opal fields to find a more reasonable buyer. The epic journey paid off. He met Tullie Wollaston's agent, who sent the samples straight to his boss in Adelaide. Tullie loved them, and telegraphed his agent to buy as many as he could afford. It turned out he could easily afford them all. The average field price of the first Lightning Ridge opals was just two pounds an ounce. Today good stones can fetch the equivalent of about half a million pounds an ounce.

The new opals were different from anything that had been seen before. Until they were found, most European and Australian opals looked like fire on snow; Lightning Ridge opals were like bright patterns painted across the night. If milky opal was seen as pure and virginal, then what would people make of its unruly, brash, chromatic opposite? The patterns coming out of Lightning Ridge were astonishing in what Tullie later described as 'their heavenly lawlessness'.[34] They were not patterns at all, he continued, 'but the gleeful spear-thrusts, the broken shining pathways of seraphic Order struggling out of chaos'.

When any new stone comes on to the market there is often a lull as buyers decide whether or not they like it – this happened recently with a bright green grossular garnet, known as tsavorite because it is found in the Tsavo National Park in Kenya. It is more durable than emerald, a brighter colour, and it is never oil- or heat-treated; it does not come from a guerrilla region and it tends to have fewer inclusions or foreign matter. It even has a nice story attached to it: it was discovered by a British adventurer, Campbell Bridges, who lived in a tree-house for five years to protect himself from lions and elephants as he developed the mining operation in the park. Yet despite all its advantages the international market is slow to come to terms with it, and tsavorite sells for a sixth of the price[35] of Colombian emeralds. Similarly, a hundred years ago it took Tullie Wollaston some time to persuade buyers to appreciate the charms of black opals – although when they did, the gem market went mad for them and there was an opal rush in New South Wales. Hundreds of men and a few women arrived from all over the country, some in stagecoaches but most on foot, pushing wheelbarrows full of their picks and their dreams.

Charlie Nettleton stayed on and became a local character but although he made some money he spent it all, and died in poverty at a Salvation Army home in Sydney, an old man with broad shoulders and big hands, slowly going blind. He was sometimes visited by two children, a brother and sister, and he used to tell them about the old days, including a Just So story about how opals came to be. He said it was an Aboriginal

Dreamtime story, dating from when the actions of the Ancestors gave rise to the landscapes, animals, customs and even minerals we know today. An Ancestral Romeo and Juliet had fallen in love without their parents knowing. The boy was told he had to marry someone else, and as he kissed his girlfriend goodbye for what he thought was the last time, they were spotted by the boy's intended bride. What they had done was taboo, and when the elders found out they had to run for their lives. They ran so fast that they turned into grass balls, which caught fire and tumbled across the land until they came to a waterhole. It was there that the elements of fire and water merged, and the lovers were entwined for ever, their passion preserved as the precious opals of Lightning Ridge.

Dawn Swane, the little girl who had visited Charlie, grew up to become a choreographer, and in 1961 she created *The Black Opal* for the Australian National Ballet, ending with a fiery *pas-de-deux* based on Charlie's stories. Her brother Peter became a miner at Lightning Ridge, but did not live to be an old man telling yarns. One day in the 1980s he was killed outright in his claim, when the roof collapsed.

Noodling and Jackhammers

Perhaps because of all the accidents – but maybe also because even Outback Australia is embracing compensation culture – it is now hard for casual visitors to get down a good mine at the Ridge. Owners are nervous: if you hurt yourself you can sue, and people apparently do. However, I had been given an introduction to Peter and Lisa Carroll who had lived at Lightning Ridge since 1991. They were mostly opal dealers but, like everyone else, they had a claim or two going. 'Sure you can go down my mine,' Peter said, when I contacted him. 'Just make sure you don't fall.'

He arranged for the two other members of his syndicate,

Peter Allan and Mick James, to show me the mine in the Coocoran opal field about twenty kilometres outside town. They had taken it over a few years ago, and it had last been worked some time before that. 'When we first broke through into the workings it was like a cap of vinegar in your nose,' Peter Allan remembered. 'Mines go stale after they've been empty a while.' So far they had not found much, a few bags of precious opals – and an intruder. 'It was a Serbian guy who thought I'd gone for the night,' said Peter. 'I marched him off and called the police. I was the first person in Lightning Ridge ever to make a citizen's arrest.' After the ratter claimed not to understand English he was let off. Usually they aren't harshly treated today, Peter said. 'Miners did the punishments themselves, in the old days.' This story ended happily, though. Some months later Peter's car battery went flat on one of the roads around the Coocoran. Eventually a man stopped to give him a jump start. It was the Serbian. 'Things happen in the Ridge you don't expect,' Peter said. 'I don't blame him too much now – he just needed a few dollars to keep him going.'

At a bar the night before I had been given a different angle on ratting by two old-timers. They pointed out the 'biggest ratter in town' sitting at a table not far from us, his Mercedes parked outside. 'If they steal from you they're bastards,' they said. And if they steal from someone else? 'They're legends.'

When we got to the bottom of the Coocoran mine, about ten metres below the surface, I could see that it wasn't a ballroom but it was big enough for a tidy tango if you made sure you didn't trip over the electric cables. The rough pink walls were covered with uneven stripes, like the fingernail marks of a giant prisoner trapped in a dungeon: it was the signature of a jackhammer as it tested for opals. Mick picked up a jackhammer, and began to pound it through the sandstone. The noise echoed round the cavern and multiplied into a cacophony. He handed it to me. It was unexpectedly heavy, like holding a motorbike on your shoulders. I couldn't admit I wasn't strong enough to handle it so I braced myself and held it against the wall. It slithered away petulantly and I almost dropped it. 'You've got to hold it straight,' Peter said. 'And you've got to *intend* to dig, you can't fool it.' So, I intended to dig, and for a few minutes the rock came out in lumps and fell at my feet.

Even with all the noise of the hammer and the weight, people say that once you get used to it opal mining is an extraordinarily meditative activity. You are usually on your own, concentrating

Peter Allan and Mick James in the Coocoran mine

solely on texture and sight. Is this area of wall harder or softer? Is that a glint to the side? A seam in front? After a while, thoughts turn to shorthand. Hard? Soft? Pink? Grey? Colour? Potch? Soon you have no idea of the time. 'You could have been there a few minutes, but more likely it's been hours and when you come up it's already dark,' Peter said. One miner had been down in his claim all day, as time changed pace and thoughts turned to dust, when all of a sudden the wall he was excavating crumbled and there, in front of him, with dust on his face and a wild expression in his eyes, was a man. They both screamed. The other man had been digging the neighbouring claim, and had broken through the dividing walls.

There were new opal words to learn that day. 'Blowers' are the enormous vacuum hoses that suck up the earth and rock and hoover them up the shaft into the back of the truck. 'Puddlers' are giant rotating tumblers as big as houses, coloured pink with the dust of Australia. The Coocoran puddlers are parked in a line along the shore of the dried-up lake: they roll the rubble around for a day or two, mix it with bore water, then push it along a rough conveyor belt where it is checked for anything that shines. We found some beautiful opal pieces at Peter's puddler – blue and turquoise, like an iridescent sky – although they were neither beautiful enough, nor big enough for the claim to start paying its way.

But my favourite opal word was still 'noodling' – which was what we did when the sorting was finished. At the Coocoran there was a great tip the size of several fields where all the rejected tailings were piled in heaps, and although at first the place seemed deserted it was soon evident that a dozen or so people were scattered in every direction, crunching over stones and putting some, occasionally, into buckets.

'Noodling' is a word of uncertain origin. But in the jazz world it refers to a casual improvisation, playing apparently without purpose, waiting for a good sequence to come by accident, and that is what we did at the tailings, riffling idly through the rubble, waiting for something colourful to turn up. Mick had told me about a tourist who had been walking along a road at the Coocoran two weeks before when she spotted a glitter. It was a red opal, one of the rarer types. 'Turned out to be worth thirty thousand dollars,' he said. After that I kept my eyes greedily on the ground, but all I found were some scraps of low-grade potch with the occasional firework in them. They were pretty, and appealed to my enjoyment of sparkly things, although they weren't worth anything. 'What are they?' I asked Peter.

'Silica gel,' he said, but admitted this still left a lot of unanswered questions about what opals really were.

What Are Opals?

To find out one possible answer I had arranged to visit a former miner called Len Cram, who lives in a neat bungalow on a tidy road behind Morilla Street in Lightning Ridge town. We sat nursing mugs of coffee in his small book-lined study and he told me that he had visited the European source of the stone in the hills of Czernowitza: where Senator Nonius' opal had come from two thousand years ago.

Before he went, people had warned him to be careful of the gypsies who lived there, and on his first night the advice seemed justified. As he and his interpreter lay in their rooms in a rented bungalow they were kept awake by the 'plang' 'plang' 'plang' of bullets hitting tin cans in the woods close by. They were told it was the gypsies, practising. When they went up to the mine the next morning they noticed two young men watching them from behind a tree. 'They were like blackfellas in Australia, totally silent coming out of the bush,' Len said. His interpreter was nervous but Len was determined to get into the mine and asked the two boys to help. They fetched some older relatives who agreed to take him, although the interpreter declined to go because he was frightened. The entrance had been sealed by the Communists and was hidden by trees and bushes but the gypsies had dug a hole to get in.

When they squeezed inside it was like going into a refrigerator. They passed through a Roman archway and followed the horizontal tunnel for eighty metres or more until they reached a shaft. The mines were renowned for their depth. Some people said they went down three hundred metres and that to prevent the opal cracking it was brought up ten metres a year and left until it stabilised – like deep-sea divers avoiding the bends. As Len stood at the top of the well he felt nervous. In torchlight, the faces around him no longer seemed friendly. He realised how alone he was, deep in a mine, carrying valuable cameras, and with a huge drop in front of him. So, using sign language, he tried to communicate that he was an opal-miner, like them. 'And they understood, and from then on we were blood brothers.' That night there was gunfire from the camp, and when Len went back the next morning to take some last photographs, one of the elders he had met the day before came silently out of the woods to greet him. 'He said to me, "God bless you," in English. He must have practised it all night.'

Opal is like that: it defies first impressions, Len said. And for him this was also true of its formation. He has a theory that almost everything we believe about opal is wrong. For years he had accepted the conventional explanation of liquid silica filtering down through the rocks over aeons, but then, after a business deal went catastrophically wrong and he had to rethink his life, he began to wonder more seriously about the origins of opal. And he realised that some elements of what he had been told didn't fit the picture.

The first was the fossils. Opals are often found in the shape of fossilised wood, shells or even dinosaur bones. One of Australia's prized national possessions is a pliosaur, or marine reptile, popularly known as Eric. It was found in the Cretaceous layer at Coober Pedy in 1987, and in the hundred million years since it had died its bones had turned into opals. Today the skeleton sparkles from its display case at the National Museum[36] in Sydney. Of course, many people had noticed these curiosities before: 'Could anyone imagine a diamond or an emerald consenting to become a shark's tooth or a periwinkle?' Tullie Wollaston had asked rhetorically, as an example of how remarkable opals were. However, he did not ask why the change had occurred. Len Cram did, although for him the tipping point was not the ancient fossils. It was a strange story of a cat in a hat.

The Cat in a Hat

In the 1890s, an old miner put the dead body of his pet cat in a felt hat and buried it in his mine. The mine was left empty for sixty years or more, but when someone else took out the claim, they found the cat still in there. It should have been just a skeleton, but it was not. Instead the calcium of the bones had metamorphosed into pale pink, scintillating rose opals. 'At the time it was seen as just a bizarre story, but it made me ask questions.' Len listened out for more stories. He heard of fence posts that had started opalising at the base, and he talked to a woman who had picked up some ironstone gravel from dried-up puddles between mullock dumps at the Three Mile mine, which had already started to grow colour. All of those things seemed to contradict the old explanation of opal formation, 'and I started thinking, Well, we must have all been wrong'.

The old theory is quite simple: it suggests that what is needed for opal to form is a particular combination of water, silica and space. Millions of years ago rain seeped into the ground and dissolved the silica to form a gel, which then drained slowly through the bedrock like toothpaste until it found a suitable place to settle. Most of those places were cracks in the ground although other spaces were formed when organic materials, like roots, nuts or bones, disintegrated.

However, this theory did not explain why some cavities are filled with opal while others nearby are not. It also didn't explain how the silica gel could reproduce the internal structure as well as the external shape of the object whose place it had taken. 'Nor did it tell me how this gel had filtered through hard igneous rocks or how you could have a seam of opal in shale which is so soft it just doesn't leave gaps.' And, of course, none of the theories even began to explain the cat in the hat. Eventually Len hit on a new theory, based on opal forming through ion exchange, rather in the same way as a battery works.

The following can be skipped if you know about batteries, but I had forgotten so Len started his explanation by telling me about ions and electrolytes. Ions are atoms that have lost or gained electrons so they have an electric charge, which needs to be neutralised. Electrolytes are substances that allow the ions to pass through them in their search to pick up an equal and opposite charge on the other side. This sounded complicated until I realised it was like a dating agency: the ions are the lost souls looking for mates; the electrolyte is the agency that can help them find each other. Many chemicals can be electrolytes – athletes' drinks contain potassium, car batteries contain sulphuric acid – but the property they have in common is that ions meet them with a sense of relief. At last their days of unfulfilment are over and they can find an opposite partner. In both the metaphor and the chemistry, the process is always electrically charged, and sometimes it leads to the formation of new and different entities.

This, Len believes, is how opal is formed. The big clue was that Australian opal contains around two per cent aluminium oxide. It isn't included in the chemical formula for opal because it tends to be seen as an impurity rather than as a necessity. 'But it's always there and I began to think that perhaps it's not a coincidence.' According to Len, the process might have started with alumina and other ions in opal dirt meeting up with an electrolyte in the groundwater. The ions are encouraged to pass through it looking for their opposite partners. On the way they meet oxygen and feldspar,[37] which contains silicon and aluminium, as well as calcium and other minerals, and as they do so they form new solids, some of which become opal.

Len thought it couldn't be that simple. But the theory made sense of his questions – even the one about the cat, whose soft felt hat would have held water and electrolyte nicely. 'So in 1983 I did the first experiment I'd ever done in my life. And it worked.' He theorised about what electrolytes were in the local soil ('I can't tell you what they are'), filled a glass bottle with groundwater and some opal dirt, then shook it. 'Then I poured in some electrolyte and crossed my fingers,' he said. 'I watched it like a cat watches a bird in a cage. Three days later little pinheads of colour formed.' It was a promising start, so he repeated the experiment with a larger bottle, which he put on the top shelf in his shed. After a few days, when nothing had happened, he forgot about it. Several months later he looked at it again and nearly dropped what he was carrying. The bottle was shimmering. 'I got a hammer, smashed the glass on the concrete floor and couldn't believe it. It was 99.9 per cent opal and I walked out on air and danced with delight.' His wife was in the kitchen, and asked him if he was sick because he was behaving so strangely. He told her what he had done and showed her the opal. 'And she said, "Ain't that different from the other one," and that's the last thing she ever said about my opal.'

Len showed me the shed. The first bottle had been replaced with five hundred. There were peanut-butter jars, soda bottles, Vegemite pots . . . a recycler's dream, all looking like pots of children's glitter with greens and reds and pinks and blues in vivid anti-harmonies. They are not gem quality ('There are still a few ions wandering around that I don't know what to do with') but Len is confident that this is a mere technicality and can be sorted out.

I remembered John Keats's protestations that Isaac Newton, in his experiments with light, had 'destroyed all the poetry of the rainbow by reducing it to prismatic colours'. Was the poetry of these rainbow stones destroyed by reducing them to chemical reactions? Not really. In a way it provided more poetry – if only because it replaced the old concept of gel oozing through bedrock with a new image of atoms shooting along an electrified pathway to find their perfect partners and make sparkling gems. Since Len came up with his theory, science seems to support it. Researchers at Australian National University recently concluded from radiocarbon dating that most black opals, even the opalised dinosaur bones, are not millions of years old, after all, but were formed between seventeen hundred and eight thousand years ago.[38]

Len Cram, with some of his opals, in his garden shed

'Are you going to publish?' I asked. Len paused to gaze out of the window. Outside we could hear a bowerbird imitating a garden sprinkler, and children's shouts and mining trucks as the town went about its business. 'I've been told that there are a couple of PhDs in my shed, and I've been given an honorary one. But what would happen to the opal industry once some smart young cookies got to know about it? They'd sort out the problems and unlike some of the synthetic opals you get today you might never know the difference between what's been started by nature and what's not,' he said. 'I won't do it. I can't do it to the Ridge. It would become like Czernowitza: an empty place.'[39]

Mark Antony's Stone

The Greek playwright Aeschylus wrote, 'I know how men in exile feed on dreams.'[40] It was a description that fitted many of the Australian opal-miners and maybe Senator Nonius too. In the opal fields of Australia I had begun to understand Pliny's strange story. Perhaps Nonius' exile had been down to his stubbornness and his refusal to give in to bullies, but perhaps it really was for the love of a sparkly stone – and, with the Angel of Yowah, I could see how that might happen too. In Australia I had met and heard of many who had gone far from home, just for a chance of finding colour. And those who found it rarely left to enjoy their fortune elsewhere. Instead they mostly stayed, like addicts, looking for more.

But the question remained why a man like Mark Antony would make so much trouble over an opal, when there were innumerable other treasures in Rome. Some months after I left Australia I found a possible key to the mystery in Plutarch's biography of Mark Antony. In 42 BC he had summoned Cleopatra to a meeting in Tarsus, now in Turkey, so she could explain why Egypt had not supported him in the Roman civil war. Now that her lover and supporter Julius Caesar had died, Cleopatra needed Mark Antony's approval – and she set about getting it in the way she knew best: with a meticulously planned seduction. She sailed towards him up the Cydnus river in a golden barge with purple sails, then invited him to dinner. 'He found the preparations made to receive him magnificent beyond words,' Plutarch wrote,[41] 'but what astonished him most was the extraordinary number of lights . . . So many of these, it is said, were let down from the roof and displayed on all sides at once, and they were arranged and grouped in such ingenious patterns in relation to each other, some in squares and some in circles, that they created as brilliant a spectacle as can ever have been devised to delight the eye.' And this, I think, is a clue to why Antony wanted the senator's opal so badly. If he wanted something that would remind him of the atmosphere in which his mind and body were fatefully seduced, what could be better than a fiery opal, a stone that lets light dance in ingenious patterns around the one who wears it?

5

Peridot

'If it were to be used as a protection from the wiles of evil
spirits, the stone had to be pierced and strung on the hair of an
ass and then attached to the left arm.'
MARBODUS, *De Lapidus*

'If heaven would make me such another world,
Of one entire and perfect chrysolite!'
SHAKESPEARE, *Othello*

There is a small island in the Red Sea that has had many
names. It was once called the Island of Serpents, and earlier,
more chillingly, the Island of the Dead. The Coptic Christians
call it the Island of St John, the Greeks knew it best as the
Island of Topaz, while today it is called Zabargad Island[1] and
is located in Egypt. Two and a half thousand years ago it was
a legendary place, controlled, first, by the pharaohs and later
by the Ptolemies of Alexandria. It was said that no boats were
ever left there overnight, in case any of the inhabitants tried to
escape,[2] and that it was permanently manned by soldiers. At
that time the penalty for landing without permission was death.

The island was so barren that it was incapable of supporting
any agriculture, and in the second century BC the Greek writer
Agatharchides of Cnidus described how the inhabitants frequently ran out of food. 'Consequently whenever there are few
provisions left, the people all sit around the village awaiting the
arrival of the ship bringing their supplies. Whenever these are
delayed they are reduced to despair.' Even the snakes had left

the 'Island of Serpents', he reported, and the gulf was called Foul Bay because of the treacherous reefs that lay around it, making it dangerous for sailors. The mainland inhabitants were no help to the hungry island-dwellers either: 'Those sailing by do so at a distance, because they fear the king.'

It is still like that, in a way. The Red Sea is now a popular tourist destination for divers wanting to see the fish that swim round its coral reefs, but even today the live-aboard boats still keep away from the island. When I asked local dive companies whether they could take me there, they all said no with such nervousness it seemed the very whisper of it might be unlucky. 'We can go diving in the waters around it, but we'd lose our licence from the government if we actually landed,' one representative said, firmly off the record. Only occasionally in the past fifty years have foreign geologists and gemmologists been allowed to visit,[3] and they have reported that it is still a desolate place, with a few 'roofless brick walls' as the only sign of millennia of enforced occupation. Today the reason for keeping Zabargad secret is its strategic importance: it is in Egypt's military zone, which separates the country from neighbouring Sudan. But in the past the island was guarded for quite a different reason: for many centuries it was the only place in the known world where one particular gemstone could be found.

Roman scholars once hazarded that the Greek name 'Topaz Island'[4] might have come from a confusion with the homonym *topasin*, which means 'to guess or conjecture', and that it might refer to the way fishermen sometimes lost the island in a fog.[5] For Zabargad was never the home of the yellow stones that we call 'topaz',[6] but of a brilliant green volcanic crystal, which – being seen to its best advantage at dusk rather than in daytime – was known for centuries as 'the evening emerald'. Now we mostly call it peridot, although many people don't know how to pronounce its name, let alone how to appreciate it.

This is not surprising. Once upon a time peridots were set in some of the world's most sacred objects and were marvelled at alongside the relics. They were mentioned in the two most famous lists of gemstones in the Bible, and the Ancient Egyptian teenage pharaoh, Tutankhamen, had a beautiful specimen in one of his pendants. But today peridots are nearly forgotten. So, although most of the other chapters in this book are about what happens when people give a high value to one type or another of pretty pebble or organic substance, the story of peridot is a little different: it is about what happens to people and land-scapes when the sense of value fades.

Peridot comes from the most abundant material in the earth's mantle, known as olivine because it is the colour of pale green olives. It is the only gemstone, apart from diamonds, to form below the crust and it usually reaches the open air by what the Smithsonian Museum describes as a 'special delivery elevator', which happens when a surge of magma picks it up[7] as it rushes to the surface ready to emerge as a volcano.

Sometimes peridot falls to earth from outer space.[8] Perhaps the most beautiful of all meteorites is the type called 'pallasite', after the German scientist Peter Simon Pallas, who first described it in 1772. Pallasite is made up of peridot crystals held together in what was once a dough of nickel and iron; in cross-section it looks like a piece of contemporary jewellery, with glinting green crystals set in a filigree of silver metal. In 2003 our knowledge of peridot as a gem from outer space went one better: it became the first gemstone to be discovered on another planet. That year scientists monitoring a NASA space-craft found a large area of Mars covered with peridot crystals, and concluded that at least nineteen thousand square miles of the 'red' planet are in fact rich in green.[9]

This almost uncelebrated gemstone also has a rather extra-ordinary history on earth. For many centuries the only place to find it was the remote, fear-inspiring island of Zabargad, and even today there is a certain sense of exclusivity about it.

Although some good olive-coloured crystals are found in a few other places, like Burma, China, Zambia and Pakistan, ninety per cent of all known peridots are found in just one place. It is a Native American reservation, and it is located in a little-visited corner of the United States.

San Carlos

'You are in Bear Country,' one of the brochures at the San Carlos Permit Office stated. 'Be a courteous Guest,' it continued, and told readers that the best way to do this was to talk, sing, clap and whistle to let their ursine hosts know they were around. 'Whistle, but don't sound like a bird!' the brochure warned. I decided it would be better not to whistle at all, and carefully noted the advice on what to do if a bear made contact: curl up and play dead.

The Permit Office, where all visitors to the San Carlos Nation have to buy a daily recreational licence, was full of photos of happy holidaymakers with guns. Several were standing with one foot resting proudly on the head of a bear or an elk that was playing dead very convincingly. I was not only in Bear Country but in Bear Shooting Country. I was also in what used to be called Indian Country, although today that means something different from what it meant hundreds of years ago when Europeans first arrived in Arizona. At that time it was about ancient culture, brilliant trackers, mutual distrust and the bloody battle for homelands. Today it is, too often, shorthand for poverty.

If you look at a map of Arizona, the San Carlos Apache reservation takes up a small section of the south-east quadrant in what looks like an empty space between Phoenix and New Mexico. It is poor land, with neither grand canyons nor great industrial resources to bring it revenue. The closest it comes to a good gorge is the spectacular Salt River Canyon to the north, but the Navajo tribe own that. And the closest it has to an impressive industrial construction is the huge Coolidge hydro-electric dam to the south, but although it is on Apache land, the US government controls that. The San Carlos reservation does have the largest lake in Arizona, inhabited by species with names like 'crappie', 'sunshine-fish' and the 'Apache cutthroat' swimming tantalisingly in its waters. It also has nearly two million acres of countryside, populated by thousands of Rocky Mountain elks, pronghorn antelopes and those ever-hospitable black bears. And it has the greatest deposit of gem-quality peridot in the world, although as a casual visitor you almost certainly wouldn't learn much about it.

The San Carlos Apache Cultural Center was set up in 1995 to retell the history of the tribe to visitors and young Apaches. Some of the stories are traditional: the Apache are especially proud of what they call the 'changing woman' ceremony marking the moment when a girl becomes a woman. But most of the history in the display cabinets and information panels is about how the reservation came into being, which is not a noble story, although it is relevant to the way the tribe views and uses its resources, including peridot.

At the beginning of the exhibition there is a black-and-white photograph from 1880 showing a line of Apaches in tattered Western clothes queuing for food rations. It contrasts poignantly with the accounts of how, less than a decade before, many had been living traditional lives, able to find food for themselves on their own land. But on 30 April 1871 everything changed. That day a war party of eight white Americans, ninety-two rival Papago Indians and forty-eight Mexicans walked into a public area near the Camp Grant army base,[10] pulled out their guns and fired. Unarmed Apache families lived outside the camp – people who, only three months before, had trustingly surrendered to the authorities in return for a 'safe' place to stay. On that Sunday morning, 128 people, mostly women, were murdered between seven and eight o'clock. Just one adult survived – a woman, who was permanently paralysed by bullets – and the only others were twenty-eight babies in their papooses, who were taken to Tucson to be sold as slaves to other Indian tribes. The vigilantes, led by William Oury, a fifty-four-year-old Virginian, justified their actions by saying they had taken revenge for the murder of several pioneers, who had found gold and other valuable minerals in the hills of Arizona, and had therefore decided that the Apache land should be theirs. 'Through the greater part of the year 1870, and the first part of 1871, these Indians had held a carnival of murder and plunder in all our settlements until our people had been appalled and almost paralyzed,' Oury said, in a presentation he made to the Arizona Pioneers' Society in 1885.[11] He didn't need to defend his actions: the European community of Arizona was almost entirely on his side.

No one was ever punished for the massacre: after a short court hearing, the white judge directed the white jury to acquit the whole gang. Yet the news of what was quickly dubbed 'the Camp Grant Massacre' divided the nation: the north was highly critical, while southerners tended to favour Oury and his men. The camp commander expressed public disgust, but he might have been biased: he had been making a lot of money out of the shops he had set up in the settlement. As for the Apaches of San Carlos, this event became their nemesis: from that time on they had little chance to decide their own destiny or generate their own wealth.

The public called for more reservations to be set up, ostensibly to protect the Native Americans but also to stop them trying to reclaim their land. The following year Camp San Carlos was founded as a detention centre for thousands of Yavapai, Chirica-hua and Western Apaches, overseen by a white administrator, or 'Indian agent'. The intention was to convert, suppress and assimilate them, using the standard weapons of missions, munitions and politicians. But, as happened all over America, the result was a mess. 'Do Indian agents steal?' was a popular catchphrase at the time, which equates roughly to today's 'Is the pope a Catholic?' The administrators were so renowned for their corruption that no one could be bothered to do anything about it. At San Carlos the situation was worse than most. The tribes thrown together so casually were all Apaches, but many were also traditional enemies. There was constant infighting between the groups, and those undignified food queues also became the norm. A new ethos of dependency grew up, and ancient ways of life disappeared. By the beginning of the twentieth century most people had given up their *wickiup* tents and were living in Western-style houses – from whose cheap windows they could see their land, influence and precious natural resources seeping away, like water on dust.

I heard one joke several times in Arizona. It tells how, in the mid-1960s, an Apache elder and his son were driving in the desert. To their surprise they came across a space crew practising for the moon landings. The old man became excited, and asked if he could give the astronauts a message to deliver to the moon. The NASA officials saw this as an excellent PR opportunity and called for a tape-recorder. The elder spoke into the microphone, but when the official asked the son to translate, he grinned. Later the NASA people took the tape to an Apache village, where the people laughed and also refused to translate. It was only after they hired a government interpreter that NASA learned what the message meant: 'Watch out for these bastards,' the old man had said. 'They've come to steal your land.'

The old man had a point. But while all those thousands of hectares of land were being appropriated, one of the few natural resources that the Apaches were permitted to keep was peridot. Which is ironic, because the histories of the Apaches and peridot have something important in common: both revolve round a theme of tribal ownership.

The Mystery of the Seventh Seal . . . or Perhaps the Second or the Tenth

For many years peridot was considered among the most precious stones in the Judaeo-Christian world. When Moses came down from Mount Sinai it was said that he had not only the Ten Commandments in his hands but also a list of twelve stones, which were to be placed on the 'breastplate of judgement', worn by the high priest Aaron. They would correspond 'to the names of the sons of Israel, twelve like their names, engraved like seals, each with the name of one of the twelve tribes'. With their vast range of colours and textures the gems could be said to represent the diversity of the human landscape – each one different, yet each one precious to God. Over the centuries the original meanings of the Hebrew words have been lost and there have been many debates about which old word refers to which modern stone. Peridot, for example, has variously been ascribed to *pitdah*, the second stone in Moses' list, and to *tharshish*, the tenth.

Much later, in the first century, St John used a similar list to give credence to his vision of the heavenly city of Jerusalem, described in the Book of Revelation.[12] 'And the foundations of the wall of the city were garnished with all manner of precious stones,' he wrote. 'The first foundation was jasper; the second, sapphire; the third, a chalcedony; the fourth, an emerald; the fifth, sardonyx; the sixth, sardius; the seventh, chrysolite [peridot];[13] the eighth, beryl; the ninth, a topaz; the tenth, chrysoprase; the eleventh, a jacinth [sapphire]; the twelfth, an amethyst. And the twelve gates were twelve pearls.' For years this list, and the earlier Mosaic list, was thought to show the most precious gemstones in the Mediterranean world. However, in reality it revealed something different: it was a list of the stones that made the best and most prestigious seals.

It is hard to overestimate the role of seals in early Mediterranean and Middle Eastern culture. Every official transaction

Ancient Egyptian seal

was supported by a seal: it marked an exchange of land, property, cargo, grain, alcohol, letters or decrees. If you owned a jar of wheat or wine you closed it with your seal to show that it was yours; when Pharaoh promoted Joseph to become the highest official in Egypt he put a seal ring on his hand as a mark of his new power.[14] In Persia, even until very recently,[15] letters were seldom written or signed by the person who sent them and their authenticity depended on the impression of a signet ring. Three thousand years ago seals were so important to the Jews that each of the twelve tribes of Egypt had an individual one, each of them prescribed by God.

All of this made the occupation of seal-cutter one of trust and danger. Seal-cutters had to keep a register of every ring they made, and the loss of a signet ring was considered a calamity. As the poet James Fenton wrote,[16] it was as if 'the Barclaycard has been torn up and the PIN number cancelled'. Or perhaps it was worse: in antiquity, to lose your ring was to lose your identity. No wonder that the best signet stones, like peridot, jasper, sardonyx and sard, were highly valued: they were soft

The high priest's breastplate; the original meaning
of the Hebrew words has been lost

enough to be carved, hard enough to keep their lines, unique enough to be easily identified and pretty enough to be a fashion statement. And no wonder that when seals went out of fashion we forgot the stones from which they had been made. Who now knows that the difference between sard and sardonyx is that the latter is striped?[17] Or even that they both take their English name from the island of Sardinia where they were once found? And who now, outside the industry, knows the origin and history of chrysolites or, as we call them, peridots?

'It's Always Been There'

With all the information in the Center about the Apache people's loss of their land, it was surprising to find nothing about their gain of peridots. Given that the San Carlos tribe owned nearly ninety per cent of the world's supply I would have expected at least an information panel and a sample or two. But there was no mention of it. The man at the counter, whose name was

Franklin, looked at me with some surprise when I asked about the omission – he hadn't thought about it before. Then he came up with a reason: 'It's probably because this Cultural Center is about stories. That green stone, it's just there. It's always been there.'

He offered to show me where it had always been, and we went outside. In front of us was Highway 70, a slim line streaking delicately across the desert like a backdrop for a Roadrunner cartoon. We walked along it for a short way, then looked north. Franklin swept his hand across the landscape. 'That's peridot country,' he said, pronouncing the *t* as all the Apaches did, and as I came to do after the English pronunciation of 'peridoh' started to sound pretentious. It was the most Wild West scenery I had ever seen, with rude-looking saguaro cactuses everywhere, limbs springing out of them. The whole place looked like a set for a John Wayne movie. In front of us the landscape rose up into a long hill with a gentle slope on one side and an abrupt end on the other, as if someone had stopped a movie camera's panning movement very suddenly and it had been cut off in mid-flow. 'Which bit is the peridot mine?' I asked.

'All of it,' Franklin said. 'All of that hill.' Some people, he went on, call it the *mesa* because it looks like a table and if you go collecting up there you can eat off what it provides. 'But we call it the *zitldega*, which means "burned mountain". You can't see it very well from down here but it's really the remains of a volcano. That's where they do all the mining.'

On the Mesa

Franklin promised to take me there if I waited until he finished at the Center, so I sat down outside in the sunshine for half an hour and watched the visitors go in and out. One family was from New York. The boys were wearing chinos and blue shirts – little versions of their father. The mother wore Prada shoes.

'Your great-great-grandmother was Apache,' they told their children, as they went in. After rushing through the Center they declined to leave a donation. It seemed that four generations and ten minutes of their holiday was as close as they needed to get to their native American heritage.

At five o'clock Franklin was ready. We got into my car and he directed me along the main road. Then, at a point where I could never have spotted a turning, he told me to drive north into the desert along a sandy white track. We climbed and climbed, and turned and turned, with me trying to remember the way. But the only landmarks were the saguaro cactuses, whose hairy arms pointed authoritatively in different directions, like one of those jokes about arriving in the land where half the people lie and half the people tell the truth, so how do you find your way?

Then, before it seemed that we had arrived anywhere, Franklin told me to stop the car – I could park in the middle of the road as no one would be passing this way. We got out and headed over a small ridge into an area that looked like another planet. Millions of years ago the volcano had vomited a spume of magma froth, which had turned into a massive formation of battleship-grey basalt, with little bubbles running through it, making it look like an old sponge. But although grey basalt is found in volcanic landscapes all over the world, the basalt of the San Carlos *mesa* was different from almost anywhere else, mainly because the landscape is covered with large, irregular lime-green circles where little crystals of peridot had formed in blotches. It was as if the landscape had been devised by the illustrator of a children's book: Green Spot Land – a place where cartoon giants played.

Franklin said the Apache called this peridot-filled rock 'the green stone that floats on water', because it was full of air bubbles and looked like pumice. However, it doesn't float and, despite the holes, is quite heavy. A few days later the samples I collected were heavy enough to make the man from the airline grimace theatrically when he picked up my suitcase. 'What have you got in here? Rocks?' he asked.

I grinned. 'They promised me they were light ones.'

From the *mesa* we could see Apache country – a Martian landscape that stretched to the horizon. At least there were no bears: there was nowhere for them to hide. Once upon a time Apache land would have stretched further than the horizon, through New Mexico almost to Texas, but as white men found gold, silver, turquoise and copper beneath its surface they carved up the territory like children sneaking to the fridge and slicing off a chocolate cake bit by bit: hoping at first that the loss wouldn't be noticed but ultimately not really caring. Gem-cutters are accustomed to cleaving and polishing, but they always try to end up with the best bit in the centre. The opposite happened with the San Carlos Apaches, for whom the old ownership magic of peridots did not work: they were left with the bits no one else wanted.

Franklin pointed out the little township called Peridot far below us: it was made up of twenty or so houses with dusty yards, all grouped round a crossroads. Arizona is full of places named after what was found there. There is the town of Quartzite in the west of the state, and one in the south called Ruby, where pink agate was once wrongly identified. Even Globe, the town nearest the San Carlos reservation, was given its name to celebrate an almost perfectly round boulder of Indian silver that was found there in the 1870s, inevitably leading to the loss of more Apache land. Globe, Ruby, Quartzite and Peridot were lucky: one town in western Arizona, with a population of 250 souls, is called Chloride.

Franklin moved towards what seemed to be a series of half-caves dug into a shallow crumbly cliff. This was his area. 'Each person has the bit they think they own, but it really all belongs to the tribe,' he said. Only tribal people are allowed there, 'which is why the white guys have to deal with us. They can't come here on their own.' There were two different ground-soils on Peridot Mountain, he said: one was soft and friable, and in it you could find stones with hardly any fractures; the other was so hard you had to use a chisel. A few years ago this area had been untouched desert, but someone had lent Franklin and his friends a bulldozer to clean off the topsoil, and then they had used dynamite. 'It can destroy some of it, but the good thing is that after a blast you can just pick stones off the ground. Easy.' Later I learned from a dealer in Globe that there was a difference between the majority, what she called the 'blast-it' brigade, and the minority of peridot miners who take hours to chisel the individual crystals out of the un-dynamited rock. It is a tension between quality and quantity. The latter, who are mainly women, acquire better crystals, but the former get more.

Franklin picked a little peridot crystal off the ground, and we looked at it in the light of the dying sun. It was the right time

The peridot mesa, San Carlos

'A *town called Peridot*'

of day to see the 'evening emerald' and I could easily appreciate how, with such a yellowish green hue, it held its colour in twilight more tenderly than the bluer true emeralds do. It really did seem to glow a little, and I could understand why early lapidaries pronounced it a good talisman against the terrors of the night. It seemed, however, that Agatharchides[18] had over-stated the case when he said – clearly without having witnessed it – that peridot is 'invisible during the day since it is over-whelmed by the brightness of the sun; but when night falls, it shines in the dark and is visible from afar wherever it may be'. He even claimed that it was so luminous that the security guards on Zabargad did the rounds of the island by night: every time they saw a stone that had become visible in the dark[19] they covered it with a bowl to act as a marker. 'In the daytime they then go around and cut away the marked rock and turn it over to the craftsmen who are able to polish it properly.'

The strong green of peridot comes from its high iron content. While gems like emeralds, rubies, sapphires and diamonds have gained their colour from tiny quantities of chemicals that are there incidentally, iron is an integral part of the peridot's chemical formula[20] and makes up at least ten per cent of its mass. This means that while beryls, corundums and diamonds can be all sorts of colours, peridots are only ever green.

Some sources suggest that the word 'peridot' comes from the Greek *peridona*, indicating 'plentiful', although since the gem was rare in classical times, this seems unlikely. The *Oxford English Dictionary* is unable to give an origin for the word, although it speculates that it may come from Middle English. What we do know is that when 'perry' is found in Anglo-Saxon place-names it indicates 'brightness',[21] and the Anglo-Saxon word 'dot' means a little swelling or button, as well as the point at the end of this sentence.

If 'peridot' once meant 'bright spot' or 'bright button', it would have been an apt description for the cheerful gem we were scrutinising – which might also have been called 'lime-stone' if that name had not already been taken. For the green of peridot is a perky lemon-lime colour, which many consider very pretty. In terms of green, peridot is the yellowy colour of a summer meadow full of buttercups, while emerald is a stronger colour, more like a spring lawn just after rain. Perhaps if it had been a little harder, a little stronger and a little better known, this August birthstone might have been valued more highly than it is now. Although if it had been harder, stronger and more valuable, its biggest deposit would certainly not still be owned by Native Americans.

There was no time for me to see the mining process before it got dark, but I could come back tomorrow, Franklin said. He was sure someone would show me how they extracted peridot crystals from their basalt bed. 'Just follow the same way back,' he said, with the ease of a man descended from some of the world's best trackers.

As we drove back to the road I paid particular attention to the rhythm of the twists in the track and the saguaro cactuses in the turns, but I was not confident that I could manage it on my own. This was the route to the world's greatest supply of a once precious stone, and it was not even marked.

Peridot Thrones

The contrast between this stone's past and its present was most poignant on those almost undiscernible tracks in the American desert. How could it be that peridot now was so little loved, yet when peridots were given to the Ptolemaic Queen Berenice of Egypt, in around 300 BC,[22] they had caused a sensation? A scholar called Juba reported in the second century BC that when the king's prefect presented them to the queen 'she was wonderfully pleased with them; and that, at a later period, a peridot statue of four cubits in height was made in honour of the wife of Ptolemy Philadelphus and consecrated in the 'Golden Temple'. As late as the sixteenth century peridots from Zabargad were so precious that an Ottoman sultan's favourite throne was covered with them. The Gold Festival Throne, or Bayram Tahti, can be seen in the high-security treasure house in the Topkapi Palace Museum in Istanbul, Turkey: it is made of walnut wood, plated with gold and studded with 957 peridots. It is a rare example of a porta-throne: high and grand enough to be imposing when carried into the outer courtyard during feast days, but easily dismantled if it started to rain. It was given in 1585 to Murad III by his new son-in-law, Ibrāhīm Paşa, as a celebration of the relatively new Ottoman colony of Egypt,[23] which suggests that, when it was made, peridots were perceived by the Ottomans as truly fabulous stones.[24] The new Egyptian rulers valued them so highly that, like their forebears long ago, they set armed guards on Zabargad, with orders to sink all unidentified ships and kill intruders.

The Ottomans, and indeed most people involved in the gem business at the time, would have weighed the stones using the same measuring system as we have today. The 'carat' is an archaic measurement that probably originated in the bazaars of the Middle East and Asia, based on the weight of carob seeds – *keration* in Greek. Jewellers chose the seeds because they were fairly uniform, and therefore trustworthy for measuring tiny and expensive gems. But the scale was still approximate and even in the nineteenth century when some attempt was made at standardisation, a 'one-carat' peridot could still weigh anything from 199 milligrams in Lisbon to 207 milligrams in Venice, which was a problem for international traders. In 1877 several prominent merchants, from London, Paris and Amsterdam, met up to sort out the confusion. In the kind of pan-European spirit that today would endear them to the Brussels bureaucrats they agreed that in future 'one carat' should be the same wherever you were, although the efficiency of their decision was somewhat undermined by the agreement that this uniform weight would be exactly 205 milligrams. Thirty years later the next generation regretted the odd number and from 1907 in Europe and 1913 in the United States a carat was agreed to be the more manageable figure of one-fifth of a gram.[25]

Before the Muslims took over the island in the sixteenth century, Zabargad was the source of some of the peridots most sacred to the Christian world. In the twelfth century the city of Cologne obtained some of the most important Christian relics, said to be the bones of the Wise Men or Magi, who had brought gifts to the Christ child. To celebrate the relics, the city's merchants built a cathedral so beautiful that people said the architect had tricked the plans out of the devil himself. The reliquary, made in around 1190, is almost as exquisite as the cathedral. It is a multi-tiered gold box, surmounted by the risen Christ and covered with gems, the most important of which is a large peridot of 200 carats or more, placed in the centre and presumed to have been brought back from Zabargad by crusader knights. The green would probably have symbolised the new life that the Wise Men were celebrating, while the choice of peridot would have had spiritual and magical benefits.

Almost all gems were thought to have supernatural powers in the Middle Ages and right up to the late seventeenth century. For example, the Victoria and Albert Museum owns a Tudor brooch made of three gemstones: a garnet, a sapphire and a peridot. The stones represented different magical protections,[26] and the setting was open at the back so that their properties could be transmitted directly to the wearer's skin. He or she would have believed that while garnets were good for the blood and blue sapphires for clarity of the mind, peridots offered particular protection against evil spirits. They were also said to protect against adversity, although they do not seem to have helped the slaves imprisoned on Zabargad. Nor, indeed, has ownership of the peridot mines done much for the Apaches, in terms of protection from financial adversity at least. As I was to see that evening, their main income comes from a different source altogether.

A Gamble

The western border of the San Carlos reservation is marked by a series of structures that have become almost as strongly associated with Native American culture as wigwams. They are a casino and its attendant cheap motel. On Native American land the casino operates legally, although gambling is banned elsewhere in the state. After I had left Franklin and driven back to the border, I checked into the Apache Gold motel. 'Excuse me, ma'am, will you be using the casino this evening?' the receptionist asked. I had some notes to write up, and said I probably would not. He glanced around to make sure no one was listening, then whispered that if I said I would, I could have the room cheaper *and* a free beer and buffet dinner. 'It's our special gamblers' rate,' he said. 'Everyone who comes here does it.' In which case, I said, he could mark me down as a gambler – although when it came to it I wished I'd paid for my dinner: the buffet was terrible.

In a way, the San Carlos casino is the flip side of San Carlos gem-hunting. The former is full of people hoping to strike it rich without working; the latter is full of people hoping to strike it rich having sweated a little. But their motivation is the same. In both, one lucky movement makes all the difference – you pick the one machine or basalt plug that holds the treasure, and which will spill it out for your own gratification.

All the casino's machines had names, and when I saw the 'Real Gem' I knew it was the one for me. But a man had just sat in front of it, so I went to get my free drink and watch the people who – whether tribal, local white or tourist – all wore the same glazed expression. Many of the peridot miners apparently came in when they got a good haul, and spent it straight away. 'Tribe pays the tribe,' said the barman, with a shrug, as a group of what I took to be young Apaches were getting rowdy in a corner. 'At least if they spend it here it keeps the money in the family.'

When I got back to Real Gem the same man – a plump cowboy type with big boots and a hat – was still in 'my' place. So, bypassing the other machines, with names like 'Wild West' and 'Apache Bandit', I settled down at 'Diamonds Are Forever'. In fifteen minutes I had won twenty dollars – no wonder this place wasn't making money. Then I saw that my rival at Real Gem had won $232, paid out in 928 quarters. It was like mining. You use whatever resources you have to get yourself a good site, pour money in, wait for as long as you can afford to, and ultimately it is down to luck and a degree of persistence as to whether it pours out again. If your neighbour gets a bigger haul than you, well, it's natural to feel a little jealous.

A Peridot as Big as the Ritz

Pansy Cassavetes is one of the main gem-dealers inside the reservation. I could not get through to her on the phone so the next morning I called at her small house on the edge of Peridot. Outside, and next to a placard on the door that said, 'God Bless America', a handwritten sign informed visitors that she was out: anyone with gems to sell should return at five. I had an appointment to visit the Tribal Office at four, which gave me almost the whole day to spend in the hills, looking for stones.

As I was trying to work out which way to go, I saw a tall man in his early thirties loping towards me in tracksuit trousers and a black shirt. He looked like the archetypal Apache in a western, with long dark hair and deep-set eyes, although when we started talking he was quick to tell me he was only half Apache. 'My other side's Creek,' he said, 'but I don't speak either. I grew up in cities.' His name was Frank and he was Franklin's son: he'd heard from his father that I might want to go up to the peridot *mesa* today. As I started the car the radio came on loudly and he winced. 'Hangover,' he said. 'Went to the casino last night with some friends and I feel terrible.' I'd seen him there, I said.

We picked up a couple of his friends – a woman in her thirties called Shannon, then twenty-three-year-old Sean. All three were unemployed, and this was the norm: the unemployment rate in San Carlos is seventy-six per cent. 'Outside the reservation, you see news stories of people worrying about a recession,' Franklin had told me the day before. 'In the reservation we don't worry about it. Our recession has lasted for generations.' It was one of the most destructive possible things in a community, he said.

'Boredom, that's the worst thing.' Frank took a different route from the one his father had shown me, and as we climbed higher, he pointed to a slightly raised plug with three cactuses on top. 'There was a lady from New York who visited some years back,' Frank said, 'and she said if we dig deep enough this whole bit of the hill is one big peridot.' I knew that I would never again sing 'There is a Green Hill Far Away' without thinking of the dusty hillock to which Frank was pointing, with its three cactuses and their outstretched arms.

In 1922 Scott Fitzgerald wrote *The Diamond as Big as the Ritz*. It begins with a teenager's excitement at being invited to spend the summer at a schoolfriend's mansion in Montana. The visitor is amazed by the crystal baths filled with rosewater and that the dinner plates are thin layers of diamonds. But there is a high price to pay for staying with these billionaires: Percy's friends have a lovely time but then they have to die. A diamond as big as a hotel is concealed beneath the house, and the parents do not want anyone to know about it, so their children's friends are murdered at the end of each summer. A pragmatic solution to the problem of play-dates.

Yet even if this hill had been made up entirely of large, un-flawed crystals, and even if peridot were as fashionable today as it was in Queen Berenice's time, it would probably have done the native people of San Carlos little good. If these evening emeralds had actually been real all-day emeralds, then in the 1860s Arizona's pioneer society would have spoken of little but the gem rush. Saloon bars and brothels would have opened, the entire *mesa* would have been flattened and the desert would have swarmed with stakeholders. Instead there were only bees, little black ones that made the hills hum, although in this bare desert I couldn't see where they would find any pollen to feed their queen.

We arrived at a huge crater, much bigger than the one I had seen the evening before. It was more than believable in this landscape that peridot was an extraterrestrial stone: it felt as if the whole place was extraterrestrial. In the very centre, dwarfed by the landscape, a tiny figure was hitting a rock with a small hammer. I went to talk to him. He was hoping that a bag of crystals would solve his cash-flow problem, 'though it hasn't yet'.

'Does anyone get rich on peridot?' I asked.

Everyone laughed. 'The guy who runs this mine gets some money. Me, I just come up here for something to do,' Frank said.

They gave me a rock hammer, showed me how to use it, then went off to their favourite corners, while Shannon sat on a small outcrop, smoking cigarettes, and watched us. When you hit the rock properly, it is like taking a piece of clay out of its mould: a little dark grey bomb of volcanic material falls out, and inside it there are lots of little green sugar crystals to sift, and hopefully a few clearer ones hidden inside as well. But you have to be careful not to damage them: they are worryingly fragile. On Friedrich Mohs' league table peridot scores around 6.5, which means it is among the softest of all the translucent gemstones, softer than emeralds, garnets, tourmaline and even quartz, on a par with tanzanite and jadeite, and harder by just one point than glass.

The others complained that the sun was too hot for their headaches, but they soon found spots of cooler shade and we fell into a quiet rhythm of tapping. It was a mesmerising process.

The calm was broken by a shout. 'Found some!' said Sean. He showed me a couple of cubic crystals as big as poker dice, but they were cracked.

'Yeah, the dynamite sometimes does that. It's a bummer,' said Frank.

An hour or so later, when we finished for the afternoon, I bought their findings from them. I paid forty dollars for what I guessed correctly was a bag of worthless green crumbs in gratitude for their help. Then Frank asked me to drive them to the casino food store to spend it.

Shannon did complex mental calculations on how to use the money, taking local taxes into account, and we processed triumphantly through the dingy place – which smelt of fried chicken and ancient coffee – filling a shopping basket. All the money, to the last nickel, went on beer, snacks and giant buckets of popcorn covered with cheap margarine. Then we drove back to Peridot and I dropped them at the stream bed so that they could drink among the trees without their parents spotting them. If you still live at home, you'll get hell from your parents if you break the house rules, no matter how old you are, Frank said. They then trooped off towards the creek – Frank so tall, with the beer case balanced on his head, Shannon cradling the junk-food bags in her arms like a contented Madonna, and Sean leaving a trail of nachos behind them like Hansel and Gretel. I sat and watched them go. It felt as if I was seeing the deciding scene in a movie where the audience realises for the first time that for some of the characters there might not be a turning point. Then they turned and waved, and I waved back.

Living in Two Worlds

The Tribal Office was a pleasant building of white rock-like breezeblocks. Behind the receptionist was a poster with a picture of a handshake and the words '*tit daanotjoo le*'. What did it mean? 'Love one another,' the receptionist translated.

'How do you pronounce it?' I wondered.

'Ramona, how do you pronounce it?' she called to a passing Apache woman.

'I don't know,' she said. 'My Apache's not that good.' It turned out that no one who was around knew how to say it.

'We're forgetting,' said a man, going out of the door jingling car keys. 'We can't help it. It's happening.'

Some minutes later I was invited to go through to meet Kathy Wesley-Kitcheyan, the first woman to be made chair of the twelve-thousand-member San Carlos Apache tribe. 'Our people are living in two worlds,' she said, 'and neither of them are easy ones.' But peridot mining was not a solution for poverty. 'You're asking me about my dream for the peridot? My dream for the peridot is that it stays exactly as it is.' She did not want white contractors moving in with their bulldozers and mining equipment, and she did not want it to be a big business controlled from outside or even from inside. She had seen what big business did for the Apaches: 'In past years we have had people coming in trying to implement a kind of mining programme, and it doesn't work.'

The point, she said, was that the land is sacred. She was not just talking about the peridot *mesa*: 'The entire reservation is sacred.' Once, in the past, Globe was Apache, Tucson was Apache, even parts of New Mexico were Apache. Now they had only the reservation. 'If you read about Apache history it makes a person angry. I feel the pain and sorrow at what my people have gone through, and I don't want anyone else to take over our land any more for any reason – not for peridot or anything.' As I left her office, we shook hands. 'Are you surprised at my answer?' she asked.

I had to admit that I wasn't.

Lady Miners

Back in Peridot township, Pansy Cassavetes was waiting for sellers to arrive with their little bags of green crystals. She invited me into her house for a soda. She had been born on the reservation but when she was twelve her parents had sent her to the Indian school in Phoenix, part of the Federal government's assimilation programme of putting Native American children through a strict boarding school system so they could learn how to speak, eat and behave in the way of white Americans. 'That first day I looked around and thought, Gee, a lot of kids here run away, I wonder whether I will.' But she didn't. At home they were living without a gas stove or a refrigerator, and at school she found, to her delight, that she didn't have to haul water or chop wood. 'I didn't mind too much if we had to pay a fine for speaking our language. For me it was heaven.' So, like many Apaches, she grew up between cultures – living in St Louis, Dallas and Pittsburgh – and when she came back to the reservation she went into a business that needed contacts in both worlds. 'I started mining first of all, but buying peridots was easier than digging.'

In the 1970s buyers paid little for the stones, which were traditionally bought by weight from the miners. 'They paid maybe five dollars a pound. But we didn't know any better.' Today the price is higher: for a bag with some good crystals in it, they can pay around ninety dollars a pound. But, Pansy said, there were few good crystals coming out of the ground now. 'We don't have equipment. We need a 'dozer and someone to blast it for us.' Until two years ago a white man had come out from Globe to do the heavy work, but he died 'and everything just went down after that'.

Pansy had got to know Elsa Hart, the 'Lady from New York', when she had come to San Carlos in the early 1980s to look at the mining opportunities. She had wanted to help the Apache make it a proper business but the venture ended in discord when the tribal council accused her of doing it for profit. 'It wasn't fair,' Pansy said. 'She was a caring person.' When Elsa had got married she invited Pansy to the wedding in New Jersey. 'She wanted me to go in my native dress, so I did. And all those people there asked me if I still lived in a tepee, and wanted to know if I had horses, and what kind of food did I eat . . . They didn't know that I ate pretty much the same as them.' Few of those kind, educated people in New Jersey had had any idea of the reality of reservation life, she said, glancing round her simple house, with its carpet and the photos of her 'boy', aged twenty-two, his young wife and their two babies . . . and at the empty spaces where there might have been other photographs – of the brother who had become an alcoholic, or the nephew who was in prison for dealing drugs. 'Somebody needs to write a book about Indians: a modern one, just to say what it's like here.'

Worth Dimes Not Dollars

Whatever life on the reservation is like, it has hardly been improved by the peridots. Pansy Cassavetes' simple room is emblematic of the story of these gemstones. Back in the Red Sea, Zabargad Island lies abandoned because nobody loves its bright green button stones enough to mine there. And the American place called Peridot has not become rich either. It is not an area of millionaire mine-owners exploiting the land and workers; nor is it a town where ordinary men and women have become rich from the treasure buried underground. Instead Peridot is a hamlet where some people are born and a few more die, and sometimes, somewhere in the middle, they take a pick and a stick of dynamite up the hill to see if what they can find will pay for their next meal or drink.

6

Emerald

'The Shah of Persia has a little casket of gold studded with
emeralds which is said to have been blessed by Mahomet and
has the property of rendering the royal wearer invisible . . . as
long as he remains celibate.'
WILLIAM JONES, 1880[1]

'Emeralds are so commonly flawed that a "clean" emerald is
said to be unknown.'
ROBERT WEBSTER, *gemmologist*[2]

Carroll Chatham was fifteen when he blew out the windows of
his neighbour's house. He had read in a school science book
that diamonds were nothing but graphite in a different form, so
he poured a mixture of graphite and hot melted iron into a
crock of liquid nitrogen, hoping that when it all cooled down
the carbon would form into pretty crystals. What he had forgotten (or perhaps his 1930s textbook hadn't told him) was that
what he was effectively making was a smoke-bomb. He was
lucky he was not in the laboratory he had set up in the basement,
but instead was crouched on the pavement just outside the
house. His father was furious. 'Get a new hobby, Carroll,' he
said. So he did. And by the time the young Californian had
reached his twenty-first birthday he had made his first emerald.

This was not a completely new idea: alchemists had been
trying to make gemstones for hundreds of years. The Greek
scholar Democritus of Thrace was hailed for his ability to make
imitation emeralds. According to Seneca, he 'could put the fire

and colour of an Emerald into a common pebble'.[3] As early as 1848 the German scientist J.J. Ebelman produced 'reconstructed' emerald by fusing powdered beryl with boric acid, although he only ever produced tiny crystals. Then, at the turn of the century, the French scientist Auguste Verneuil had a similar dream for rubies. In 1902 he made 'ruby soup' from powdered aluminium oxide over a very hot flame, hoping that it would harden to something very like a ruby. It did, and the little 'verneuils' were certainly cheap to make, but they weren't quite good enough. It was rather like the comparison between two school photographs, the first taken with all the children sitting in ordered rows, the second when they have just been told they can leave. The same elements are present in both but there is a key difference in what you might call the attitude. The verneuils were like the second photograph: they had the constituent parts, but lacked order. Later Verneuil synthesised sapphires by a similar method but he never succeeded in making emeralds. Thirty years later, Hitler's scientists at I.G. Farben produced synthetic emeralds, hoping to augment the war chest – they were called 'Igmeralds' in a 1948 article in *Science Illustrated*[4] – but they were very small and the company soon gave up experimenting because it was so costly.

What Carroll Chatham had developed in the summer of 1935 was different from all of these. It was a method of growing an emerald as a crystal, rather as it would grow in nature, and it could create gems that weighed ten carats or more. Indeed his largest was 1014 carats, and now belongs to the Smithsonian Institution. The process is still secret even after all these years – the Chatham laboratory has strict educational criteria for its employees and will only hire people without school-leaving certificates. People with PhDs are definitely not allowed to join. What we do know is that it is a 'flux-growth' process, and that it starts with a small sliver of natural emerald, around which the synthetic crystal is encouraged to form. We also know that it is vulnerable to power cuts and surges: at the Tucson Gem Fair of 2003 the company was selling off a small collection of blackened, burned emeralds, the result of power cuts in California the previous year.

Chatham began by looking at geodes, the cavities in which certain gemstones form. He had noticed that emeralds occurred when superheated water had passed in and out of a geode, melting the minerals around it and – sometimes – allowing crystals to grow. Even with this clue it had not been an easy process. His first emerald, in 1935, had happened almost accidentally after he had been about to give up on his experiments because he had seen no results. 'I was disgusted, I more or less forgot about it,' he told an interviewer twenty years later.[5] Then, having left the mixture for far longer than he had meant to, he went to check it and found a dark green, impure stone that weighed about a carat.

It was the last gemstone he produced in his laboratory for three years. No matter what he did to reproduce that experiment, he kept failing. 'I was about to give up when I remembered something I had done that I hadn't bothered to put down in the notes – it was so simple, something that didn't seem to have any more to do with the experiment than moving a book from one end of the table to the other . . . But I decided to try it,' he said. 'And that was it. I've never had an absolute failure since. I don't understand it completely to this day.'

It takes nine months for an emerald crystal to grow by the Chatham method. The result is a gemstone that looks, to the naked eye, just like the natural stone to which it aspires, although to the knowledgeable gemmologist it has certain signature inclusions – feathery wisps and veils, and sometimes little platinum crystals that have come from the metal crucible. Like the best natural emeralds, however, they tend to be perkily bright, like little sweets, or like the stones that the gem writer Thomas Nicols had seen in 1692, which were 'of so excellent a viridity or spring-colour as that if a man shall look upon an emerald by a pleasant green meadow it will be more amiable than the meadow'.

When the jewellers of America looked upon Carroll Chatham's new discovery they did not, however, feel even slightly amiable. A short time after he had perfected his process, the shy young scientist and his new wife, Barbara, went on honeymoon to New York. They took the opportunity to show their emeralds to one of the city's top jewellers. But they were as green as their own stones: and when they walked into the Van Cleef & Arpels showroom on Fifth Avenue, they did not find quite the reception they had hoped for. Chatham opened up a little paper packet and out spilled some hundred carats of the most beautiful stones the manager had ever seen. 'What do you think of these?' he asked.

The manager called over his secretary, pretending to admire the emeralds but telling her in French that he would keep the couple talking while she called the police. He could see that they could not have afforded such stones and was convinced they had stolen them. Barbara had studied French and knew what the man was saying. 'So I whispered to Carroll that we should run, and he scooped up his emeralds and we ran straight out of the shop,'[6] she recalled, many years later. That afternoon they had both learned an important lesson about created gemstones. Even if it had taken hundreds of years of alchemy to reach the stage where someone in a laboratory could create a crystal, the really difficult bit is not actually the making of them. It is the selling that is the challenge.

But why? If created emeralds cost a fraction of the price of natural ones and look virtually identical, why should it be so hard to persuade consumers to buy them? In *The World of Goods*, the British anthropologist Mary Douglas describes the desire for luxury goods, like gems and expensive champagnes, as being less about pure display and more about giving out a complex set of information about our status in the community. What we display, eat and wear is not simply about our own entertainment: it also says a great deal about what and who we are. How we admire those who get it right – the film stars who dazzle with just the right amount of taste at movie premières, or the presidents' wives who appear effortlessly stylish. And how we mock those who get it wrong. In Douglas's example, a hostess in 1890s New York tried to surpass a rival who always presented each of her guests with a jewel when they visited. So she folded a crisp hundred-dollar bill into each napkin, and was surprised by her guests' derision at her generosity.

We may think we buy expensive jewels 'because they are beautiful' but that is only part of the story. We usually buy them not only because they mean something to us, but also because our buying and wearing them conveys something to others. The symbolism of emeralds is a complex puzzle, different probably to everyone who owns or would like to own these vivid green stones. But to start to unpack the puzzle and understand the ornate history and geography of these stones, we can begin with one of the greatest, most effortlessly stylish socialites of all: Cleopatra, Queen of Egypt.

Cleopatra's Emeralds

Cleopatra came from a long line of rulers, of whom the first had been Alexander the Great's henchman, General Ptolemy. She inherited the Egyptian throne after her father died in 51 BC, when she was twenty. But tradition dictated that she should marry her twelve-year-old brother Ptolemy XIII, and if the new Queen was not impressed by this, her younger sibling was not overjoyed either. Two years later Ptolemy sent his sister into exile in Syria and it was from this time that Cleopatra began to make an international name for herself. As she amassed her forces and supporters (and later on once she had regained her throne) she became known throughout the Roman world and beyond for her affairs with powerful men, her charisma, her ruthless determination – and her jewels.

The first mention of Cleopatra's interest in emeralds is an account of her famous seduction of Julius Caesar after his victory over General Pompey in 49 BC. She was twenty-two, and desperate for the Roman to support her against her brother. The majority of writers at the time were most interested in the fact that Caesar's advisers were furious and made it known that she was 'whoring' to gain Rome. But it was the upstart poet Marcus Annaeus Lucanus who really went into *Hello!* magazine-style prose in his ten-volume epic *The Civil War*.[7] In it he described the interior of her home, including the agate porphyry columns of her sitting rooms, the ivory hallways, jasper couches and the Indian tortoiseshells scattered around her boudoir 'with frequent emeralds studded'.

How could the Roman general resist her as 'laden she lay . . . faint beneath the weight of gems and gold'? Of course he could not. For Caesar that first evening with Cleopatra was a lesson in how to use luxury to exhibit power, and when he returned to Rome he immediately introduced sumptuary laws, limiting luxuries like purple togas and certain gemstones to Caesar's use alone.

For Cleopatra, it was perhaps an even more important lesson in how to use luxury in a slightly different way to gain influence. After her younger brother had been defeated and she was Queen of Egypt in her own right, she sent soldiers and workers out to every gem mine in her dominion, because by then she had learned – as so many rulers have learned ever since – that her royal popularity depended largely on her royal glamour. Jewels told the world that even if she had once been ejected temporarily from the throne she was still a queen.

Today people wear emeralds because they want to wear something that is beautiful but not as brash as diamonds. But two millennia ago, emeralds 'said' something different. They were among the most expensive jewels of the Roman and Ptolemaic world, the equivalent of the flashiest diamonds today. And they had another role, as well as being the ultimate in Ptolemaic bling. Since they were also synonymous with Egypt at the time, for Cleopatra to wear them, or give them as presents, engraved with her portrait,[8] as she liked to do, was rather like a green tie or scarf worn by an Irish president, or a British-made Bentley driven by Queen Elizabeth II: a practical but emblematic sign of patriotism.

Cleopatra's Emerald Mines

Queen Cleopatra's Emerald Mines. When I first heard of them they sounded almost fictitious – rivals in romance to King Solomon's mines in southern Africa, or Prester John's treasure in Asia. Yet these mines really existed. In fact, once upon a time entire cities in the southern desert of Egypt were filled with men whose lives were dedicated to finding jewels for their Greek queen. According to nineteenth-century travellers and twentieth-century archaeologists, there are still traces of these places to be found in the sandswept ruins of an otherwise empty desert, and when I heard that, I knew I had to see them for myself.

Before I went, I contacted Dr Ian Shaw of Liverpool University, a specialist in historic Egyptian mining operations. We went to a Sudanese café near the university and before the food arrived he took four gem specimen boxes out of his briefcase. 'These are the remains of the mines of Cleopatra,' he said, emptying out the contents. They were tiny pieces of green stone – pale like pistachio, not much bigger than granulated sugar and full of imperfections. Inclusions are so common in emeralds that there is scarcely a stone that doesn't have them. It means you have to be particularly vigilant when you buy emeralds – not only because of the synthetics, but because for centuries

people have been putting so much oil,[9] and more recently poly-
mers, into the natural stones to disguise their fractures that
almost no one ever bothers to disclose the practice any more.
Jewellers call the inclusions *jardin*, or 'garden', because they
look like a wilderness growing within the crystal, and if you
look at a gem-quality emerald under a microscope it is like
diving on a reef: full of intriguing growths and bubbles and life.
But if you were to look at these Egyptian stones under the
microscope it would be like swimming in mud. I felt momentarily disappointed. Dr Shaw agreed that they weren't up to
much. 'These are the bits that were discarded by the miners,' he
told me. When Dr Shaw was a child he loved reading books by
Rider Haggard, and medieval stories about the mysterious
Prester John – the king of a mythical eastern kingdom, who
was famous for carrying a sceptre made from a single huge
emerald.[10] 'I loved those stories. In fact, I liked anything that
involved treasure-hunting,' Dr Shaw said. 'Of course, when you're
an archaeologist you can't actually call it treasure-hunting.'

He drew a little map on a paper napkin, showing how to
reach the mines from the Red Sea. It involved covering two and
a half sides of a square: going in from the coast, turning south
along desert tracks, then turning back east again. He added two
Xs to mark the spots where the main emerald mines were – and
then it really looked like a treasure map. One place was called
Sikait, which was where ancient temples had been cut into the
rock two thousand years ago, and the other was called Zubara.
They were both found on different slopes of Mount Smaragdus,
or 'Emerald Mountain'.

Apart from temporary Bedouin encampments there were no
settlements anywhere nearby, Dr Shaw said. In fact, when he
first visited, ten years before, there was so little to mark the
emerald mines that they almost missed them. Getting there
would not be easy, he warned, and once I did find a willing
driver I should make sure he had a global positioning satellite

(GPS) system. The sites were devilishly difficult to find, he said, 'and the sand is limitless'. 'Is there anything in particular I should look out for on my journey?' I asked, expecting a list of archaeological sites. 'Oh, yes,' he said. 'Scorpions.'

To the Desert

As Dr Shaw had warned, it was not easy to organise an expedition into the desert and there were plenty of false starts. But finally I located an agency with the right contacts to get permits to visit the emerald-mine areas, which are usually closed to visitors. Thomas, my guide, had warned me that there was a 'ninety per cent chance we will get to Zubara, and perhaps a fifty per cent chance that we'll be allowed to go to Sikait'. But I was optimistic, and a few weeks later found myself in southern Egypt, in a white jeep heading south along the Red Sea coast past huge tourist resorts and looking out at the limitless sand. This was the Costa Diver, and the concrete went on for miles. But after a checkpoint just north of Marsa Alam there were just empty dunes and the dusty town, with its petrol station, camel traders, five thousand souls, and a host of white diving boats, cruising offshore like sharks.

We bought extra water from a small shop run by a man with one glass eye. It was a good omen for the journey: emeralds are frequently associated with eyes. Nero apparently used them as lenses in his theatre binoculars, in order to watch the games more vividly,[11] and polished stones from the beryl family, of which emerald is the most valued member, were used in spectacles for so long that the German word *brille*, meaning 'glasses', is derived from 'beryl'.

In many ancient mythologies placing emerald eyes in statues was said to give them mystical powers. The Romans told a legend of a marble statue of a lion in Crete, which had eyes made of emeralds and which stood on a cliff overlooking the

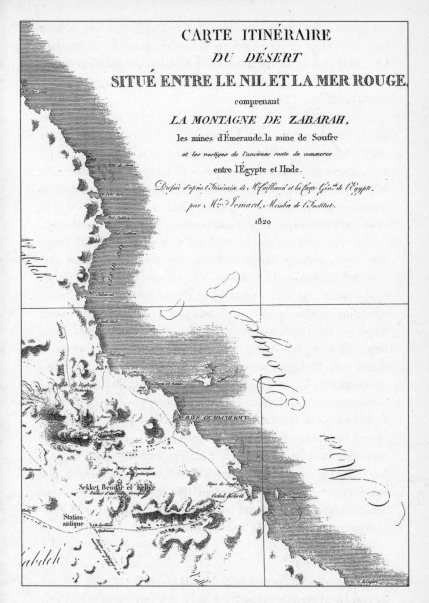

The emerald mines of Egypt: Caillaud's nineteenth-century map

sea, near a fishing village. However, the brilliance of its gaze was said to scare the tuna away and it was only when the fishermen prised out the precious stones that the shoals returned to their nets.[12] Linking emeralds with sight was not limited to the Mediterranean. The ancient Bamiyan Buddhas in Afghanistan – destroyed by the Taliban army in 2001 – were believed by the local people to have once had their eye sockets set with great emeralds which could be seen by travellers from many miles away, glinting in the sunshine and leading them to safety.[13]

You couldn't see any emeralds in Egypt from miles away, of course, but a little further south of Marsa Alam was the next best thing: Smaragdus.[14] It was the tallest peak in a jagged range directly to the west, and in its shadow were the emerald mines of Zubara. No one knows how old they are, although the first recorded reference to them was in 24 BC when the Greek writer Strabo wrote in his *Geography*[15]: 'Then follows the isthmus, extending to the Red Sea near Berenike . . . [where] stones are found by the Arabians who dig deep subterranean passages.' This suggests they had probably been established some time before that, perhaps even in the time of the pharaohs. Emeralds were certainly known in ancient times: a ruler called Ptah-hotep, in around 2200 BC, wrote that 'Good words are more difficult to find than the emerald, for it is by slaves that it is discovered among the rocks of pegmatite.'[16] From the coast the foothills of Mount Smaragdus looked very far away and very dark.

I looked back at my table-napkin treasure map. We were not travelling two and a half sides of the square at all: we were going straight in to Zubara from the coast. 'Do we have GPS?' I asked, remembering Dr Shaw's advice.

'No.' Thomas laughed. 'We have a Bedouin guide, and I remember the way.'

As he said that, our driver, Mohammed, turned the car off the road and on to what seemed like a random expanse of sand. Then a pickup truck drew up beside us. It was piled high with mysterious shapes under a canvas cover. 'You didn't think we just had the one car?' Thomas asked. So now, in addition to Thomas and Mohammed, there was Ali Saz, the second driver, as well as Naim the cook, Aderup the Bedouin guide, and piles of food, spares, tools and enough water to last us all for several days.

With two vehicles and a support crew of five, it suddenly felt like a huge expedition. However, in comparison to a group of six Englishmen sent on a survey to the same area in 1899, we were almost invisible. Their group had included three surveyors – led by one Donald McAlister, who had to map the area and write it up – and three Cornish tin-miners, who would actually get down the mine tunnels. Their baggage train had included 130 camels, each carrying 150 kilos of tents, equipment and other supplies for the men to survive the rigours of the desert for four months while they went searching for emeralds.

And what a desert it was. Once upon a time when the continents were one, this was apparently the South Pole. Now in October the average temperature was 37 degrees centigrade, while in the summer the heat is almost unbearable. An ancient inscription from the Middle Kingdom period,[17] around 1900 BC, describes the sensation of the Egyptian desert with poetic simplicity: 'The highlands are hot in summer,' it reads, 'and the mountains brand the skin.' It was easy to see what the writer had meant.

I had expected the 'Eastern Desert' to be made up of endless dunes, not this rocky, camel-coloured landscape with its wide, flat *wadi* valleys that look just like dried-up stream beds, which in a way they are. Once in a decade or so there are floods and it is those flashes of water that have made the landscape into the shape it is today. 'They are really serious events,' said Thomas. 'There is cholera, the roads collapse, people can't travel and everything is destroyed.' But afterwards, he said, the water stays in the reservoirs and people and animals can survive there for several years. In Cleopatra's time the rains came almost yearly – if they had had the same weather patterns as today, with the goods supply system they had then, they would never have been able to keep the mines open.

The landscape was impossibly bare: the only vegetation was brushwood and the occasional acacia, a tree that needs very little water to survive. Acacias were the sacred trees of Hathor, the Egyptian goddess of mines, perhaps because their roots tended to seek out the same cracks and crevices in which gemstones and valuable minerals were found. From a distance it looked as if parakeets were perched in their branches, but as we approached we could see that they were not birds but the belongings of the local Bedouin, called the Ababdeh,[18] who leave their food and clothing hanging on the branches so that wild animals cannot steal them. In the past the Bedouin often believed in the curative and magical powers of gems: they would wear them as charms called '*hurruz*'. According to a legend from the stories of Solomon, these gems are jinns that have been turned into stone, and can bestow strength and protection.

After several hours we turned into a valley with a Muslim cemetery at the entrance. This was Zubara. The hundreds of jagged headstones testified to the many centuries this area had been mined, even after the Ptolemies and the Romans had left. Most of the graves had been robbed, as if the miners had suffered a final indignity and had themselves been mined for emeralds. Beyond the cemetery were the ruins of two-thousand-year-old houses and office buildings, and on the rockface was a fine inscription in French telling us in bold capital letters how an engineer called Leonidas 'had explored these mines between 22 November 1846 and 18 January 1846 [*sic*]'.[19] And there was another, even more fascinating, sign that we had at last arrived at the famous Mount Smaragdus. The ground had changed. The rocks were different, and they were shining.

The foothills of Emerald Mountain

'The Bedouin leave their food and clothing hanging on the branches'

Emeralds in Egypt form in a rock called mica-schist. It is a metamorphic rock, which means that it was created when an extreme event – like a volcanic eruption or the tremendous heat of two continental plates crashing into each other – causes existing sedimentary rocks to turn into something quite different. Temperatures have to be extremely hot: if these rocks had been formed in cooler circumstances we would have been seeing slate on this valley floor, and no emeralds in its walls. Schist is named from the Greek *skhistos*, meaning 'split', from which we get the prefix 'schizo-': and it is indeed a rock with a splittable personality. Its minerals have aligned themselves in one direction, which means it slides off in parallel layers like a harder form of slate. So what we were seeing glittering in the dust of this remote place were slim slices of black schist decorated with silvery mica and these told us, as they had told the Egyptians more than two thousand years before, that this was a place where emeralds might have grown.

Further into the valley there were some large, square houses, containing well-constructed ovens and with some fine schist tiles still marking out the floors, testament to the importance once given to these emerald mines. Egypt became a Roman province in 30 BC, soon after Cleopatra had killed herself, and for the next three hundred years the country was ruled from Rome. After that, when the imperial capital shifted, it was ruled from Constantinople, now Istanbul. Right through their occupation, the Romans' chief aim was to extract as much money as they could from their colony[20] and so, shortly after they had taken over, they seized control of all the gemstone mining operations throughout the country. The expensive construction of some of Zubara's buildings suggested that the Romans organised the mines as a multinational business, sending down their representatives to oversee the work and ensure that most of the profits ended up in official coffers not private pockets.

The findings of the miners during those years filled the

jewellery boxes of rulers and aristocrats in Rome and beyond. Just over seventy years after Cleopatra's death, the Emperor Caligula's wife Lollia Paulina was seen at a party dressed fabulously in 'alternating emeralds and pearls, which glittered all over her head, hair, ears, neck and fingers'.[21] Pliny had been at that party when he was sixteen, and it had presented such a scene of careless opulence that he never forgot it. As he wrote many years later in his *Natural History*, Lollia Paulina could not help but tell everyone that her jewels had cost forty million sesterces – the equivalent of twenty villas in fashionable Rome, or a year's wages for forty thousand soldiers. But she was playing the emerald game too hard: the gems were not giving quite the right information she needed to maintain her social status, and behind their smiles the guests were disapproving. The pearls and emeralds were the proceeds of her grandfather's extortion and corruption, and he had been forced to commit suicide because of his crimes. 'He took poison so that his granddaughter could be seen in the lamplight covered with forty million sesterces!' Pliny wrote in disgust. One hopes that Lollia Paulina enjoyed her brief moment of bejewelled celebrity since the following year the emperor divorced her, and she was moved unceremoniously to the suburbs to make room for his new lovers.

The fashion for Egyptian emeralds continued throughout the Roman period and beyond. The British Museum owns a glamorous mummy portrait of a second-century Egyptian woman wearing a gold and green necklace around her pale throat. At about the same time the social commentator Clement of Alexandria wrote caustically of how amethysts, emeralds, peridots and jasper were 'among the stones which silly women wear fastened to chains and set in necklaces'. A note by the historian Aelius Lampridius[22] gives a useful peep into the trousseaux of wealthy Roman women in the third century: stating that Junia Fadilla, whose fiancé was murdered, retained the following wedding presents after his death: 'viz: necklaces of single pearls, nine; hair-nets of emeralds, eleven; bracelets with clasps of true hyacinths [zircons], four'.

A handful of those Roman emeralds might have come from the Habachtal region of Austria[23], where some emeralds were mined during Roman times. Recent studies also suggest that some rare Greek and Roman emeralds might have come from eastern Afghanistan.[24] But the majority of these green gemstones in Ancient Rome came from Egypt, and in its day Zubara was a busy place. The centuries of activity meant that pottery remnants lay everywhere, dating from Greek, Roman, medieval and more recent periods. I had read about this, but nothing had prepared me for the quantity. There were numerous intact handles and bases of large water amphorae and I even found the lip – like the mouth of a tiny cream jug – of an ancient oil-lamp. Not long ago it was common to find intact amphorae there, Thomas said, 'But then on our last visit we found them smashed on the hillside'. It was some archaeologists who – having studied, photographed and recorded the artefacts – then destroyed them so that no one else could profit from them.

As I looked up towards the hillside, I realised that all around the valley walls there were numerous heaps of rubble: tip heaps, spilled out by miners as they dug in their labyrinths. In some cases they were the only clues to the existence of the emerald mines, since the entrances were so well hidden. But others had been carefully cleared, so that from below I could easily trace the paths that led to them. The person responsible for most of the clearing in recent centuries was a Frenchman. Not the engineer Leonidas who had so triumphantly inscribed his name on the rock in the 1840s, but a young mineralogist who had arrived nearly two hundred years ago with an expedition party scarcely bigger than my own. Today he is described with some admiration as the foreigner who rediscovered 'the lost mines of Cleopatra'.

'The Pasha's Emeralds'

Frédéric Cailliaud was born in Brittany in 1787. Throughout his childhood he had heard reports, mostly from Napoleon's corps of soldiers, scholars and engineers, who were in Egypt at the end of the eighteenth century, of how Egypt was the cradle of a lost and wonderful civilisation. In 1815, tired of a Europe that seemed permanently at war, the twenty-eight-year-old Cailliaud took a ship to Alexandria, hoping to find an adventure. What he found was a country besieged by tourists and treasure-hunters. Egypt was *the* destination of the moment. Ancient sites were in chaos as Europeans descended *en masse* to look for the latest fashionable form of buried treasure. As Cailliaud wrote in his memoirs,

> The whole space occupied by the ruins of Karnak was covered with lines of demarcation, separating the quarters of the French, English, Irish, Italians, etc. Some European ladies were traversing the ruins and making their way into the catacombs. Like other voyagers, all were eager to collect or purchase antiquities, alike insensible to the fatigues or the heats; at all hours of the day and night they may be found exploring the plain or the tombs.[25]

A year after his arrival Cailliaud was appointed official mineralogist to the pasha, the ruler of Egypt under the Ottomans, and his first mission was connected with emeralds, which were then popular in France. The demand for all precious stones had dipped during the French Revolution, but by the turn of the century lavish and ornate jewellery was back in fashion. Not only was green Napoleon's favourite colour[26] but the emperor also longed to re-enact the glories of Ancient Rome. It made sense that a stone with such classical connections should be the new French emperor's favourite. During his rampage through

Europe he had briefly conquered Rome and sacked the Vatican treasury, taking much of its wealth with him including a large emerald that he took a personal interest in. Some years later he returned the stone to Pope Pius VII, set as the centrepiece of a spectacular tiara. It met with a mixed reception: the return of the stone was welcomed but its form was insulting – Napoleon had deliberately made the tiara too small for the pope's head.[27]

The emperor liked to give emeralds to the women in his life. According to the celebrated nineteenth-century society artist Jean-Baptiste Isabey, in around 1809 the Empress Josephine sat for her portrait in miniature just before it was announced publicly that Napoleon was divorcing her. When Isabey asked what jewels she wanted to wear for the picture she looked at him sadly. 'Paint me in emeralds,' said the empress, showing him a necklace her husband had given her in happier times. 'I want them to represent the underlying freshness of my grief,' she said, adding that she had learned that certain Englishwomen, 'abandoned by their husbands', wore green to show that they had been forsaken.

The emerald necklace played another small role in history. A few months after Isabey had painted it into his miniature it was stolen from Josephine's château outside Paris. Napoleon feared his enemies might accuse him of arranging the theft, so he sent the director of police an urgent order to find it. At the time[28] the main task of Napoleon's undercover police force was to sniff out political enemies and they were quite unused to tracking down criminals, so they employed the infamous outlaw Eugène François Vidocq to ask around the Paris underworld for them. Within three days he had found the emeralds, and, in gratitude, Napoleon pardoned him. Later he became France's most celebrated detective, a master of disguise and surveillance, and the first chief of the Sûreté.

With emeralds so much in the headlines, and with so many of France's newly rich wanting to emulate the imperial family, it was no wonder that the pasha asked his official mineralogist to take a fresh look at some of Egypt's ancient resources. However, when it came to giving even approximate directions, the pasha was as lost as the mines. No one seemed to have any idea of where they were. But Strabo had reported that they were 'near Berenice', and in the thirteenth century the traveller Muhammad Ben Mansur had confirmed this, describing the mines as being on the borders of 'the land of Negroes and yet belonging to the kingdom of Egypt'. So that is where Cailliaud and his small expedition of six men headed: south. All they had to help them were a few scraps of classical references and some Bedouin songs, which told of holes in the mountains where green stones were found. However, using maps, mineralogy and the help of the local Ababdeh tribesmen, they narrowed down their search to a few promising *wadis*. On 8 November 1816, three months after they had left Cairo, they came across the first sign that they might be successful. 'After five hours' march, we arrived, through a valley, at the foot of a great mountain that the Ababdeh called Zabara,' Cailliaud wrote.

They passed the same Muslim cemetery that I had, saw the same gleaming mica-schist on the ground, and noticed the same holes in the hillside. However, they didn't have the advantage of knowing for sure that this was the right place. 'When we came to the caverns we found they had been originally mines,' Cailliaud wrote, 'but I was at a loss to know what sort of mine they might have been.' He set three Arabs to clear an entrance and then, 'as I was resting from my exertions, sitting on some pieces of rock, my eye suddenly glanced on a fragment of emerald, of a dark green. My surprise and joy made me forget all my tiredness and, impatient to enter the gallery, I encouraged the Ababdeh and began to labour with them. It was not long before we entered the mine.'

Within a hundred paces the path became dangerous. 'The frightened Arabs turned back; my interpreter, finding the way too narrow, hesitated and stopped short; I alone continued to descend for the space of three quarters of an hour.' Then he found his route barred by enormous blocks of mica, which had fallen in from the roof, and he was unable to clear them. 'When just on the point of re-ascending, disappointed at having discovered nothing remarkable I perceived, among these masses of mica, a six-sided prism of emerald. I carefully removed it, letting it remain in its ore.'

Eventually Cailliaud's torch began to die so he had to go back 'and this was toilsome clambering. At length the voice of my interpreter interrupted the profound silence, and guided me to the place where he stood. His first question was: "Have you got any emeralds?" I answered in the negative, but in such a tone as to make him believe I had my pockets full. This thought was a greater punishment to him than any reproaches of mine.'[29]

I had reread Cailliaud's account just a few days before I left for Egypt, and it had worried me. How was I going to be able to see what Cailliaud had seen in those abandoned places? How would I dare? I didn't want to be like Cailliaud's interpreter staying anxiously at the cave mouth, wondering about the emeralds that might lie inside. So I contacted the Derbyshire Caving Association, and two days later met caver Matt Robbins in Matlock, to explore the lead mines below the quaintly named Heights of Abraham. There were three main tips for exploring mines, he said. One: wear a hard hat. Two: remember to take not just one spare torch but two. And three: always go into a small hole feet first. 'That way you know you can get out if you get stuck,' he said, as we squeezed along passages so narrow that I had to move the battery pack on my belt to wriggle through.

The Emerald Mines

Now, equipped with a hard hat and a head torch, I felt ready to enter Cailliaud's labyrinth. But first I had to find it, and there were hundreds of holes in the mountains to choose from. As I eased my way into the most likely-looking one – a metre high and surrounded by rubble – I was glad of my training: crawling through spaces the size of a handbag is excellent preparation for crawling through spaces the size of a suitcase. In comparison with some of the puddle-filled fissures I had wriggled through in England, this Egyptian mine seemed like luxury. However, I couldn't help remembering the scorpions. It is hard when you're squeezing into a mine full of fallen stones not to disturb anything for fear of what might lurk beneath. Brushwood concealed the entrance, and although I pulled it out of the tunnel as best I could the thorns worked their way into me as I eased down, feet first. There was Roman pottery everywhere, most of it rough but a few pieces had been glazed with red, like the Samian ware that was so prized at the time. This was clearly a better class of mine.

About ten metres in, I saw something unusual. Small lamp niches had been dug into the walls, about a metre above the floor. Unlike the roughly hewn versions I had seen in other caves, these had been carved out as if someone had cared about what they were doing. Then I saw a large empty niche on the left wall. It was about seventy centimetres high and ten deep, with a square ledge and a rounded top like an arched window. I continued on for another thirty metres and there, in the right-hand wall, I found a double niche. This time there were two regular arches – as if they had once housed small statues. The tunnel ended some twenty metres further on, not in the jagged, dissatisfied way of most mines but rounded, as if this was its intended ending. I roared back in great excitement. 'Have you found emeralds?' Mohammed asked. 'No! Better!' I said. 'I think I've found a shrine tunnel.'

Years before I had seen something similar in a silver mine at Potosí, in Bolivia: a little underground shrine dedicated to the devil that controlled the mine, on which the miners piled coca leaves and cigarettes as offerings. Underground shrines in Egyptian gem areas are not altogether unknown – there is a particularly interesting example, in the ancient turquoise mines of Serabit el-Khadem in the Sinai desert, dedicated to Hathor. However, they are rare – so perhaps this one was further testament to the value of emeralds.

While I had been in the tunnel, Thomas and Mohammed had filled the time looking for little green crystals in the tip heaps. 'If you get this colour fixed in your mind's eye, then you will find emeralds,' Thomas promised. I joined them, but I didn't find emeralds. Not yet. Instead I found a fragment of Roman glass, a bright blue-green colour half-way between emerald and aquamarine. Green glass has a curious role in the history of emeralds. In 529 AD the Byzantine emperor Justinian passed a code ruling that emeralds, as well as pearls and sapphires, were reserved for the aristocracy. In the San Vitale church in Ravenna, in northern Italy, two astonishing full-length mosaics show Justinian and his wife Theodora. They are wearing multi-tier crowns, earrings, brooches and long ropes of pearls, sapphires and emeralds.

The depiction of those gemstones gave a clear message that the people in the picture were not simply extraordinarily powerful: they were exclusively powerful. The laws emerged partly from the hierarchical nature of the Byzantine world – no *nouveaux riches* should look as *riche* as the imperial family – and partly because gold and precious stones were the basis of international trade.[30] The income from exchanging them with foreign kingdoms like India was needed to maintain the army, and Justinian had no desire for his currency to be tied up round the arms, necks and fingers of his populace.

From around this time, therefore, green glass beads had a

currency of their own. When women of high social standing were unable to buy emeralds they commissioned necklaces made of hexagonal green glass beads.[31] They were of very high quality, so unless their rivals looked closely they probably would not have known for certain that their wealthy neighbours' jewellery was simply a fabulous fake. And, on the lines of Mary Douglas's theory about jewels as information, it was a clever way for women to pass on subtle social messages about status – even if the usual means of doing so was forbidden to them.

The Road to Sikait

Zubara and Sikait are only twenty kilometres apart as the falcon flies but there is no driveable pass connecting them. If we had had camels we could have headed straight across the mountain passes to reach the other major source of Egyptian emeralds, but as it was we took a long, bumpy drive back to the coast, then went up another *wadi* that began a little further south. It was originally named Wadi Gemal, meaning 'valley of the camels'. Now the meaning has shifted and it is often called Wadi Jamil, which means 'beautiful valley' and is a good name for the national park being created there by the Egyptian government. However, despite its newly acquired park status it was as remote and wild as anything we had seen and it was hard to believe that this was once the highway to the Nile, the main road linking the port of Berenice to what Rudyard Kipling once called the 'market garden' of Egypt.

Once upon a time this stretch of sand without markings or tracks was a real Roman road along which 'emeralds, gold and singing boys'[32] were transported, with other luxury goods such as frankincense, myrrh and Indian pepper. As I travelled through this place, which was once great and now is nothing, I realised how easy it is to lose a few mines in such country. If you shut down an enterprise and the people move elsewhere, then the trails through the desert disappear quickly. In a few decades there is almost no sign of civilisation at all.

What there were very clear signs of, however, was geology – in its most dazzling show-off form. The pink cliffs of Wadi Gemal had strips of black rock and shiny quartz across them, in crazy designs like a toddler's felt-tip scrawlings, although it was anything but random. Instead these were the graffiti of ancient prehistory saying: 'I woz here' in a spectacular way, testifying to a day many millions of years ago when the continental plate of Africa had crashed into the oceanic plate of the Red Sea, and everything buckled and clashed and turned somersaults so as to accommodate the new situation.

This history of physical violence, as shown in that rockface full of spectacular serpentine veins, is one of the keys to understanding the story of emeralds. The beryl family of gemstones has a complicated formula. Beryl is made of beryllium, aluminium, silicon and oxygen[33] and is one of the rarer elements in the earth's crust.[34] The extra element that makes emeralds green – chromium, meaning 'the colour element' – is even less common. Beryllium forms in different places from chromium so there is literally no reason on earth for them to meet. It is only by accident – for example, by two opposite tectonic plates bumping into each other one day while heading in different directions – that the introduction is made.

If instead of chromium, a drop of iron had been present to meet with the beryl as it grew beneath these mountain ranges, we would have been on the search for Cleopatra's Aquamarine Mines – and we would be looking for those pale blue sisters of emeralds named after the colour of clear deep salt-water and consequently believed to be lucky for sailors. People who travelled by sea during classical times often wore them to appease the sea-god Poseidon or, if the waves became rough, they would sometimes even throw them into the sea.

If there had been manganese present instead of chromium

when the beryl crystals were forming, we would now have been looking for a peach-pink stone whose name is the epitome of nineteenth-century American capitalism. John Pierpont Morgan was the son of a powerful banking family in New York. Since boyhood he had suffered from a particularly horrible form of acne, which made his nose pink and bulbous. Although in adulthood he could joke that his nose was 'part of the American business structure', the affliction gave him a permanent sense of his own lack of beauty – which was perhaps why he looked for it elsewhere.[35] Morgan moved rapidly from one interest to another, collecting only the best specimens, whether snuffboxes, tapestries or fine art, then moving on. When his sister once asked him if he was interested in meeting a top dealer in Greek antiquities, he famously replied, 'I have done with Greek antiquities; I am at the Egyptians.'

With the help of the Tiffany's jeweller Frederick Kunz, he bought some of the finest mineral collections in the world, including one from the Philadelphia industrialist Clarence Bement, and then – when he had done with stones – he gave it all to the American Natural History Museum in New York. The collection was so extensive that it filled two railway boxcars.[36] As a sign of gratitude, a new form of pink beryl, discovered on Madagascar in 1911, was named 'morganite'. When it comes out of the ground it is usually a pale salmon colour and quite unremarkable, but after being heated it can look vivid, like a bowl of raspberries in the summer sunshine. Morgan loved it – even though (or perhaps because) it was the exact rosy colour that had plagued him throughout his life.

The Emerald City of Sikait

When we arrived at the ruined city of Sikait the whole place was lit up briefly with the colour of morganite. It was late afternoon, and we had reached it by walking across the hills along a rocky Roman track, just as the ancient traders had done. The cars had gone separately along the *wadi* and Naim, the cook, was already sitting on the ground rolling dough to make bread in the way Bedouins have for centuries, by burying it in burning sand. Behind him was the larger of the rock temples Dr Shaw had told me about, and we caught sight of it just as it blushed bright pink in the last light of the sun. The temple had been built during the time of the Ptolemies, with four columns, three altars, and a great stone lintel linking them.

Inside there were graffiti signed by Lanoninas de Crete, who had stood there with his penknife on 5 June 1844. Above them, earlier carved signs showed what looked like the sun over a horned moon: the symbol of Hathor, invoked to protect the emerald mining. The temple had an altar niche like those in the tunnel at Zubara. At some point someone had dug energetically into the back of it to see if any treasure had been hidden there – a little cache of emeralds, or perhaps even some concealed workings. The treasure-hunters would have had some justification in suspecting a hidden mine: the ancient turquoise mines in the Sinai had often been built in the form of galleries, with pillars and carved reliefs at their entrances, rather like this. But had they studied their history and geology a little better, they would have saved themselves the effort. This place was simply the processing centre for polishing the stones and possibly trading them; the mines were somewhere else.

All over the hills I could see the outlines of houses and temples, or perhaps churches, that had once been full of travellers and traders, soldiers, slaves and priests. 'Great was my astonishment to find in the desert at so remote a distance a town in such good repair,' Cailliaud had written, when he returned to Mount Smaragdus for a second time and found Sikait. 'It was highly amusing for me to stroll from house to house, from chamber to chamber.' He found lamps of burnt earth and fragments of glass vases, as well as granite stones that had been hollowed into

'Once this was the highway to the Nile'

Naim making bread in the desert

Cailliaud's drawings of Sikait's temple (left) and town (below)

mills for the people to grind their grain. 'With unbounded satisfaction I greeted and hailed a town, hitherto unknown to all voyagers, which had been uninhabited for two thousand years, and was almost entirely standing.' The silence of these ruins was unlike the silence of deserted places in Europe where rain has washed away so many traces. At Sikait, where it is so dry, there is a sense that the people left only a short time ago, and that if you look hard enough their fingerprints will still be there in the dust and on the ancient pottery. What traces might be left in two thousand years' time of the concrete resort towns we had seen by the Red Sea? Much less than this, I suspect.

Archaeologists had discovered many artefacts in these foundations, including a coin from Nabataea – indicating trade links with what is now Jordan – as well as pearls and beads from as far away as India and Sri Lanka.[37] The jewellery indicated that there must once have been a sizeable population of women – perhaps some prostitutes. There was a garrison at Sikait, so it is reasonable to assume there were brothels as well.[38]

Ghosts in the Wadi

For a long time beryls have had a reputation for letting their owners see strange things from the spirit world. In 1696 John Aubrey, the English antiquarian, gossip and seeker of the arcane, wrote in his *Miscellanies* that 'A berill is a kind of crystal that has a weak tincture of red. In this magicians see visions.' In Ancient Roman times, when these mines were being worked, emerald was said to be the official gemstone of the messenger god Mercury, who was not only the god of paths and roads, but also of sleep and dreams. Perhaps because of this, or because of something in the air, people tended to have odd dreams in the valley. Cailliaud mentioned several times that the Ababdeh were convinced there were bad spirits in the Sikait valley. '[On one occasion] I called for ropes and nobody answered,' he wrote, 'so terrified were they of ghosts.' My own guide, Thomas, spoke of how once he had awoken in the middle of the night and seemed to see a band of ten centurions marching down the centre of the *wadi* towards the Nile. 'They didn't stop for tents or people,' he said, 'but they seemed very real.' On another occasion he had been there with a girlfriend and had a nightmare that she was being raped by ghosts. 'The strange thing is that when she woke up she had dreamed the same thing.'

Hours later I woke in the darkness and it was very still. I saw no centurions, but I remembered a poem by the Roman writer Sextus Propertius, who had lived around the same time as Cleopatra. He had imagined his lover, Cynthia, returning to him as a spirit, or 'shade', and berating him for forgetting her so soon after her cremation. The fire had scorched her dress on one side, he wrote, and the heat of the pyre 'had cracked and dulled the beryl ring she used to wear on her finger'.[39] As I lay there imagining Cynthia striding across the *wadi*, I could understand the Ababdeh superstitions: this was an eerie place, much more so than Zubara had been. But even so, with the moon lighting up the landscape like a football ground, there were certainly no shades to be seen in the valley of beryls that night.

The Mines of Sikait

The next morning we went, finally, to the greatest source of Cleopatra's emeralds, several kilometres further north at the throat of the *wadi*. Probably the town and the mines were separated for security reasons: it is a common rule in gem areas that if you keep the traders away from the source they are more likely to buy through official channels. We parked at the bottom of the hill, and in front of us was a great Roman causeway, curving up the hill towards some quite complete ruins. There were beacon-posts on the summits, watchtowers and guard-posts on all the passes, which showed how highly valued these mines had once been. We crunched our way round the lower structures where the miners would have lived. Most would have been cramped dormitories, locked and guarded by soldiers, but the high end of one faced east and was built in three tiers, with the best pottery fragments scattered around it. It might have been a church.

The mining here was primitive. Donald McAlister had warned in his 1900 report to the *Geographical Journal* that: 'The anci-ents simply excavated, in the likely emerald-bearing schist, a network of long and very tortuous passages just large enough to allow of the body being dragged through.' He and his com-panions had spent several weeks at Sikait visiting more than a hundred mines, 'some of which took more than an hour to crawl through'.

We found many caves above the ruined settlement, each with a number painted in faded white pigment on the outside; the highest number we found was 91. I wondered whether they might have been McAlister's markings. Most of the tunnels were shallow and when I shone my torch into them I could see the back wall; others went straight down into deep shafts and were impossible to explore without ropes.

Then I found a cave on which the markings had rubbed off. There was a short tunnel from the entrance, and what appeared to be a deep drop beyond. I squeezed down the passage, then dropped into the labyrinth about two metres below. At last – here was an emerald mine to explore. Three tunnels led off from there, and the chisel marks of long-dead miners were like graffiti leading me down. I couldn't help wondering whether the men who had made them were slaves or free men. The archaeologists had been undecided: Dr Shaw said there was a word in hiero-glyphics spelled 'mšc' and pronounced *mesha*, which referred both to an army sent to war and conscripts sent to quarries. 'Military expeditions or quarrying expeditions were seen as similar – both involved going out to a remote and dangerous place, and not necessarily choosing to do so,' he had said.

We know nothing of conditions in the emerald mines, but in the second century BC the Greek historian Agatharchides described the situation in the Nubian gold mines, just a few hundred kilometres to the south: 'For the kings of Egypt collect together and consign to the gold mines those condemned for crimes, and prisoners of war and, in addition, those who have been the victims of unjust accusations . . . sometimes alone and sometimes together with their whole families. Those convicts, who are numerous and bound with fetters, work at their tasks continuously during the day and throughout the whole night, being allowed no respite at all and rigorously prevented from all possibility of escape. For barbarian soldiers who speak different languages are appointed to be guards so that the prisoners cannot corrupt any of their warders through conversation or some human appeal . . . This is accomplished with so much and such great toil, because nature, I believe, makes it clear that gold is laborious in origin . . . the desire for it is great and its employment lies between pleasure and pain.'[40] Perhaps if there was slavery at Sikait that is another reason for the distinct separation of the town and the mines: the owners had to make sure that the workers did not escape.

After a while the marks and scrapes on the tunnel walls seemed to resemble hieroglyphics and shapes – it was like gazing at the night sky over the desert and making pictures in it, a bat, a swan, a flying horse, a hornet . . . Except in this case the hornet at least was real and rather angry. I had knocked my hat against its nest – there were several on the ceiling, looking like a series of reversed egg-cups which of course is almost what they are – and it was trying to attack me. I ducked my head, ignored it and crept on. This place went on for miles: I kept checking back to make sure I knew my way back to the light as the multiple tunnels divided, then swung underneath themselves and round corners, always going down. Then I realised I was approaching a large, deep hole. I moved forward, and a white-bellied creature flew up into my face. At first I thought it was a bat, but it was more like a martin, with its beak open, sounding an alarm. It was joined by its mate and they both flew up and around me, then back up the tunnel. How many generations was it since someone had disturbed their ancestors on their nest? Perhaps the last people to do so had been the three Cornishmen who came with the British expedition a hundred years ago, and who must have been realising by then that however many mines they crept through they would never find valuable seams of jewels. Like me, they had reached the mines, but had not found the emeralds.

Mohammed outside tunnel 91

In the emerald mine

Then, as I paused at the side of the deep underground well I saw something that made me glad I had gone so far. There, balancing on the edge of the precipice, was a small flash of green, a little emerald crystal. It was not worth anything because it was full of gardens and fractures – deeply flawed and fascinating, like Queen Cleopatra herself – but it gave me my first real sense of the elation in finding something sparkling amid the silence and darkness of an ancient mine. Had the others not been waiting anxiously several hundred metres above me, I might have gone on searching for hours to find more of them – better, prettier, bigger – until, as had happened to Frédéric Cailliaud on Emerald Mountain two centuries before, my torch began to give out.

The Jewel in the Crown

Two days later, it was late afternoon in Cairo's Egyptian Museum. The place was full of cases and crates in dark corners, as if everything had just arrived from somewhere, or was about to be packed up to go somewhere else, although that is how the museum always is. I had found Cleopatra's emerald mines, discovered their stories[41] and discarded crystals. But I had not yet seen the precious green stones for which those unnamed slaves or conscripts toiled underground for so many years. I had hoped to find little emerald rings, so tiny that they could only have fitted on the fingers of children, or on the top joints of adult fingers, which, according to pictures and statues, is how they were sometimes worn.[42] But despite Egypt's reputation for mining these stones, I had so far found no emeralds in the museum. Perhaps Propertius' dream of his dead girlfriend's ring was an indication not only of the lasting nature of passion but also of a Roman habit of burning rings with the one who had owned them, which would explain why so few remain.

The guards had called closing time, and I was about to leave when, in the last room, far from the other visitors to the museum, and in a dusty case, I caught sight of two crowns. They were old-fashioned, like the headgear worn by kings in children's books, and the marks where the silver had been hammered into shape were still apparent. They had been found in the graves of a fifth-century king and queen of Ballana, in Nubia. Almost nothing remains of them: not their names, not their dates, not their achievements – indeed, we don't even understand their written language. We have only their bones, some of their belongings and the crowns, which, when their burial mound was excavated in the 1930s, were still placed optimistically on their heads, showing they had claimed kingship in the next life as well as in this one. The silver crowns are inset with jewels. Most are red carnelians but at the front, just beneath the silver images of rams that were symbolic of sovereignty to these forgotten people, there are two green emeralds. They are big stones, the size of quails' eggs, still in their natural hexagonal form, and they are much darker than the emeralds with which we are familiar from Colombia. But although they are dulled, without a flash or scintillation to make us desire them in this century, the fact that they were placed so prominently on the Nubian crowns suggests that, for that culture at least, Egyptian emeralds had been the most valuable stones in the world.

But, like the reigns of the Nubian kings, the Ptolemies, the Roman emperors or any earthly dynasty, the time of Egyptian emeralds would pass. The mines continued, on and off, until the sixteenth century and then, with the exception of the pasha's experiment in the 1810s and a few later unsuccessful attempts in the early twentieth century after McAlister's expedition, they closed for ever. Partly because the existing seams were running out but, more importantly, in the early sixteenth century a much greater source was found that would outclass all of the emeralds that had ever been known in the Old World.

Colombia

When Spanish settlers first landed on the shores of America in the early sixteenth century they had guns in their hands and stories in their heads. The guns were mightier weapons than anything the local people had, and the stories – of fabulous hoards of gold and precious stones – were the reason they were there, in the belief that such things would make them happy. When the Spanish colonial machine first ground into gear after Columbus found the New World in 1492 it was hard to persuade men to leave their homes and travel as strangers to a strange and dangerous land. But once the legends of treasure started spreading through the exciting diaries of Amerigo di Vespucci and others, published in a deliberate PR exercise[43] by the authorities, volunteers signed up in their thousands.

The most famous myth was about a city built entirely of gold, which became known as El Dorado. But another story that drove the early conquistadors insane with greed was about an enormous emerald. It was first recorded by a man who called himself Garcilaso the Inca: his father had been an army captain who arrived in Peru in the 1530s, and his mother was an Incan princess. In Manta, he wrote, on the Peruvian sea coast, 'there used to be people who worshipped an emerald that was as big as an ostrich's egg. On feast days it would be taken out from the temple and shown to the crowds of people who had walked for many miles to see it.'[44] He recounted how the priests had devised a clever system of wealth accrual: they persuaded the ordinary people that small emeralds were the daughters of the sacred stone, and that no other gift would be quite as well received as the return of its children. In this way they had accumulated an incomparable treasury of emeralds, and although when the conquistadors arrived the sacred stone was long gone, its precious daughters remained locked in the temple treasure chests 'and were discovered by Pedro de Alvarado and his companions, among whom was my father, Garcilaso de la Vega'.[45]

But this treasure trove was not enough: the Spanish wanted more. The local people didn't want to tell them anything – they believed that the light in the stones was the essence of divinity, and they wanted to protect them. But the rack, the bonfire and other techniques honed by the Spanish Inquisition were ultimately more persuasive, and the source was revealed as a dramatic mountain ridge seventy-five kilometres north-east of what is now Bogotá. There, in 1537, the Spanish opened their first emerald mines, in a place they called Chivor, named after the Chibcha people who had once been the landowners and were now slaves. It was the same area from which the myth of El Dorado had sprung, based on the tradition that once a year the local king-priest was carried to the centre of the lake of Guatavita where his attendants covered him with clay and gold dust until he glittered. In the culmination of the ritual, this representative of the sun-god dived into the sacred waters as his subjects threw in their emeralds, or statues made of beaten gold.[46]

The stones were better than anyone in Europe, Asia or Africa had ever seen. Most Egyptian emeralds were pale, full of flaws and rather small. These gems were different: they had formed in a different way from the schist deposits of Sikait, having been created millions[47] of years ago when the Andes mountain ranges were being formed. At that time hot water was forced up through layers of sediments to the surface, dissolving and carrying with it the elements that make up emeralds. In most places the water simply dissipated when it reached the air, but in some areas it met an impermeable layer of black shale and was forced to stop. As the pressure built up, the water formed underground pools, some of which cooled slowly, allowing crystals to form at the edges. This process means that the Colombian gemstones are often larger and clearer than those found elsewhere. It also means that if you come across thick black shale in the Andes there is a chance, at least, that you will find emeralds too. When you think of 'emerald green' it is probably the Colombian shade that comes to mind: a brassy, grassy, saturated colour at the very centre of the rainbow spectrum. And if the Chivor stones were good, the stones from a new mine, found in 1567, were even better. It was called Muzo, 105 kilometres north of what is now Bogotá, and it was the best emerald mine in history.

The market went mad for the new jewels. The missionary Joseph d'Acosta wrote in an account[48] of his years spent in the New World that the ship that brought him back to Spain in 1587 carried two chests in its hold, each containing a hundred-weight of emeralds, weighing around half a million carats – about a hundred kilos. The wreck of the *Nuestra Señora de Atocha*, which sank in 1622 off the coast of Florida and was located by divers in 1985, gives a more physical idea of the extent of the trade: more than six thousand uncut stones have been found around it, as well as several pieces of elaborate emerald jewellery. One of the archaeological assistants recalled an extraordinary moment. One day when he was working underwater 'he looked up and saw hundreds of sparkling green emeralds floating down through the water toward him'. They had been sucked up in an underwater 'vacuum cleaner' used to clear silt from the wreck. 'The airlift released the jewels just under the surface of the water and everyone caught in the emerald rain shower delightedly picked up as many of the "rain-drops" as they could.'[49] But, dramatic as it was, the shower represented only a fraction of the treasure that went down with the ship. A document unearthed by Mel Fisher, who found the wreck, suggests that there might still be more than 125,000 carats – or 25 kilos – of emeralds still to find. And the *Atocha* was only one ship out of a fleet of three, making just one journey of so many across the Atlantic during those years.

In the first years the gems were worn almost exclusively by

the Spanish royal family, communicating their country's newly found (or newly stolen) wealth and power. The fashion at Castille in the sixteenth century was for dark clothes contrasted with white lace and collars so high that only the face and hands were revealed. Colourful jewellery[50] would alleviate the dullness, and the bright new emeralds and pearls from North America were perfect. From the middle of the sixteenth century the fashion was adopted by virtually all of the European courts.

However, one of the most important factors in deciding the value of any gemstone is neither its beauty nor its welcome brightness against a black dress, but its scarcity. In 1150 the Muslim lapidary writer Teifaschi had valued emeralds above diamonds, rubies and sapphires because at the time they were the rarest. But when emeralds were coming in by the half-million carat-load for more than a century after the conquest of the Americas, the market virtually collapsed. In his English lapidary of 1652, Thomas Nicols told the story of a Spaniard in Italy showing a jeweller an emerald 'of an excellent lustre and forme'. The jeweller valued it at a hundred ducats. Then the Spaniard showed him an even larger, finer one, which he valued at three hundred ducats. 'The Spaniard drunke with this discourse carried him to his lodging, shewing him a casket full. The Italian seeing so great a number of emeralds, sayde unto him, "Sir, these are well worth a crowne [about one-eighth of a ducat] a peece."'

If the *Atocha* had made it past Key West without catching a storm then its pretty green cargo would have been unloaded in Cadíz, and sold on in small lots to Europe, but also to Persia (now Iran) and India, where shahs and maharajahs paid immense prices to own the world's most beautiful emeralds. Emeralds carried a strong sacred symbolism for Muslims. Green was the colour of the Prophet Muhammad's cloak, and it was therefore the colour of Islam, as can be seen from the flags of many Islamic nations today. By wearing emeralds, the Middle

Eastern and Mughal rulers were not only demonstrating that they were impossibly wealthy and powerful: they were showing that they were protected by Allah.

By the seventeenth century there were so many South American emeralds in the Middle East and India that when the French jeweller Jean-Baptiste Tavernier visited in the late 1670s he was moved to remark that no true emeralds occurred in the East at all. 'The majority of jewellers and artisans, when they see an emerald of high colour inclining to black, are still accustomed to call it an Oriental emerald in which they are mistaken,' he wrote from India. 'It is true that since the discovery of America quite a few rough stones have often been carried by the Southern Sea from Peru to the Philippine Islands, whence they have been exported in due course to Europe, but that does not justify these being called "oriental" ,' he added strictly.

The Topkapi Dagger

Among the most famous emeralds in the Islamic world are three huge South American stones, set in the shaft of a dagger. It is called the Topkapi Dagger and is one of the most precious items in the Topkapi Palace Museum in Istanbul, although the fact that it is owned by Turkey rather than Tehran is just a matter of timing. In 1747 the newly commissioned dagger was one of the celebrity items in a chest of gifts sent from the Ottoman Sultan Mehmed I to Persia's ruler Nadir Shah in a gesture of thanks for a nice new throne and some political favours. But the Ottoman ambassadors had hardly reached Baghdad when they heard that Nadir Shah had been assassinated in an uprising. So, with diplomatic pragmatism they turned back, taking the dagger with them.

Had it arrived at its intended destination it would most certainly have been included today in an even more spectacular collection: the Iranian royal treasury. Officially the Islamic

Republic of Iran disapproves of its jewellery collection. 'The Treasury on one hand depicts the culture and civilisation of the Iranian people who have had an adventurous past,' explain the curators,[51] 'and on the other hand repeats the silent tears of oppressed people who worked hard [so that] the rulers could show off their arrogance and power with their gold and jewels.' It is a reminder, they say, of 'a bloody and painful history – a history that should under no circumstances be repeated again'.

The collection is lodged in the deep vaults of the Melli Bank in Tehran, as collateral[52] for the country's monetary system. It is, however, despite the reservations of its owners, on public view – although security is tight. Visitors have to pass through several metal detectors and thick security doors before they can see, in the half-light, some of the greatest treasures from the Muzo and Chivor mines, dotted among some of the greatest treasures from everywhere else. 'Holy schmoly!' exclaimed the young American visitor in front of me, and I had to agree: the collection is almost unrivalled in quantity and, sometimes, in quality. Most of the emeralds are 'old mine' because nothing like them has been found since those first intensive years of South American mining. The collection includes crowns, thrones, snuffboxes and bejewelled water-pipes. One crown weighs more than two kilos and was used by the last shah, Muhammad Reza Pahlavi. It contains 3380 small diamonds, two sapphires and 368 natural pearls, but its greatest gems are five large emeralds, totalling 199 carats. Muhammad Reza Pahlavi's father – a soldier who had toppled the then shah in 1923 – had designed it to resemble the crowns of the Persian Sassanid kings, who reigned from the third to the seventh century. He needed regalia to prove that he belonged in his new position and chose emeralds because they were the colour both of Islam and of ancient kings.

One of the last exhibits is a golden globe. It is encrusted with 51,000 precious stones that were sitting around loose in the

Treasury when Shah Nasser ud-Din decided to do something with them in 1869. His craftsmen's skills evidently lay more in jewellery-making than in geography: the land masses, in sapphires, rubies and diamonds, are very approximate, although an English visitor was impressed that Britain, in contrast with the rest of Europe, was traced entirely with diamonds. But the oceans are its glory, made entirely of vast, fathomless South American emeralds. Had it been created in a different century by better craftsmen it might have been a wonder. But in fact it is an ugly, pointless, excessive object – which is even more tragic when you consider its cost in human suffering, not only in Iran but half a world away, in Colombia.

The conditions at Chivor in the 'old mine' years were so inhumane that in 1593 the president of the New Kingdom of Granada, now Colombia, Panama, Venezuela and Ecuador, issued an unprecedented decree explicitly protecting the rights of the enslaved emerald-miners. Nine years later Philip III of Spain ordered that it should be enforced. But it was too late: too many local people had died, and production declined. In 1675 Chivor was closed, although Muzo continued working, first for the Spanish and later to satisfy French demand, led by Napoleon's quest for an empire like that of ancient Rome. But in the 1830s even Muzo's production faltered when it faced intense competition from another blockbuster discovery of emeralds, this time in the Urals of central Russia, where a charcoal-burner had seen something sparkle in the roots of a dead pine tree. As had happened in Egypt, the South American mines were virtually forgotten as the world's wealthy buyers rushed for something new.

By the late nineteenth century there was no longer any trace of Chivor's mines to be found at all. Which makes the achievement of Pacho Restrepo, an engineer, all the more remarkable. He did not have anything as useful as a treasure map to guide him: his only clue was a single sentence from a seventeenth-century manuscript that had been found in 1888 at a Dominican convent in Ecuador.[53] Chivor, it said, was located at a place 'where you could peer through a mountain pass and see the plains of the Orinoco River'. Restrepo spent eight years climbing mountains and peering through their passes, only too aware of how easy it would be to stand on the site, then walk away from it without realising he had arrived. In the end it was a combination of hunger, boredom and coincidence that found the mine for him. One day in 1896 one of his men caught sight of a groundhog-like animal, known as a *buruga*.[54] It fled down a hole and the man chased after it. When he emerged some minutes later, he wore a strange expression. 'Señor . . .' he said. He had found himself in a tunnel made by the picks of long-dead Indian slaves – and Restrepo realised that the mythical emerald mines of the Chibcha Indians were found once again.

The mines are still open today – although visiting them is foolhardy for all but the best-connected. The businesses are run by emerald barons as powerful as the cocaine kings, each mustering private armies, and the mountains around are full of armed smugglers and guerrillas. Kidnappings are frequent. At one point during my research I approached the American gemmologist Joe Tenhagen, who has visited the area regularly since the 1970s, and told him I was considering paying the mines a visit. 'How good are you with a gun?' he asked, looking at me doubtfully. 'Because you'll probably need to carry at least two.'

Don't Tell Anyone . . .

In 1994 Tom Chatham, son of the emerald inventor Carroll, went to the emerald fields of Muzo with a helicopter-full of international emerald-dealers. They had been invited by the mine-owners and were guarded by soldiers from the private armies. Chatham, who has been managing director of Chatham Created Gems since his father died in 1983, always carries a few samples in his pockets. He gave one miner a small synthetic crystal as a present. The man followed him, with urgent advice: '"You should keep this quiet," he whispered. "Don't tell anyone here." I said, "We've been in business for sixty-five years," and he said, "Not in South America you haven't." And then he suggested I go into business with him.' His father, Chatham said, had had so many underhand offers of 'business partnerships' that he had filled a thick folder called 'the Crazy File' with the most bizarre propositions.

'Was it not tempting to create emeralds that could be passed off as natural?' I asked Chatham, when I met him in his office in downtown San Francisco. Others had tried, he told me. Pierre Gilson, for example, was a maverick French scientist who made his name by creating opals, but had later fabricated turquoises and emeralds as well. 'He was a crafty guy. He thought it was great fun to let stones slip through the system,' Chatham said, playing absently with a small bowl of his own gems, letting them slip through his fingers as if they were little sweets. Other synthetic-stone producers are the same, he said, but for different reasons: 'They feel unappreciated and want to strike back at a system that doesn't help them.' He understands their point of view, 'But I always say to them, "Trust me, you won't make more money in the long run that way. The only way forward in our business is full disclosure."'

He said he had received an early lesson in the importance of trust in the synthetic gemstone business. 'Dad was a typical mad inventor,' he said fondly, and recalled the scars on his father's hands, gained from trying to reinvent fireworks when he was thirteen, and the plans he made to devise, in turn, a cure for cancer, a car that ran on atomic energy, and a way to desalinate ocean water that he hoped might end the world's water-shortage problems. Carroll Chatham had loved science more than business, gambled more than he invested, and preferred to spend his time in the laboratory, trying to make rubies, alexandrites, opals and sapphires (all successfully), rather than on the sales circuit refining his bottom line. This meant that, for the first two decades, he sold his entire production to a mysterious Englishman with an office in Lausanne and the ability to spin a line. 'Dad was a really simple guy in terms of business, so this was the easiest thing for him. But then when I became a teenager I started to ask this guy lots of questions,' Chatham remembered. 'I would ask him, "So where do you sell our products?" And he would blow me off with vague answers, saying they were polished in Idar-Oberstein in Germany, then sold in dozens of places.' But Chatham was not satisfied, and then the buyer made a crucial mistake: 'He offered me a Swiss bank account. He said, "How about we set up a little account for you, if you lay off these questions?" He was offering me fifty thousand dollars to keep my mouth shut,' Chatham said. 'And I said to Dad, "This is not good. We don't have the slightest idea of where we are doing business."'

Soon afterwards, when he had finished a degree in mathematics and chemistry, Chatham joined the company and took over the marketing. The key to their success, he decided, was in a new approach to selling. In Cleopatra's time, exclusivity had been a vital part of emeralds' appeal; for Chatham the key word was accessibility. 'Try going to any gemstone supplier around you and asking for ten emeralds of seven by five millimetres oval, matched colour,' he said. 'They'll give you a look to kill, and say it's impossible. It would take months.' So he did what the miners of natural stones would not do: he cut the crystals to order, sometimes ten thousand at a time. It cost dearly, with many of the emeralds ending up at only fifteen per cent of their original size, but at last after years of struggle, the big orders began to come in to the Chatham laboratory.

In the past only the rich could own precious gems like this – perfectly formed, brightly coloured emeralds with no enhancements. But now many more people can have fine emeralds, bought on the Internet or through their local television shopping channel for around $550[55] a carat (about a fifth of the price of a natural stone) ... and nobody but their neighbourhood gemmologist will ever be able to tell the difference.

Cleopatra would have hated it, but she was a creative, enterprising queen. She would simply have found something else that only she could own and display – and of which the rest of us could only dream.

Sapphire

'It frees a man from prison and looses heavy fetters; it is good
for effecting reconciliation and is better than any other stone
for seeing in the water the signs which reveal things hitherto
not known.' *Medieval lapidary*[1]

'Who would think that so pretty a toy would be a purveyor to
the gallows and the prison? I'll lock it up in my strong box
now, and drop a line to the Countess to say that we have it.'
SHERLOCK HOLMES, in 'The Adventure of the Blue Carbuncle'[2]

When I was twenty-three, my parents found a sapphire in the
secret drawer of a writing desk. They were not surprised to find
it – they had put it there themselves nearly thirty years before.
But they were surprised that they had forgotten it: it had been
one of the first gifts my father gave to my mother when they
met. At the time they couldn't afford to have it set into a ring,
so they hid it away in a manila envelope, and didn't think about
it for years. At the time of its rediscovery I had just lost all the
small jewels I owned: a topaz ring dropped into a river, gold
earrings ripped out in a mugging in New York, and an amber
bracelet stolen in a burglary. In fact so complete was my history
of jewellery loss that it began to look as if I wasn't supposed
to own any gems at all. So when my mother offered me the
sapphire I said no. I couldn't bear to lose it too. But later I
agreed and I still have it, set in a ring. I wear it all the time.
Whenever I visit my parents' home my father cleans it. When it
gets too opaque I know it's time for another visit.

After having been so indifferent about owning it, I was surprised to find that this little stone captivated me. I would look at its clarity and its pale, pure colour, and I would think of it growing slowly in the earth, a clear crystal in the midst of darkness. It gave me a sense of perspective: it had been around for so long. But I realised I had no idea how long, or how it had moved from the earth's crust to the surface. I imagined that it must have come from some kind of mine – perhaps one full of labyrinthine passages like the emerald mines of Egypt, or an open-cast one, like the amber mines of Russia. But I didn't know what kind of person it might have been mined by, or even how it had been cut. My only clue was that it had been bought on the island of Sri Lanka. So I decided to go there to find out more about it. Not because it is special, but because it is not. It is an ordinary gemstone, yet like most other ordinary gemstones it has a good story to tell, if you go looking for it.

The Island of Gems

Sri Lanka lies just fifty kilometres off the southern tip of India. For twenty years it has been shaken by civil warfare and when today people talk about that bloodshed they say their island is in the shape of a teardrop. When they think about the country's natural wealth they tend to describe it differently – as the shape of a jewelled pendant. It is a good description: Sri Lanka is one of the very rare locations where gemstones occur in abundance. It is literally a treasure island. It is said that King Solomon and the Queen of Sheba wooed each other with coloured stones from this place[3] and that the Ancient Egyptians imported gems from here too, placing them in their burial chambers to delight the dead in their next life.

The first local record of the gems of Sri Lanka appears in the Buddhist *Mahavamsa Chronicles*, dating from around the sixth century. They mention a 'gem-encrusted throne' that was fought over by two rival kings, an uncle and his nephew, in the northern part of the island. The younger king had inherited the throne from his mother but his uncle wanted it and they went to war. According to the *Chronicles*, the Buddha visited them, and taught them his philosophy of non-violence. When the kings realised their foolishness they decided to give him the throne. But he wanted them to learn to share their resources and to understand the illusion of worldly things, so he gave it back to them, saying they should both have it.

Europeans have told stories about the jewels from this island for more than two thousand years. In the third century BC, the historian Megasthenes came back from a diplomatic mission to India full of tales about an island to the south that had more gold and pearls than India itself, while Pliny called it the Island of the Antichthones, meaning 'the people who live at the opposite ends of the earth',[4] and described it as a paradise of democracy and fair-living.[5] He specially emphasised the island's natural wealth, saying that the people 'have a marble which resembles tortoiseshell, pearls also and precious stones, and these are all held in high honour. Their articles of luxury surpass our own, and they have them in great abundance.' However, he added, 'It appears that we excel them in the art of deriving enjoyment from opulence.'

Around 1294 Marco Polo, his father Niccolò and uncle Maffeo were probably the first[6] Europeans to visit the island, when they stopped off there for provisions and purchases on the long journey back from China. They had previously known it only from myths and market rumours and, as Polo said in his journals, they found it to be 'the finest island of its size in the world', partly because of its beauty, but mostly because 'from its streams come rubies, sapphires, topazes, amethysts and garnets'.[7] By then 'Seilan', as the Venetians called it, was already a recognised brand name for some of the most precious jewels in the world, and the Polos had seen the island's gemstones many times during their travels. Indeed, the great Kublai Khan, for whom the merchants had worked for seventeen years, had bags of jewels in his treasury, and he sometimes showed them to friends and visitors as a treat. The khan had cornered the market for gems, paying top prices to merchants who brought their stones to him although, as Polo noted, whatever prices the khan paid, he was always the real winner because he used paper currency, unknown in Europe at the time. 'He buys such a quantity of those precious things that his treasure is endless, whilst all the time the money he pays away costs him nothing at all,' Polo wrote, amazed at the credulity of people who would exchange gems and gold for little bits of paper. In one of only two jokes in his entire memoirs he commented that, when it came to acquiring gold and precious stones, 'you might say [the khan] hath the Secret of Alchemy in perfection, and you would be right!'[8]

The Chinese continued to set great store by the richness of Seilan long after the power of the Mongols had waned. At the beginning of the fourteenth century the Ming dynasty emperor sent an officer on the long journey to the island to buy a ruby of unusual lustre and size. It weighed more than 150 carats and was always brought out at parties. 'Every time a grand levée was held at night, the red lustre filled the palace and hence it was designated "The Red Palace-Illuminator"'.[9] The Chinese honoured the origin of the gems in their word for a certain variety of dark red ruby: they called it *si-lan-ni*, which probably came from their pronunciation of 'Seilan'.[10]

As befits a rich island that has been the centre of international trade since before its written history began, Seilan has had many names. The colonial Portuguese called it Cilão, the colonial Dutch Zeylan, and the colonial British Ceylon. The Indians called it Ratnadeep, meaning 'gem island', the inhabitants called it Sinhala, from the Sanskrit for 'people of the lion' and ever since 1972 it has been known throughout the world as Sri Lanka, meaning 'magnificent island', just as Marco Polo described it.

The Ancient Greeks called it Taprobane, confusing it with Sumatra, which is much further east, and the Arabs, who traded there for centuries, called it Serendib – from which, in the eighteenth century, the English writer Horace Walpole coined the word 'serendipity'. He was inspired by a fairy-tale about three princes from a distant island who 'were always making discoveries, by accident and sagacity, of things they were not in quest of',[11] suggesting to travellers ever since that marvellous, chance adventures could happen there.

Gem Scams

The frustrating thing about planning a journey was that my father could remember so little about buying my sapphire. I wanted him to tell me of how he went into a small dark shop one afternoon and, as cups of sweet milk tea were brought to him, he was shown more and more stones in order to choose just one. I wanted him to tell me how the salesman had played the age-old jeweller's trick of 'washing his eyes' by showing him poor-quality stones first, then moving on to finer ones so that he ached to buy the most expensive. I wanted to hear about the slim, long-fingered tweezers with which the stones had been handled as they were held up to the light. I wanted the whole story spun out as a thread to tie around my little stone, to understand it better. But although my father agreed it might have happened like that, he wasn't sure. 'It was more than forty years ago,' he protested. 'All I remember is that I bought it in a small shop in Colombo, near the Galle Face Hotel, and I tried to bargain hard.' So, hoping that serendipity would play its part, I arrived in the capital of Sri Lanka on a warm January day to find out more about the country's sapphires, and my own in particular.

The area around the hotel, near the fort, had probably not changed much in the past forty years. The traffic was probably worse and noisier and created a cloud of shimmering grey fumes somewhere below waist-level. But cocktails were still drunk on the elegant terrace, the faint thwack-applause sounds of a cricket match from the nearby club ground hung in the air, and on the ocean hundreds of container ships spread out to the horizon, testimony to the fact that this island has been trading with the rest of the world for thousands of years, and that trade is still brisk. I asked the concierge how I should set about discovering the origin of my stone, and he gave me some wise advice: 'Madam, a shop will not be likely to give the answers you require. Go to the National Gems Authority. They will help you, I am positive.'

The National Gems Authority, I learned, is the main place for buyers to have their precious stones tested. It is staffed by gem detectives, who are employed to tease the secrets from the stones and establish whether they are natural and, if so, whether they have been treated. It seemed an ideal place to start finding out more about my own sapphire. However, when I reached the address I had been given at the hotel, the building was empty. A man was sitting on the pavement outside eating a bright yellow sponge cake beneath a broken sign indicating that the Authority had been there once. 'It's moved,' he said, and he spat on the ground beside him. He didn't know where it had gone, but pointed to a handwritten notice pasted roughly on to the wall, which seemed to give directions to new premises just a short taxi ride away.

But there was a complication: sixty elephants were processing into town in preparation for a major Buddhist 'Poya' festival in Victoria Park, and it seemed that the entire population of Colombo was stuck in traffic behind them. As we waited, the driver talked about elephant parades. When rajahs ruled the island, they used sacred-elephant processions to show off their wealth. Every major feast day was marked with one, with the animals and their mahouts sparkling with rows upon rows of sapphires, topazes and rubies set all about them. It was a marvellous sight – and incidentally was very good for the gem business. A sapphire that has been set into an elephant's tusk and worn in a sacred parade was believed to have been blessed by the Buddha: 'They could sell them for twice the price if they said they had been worn by an elephant,' he added, blithely charging me what I later learned was exactly twice the normal price for a taxi fare.

As I wandered up and down a dusty street, looking for what I began to suspect was a non-existent address, a smart young man came up to me and asked if he could help. He appeared to know what I was looking for, walked me to a small shop, then disappeared. The door was unmarked and I had some reservations, but I went in anyway. A man was sitting in the dark, his face up-lit by a rainbow of stones in the display table in front of him so that blue and yellow lights danced round his chin, like the fairy dust around an animated cartoon genie. Was this the National Gems Authority? Perhaps, he said, shaking his head in the way that means assent in Sri Lanka. I showed him my ring and said I was looking for advice. He said his advice was that I took home a handful of sapphires and sold them for a profit. 'You will double your money, guaranteed,' he said. I said I was more interested in learning about stones than buying them, and he said he would help me do both. When I insisted, he became angry. 'Why do you not listen to me?' he shouted. 'I can make your fortune.' Two men in suits appeared silently from a side door and stood behind him, their hands behind their backs. I wanted to leave, but the manager still had my ring. 'OK,' I said. 'If I did buy stones to sell in England for a profit, then I'd like them to be just like the one in my ring. What is it? And how much does it weigh?'

We both looked at it again. What I saw was a pale blue oval stone, about the size of a sweetcorn kernel. It was a bit grubby, was set very simply in claws of white gold, and it was full of my own memories as well as being a reminder of my parents' love for each other. The jeweller would have seen something quite different. Dealers usually look at four factors: colour, cut, clarity and carat – known as the four Cs. There is however a fifth C, certificate, which is becoming equally important. The certificate informs buyers of whether or not their stone has been treated, heated, coloured, coated, dyed, diffused, lasered, oiled or sealed with epoxy resin, all of which are possible, and too many of which are hard to detect outside a laboratory.

The most valuable natural colours depend on both fashion and rarity, although it is a reliable rule that the most saturated stones, which reproduce the sparkle of sunshine after rain, are the most expensive. To achieve the highest price the cut must show the stone off to its best possible brilliance, and in terms of clarity, a stone should not be too milky, or have too many unsightly inclusions. But, of course, the final thing that makes all the difference is the weight.

The man was now squinting at my stone to assess how heavy it was. He couldn't weigh it without removing it from the setting so he had to make an approximation. He guessed that it was around one carat, and I found later that in this, at least, he was telling the truth, even though he used it to augment his sales pitch. 'You must buy some from me that are more than a carat for your maximum profit. They are cheaper with cash,' he added greedily. I was anxious now to leave, and asked to look at my ring again. When he held it out to me I took it, then headed straight for the door. I didn't look back, either at him or at his two tough colleagues.

I must look even more naïve than I am, I thought, as I walked down the street into a chaotic parade of elephants. The incident was depressing: on the Island of Gems, I evidently had 'dupe' written across my forehead. Still, I had at least found out how much my stone weighed and had avoided being cheated out of any money, and an hour later I had also found the real National Gems Authority. When I arrived, the receptionist tersely pointed to the clock, which read '16.48'. The Authority had closed three minutes before, and would not open again for several days because of the holiday. However, she took pity and I was shown through to an almost empty room in which a man was sitting on a chair. Surreally, this was the only furniture: the desks had still not arrived. When I told him of my quest he pulled some papers out of his briefcase and began to fill in a form, resting it on his knee. It was in triplicate, with lots of filmy bits of carbon paper. Blue carbon paper is very common in Sri Lanka, not only because of the bureaucracy but also because it is one of the simplest ways to 'improve' poorly coloured sapphires. If you roll a pale, uncut stone in carbon paper, enough blue will lodge in the pores to make it look like a fine gem with a rich colour . . . although of course as soon as you start cutting, the sapphire's ordinary colour returns.

The form-filling had gone on for several minutes when the door opened and a man rushed in. He spoke rapidly in Sinhalese, then turned to me. I explained about my sapphire and he held it up to the light shining through the windows. There were gem deposits all over the southern two-thirds of Sri Lanka, he said, and you can rarely know for certain which area a stone has come from. 'There's Rakwana, Gampata, Elahera . . . so many. But it's blue like cornflowers and it has a little violet in it . . . it looks like it's from Ratnapura.' He then took out a loupe, which is a small jeweller's magnifying-glass, and held it close to both the stone and his eye to examine it. 'This was bought a long time ago,' he said. 'Maybe fifty or sixty years?' How did he know? He laughed. 'Nobody cuts like this any more.' And he was gone. 'He doesn't work here,' said the man from the Authority, putting away his forms and preparing to go home. 'He was just visiting.' But although I didn't find out who he was, he had given me the clue I needed. The next day I left early for the township whose name literally means 'the city of gems'.

Many of us have read about the city of gems even if we don't

A nineteenth-century woodcut of Sinbad the Sailor on his raft

remember it. It appears, unnamed, in the story of the Sixth Voyage of Sinbad the Sailor. In that adventure the hero is ship-wrecked on an unknown shore, and just as he is succumbing to the usual traveller's self-recriminations (along the lines of 'Why did I come to this awful place when I was doing so well at home?') he notices a flow of water going into a cavern from the seashore. Listeners who have already swallowed stories of flying carpets and cannibals in previous adventures, need only a small leap of faith to join Sinbad on a home-made raft drifting inland along the river. He then notices something strange about it, apart from the direction of the flow. The 'banks were covered with glittering jewels and the bed was studded with myriads of rubies, emeralds and other precious stones, so that the entire river blazed with a dazzling light',[12] and the river soon carries Sinbad to a wealthy, democratic town where he makes his fortune.

The story is based on real-life accounts by Muslim travellers of going to Serendib from around the fourteenth century.[13] The river Sinbad sailed along so merrily is today called the

Kaluganga. It still winds its way down from the ancient gem city of Ratnapura before meeting the sea at the small town of Kalutara. But, most importantly, according to all reports, it still carries gemstones in its flow.

The City of Gems

My own journey to the city of gems was not on a raft flowing up a gleaming river, but in a small and smelly minivan, which tooted its way along muddy roads for three hours from Colombo, climbing slowly away from the sea and upwards into the hills, past numerous tiny villages where children played cricket barefoot beneath sheltering palms. It dropped me at a petrol station on the main street of a dusty town, and looking around it was hard to believe that this was the place that fairy-tales were made of.

On first impression Ratnapura was a rough, brown-coloured town with rough, brown-coloured roads. Everything was corrugated-iron, wood and unstable concrete, and it seemed that there were far more shoe-shops and poorly stocked grocery stands than jewellery stores. There were few immediate signs that since at least 600 BC this had been one of the world's most important sources of gems – even the Sapphire Snooker and Gaming Hall had seen better days. However, somewhere behind all those tatty shoes and shutters, there had to be the successors of the smart-talking traders who had sold their sapphires to Marco Polo. They were still there doing business in the city of gems, I knew. It was just a matter of finding them.

I was lucky to have got this far. The area was once a secret military zone owned and controlled by the royal family, and foreigners had no business here. The British first learned about it in 1762, forty years before they officially took control of Ceylon.[14] That year John Pybus, an employee of the East India Company, was sent to the island on a secret mission. The King of Kandy, which was then the royal capital, had recently sent an agent to Madras asking for help in ejecting the Dutch colonists who had long outstayed their welcome. The ignorance of the British about Ceylon is shown by the very basic questions Pybus was told to ask. He had to find out whether the king controlled the whole island, what the weather was like, what the people believed in, whether they mostly lived in towns or villages, what forts the Dutch had set up and, most importantly, the potential for trade. Without a clear promise of financial returns, the East India Company had no intention of doing anything for anyone.

Pybus gleaned plenty of information about the main commodities, cinnamon, pepper, pearls and elephants, but nothing on precious stones: 'There are several parts of the Island under the King's Jurisdiction, at which Guards are constantly kept, and where Rubies, Sapphires, Topazes and Stones are to be found, but they cannot be dug for without the King's express orders, for all that are found are reserved for his use,' he wrote with disappointment.

Although Pybus did not see where the precious stones came from, he did at least discover where most of them ended up. The handwritten account[15] of his journey through the palace at Kandy makes delightful reading, not least because of his numerous arguments with court officials about etiquette as he resisted requests to remove his hat and his shoes. Pybus was also asked to kneel before the throne – which to him was the last straw. He might have done well to recall the Greek story – popular among gem historians – of Ismenias,[16] who was sent as an envoy to the Persian king in the middle of the fourth century BC. Like Pybus, he was instructed to prostrate himself before the throne and, also like Pybus, found the idea demeaning. Instead he took off his gem-encrusted ring and dropped it, 'whereupon he stopped and picked it up', satisfying both the king's desire for respect, and his own desire for self-respect.

Pybus was less wily than Ismenias and eventually submitted to palace protocol. But when he looked up sulkily from the carpet he was impressed to see that the king of the Land of Gems was glittering and shimmering as he sat in his ceremonial hall. 'The Upper Garment seemed an open Robe of Gold Tissue with a close vest underneath and a broad belt richly embroidered with Gold round his Waist,' Pybus reported. 'He had upon his Head a Cap of Scarlet Cloth Embroidered with Gold much in the form of an American Cap, upon the top of which was a small Crown set with Precious Stones, several rings on his fingers, a short Dagger in his left hand, the Hilt of which was Gold set with Precious Stones.'[17]

Pybus did not name those stones, though when the last King of Kandy was finally captured by the British in 1815 his treasure house was found to be full of rubies, white topazes, yellow cats' eyes, and most of all of sapphires: the stones believed by the kings to protect them from harm.

Sapphires have also been royal stones in the West for many centuries. The oldest European crown still in existence[18] – made for the seventh-century King Recceswinth of the Visigoths – includes a circle of gold set with sapphires and pearls, with an extraordinary fringe of twenty-four pear-shaped sapphires hanging from it, like the corks on an Australian hat. Unlike many other gemstones, whose fortunes have ebbed and flowed, sapphires have maintained their status. The British coronation ring, 'the Wedding Ring of England', is designed round a central sapphire. It was made for the coronation of William IV in 1831 and has been worn at every coronation ceremony since – except that of Queen Victoria, whose fingers were so small that the ring could not be reduced to fit. A new ring was made, although unfortunately it was forced on to the wrong finger, 'causing Queen Victoria to be in great pain'.[19]

Perhaps sapphires owe their staying power as royal stones to their parallel status as holy stones. A famous example is

Edward the Confessor giving his sapphire to the beggar

St Edward's Sapphire, probably the oldest stone in the British Crown Jewels. It was first supposedly set in the coronation ring of Edward the Confessor, who became king in 1042. According to legend, one night Edward met a beggar, and gave the man his ring. Years later, some of the king's envoys in Syria met an old man at an inn. He said his name was John the Evangelist and asked them to return the sapphire to the king with a message that they would meet again soon – in paradise. Soon afterwards, in January 1065, Edward died and was buried with the ring on his finger. It has since been disinterred, and is set in the centre of the cross on Britain's Imperial State Crown. Recent tests have proved that the stone originated in Sri Lanka.

Soon after the death of Edward the Confessor, sapphires became the bishops' gemstone of choice.[20] This was partly because their colour is symbolic of heaven, but also because in medieval times sapphires were believed to soothe discord and promote pure thoughts – which was particularly appropriate after the eleventh century when all priests were required to be celibate. Today bishops often choose amethysts rather than sapphires. Not only do these purple stones represent the communion wine but they are also cheaper – useful now that bishops have to pay for their own rings. The current Archbishop of Canterbury, Rowan Williams, wears an amethyst, a gift from his wife's father who was also a bishop. I asked him whether he thought of the communion wine when he looked at his ring. 'Actually,' he smiled, 'I usually just think of my father-in-law.'[21]

The Most Beautiful Sapphires in the World

It might once have been a place where holy stones were found in plenty but over the next two days I found Sri Lanka's city of gems a hard place, abrasive as corundum. It was as if the people were so used to looking down at the ground searching for treasures that they did not look up to welcome a stranger. I grew to recognise a low scream, coming from unmarked doors: it was the sound of lapidary wheels grazing against sapphires and polishing them into facets, and several times I stepped from the street into small rooms where young women sat in the dark, lit by a single overhead bulb, cutting tiny stones the size of match heads. When I asked their managers if I could learn to cut I was told it was impossible. 'Not in Ratnapura, madam. Buying you can do, cutting you cannot,' said one man with firm courtesy.

To try to find out more about where sapphires come from, I went to a private gem museum just outside town. It was closed when I got there, but the white-clad owner, Mr Purandara Sri Bhadra Marapana, opened the door with an energetic,

'One, two, three, four,' as he shot the bolts. It was full of dusty minerals, each labelled with their place of origin, and it was here that I learned in just how many places sapphires are found. I was astonished to discover that sapphire is the only precious stone ever to have been found in Britain, with a small but historic discovery made in the 1980s on the island of Lewis in the Outer Hebrides.[22] Brazil, Burma, Laos, Madagascar, Nigeria, Thailand and Hainan Island in China have all yielded good-quality stones. In China, a source was discovered in the 1960s by a farmer who was paid just 1.6 yuan, or less than a dollar, for his pains.[22]

The best stones in the USA came from Montana after Jake Hoover, a 'hard-drinking womanising raconteur,'[23] stumbled over blue pebbles in the Lower Yogo Creek in 1894. The resulting sapphire rush lasted until 1923, with some 2.5 million carats found to supply the dizzy high spending of the Jazz Age. The Australians started to find sapphires at around the same time as the Americans, but although some were first class, most were ink-dark and, in the early years at least, the term 'Australian sapphire' was something of an insult. However, new treatments have changed all this. Many Australian sapphires are exported to Cambodia or Thailand and sold as local stones. By that time many are unrecognisable: they have been doped with heat and so many chemicals that they look bright and alert, like the Asian sapphires they are sometimes claimed to be.

Sri Lanka has always been the chief source of sapphires although, as the gem museum explained cheerfully, it has not always been the best. That place was held – for a decade in the late-nineteenth century – by a remote hillside in the Himalayas. The discovery of Kashmir sapphires is the subject of many conflicting stories, but the one thing they have in common is the element of serendipity. In one version, a hunter clambered away from the main trail, looking for a piece of quartz to act as a flint in his rifle but instead found a dark stone that did the

The Angel of Yowah

A mullock hill in
moonlight,
Coocoran opal
field, Australia

Len Cram's jars
of homemade
opals

The Canning Jewel: a baroque pearl in the
shape of a merman's torso

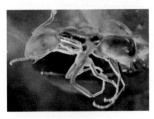

Our Lady of Częstochowa: clothed in amber at St Bridget's in Gdansk

Forty-million-year-old insects in Baltic amber

Amber for sale in Mariacka street in Gdansk

Christ in Judgement. From the Pala d'Oro altar in Venice

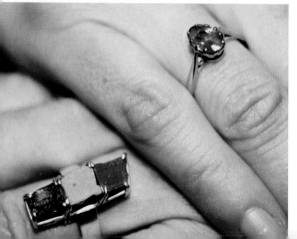

The author's sapphire
from Sri Lanka; and
her engagement ring
made of mosaic
stones from
Constantinople

The Byzantine Empress
Theodora, with emeralds.
Ravenna, Italy

Franklin at Peridot, Arizona

The Valley
of Emeralds:
Zubara in
Egypt, with
the walls of
the houses
still clearly
visible

Tom Chatham, with an emerald
made in California

Roman Mummy Portrait:
Egyptian woman with an
emerald necklace, from the
second century

Miners in Sri
Lanka look for
sapphires in
Sinbad's river

A Sri Lankan illam miner prepares to descend into the sapphire mine without a ladder

Pink umbrellas in the ruby market of Mogok

Mogok Lake, where rubies once were mined

The diamond quarter of Antwerp

The Hope diamond illustrated in
Edwin Streeter's book

Watching the Hope.
At the Smithsonian
in Washington

job much better – until it was recognised as a precious gem. In another version the sapphire arrived in the hill station of Simla with a cargo of borax. The merchant who was checking it threw it on to the street, hitting a man called Alexander Jacob. As well as being the inspiration for Kipling's charismatic Lurgan Sahib (who teaches Kim how to spy) Jacob was one of the most important jewellers in India. He recognised the ammunition, walked into the shop and offered to pay for information on where it had come from.

Whichever version is true, the sapphires came from just south of the Zanskar valley where there had been some sizeable landslides in 1880. By spring 1882 the area was crowded with coolies, miners and geologists, living in tent villages at 13,100 feet. Most trekked for a week to get there, following narrow paths and crossing gorges on shaky rope bridges. In the beginning they were removing stones as 'large as polo balls' from the site and selling them privately, but by August the Maharajah of Kashmir had sent his own regiment to take possession, and all private mining enterprise was forbidden. Even today a law in Jammu and Kashmir state dictates that no one may possess sapphires without a licence.[24]

The sapphire rush lasted only a decade before the seams ran out. Occasionally there are rumours that mining operations are planned but so far all attempts have been unsuccessful: little more has been found in those mountains. However, in those few glory years, Kashmir stones were identified as the most beautiful sapphires ever found. Today they are the standard against which all others are measured. 'Velvety' is the word most often used of them although it is not adequate to describe the experience of looking at one. It is like swimming through a pool of tropical water, like the iridescence on a peacock's neck, like the moment, in the mountains, before a storm begins.

The closest visual match to a Kashmir sapphire today is not a sapphire at all, but a stone called tanzanite, discovered in

1967 near Mount Kilimanjaro in Tanzania. This intense violet-coloured jewel – which has been described as the colour of film star Elizabeth Taylor's eyes, or as what sapphires would look like, if they could[25] – is among the top five stones currently being bought in the United States, thanks partly to its availability on retail TV channels like HSN, QVC or the Gem Shopping Network. Tanzanites were the first gemstones to achieve celebrity not because they were worn by a film star, but because they *were* a film star. In 1997, *Titanic* was framed around the fictitious story of a blue diamond that was lost along with the ocean liner. However, according to film lore,[26] when the director James Cameron was looking around for an appropriate stone he rejected blue diamonds because they appeared too dark, and blue sapphires because they appeared too dull. Instead, he decided, the stone to play the role of his diamond would be a tanzanite.

Serendipity

After all his energy in opening his little gem museum and showing me round, Mr Purandara Sri Bhadra Marapana sank into a kind of funk when it came to talking about the stones. He had never wanted to be a gemmologist, he admitted. In fact, the whole thing had been an unfortunate accident. Ratnapura children collect stones as others swap stamps or trading cards. 'You buy a few and sell a few. If you lose your pocket money you do something else. If you double it you go into gems.' He had more than doubled his money, and it was only later, as an adult, that he realised he didn't really like jewellery. 'It doesn't suit me,' he said, spreading out bare hands. 'The only things I wear are my two wooden rosaries.' Did he know where I could learn to cut or identify stones? 'Not really,' he said. 'I do not think you will find someone who will teach you. Ratnapura is not that kind of place.'

His *ennui* was catching. I had followed other false trails during my first few days in Ratnapura, and it was beginning to seem that the origin of my sapphire would prove more elusive than I had thought. However, it was just then, on my return to town in a three-wheeler taxi, that serendipity kicked in.

'Short-cut?' suggested the driver. I agreed. Later I learned it was a long-cut – we were after all running on the meter – but the money was well spent. A mile before town we passed a sign advertising 'Ratna Gems Halt: Family Hotel and Lapidary', and I stopped the taxi and went in. It was a simple guesthouse built on a hillside so it was all steps. A good-looking young man was sweeping the upper floor. There was a room available, he confirmed, and there was also a gems shop, which was owned by his father-in-law. After I had booked in, he took me down to the lower level where the family lived. Next to the house there was a plain room with a white-tiled floor and the shutters closed. At the back I saw an unattended lapidary wheel, and at the front a man sitting at a desk. He had a torch on his forehead and as he stood up the light shone in my eyes. He introduced himself as Jayarathna Watadeniya, the young man's father-in-law. He was a big man with a relaxed expression, and I liked him immediately.

I explained that I had come to Ratnapura to learn about gems, but it was hard to find anyone to teach me. Did he have any advice? He paused, assessing me with his dealer's eye. Yes, he said at last. If I wanted to learn, he could teach me about stones. He handed me a bundle of much-thumbed gemstone books in English and French. 'Read these,' he said, 'and tomorrow you will have your first lesson about sapphires.'

Sapphires Are Not Always Blue

It turned out that the lesson would involve a trip with Jayarathna to the gem market. But before that I had preparatory homework to do. First, for example, I had to absorb the surprising fact that sapphires are not always blue: they can be brown, yellow, white, purple, pink, green or even orange. They can even be several colours at once: green at one end and blue at the other, or yellow striped with pink, like a sponge cake. Some sapphires can even be green in the daytime and violet-blue at night, in which case they are called 'colour-change' and – if they are natural – are expensive. A tri-coloured sapphire sold in London in the nineteenth century was cut into a figure of the Chinese sage Confucius: the head was colourless, the body pale blue, and the legs yellow,[27] like a tropical beach scene under a morning haze.

The only colour that sapphires cannot be is red, because 'red sapphires' are actually rubies. The only difference between sapphires and rubies is that rubies contain chromium – meaning, curiously, that the element which makes emeralds green also makes rubies red – and sapphires contain iron and titanium. Although Indian scholars have known since ancient times that rubies and sapphires were twins,[28] Europeans were slow to catch on. It was not until 1782 that the French scientist Romé de l'Isle looked at the two gemstones under his microscope and saw that they were crystallographically similar. The study was taken up by Abbé René-Just Haüy, who had had plenty of time to think about it when he was imprisoned during the French Revolution. His captors thoughtfully provided him with crystal samples and a microscope to enable him to continue his experiments undisturbed in his cell. He described ruby and sapphire as a single species of mineral, which he admiringly called '*télésie*', meaning 'a perfect body'. Today we call it 'corundum', from the Sanskrit 'kuruvindam', meaning ruby.

Today most of the non-blue or -red samples of this perfect-bodied gem are described in English as 'fancy' – as if they had been forged by caprice or whimsy. However, until about a hundred years ago they were generally known as 'Oriental'. Purple fancies were called 'Oriental amethysts' and for a long time were more valuable than diamonds. They are still rare, and today the finest come from Burma, Sri Lanka and Vietnam. In the nineteenth century the most famous purple sapphire in Europe was owned by the banker Henry Hope, and 'it has the peculiar property of transmitting by day-light the most beautiful and perfect violet colour; but by candlelight a decided blue'.[29] The most prized of all fancy sapphires are those known in Sri Lanka as 'the colour of lotus flowers'. In Sinhalese the word is '*padmaraga*'; English has inherited it via a German mispronunciation and so we call it 'padparadscha', by a sort of mistake. The Natural History Museum in New York owns the biggest natural padparadscha in the world: it weighs 100 carats and is a deliciously energetic colour, like papaya.

The difficulty for buyers is that a new treatment has been developed in Thailand, called 'beryllium bulk diffusion', which involves cooking low-quality pink sapphires with a solution of beryllium oxide to make them appear a delicate padparadscha orange. Some can be detected by looking for a pale yellow line enveloping the pink like a halo. However, recently the American Gem Trade Association warned that[30] treaters have found a way to diffuse the yellow aura through the stone so it cannot be distinguished with the naked eye. This was just one of the tricks I would have to look for in the gem market.

Gem Market

The next day we went to the main street-market for all these fancy gems, which takes place almost every morning on the edge of Ratnapura. It is not a market in the usual sense with stalls and stands. Instead, it is more like a cross between a stock exchange and a school playground, with traders rushing around to show each other their latest finds. White is believed to be an auspicious colour so they all wear fresh white shirts and lungis. The more successful traders were wearing new cotton; the clothing of the poorer ones had been washed so often in laundry blue that it had a purple shimmer.

This was where Jayarathna had started trading as a young miner, swapping stones for cash at the edge of the market. Today his circumstances have changed and he drives into town every morning in a large four-wheel-drive vehicle, and sets up in the middle of the street. As one of the well-known Ratnapura buyers he can sit in comfortable air-conditioning waiting for the traders to come to him. And that was how he did it, with the car windows open and an anxious crowd outside. He showed me how to hold out my hand for the gems to be placed on it, then to look at each stone carefully through a loupe, the glass held close to my eye to suggest that I knew what I was doing. It was an immediate lesson in the richness of Sri Lanka's gemmology. Lemon topazes, pineapple citrines, orange garnets, milky moonstones and, of course, sapphires and rubies of all qualities, shades and sizes appeared in turn, while Jayarathna explained what each of them was.

I could see how in ancient times people found it hard to tell the difference between sapphires and other blue stones. The most confusing were blue spinels, which were not dissimilar to sapphires although instead of being pure aluminium oxide as sapphires are, they are magnesium aluminium oxide, which makes them softer and a little darker. You can see the difference if you remember that spinels tend to green and sapphires to violet. It is similar to the difference in painting between ultramarine and azurite: ultramarine is the colour of heaven while azurite is the colour of the sea.

At one point I was shown some particularly gaudy stones, quite unlike anything that had appeared so far. It turned out that they were not from Sri Lanka at all, but Madagascar. Although gems have been sourced from there for a century or so, it was not until the 1990s that marvellous gem finds were uncovered. They are now so cheap and plentiful that Ratnapura dealers sometimes fly to Africa to bring them back to Sri Lanka to sell to foreigners who do not know the difference. However, once you have seen it, it is obvious: the Madagascar stones tend to be brasher, more *nouveaux riches*, while the Sri Lankan ones are somehow subtler, more polite.

Suddenly the crowd seemed to clear from around the car and a young man in fresh white cotton came towards us. He placed a large blue stone in Jayarathna's hand, some five carats in weight, big as a coat button, with a white six-pointed star in the centre, stretching to the edges. It was a star-stone – one of the most prized Sri Lankan sapphires. Star-stones are always polished in cabochon shape. In fact, before cutting skills were improved in the Middle Ages almost all precious stones were prepared like this, with smooth, rounded surfaces, in the shape of semi-spheres, like domes.

In many cultures star-stones were thought to be love charms. Helen of Troy was said to have owned one – and to have owed her conquests to it. The great nineteenth-century Middle Eastern traveller and seducer Richard Burton had a fine one. Apparently its fame preceded him wherever he went, 'assuring him good horses and prompt service upon his arrival, in return for which the natives would receive a glimpse of his gemstone'.[31] Some Sri Lankans believe that if you have ever owned a star-stone you will always be lucky, and the mystery is heightened by the fact that, if the stone is divided into several pieces then each of them, when cut and polished, will also display a star. It is like a hologram: cut it into a hundred pieces and each will contain the whole design.

The stars are caused by 'silk', the name given to the needles of titanium oxide that are sometimes trapped inside a sapphire

Star sapphires – the lucky charms of Helen of Troy

as it grows. When the silk comes in random patterns it looks like contrails left by aeroplanes flying through a spring sky. However, sometimes it forms more symmetrically. Sapphires tend to grow naturally as six-sided prisms, and when the needles follow the three principal axes of the crystal, a star is born. The phenomenon is called 'asterism'.

Probably the most prized star sapphire in the world is the Star of India. It weighs 563 carats, is bigger than a golf ball, was mined in Sri Lanka and presented to the New York Museum of Natural History in 1900 by the multimillionaire banker J. P. Morgan. In 1964 the Star became the gem of the year when it was stolen from the museum in a spectacular jewellery heist. That year Jack Murphy, a Californian surfer,[32] and two friends were inspired by the movie *Topkapi*, in which thieves burgled Istanbul's Palace Museum by lowering themselves from a window on a rope. Murphy and his friends mounted a copycat operation at the Natural History Museum in New York, having noticed an open window on the upper floor of the Morgan Hall where the jewels were kept. One night two hid upstairs, climbed down a rope and landed beside the display cabinets. They were lucky there was only one alarm in the whole place. It was fitted to the Star of India and the thieves were relieved to find the battery was dead (and in fact had not been replaced for years). They were eventually arrested in a hotel room in Florida, trying to ransom their hoard, and leaving the gems in a phone booth, as the designated pickup point. The court case became a *cause célèbre*, and the female public swooned over wild Jack Murphy, the beach-boy thief who had once played the violin with the Pittsburgh Orchestra.

The star crystal we were looking at was probably natural, but even in the Ratnapura market, so close to the source, there was a high chance of being sold a fake. 'Many are synthetics,' Jayarathna said, and made arrangements for the man to bring the stone to his shop later so that he could examine it properly. When he makes an expensive purchase he ensures that he knows the seller personally, in case he wants his money back. The key for any amateur buying gemstones in a market like this one is either to do the same or to spend only what you can afford to lose if your purchase turns out to be worthless.

Another stone appeared in my hand: a shining blue sapphire with – through the magnifying-glass – almost no impurities. Jayarathna broke off from his own negotiations over a rare hessonite garnet. 'Be careful,' he said. 'It's probably heat-treated ... This is one of our greatest problems of all.'

The Power of Fire

According to Greek legend, the world's first ring contained a blue sapphire. It was worn by the impetuous Prometheus, who stole the secret of fire from the gods. In punishment for his impudence, he was chained to a rock for eternity with an eagle pecking out his liver. After many aeons, the hero Heracles killed the eagle and asked for the prisoner to be freed. Zeus, the ruler of the gods, agreed, but with one condition: Prometheus had to wear a ring forged both from his chains and the rock as an eternal reminder of the consequences of his actions. The rock fragment he was forced to wear was said to have been a sapphire, the stone that is the same colour as the centre of the hottest flames.

If the first sapphire ring was worn by Prometheus then it is appropriate that fire is particularly relevant to the sapphire story today. Some say that fire is the greatest gift to sapphires, others that it is the greatest curse. Either way it is a force that, once let loose, cannot be stopped. The issue is heat treatment of stones and its use has been likened to steroids for body-builders: the drugs make them perform and look better than they could naturally, but if they test positive their value plummets, and if they persist they will be damaged inside. Heat treatment has been going on in one way or another for thousands of years.[33] The two-thousand-year-old sacred *Puranas*[34] of India state that gems may be cooked and improved over a fire; the early-sixteenth-century-traveller Duarte Barbosa reported that, 'When the gold-smiths of Ceylon come upon any [gemstone] which is good they place it in fire for a certain number of hours, and if it comes forth whole its colour becomes very bright and of great value.' The clause 'if it comes forth whole' is important: heating stones is for gamblers, not for those who play safe.

The reason why it works is complicated, but it is worth understanding because it helps to explain why sapphires appear to be coloured. Colours happen in several different ways. Some, like the iridescence of opals, are purely physical, with the texture of the surface refracting the light into shimmering colour. Most objects, though – whether flowers or paints, sapphires or beach-balls – get their colour because they are undergoing a trans-formation as we look at them. The difference between physical and chemical colour is like the difference between a painting and a performance. A painting is static, but in a play or a ballet the performers are constantly shifting and changing: as soon as the movement stops, so does the performance. The chief actors in the drama of blue sapphires are iron and titanium impurities. In darkness a sapphire has no colour, but when it is taken into the daylight the metaphorical theatre lights are switched on and the dance begins. Free electrons hop from the titanium ions to the iron ones and the result is a shift of energy that our brains translate as 'blue'. When we look into a bright stone and are captivated by its colour, what is actually happening is that we are watching a constant metamorphosis: the sapphire is performing for us – as well, of course, as for the light.

The system is not perfect. Iron can take one of two forms, which confusingly can be called ferrous or ferric. The former has two free electrons, while the latter has three, and the issue, as far as the colour of sapphires is concerned, is that only the ferrous ions (with one free electron too few) are hungry for the titanium energy exchange. The ferric ions are sated, so sapphires containing them tend to be pale or colourless, reflecting that there is not much happening inside. Heat changes the ferric iron to ferrous and the results can be startling: deep swimming-pool blues emerge from something very ordinary indeed. The process has been perfected and improved over the past decade and today stones that, only ten years ago, would have been worthless can be transformed into beautiful, valuable gems. Legally the process doesn't even have to be mentioned. One might say, paraphrasing Marco Polo, that the heat treaters have the secret of alchemy to perfection.[35]

It is a secret of the gem trade that terrifies many legitimate traders and assessors. So far – although kilos of newly treated stones are exported from Thailand, Cambodia and Sri Lanka – the market has not responded with any level of either panic or disdain. 'But what if people find out?' wondered a trader I met at the Tucson Gem Fair, who preferred not to be named. 'Would they be happy that they are paying thousands of dollars for something that started off brown and cracked and completely worthless?'

Jayarathna put the blue stone back into the dealer's hand. 'She doesn't want it,' he said.

The man grinned: he knew what he had, and that he would sell it eventually to someone who didn't know – or didn't want to know – the difference.

The Illam Mines of Ratnapura

The person who bought the treated gem would probably be a foreigner. In Ratnapura it seems that every man in the town has dabbled with some aspect of the trade at some point, either as a dealer or, more commonly, as a miner, and they are almost all experienced amateur gemmologists, with skills that would take years to learn elsewhere. After all, this is a place where 'gem' is a verb, and 'gemming' an activity. Everywhere in the Ratnapura valley there are gem mines. You can recognise them by the small thatched roofs built over the shafts, which make it appear from a distance as if every paddy-field has its private toilet. However, these are mostly small-scale family affairs. To see the real thing Jayarathna had arranged for me to spend the afternoon in the jungle outside the town, where mines are run as businesses and where whole village economies depend on the success of the gemming.

My guide was a friend of Jayarathna's called Galla who, as we drove into the countryside, gave a running commentary on the paths off the main road beyond which treasures lay. 'That was a big mine when I was a boy,' he said, pointing down a path between two biscuit shops. 'That one, very useless always,' he said of the next, which led off from a latrine. The best story came from Tiriwanakatir Hindu Temple on the outskirts of town. In 2002 a government road-construction gang had been sent to widen the street outside the temple and had been surprised to find sapphires, spinels and rubies dropping from their spades. They had hit a gem deposit. As soon as the word was out, the locals secretly commandeered the nearby houses, dug cellars and tunnelled towards the roadworks. The bonanza ended when a house collapsed and the police were alerted. They went in with guns and arrested more than a hundred muddy villagers from their spontaneous underground excavations. It was a literal example of highway robbery.

When, as usually happens, there are no serendipitous road excavations to help identify where the gems are, the miners use a clever method of divination. Corundum is, of course, one of the hardest of minerals. On Mohs' scale it scores nine. Indeed, it is so hard that it has sometimes even been called 'diamond' or 'adamant', and it is this quality that the miners exploit to locate their island's buried treasure. They lower metal rods into small bored holes, rotate them vigorously and remove them every few metres. When the rod comes up grazed, the miners will dig, because this is where sapphires and rubies are most likely to be discovered: other less precious minerals would not do so much damage.

After about seven kilometres we stopped and set off down a path. A reptile the size of a small cat slithered over my feet. I jumped, but Galla laughed: it was a rat-snake or garandiya. 'Not dangerous, just fat,' he said. When we reached the gems camp in a jungle clearing it was a startlingly uniform colour. Orange sand merged with orange trees, and even the two roughly constructed huts protecting the mine shafts were rusty red from the corrupted iron on their roofs.

There were fourteen men altogether: six at the surface, the others down below. They worked on a co-operative basis meaning that at the end of the season the findings were divided between them and the owner, who took half, plus an extra cut for the generator. This meant that each man would receive around three per cent of whatever the gemstones earned locally.

Because of the high mark-ups from Sri Lanka to Europe and America it also meant that, for example, if a sapphire sold for three hundred pounds in Hatton Garden, each miner would have earned about a pound. Despite this, some miners become wealthy: it's just a matter of waiting for a break. What would they do if it happened?

'I would buy land and plant tea,' said Dinapaula, who was forty-nine and a father.

'I would buy a house,' said his friend, who was younger and single.

'And I would buy a gem mine, and have other people mining it for me,' said a third.

The others nodded in agreement: they knew where that dream came from.

They showed me the 'sapphire telephone' or 'talking pipe', made of long pieces of bamboo through which they communicated with the men underground. *'Aybowan*!' I called, in the Sri Lankan greeting.

'Hello!' echoed back from far below. Even through a bamboo pipe booming forty metres underground, to men who rarely had foreign visitors, my English accent was unmistakable.

Open-cast mining of gems is banned on the island so many of Sri Lanka's sapphires come from mines like this one. They are piped to the surface to the strange, pained music of a generator howling at varying pitches as it powers a series of ancient water- and air-pumps. These were vital: there had been only three gem-mine fatalities at Ratnapura in recent years, all at a site where the generator had broken down, allowing poisoned air to hang in the mine. One man died instantly, his two friends more slowly, when they tried to rescue him. After hearing that story, I thought the horrible sound began to seem almost gentle.

I wedged myself against the wooden supports and crept to the side of the shaft. It was very deep. At first all I could see were black shadows, ochre mud and air-pipes, but then I realised

The sapphire telephone

that, far below, something was moving – and it was coming closer. In a few moments a boy emerged, covered with yellow earth and full of energy. He looked like a laughing jewel: a clay figure with a contagious smile. His name was Damit Nasander, he was nineteen and had been a miner for nine years. 'Though it's not allowed for children to mine any more,' his colleague said hurriedly, as he saw me writing this down. No one could quite agree on the new legal age: some thought sixteen, others eighteen. How old were the youngest miners here? They consulted each other. 'Eighteen,' they said.

'Come down the mine and see it,' Damit said. It was just the invitation I had been hoping for. I approached the shaft with confidence, then stopped, looking carefully at each of the four sides. 'Where's the ladder?' I asked finally. Watching the ease and speed with which Damit had come up, it hadn't been at all obvious that he had been using a long, thin bamboo pipe tied to the earth wall with rope round it for grip. For a moment I played with the idea of trying it anyway, but the mud made up my mind for me. Even with the rope round it, the bamboo was like a fireman's pole. Going down might be possible, but to climb back up would require strength. I was no Murph the Surf, able to ascend and descend five storeys on a rope, and this was more like fifteen. Reluctantly I conceded defeat. I would have to rely on other people's descriptions.

'What is it like down there?' I asked.

'Warm like Ratnapura night-time,' said a serious-looking man called Sunil Bandera.

'Yellow and dark,' said another.

'Small and your feet get wet,' said a third, as his friends laughed.

At the gravel layer all the outgoing tunnels are flat, fanning out from the central shaft for about twenty metres in every direction. Sometimes they stretch further, especially if, as sometimes happens, the miners break through into the musty air of ancient tunnels. 'Maybe they were dug ten years ago, maybe a thousand, we cannot know,' said fifty-four-year-old Piasena. 'We just go inside to look at them sometimes. Perhaps the old miners left something nice for us.'

Some of the old mines reveal the presence of people much earlier than even a thousand years before: miners in the Ratnapura district have found Stone Age pottery and flints at the gem gravel or 'illam' layer, complete with tiger and lion bones, some of which have turned partly to agate. There is no formal explanation of how this has happened, but perhaps it is a process similar to the opalisation of dinosaur and cat bones in Australia – through ionisation.

The Best-known Stone in the World

Back at the guesthouse Jayarathna had asked his son-in-law Lasantha to teach me how to cut and polish stones, and my first lesson involved shaping a piece of quartz. Quartz is silicon oxide – it is nature's glass. When pure it is clear but, like sapphires, it takes its colours from traces of other elements and it can be a rainbow. Agate, amethyst, carnelian, chalcedony, chrysoprase, citrine, jasper, obsidian, onyx and sardonyx are all quartzes, but my piece looked like none of these. Instead it resembled a rolled-up piece of yellow pastry dough, and was the size of a date. I offered to pay for it, and Jayarathna roared with laughter, saying it was worth no more than a cup of tea. But once it was placed on the lapidary wheel it gained its own value, because it was all that separated my fingers from a swiftly rotating blade of steel.

Quartz is often muddy, like ice on the road that has been mixed with dirt, and the lapidary's job is to cut away those impurities. By holding the stone against a rotating horizontal blade, on to which water dripped like a torture, Lasantha could create a flat surface like a window into a frosted world. From it we could see that one side was full of cracks, while the other was quite pure. 'Sometimes you have to chase the inclusions, and the stone gets smaller and smaller,' he said. I ground away the cracked side, until I had only half of the original. Lasantha then showed me how to fit it on to a dop, or little stick, with melted green wax that burned my fingers.

The second stage is the cutting. A different horizontal blade is used – again a flat wheel, but this time smeared with abrasives. Sometimes cutters use diamond dust but more often in Sri Lanka, when softer stones are being cut, the dust is the same basic material – aluminium oxide – that composes rubies and sapphires. In the gem trade this polishing material is, like the stones themselves, called corundum although elsewhere it is more often known as emery.

Corundum's hardness makes rubies and sapphires suitable for industrial use in the workings of watches. Pocket watches became popular in England in the seventeenth century, but they were inaccurate because of the friction in their mechanism. In 1704 the Swiss mathematician Nicolas Fatio de Duillier came up with a way of making holes in rubies and sapphires so that the metal workings would turn in them and they would act as bearings. From then on, the best watches had twenty-one basic jewelled bearings; some boasted 'a hundred jewels'[36] or more, but anything above twenty-one was pure ornamentation. Half a century later this invention enabled the British watchmaker John Harrison to make his award-winning clock 'H4', which in 1762 scooped the science prize of the century and enabled sailors to navigate longitude as well as latitude.

Different stones have different ideal cuts, partly related to the refractive index, which is the angle at which light bends when it passes through the stone, and which is different for every species. An emerald is usually cut square, a diamond is usually cut as a brilliant with fifty-seven facets, while sapphires can be either, or indeed many other kinds of cuts. My own sapphire, Lasantha said, was a simple oval cut with a square table. It was popular in the 1950s when gem-cutters had much simpler equipment. 'But it doesn't refract the light as it should do, and it's much too shallow,' he pronounced critically. 'I wouldn't cut it like that.' The ideal is to create exactly the right shape for light to pass round the inside of the stone, knocking against the edges like a pool ball and gathering energy until it emerges from the table facets with maximum sparkle. It is the capacity of gem-stones to concentrate light and magnify it that led to their use in lasers. Some of them shed such a concentrated beam that it is said they can cast their rays on to the moon.

Lasantha placed the dop on a metal grip, which swung over the blade like the arm of a record-player. By pressing the stone on the turning blade he made the flat surface called the 'table' at the top of the stone, then twisted and rotated the stone a few degrees to make other windows round the sides. By this method we first formed the top layer or 'crown', above the central band or 'girdle'. Then we cut the bottom or 'pavilion', refining it to a point called the 'culet', from the same origin as the French

Lasantha polishing quartz

Cutting stones en cabochon, *near the gem market in Ratnapura*

'*cul*', meaning 'arse'. Every time we checked the stone to make sure the new facet was the right size, before moving on to the next rotation, a set number of degrees along. At one point his father-in-law came in – it was making the wrong sound, he said – and removed a small piece of grit. 'Even a little granule can mean the angles are wrong.' At the end we had to do it all again, with a polishing blade, to make each facet shine. It is done mathematically, according to fixed geometrical tables: if you get one number wrong, the whole thing is thrown out of symmetry. Curiously, the ideal ratio between the depth of the brilliant-cut stone and the space above it is between 58.7 per cent and 62.3 per cent,[37] which is uncannily similar to the 'golden section' of 61.2 used by neo-classical architects to measure the perfect proportions of a building.

It took us five hours to finish that quartz (normally it would take just a few minutes), and what we ended up with fell far short of achieving its refractive potential: I had found out the hard way how easy it is to cut too hard or get an angle wrong if you don't watch the calibrations carefully. It was, at the end, probably worth a little less than a cup of tea. But today it is one of my proudest possessions, partly because it is the first gemstone I cut, but also because, of all the stones in the world, it is the one that, having stared into its depths several hundred times, I know best of all.

Sinbad's River

But this still left the stone I know second best, and although I now knew more about how my own sapphire had been cut, and probably where it had first been sold, I still did not understand where it had come from. How had it got to the bottom of that illam mine as bits of coloured gravel? The next day Jayarathna agreed to take me to what he called 'the other kind of mine', which he said would help to answer those questions. It involved driving to a place about ten kilometres away from Ratnapura. 'There are two things you have to know,' Jayarathna said, as we walked along a jungle path. 'First of all, sapphires and rubies are heavier than glass and sand, so they sink.' That seemed logical. 'The second thing is that you have to be careful on the bridges: they are quite frightening.' The wooden structure round the next corner was as precarious as he had promised. It spanned high above the river and swayed dramatically from side to side as we walked. In the wet season it often collapses.

But my consternation at the sight of the swinging bridge was nothing to my astonishment at what I saw from it. From the centre I could see five men in loincloths standing in the water below, up to their knees, in a shallow place just after two rivers had met and become one. They were 'gem-miners', but they looked as if they weren't mining at all: they were fishing. They were holding long, thin poles with hooks at the end which they were probing in the current like hesitant pole-vaulters looking for a suitable place from which to base a leap. This was the Kaluganga, Sinbad's river, and if the banks were not exactly covered with glittering jewels it was certain that the bed was studded with myriads of rubies, sapphires and other precious stones, because that was what the men were dredging for. It was like an antique scene, and if Marco Polo had been allowed to see where his stones had been found eight hundred years ago he might have encountered an identical sight. Even the clothes the men were wearing had probably hardly changed since antiquity.

As we walked across the bridge and towards a primitive shelter set up under the trees, Jayarathna explained that the river miners were generally much poorer than those at the illam mines. Although there are few outlays, except their time, the finds are usually small and shared between many people. 'At good times they have bread for breakfast, curry for dinner and tea through the day, but in bad times they pick jackfruits from the trees and survive on that.' The men all had bright red mouths and gums from chewing the kernel of the betel-nut palm, which is endemic to Sri Lanka and contains an alkaloid that acts as a stimulant. For the miners betel was not just an addiction, it was a necessity: 'Betel gives warm; water gives cold,' explained Sunil Kajotawata, who was in charge of the group. 'Without betel we cannot stay in the river for eight hours a day.' He pointed to his feet, which were so wrinkled from the water that the skin seemed two sizes too big. They were also lacerated with cuts and scars. 'Sometimes the sapphires are like knives,' Sunil said. 'They cut everything.'

When I had first imagined how my own little sapphire might have been mined, I had taken it for granted that it would have been like extracting opals in Australia or emeralds in Egypt: that is, excavating into the bedrock until you find a trace of the desired mineral, then digging or dynamiting it out. This was how almost every kind of gem mining that I had previously heard of seemed to work. But this is not the case in Sri Lanka. Although sapphires can potentially be mined from bedrock – the Kashmir sapphires are a good example – all the sapphires of Sri Lanka are found in what are called 'secondary deposits'. This is the result of a lengthy geological process, which started when the rough crystals dislodged from their parent rock and fell to the ground. Over millions of years they eroded from their original matrix, were swept along by rainstorms and started a long journey downhill, at first carried briskly through the mountain canyons by strong streams, like Sinbad on his little raft, then reaching the rivers and slowly tumbling downstream on the long voyage towards the sea. Shaft mining happens when people dig down to find precious gravel that was once in a river millions of years ago but which, over aeons, has become covered by clay. River mining involves stopping those precious stones while they are still making the journey to the ocean. You cannot tell by which method my own stone was found – the cutting

River mining for sapphires

removes the evidence – but when it was still in its rough state an expert would have known. River stones have a smoothed surface that testifies to how long they have been subjected to the tumbling of the water: they have the 'owned' look of a lucky pebble you've kept in your pocket for ever.

Sunil took me into the river to see how the dredging worked. The current was strong and it was a struggle to get through the fast-running water, which came up to our waists, and reach the shallower area in the middle where the men were working. Selecting a place to look for stones is like the message in *Goldilocks and the Three Bears*: if the water moves too fast the heavier gems are swept away; if it moves too slowly the lighter minerals are not removed by the flow; it is only when the treasure-hunters choose a place that is just right – like the inside of a river bend or a place like this one where two tributaries meet and the current slows in the middle – that they have any chance of success.

Earlier in the season the men had built a dam across the middle of the river to catch the material as it swept down. The drawback is that for every carat of gem material that passes down Sinbad's river there are also several tonnes of worthless gravel travelling down as well. Fortunately the river helps. A few metres upstream from the dam the men had dug a ditch in the stream bed. They were now taking the material from the dam and were scooping it into the ditch with their long poles, or *mamoti*. It was hard to understand what was happening, as most of it was taking place underwater. Then I remembered what Jayarathna had said about the gems being heavier than the sand. As the river ran over the ditch it picked up the lighter sand and swept it away, but left the heavier material behind for the men to sort manually with sieves later on: it was an effective way of using the natural power of the river to do the initial sorting. The stream does another kind of sorting too. Any stone that reaches this point intact has already been turned, crashed, rolled and knocked over many years and kilometres since it left its bedrock: the weaker ones will have cracked long ago so anything that remains should easily stand up to cutting and polishing. The abrasive scream of the lapidary wheel is nothing in comparison to the eroding power of the river.

Until then I had taken the process of what is called 'alluvial mining' for granted: I had accepted there was gravel in the ground that had to be removed to find the gems inside it. But standing in that river as sapphires and rubies flowed invisibly around me, I realised the magnitude of the forces that had made Sinbad's magical river, and wondered for the first time where the gems had really come from. Surely somewhere in those high mountains upstream from us there was a mother-rock? Sunil said he thought the sapphires originated from the gods; Jayarathna said, more pragmatically, that nobody knew where they came from. There is no primary mining of precious stones in Sri Lanka at all because geologists – even though they have tried extremely hard – have never managed to find the parent rocks.[38] 'But we have our own theories. In our mythology we say they come from Adam's Peak.' He pointed to where the clouds had momentarily cleared and I saw a mountain that looked like a child's drawing, it was so carelessly jagged.

At more than 7200 feet, Adam's Peak – or Sri Pada, as the local people call it – is one of the highest mountains on the island. But more than that it is also an immensely holy place, with what seems to be a giant footprint near its summit, more than one and a half metres long. Hindus say it is the place where Siva dances; Buddhists say it is where the Buddha once stood; some Christians say it is the original Garden of Eden, guarded by the swords of angels; and Muslims believe it is where Adam first alighted, after he had been cast out of paradise, and that it is where he remained, standing on one foot, until he had completed his penance. Chinese animists have been going there on pilgrimage since at least the third century, believing it to be the place where the first man, Pan Ku, once lived. And the legend of Adam's Peak even has traces of the story of Prometheus in it: on the way up this sapphire mountain there are iron chains fixed by pins and the last of them, according to legend,[39] is called the 'chain of the profession of faith' because to look down is to be seized by such a fear of dying that it is a rare traveller who does not pray for protection.

Along with these legends of a first famous visitor and strange iron chains, there are also many myths about the precious stones on Adam's Peak. Whether they were brought by Adam from paradise, dissolved from the footprints of the Buddha, or represented the crystal ears of Pan Ku, the stones from this place were said to be holy. Medieval Christians had a tradition that the Garden of Eden was an actual place on earth, and that the closer one came to it, the more gemstones were to be found on the ground. So for centuries medieval voyagers created and followed maps with gem sites traced on them in the hope of finding spiritual as well as earthly riches. 'You were in Eden, the garden of God,' the prophet Ezekiel proclaimed to the Israelites.

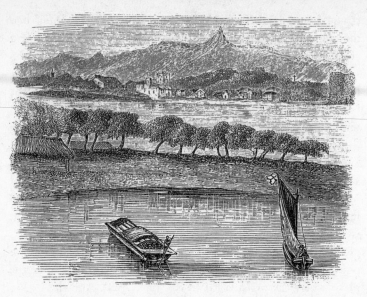

Adam's Peak – like a child's drawing of a mountain

'Every precious stone adorned you – ruby, topaz, chrysolite, onyx, jasper, sapphire, turquoise, and beryl . . . and I set you, so that you were on the holy mountain of God.'[40] And, writing this much later, I suddenly wonder whether the mysterious 'gem-encrusted' throne, fought over by the two rival mythical kings of Sri Lanka, was not a throne at all, but a mountain, encrusted with rubies and sapphires, that was to be shared by all.

I had started on my journey with a sense of awe at the millions of years my sapphire had probably stayed within the earth, but I was also confident that I would find its source, or something like it. But now, standing beside the river in whose flow it had perhaps been found, I looked at it with a different kind of wonder. Now not only did I have a geological, economic and gemmological history of my little ring-stone, but I also knew a beautiful legend about a holy place from which it had once tumbled. I would never visit its real source, or even know where that was, but instead I had learned of a mysterious mother-rock that nobody, not even with all of today's technology, can find and that might not even still be there. Best of all I had learned something that pleases me about my ring every time I look at it. I learned that my sapphire was so old and so strong that it had lasted aeons already, while the great rock it had come from had probably worn completely away.

8

Ruby

It appears that certain dangers exist, or are said to exist in
the lands where Rubies are found, such as malaria, wild
beasts and venomous reptiles. But it is possible that these
dangers may be exaggerated by the Ruby merchants in order
to hinder competition.

EDWIN STREETER[1]

'The king of Pegu wears more rubies on him than the value of
a very large city, and he wears them on all his toes . . . He
shines so much that he appears to be a sun.'
Sixteenth-century traveller LUIGI BARTHEMA

One morning in December 1885, a tall Englishman in his early
fifties could have been spotted taking his breakfast alone in the
Grand Hotel in Paris.[2] An attentive observer might have noticed
him pause over his croissant and coffee to listen with increasing
fascination to the conversation of two gentlemen sitting nearby.

They were discussing how, a few days before, on 29 November,
British forces had captured Upper Burma, whose king had been
given poor advice. His counsellors couldn't bring themselves to
tell him how close the British had come to the capital of Mandalay and had delayed until the Burmese forces had no chance
of holding their ground. Within a week the 'Glass Palace' –
so called for its mirrored mosaics – had been ransacked, and
numerous treasures had disappeared into the even more numerous pockets of the British regiments. King Thibaw, his pregnant
queen and their three little daughters had been sent into exile –

in a deliberately humiliating procession of just seven tiers of ceremonial umbrellas instead of the usual royal nine, and the British were working out how to operate their new colony for maximum profit.

There were three main reasons for the British to take Upper Burma. First, they wanted to expel the French, who already had a hold on Laos, Vietnam and Cambodia. Second, there was the teak, of which Burma then had so much and now has so little. But for those in charge of military decisions, the third was the most persuasive. For years, Europe had heard rumours about a town that was said to lie in the heart of the jungle in north-eastern Burma.[3] It was called Mogok, and some of the world's most beautiful gems were to be found there. There were sapphires, topazes, amethysts and even emeralds. But Mogok was really known for its rubies. The colour of the best of them was so saturated – so deep, so unfathomable – that Europeans struggled to describe it. The Burmese had no difficulty: they referred to it as 'pigeon's blood', although most of the foreign women who wore the stones did not think too hard about what that meant.

'Did you hear about the lease?' one gentleman asked his friend. It appeared that the French company Messrs Bouveillein & Co. had bought a lease on the Burmese ruby mines a few months before. They had paid the substantial sum of three hundred thousand rupees, or twenty thousand pounds,[4] plus a further hundred thousand rupees in bribes to the king. It was appalling timing, as far as the French company was concerned: now that the British had taken over that part of the country, including the mines, the lease would surely become worthless.[5]

This last piece of information was too much for the Englishman. He admitted that he had been eavesdropping and introduced himself. His name was Edwin Streeter, and if his new acquaintances had been in the business of either jewels or adventures they would have certainly heard of him. He owned one of the biggest jewellery businesses in London, but he was not only interested in selling. In his lifetime his fortune would be made and lost – but mostly lost – by his fascination with the origin of precious stones. By 1885 he already had such a reputation for adventure that his shop was mentioned in *King Solomon's Mines*[6] as a place where explorers would go to get their gems valued. With all his interest in remote places no wonder his attention was alerted when he found out that the lease for the fabled ruby mines of Burma might be available for the first time to British investors.

All the Rubies in Burma – £27,000 the Lot

That brief conversation with two strangers in the Parisian hotel had a profound effect on Streeter's fortune – and, indeed, on the fortune of Burma's rubies. In 1879, Streeter had published a book, *Precious Stones and Gems*, which proved to be a bestseller – finding its place on Victorian gentlemen's bookshelves filed somewhere between adventure and science. In it he explained that rubies were found in a wide range of places – Afghanistan, Australia and the riverbeds of Ceylon – but the best ones, he wrote excitedly, came from a mysterious mountainous region of Burma where 'not only are the people inhospitable, wild, cruel and avaricious but the country is infested with wild beasts and poisonous reptiles'. Yet the risks might be worth running, he conceded, for 'the Oriental Ruby is indisputably the most valuable of precious stones' and the kingdom of Burma is indisputably the 'greatest emporium of Rubies' in the world.

Upper Burma's gems had enjoyed an exotic reputation in Europe for several hundred years. The first Englishman to visit the country was the Elizabethan traveller Ralph Fitch, who reached Burma and Ceylon almost accidentally while escaping from the Inquisition, and paid for his journeys by buying and selling precious stones. Unlike other early travel writers, Fitch's diaries do not include gripping tales of unicorns with gems set in their horns, or of swooping vultures picking up diamonds in their claws. But he does describe the Burmese King of Pegu going to war in an astonishing procession of three hundred thousand men and five thousand elephants, many of them glittering with gem-encrusted costumes and howdahs. He also saw the spectacular royal jewellery collection, held in four 'treasure houses' in the capital city of Pegu. Each of these was 'woonderfull great, as high as an house' and, needless to say, covered with more rubies and sapphires than a man could conceive of. His account revealed something to which, three centuries later, Edwin Streeter and the British Army might have done well to pay more attention. Fitch had realised that the precious stones from this region meant more to the Burmese than simply denoting wealth. The reason the pagodas of Pegu were so bejewelled was because after every coronation ceremony the new king would break up his regalia and place the gems high on the spires of these towered Buddhist temples, for his subjects to see and wonder at. The national treasure houses were not spectacular for the sake of it: for the Burmese people, ownership of jewels was a supremely potent, highly visible statement of political supremacy.

Three years before Fitch's journey, in 1583, a Venetian jeweller called Gasparo Balbi had visited the same court. Unlike Fitch, he had the honour of an audience with King Nanda-bayin and was astonished to find that the custom was to take the king a gift of jewels, even though he could hardly need any more. Balbi brought a box of emeralds, which were rare in Burma although – after the Spanish conquest of the Colombian mines – they were increasingly common in Europe. He passed them to the interpreter, who handed them to the monarch with a great deal of ritual bowing. The king asked where the stranger came from, and when he learned it was Venice, he asked what king governed it. The jeweller replied that it had no king but was a republic. At that, Nanda-bayin 'began to laugh so exceedingly, that he

The King put the ruby into a glass of milk, which turned bright red. Nineteenth-century painting from Burma

A bejewelled white elephant at Annapoorna in Burma

was overcome of the cough, which made him that he could hardly speak'.[7] So ingrained was the sense of royalty in ancient Burma that it was impossible for him to imagine any other system.

Neither Balbi nor Fitch was permitted to see the place where all those rubies had come from. However, they did know of its reputation. Fitch referred to it as 'Caplan', and the place 'where they find the rubies, sapphires and spinelles . . . There are many great high hilles out of which they digge them.' He knew that Caplan was six days' journey from the city of Ava, near to the modern city of Mandalay,[8] and that it was a secret place. 'None may go to the pits but onely those which digge them.'[9]

Caplan is the place where the rubies and other precious stones are found.

Caplán is the place where they finde the rubies, saphires, and spinelles : it standeth sire dayes iourney from Aua in the kingdome of Pegu. There are many great high hilles out of which they digge them. None may go to the pits but onely those which digge them.

Much later, in 1826, John Crawfurd, a British diplomat, went on a mission to the Burmese court. When he returned home he brought with him a huge Mogok sapphire weighing 907 carats (equivalent to about three-quarters of a pack of butter). He, too, had an audience with the King of Pegu, whom he described with some amusement:

> He mounted a flight of steps . . . with apparent difficulty, and as if tottering under the load of dress and ornaments on his person. His dress consisted of a tunic of gold tissue, ornamented with jewels. The crown was a helmet with a high peak, in form not unlike the spire of a Burman Pagoda, which it was probably intended to resemble. I was told it was of entire gold, and it had all the appearance of being studded with abundance of rubies and sapphires.[10]

If all these accounts were not enough, Streeter's son had mentioned only recently his dream of one day going to find the Burmese ruby mines. However at the time, Streeter wrote, 'knowing how jealously these mines were guarded from all Europeans, I would not for a moment countenance so hazardous an expedition'. What he had overheard in Paris, though, made him change his mind: when he returned to London, he decided to put in a serious bid. He formed a syndicate, which included his second son, George, and three other businessmen. They agreed to send an agent immediately to Rangoon, and the man they chose for this task was Captain Aubrey Patton, later described as 'an adventurous speculating person known for his great proficiency in pigeon shooting'.[11] He travelled by steamer to Burma, carrying a letter of introduction to the Viceroy of India. However, when he arrived he had a shock: a serious competitor had emerged, and Streeter's syndicate now found itself bidding against the worst possible kind of rival.

Messrs Gillander, Arbuthnot & Co. of Calcutta was a hardnosed, wealthy, British-run enterprise. It had made most of its fortune by sending Indian villagers to work on plantations in Mauritius, and trapping them in a spiral of debt. Indentured labour was controversial even in those days and, as Streeter would learn to his cost, the Calcutta company's directors were not shy of employing a few underhand tricks to get what they wanted in other areas. The viceroy rejected Streeter's first bid of three hundred thousand rupees and opened the lease application to public tender – with all interested parties asked to submit closed bids. Over the next few days, Patton was a constant visitor at the telegraph office, communicating with the syndicate to find out what they wanted to do. They decided to put in a final offer of four hundred thousand rupees, about twenty-seven thousand pounds,[12] and on 15 April 1886 a telegram from the foreign secretary in India informed them that their tender had been conditionally accepted.

Streeter then sent George to Burma, with two fellow members of the syndicate and Robert Gordon, a surveyor. Their plan was to travel with the British Army as they marched towards the so-far unconquered territory of Mogok. They wanted to know what they had got for their money: where the rubies came from, what were the chances of finding more and – most complicated of all – how the payments to native miners were structured. It was typical of a colonial government that they should sell the rights in an industry they had never seen to a company that had no experience, without anyone even knowing how the traditional ownership of the land worked.

In Burma, they would discover that mythologies and stories had been woven around the stones for hundreds if not thousands of years, and that their almost casual takeover of the ancient mines would prove more complicated than anyone could ever have imagined.

Rubies the size of Hens' Eggs

Detailed Burmese history[13] was not written down until 1044, when the ambitious and literate King Anawrahta came to the throne. In the early years of his reign, he conquered the land of the Mons, which is the thin strip of southern Burma that squeezes along the coast past Thailand. The King of the Mons was stripped of all his possessions, including a star ruby as big as a hen's egg, which had symbolised his power. He was allowed to live as a slave under the new regime, but did well. When he had grown old he called his family together and asked them to help him build a pagoda.[14] He passed round a tray to collect their gifts. When it was returned to him, the donations included a magnificent star ruby, set in a ring. It was his own stone, returned anonymously by King Anawrahta. It financed the pagoda, which became a symbol of the transience of human victories and losses. And of how even fierce rulers sometimes mellow with age.

During Anawrahta's reign, the Mogok 'Stone Tract' belonged

to the crown, and the miners' livelihood depended on whether the royal mines manager gave them permission to work it. In practice he almost always did, but at a high price: officials in Mogok stung the miners for whatever they could get away with, each layer of officialdom adding a little more for itself in the time-honoured code of corrupt bureaucracies. But this was petty taxation in comparison with a more notorious rule, which would lead to the destruction of many of the most beautiful rubies ever found, and to a tragic affair that is commemorated in Mogok even today. The rule was that every large stone should be offered to the king. During some reigns the cut-off point was three carats, in others it was four or six, but in all cases it was controversial. The theory was that the king would pay the market price, but it was a rare monarch who offered a fair sum for anything found on land he believed to be his. The workers resented this.[15] They sent a few stones to the king each year to keep him happy, but many crushed their large rough stones into smaller ones that they could sell for themselves.

One man, however, gave his beautiful ruby to the king, and he suffered for it.[16] Nga Mauk was an ordinary villager – not even a miner – and at first everyone thought he was the luckiest man in town. One day in 1661 he was fishing by the river when his eye was caught by a strange glint. He waded into the water and picked up an enormous ruby. Its size varies in the telling – between sixty-one and eighty-one carats, or perhaps double that – but everyone agrees that its colour was exceptional. In the air it was a fluorescent crimson and in the water it must have been even more astonishing. Nga Mauk showed it to the village headman, and a few days later he found himself on the back of a royal elephant at the front of a grand procession heading for the capital of Ava. The story goes that the king placed the ruby in a glass of milk, which turned bright red.

Nga Mauk returned to his village, in high hopes of receiving a good reward. But back in Ava – according to legend – the king boasted about the new ruby. 'No one else has such a beautiful gem,' he crowed, while paradoxically expressing the desire to find another to match it. A foreign dealer heard of this and, by chance, had just bought an extremely beautiful ruby across the border, possibly in Yunnan or Calcutta – depending on the version of the story. He took it to the palace, but his gem didn't get the reaction he had imagined. Instead there was a surprised silence. Not only was the second stone a perfect colour match for the king's ruby, but it was also a little larger. When the two rough stones were put together they fitted exactly.

The king realised he had been cheated: Nga Mauk must have cleaved the stone in half and kept the better piece for himself. He sent his men to the village and, according to one terrible version of the story, they locked all the villagers into one house and set it alight. Only Nga Mauk's sister escaped. She was searching for herbs on the hills and looked back to see her home on fire, and the whole village burning as bright red as her brother's ruby.

Nobody knows what happened to the foreign dealer's stone: it is rarely mentioned again, although in the myths it represents darkness and tragedy. *In absentia* it was named the Kalla Pyan, or Black Water ruby. As for Nga Mauk's stone, the king put it first into his royal ring, then later into the headdress of his chief white elephant. After he died, the stone achieved legendary status. It was said that whoever owned it could claim the throne of Burma. So, it was hardly surprising that when the British forces took Mandalay in 1885, their commanding officer, Colonel Sladen, had orders to find the Nga Mauk as a priority.

But the colonel always said he never saw it. He said King Thibaw must have taken it with him, or that someone else had stolen it in the looting. Many did not believe him. And the king himself, in exile at Ratnagiri in India, always held that he had given Colonel Sladen several precious items 'for safe-keeping', and later wrote many letters petitioning for their return. The disappearance of the Nga Mauk caused major dissent in the newly colonised cities of Upper Burma, and even today many Burmese are angry with Colonel Sladen. On a train in Shan state, I met one highly educated man, who was clear on the matter: 'There is no doubt that Sladen stole it, and broke it into smaller pieces, and now it is in the Tower of London, with the Queen's Crown Jewels,' he told me, in faultless English.

The First British Expedition

On a late winter's afternoon in February 1888, the engineer Robert Gordon stood up to talk at the Royal Geographical Society in South Kensington. He had just returned from the first British expedition to Mogok and the auditorium was packed with people – including the notorious Colonel Sladen – who were eager to hear about the fabled ruby mines. It had taken forty days for the expedition to reach Burma by steamer, Gordon said, and it had taken more than half of that again to reach Mogok. Part of the reason the journey took so long was the bandits, who 'paralysed the river' and did not hesitate to shoot at the British troops whenever they had the chance. They had been around longer than the conquerors, longer even than the kings: it was said that some bandit families in the Mogok region could trace their families back to when the stones were exported to Ancient Egypt. Filching rubies was an old and well-established business.

The other problem facing the British Army was a more organised kind of resistance. The miners had hired more than a thousand local mercenaries to fight for them on the mountainous approaches to Mogok. The British prepared for a long campaign, but the Burmese stockades fell without a fight. It turned out that the man who was paying the mercenaries' wages had absconded with the money and the men refused to fight unpaid.[17]

Even with the human dangers sorted out, the road to Mogok was still perilous. Gordon described trees with such poisonous juices that a man could die from any contact with them, and the area was rife with malaria and cholera. He read out a letter from Frank Atlay, the first company manager of the ruby mines, who reported pragmatically that 'The servants are all down with fever and the native doctor as well; he will probably soon be replaced.'

When the British eventually arrived in Mogok, the town was empty. The people had fled to the jungle and it took a long time to persuade them that it was safe to return. When they did come back, several weeks later, they were a community in disarray. Ever since the British had taken Mandalay the year before, anarchy had ruled at Mogok. No one was in charge, the king was not there to take the best stones, and finders were keepers. So, after their attempt to fight the invaders had failed, the miners were justifiably worried that their newly found freedoms would be curtailed once again.

Gordon and his companions soon realised that the previous lease-holders had not been allowed to work the mines for themselves. Instead they had paid the king an annual sum for the privilege of collecting taxes as well as making personal loans to the poorer miners, 'for which they extorted exorbitant interest'.[18] They also realised that, under the terms of the new lease, if the Burma Ruby Mines Ltd. wanted to work some mines it would have to find its own new ones, rather than take over other people's. In this confusing hill country it was not easy to know where to start. In the words of a later, apologetic, report to shareholders,[19] all Gordon could do 'was to look about him in dense jungle, and start practically at haphazard anywhere'.

But Gordon, like his boss Edwin Streeter, was caught up in the wonderful adventure. And, fortunately, he was able to report to a fascinated British public that rubies were indeed coming out of the ground by the thousand – and that he had seen 'myriads of small rubies glitter[ing] in the sun'. Of course, nobody knew what would actually be found, but he could report to Royal Geographical Society members that the geological signs were positive. His speech was well timed: exactly a year later, the promise of Burmese treasure caused a most dramatic stock-market rush in London.

Burma Ruby Mines

Although the syndicate's exploration for new rubies had already started, the matter of the lease was still not settled. In 1888 *The Times* had launched a surprise attack on what it claimed was the 'unwise and improvident' decision by the British government to lease 'mines which have never been examined or even seen by a British officer'. It suggested that bribes had been involved in the decision to give the lease to Streeter's syndicate, although later it was revealed that some of the corruption stemmed from *The Times*'s employees. The newspaper's correspondent in Burma, Edward Moylan, was a barrister practising in Rangoon. He was known as a nasty character, who threatened to use his journalistic connections against judges who ruled against his clients.[20] Messrs Gillander, Arbuthnot & Co. had secretly employed him to write negative publicity against the British syndicate.[21] The plot was unsuccessful, but it delayed the signing of the first seven-year lease by a year[22] and ensured that the stock flotation of Burma Ruby Mines Ltd was preceded by plenty of publicity.

Exotic gemstones were the flavour of the era. The discovery of amazing stones in the South African diamond fields in the 1870s had received massive coverage in European and American newspapers, and as the century drew to a close almost every popular writer, from Conan Doyle to Wilkie Collins, was churning out stories about missing gems or gem-hunters. So, in 1889 the sale of shares in the Burma Ruby Mines tapped straight into the public's imagination.

The mining prospectus was published on 27 February 1889, and the next morning there were unprecedented scenes outside Rothschild's bank in London, where the application forms were distributed. 'If St Swithin's Lane had been a ruby mine itself the scene witnessed there yesterday morning could not have been more remarkable,' said the *Financial News*. Indeed, so dense were the crowds that Lord Rothschild and other bank staff could not get into the building by the front door. 'So a ladder had to be got, and the spectacle was seen of a number of great financiers entering their own office in a burglarious fashion,' the newspaper's correspondent wrote. *The Times*, having gainsaid the award of the lease to the Streeters in the first place, decided not to report these scenes, although its financial pages on 1 March informed readers that 'Messrs Offen and More (Limited) request us to state that notwithstanding the destruction of their shopfront in St Swithin's Lane, caused by the crowd outside Messrs. Rothschild's office yesterday, business was resumed this morning as usual.'

Within minutes the £1 ruby shares had quadrupled in price and the stock was oversubscribed many times. They were 'a pure gamble, even more than is usual in mining', grumbled the editorial writer of New York's *Engineering and Mining Journal*. However, he conceded that the issue had an advantage over the rest of London's mining stocks: 'There is a *possibility* that they will pay, and pay largely, while the average London mining stock is absolutely certain never to pay anything,'[23] he wrote smugly.

For a while it looked as if the gamble would pay off. The company had started well, with reserves of £150,000 and a huge amount of optimism. But it soon ran into difficulties. It was harder than anyone had expected to transport pumping equipment along bad roads, labour was difficult to hire, the payment system to the local people was almost unworkable, the British Army failed to subdue the bandits, and although bullock carts could reach the area from Mandalay in three weeks when the weather was dry, the road was impassable in the wet season. When rinderpest broke out and the bullocks died, which happened regularly, Mogok was isolated for months.[24]

Despite the problems, 1895 and 1896 were exceptionally profitable years, with plenty of stones found. In each year the company earned more than a hundred thousand rupees – a quarter of the price paid for the original seven-year lease. But at the turn of the century Verneuil found a way to synthesise rubies and, although they were never as pretty as the natural stones, the market suffered. Any glimmers of a revival were extinguished by the outbreak of the First World War. 'Work has been restricted,' George Streeter wrote, 'and native royalties in which the Company has no longer any but a limited interest, have fallen almost out of sight.'

Today, Mogok itself has fallen almost out of sight. In 1947 Burma gained independence from the British, and a decade and a half later something happened that has had drastic consequences for the Burmese. In 1962 General Ne Win came to power in a military coup, and introduced many repressive measures for the ordinary people. He was something of a gem connoisseur – rumour has it that one of his wives set up a jewellery shop in Italy to sell Burma's finest stones on the sly – and took a personal interest in Mogok. He banned private mining operations, and the government – by then called the State Law and Order Restoration Council or SLORC – took control of the area. Almost no foreigners (apart from Chinese, Indian and Nepali traders) were allowed to visit. In the early 1990s when the country opened up a little, the Stone Tract was still forbidden, and even today few foreigners are allowed to go there: the official line is that smuggling would flourish, although less formal reports suggest that the dark corners of Mogok township hide secrets that the government wants to keep, including forced labour, child exploitation and HIV.

I wanted to find out what legacy still remains of that first

British expedition and also to discover what was happening to Burma's rubies today. It seemed like an impossible quest until I talked to an adventurous gem-dealer in the United States:[25] in exchange for many hundreds of dollars the Burmese army would take me on a short visit to Mogok. The itinerary would not include any of the dark corners.

An Expedition to the Stone Tract

In March 2004 I found myself in the lobby of an expensive hotel in Rangoon,[26] handing over a substantial amount of cash. My guide was a smiling man in his early thirties called Yan Naing, who had wanted to be a philosophy lecturer until he discovered that he could not support himself on a salary of twenty dollars a month. We would meet two days later in Mandalay, we agreed, as he counted out the hundred-dollar notes again, just to check.

My visit coincided with the Myanmar Gems Emporium, the government's biannual auction of rubies, jade and cultured pearls. It is an invitation-only event for buyers, but I was lucky. As I approached the door one of the security guards sneezed. Not an ordinary sneeze but a spectacular explosion that reverberated round the lobby. I caught his eye and we both laughed so much that when he recovered he waved me in.

I entered a large hall in which several hundred people were sitting at plastic tables, popping peanuts into their mouths and consulting slim, photocopied catalogues. At the front a huge electronic board gave details in flashing green letters of which lot was on sale, and how much the previous one had sold for. The bids were quoted in neither Burmese kyat, nor US dollars, but in euros, a currency that most Burmese have never seen. In 2003 the United States adopted the Burmese Freedom and Democracy Act, which banned all imports from Burma. Cynics say that in its first years it had little effect on the gem business because no one can tell the difference between a stone that was imported five years ago or five months ago, and that now many more rubies for sale in America are labelled 'from Thailand'[27] than should be. In retaliation, Burma's gemstones are auctioned in euros.

If I had hoped for excitement, tension, verve, competition and passion, I was disappointed. The lot number was announced and a photograph was projected on to a screen while men in brown sarongs strolled round the room collecting pieces of paper, the closed bids. On the Tannoy a bored male voice asked, 'Any more bids?' then, 'No more bids?' in a tone that suggested he just wanted to get home. Someone in that room must have experienced the thrill of the chase. Did Mr Po Kong, who had just bid 93,300 euros for a lot reserved at ten thousand, feel excited – or did he agonise at the piece of vital information he had missed to make him bid so much higher than anyone else? If so, the tension did not carry to the rest of the hall where several people were asleep with their heads in the peanut bowls. It was hard to imagine the time when the gems emporium buzzed with the story of a 496-carat gem that almost escaped the net.

The ruby was found in 1990, conveniently just after Ne Win's government began to allow non-government mining companies to operate at Mogok. The best stones still had to be sent to the capital, but the miners who found the spectacular gem decided instead to despatch it illegally to Thailand, via the notorious Thai border town of Mae Sai, which is still the main place to buy smuggled Burmese gemstones. But this stone was too good to lose like that, and military intelligence followed it across the frontier. The smugglers were sentenced to life imprisonment with hard labour. And the ruby, in tune with the usual way of honouring really big gems, was given a name and sold a few months later. Since then it has almost certainly been renamed – few would want to boast that their lover had just bought them a ruby called 'The SLORC'.

A curious noise was coming from the balcony, like Chinese fortune sticks being shaken, or perhaps shamanic musical instruments. I went upstairs to investigate, and when I reached the source I realised something wonderful. It was the sound of rubies: tens of thousands of uncut red stones were being graded energetically in round metal sieves all over the balcony area, watched by Thai and Burmese dealers to make sure that no stones hopped out and into pockets. I asked one of the dealers whether the stones were from Mogok. 'No, not any more,' he said. 'These are from Mong Hsu.'

Mong Hsu is about 240 kilometres south-east of Mogok. It is closed to foreigners and the road is so bad it takes around fourteen hours to travel there from the nearest town.[28] Its gems were first discovered in 1991 when a local resident went bathing in the Nam Nga stream[29] and found pink stones between his toes. The town's population quadrupled overnight, but almost as suddenly enthusiasm dipped: the rubies were of low quality and only the best could hold a flame to Mogok's stones.

A few years later, people realised that the quality issue could be resolved by literally holding a flame to Mong Hsu's stones. Dealers discovered the high-temperature treatment that has thrown the rest of the gem industry into a tailspin of anxiety, and Mong Hsu became important again. The treatment is so good that it is usually impossible to tell with the naked eye whether rubies and sapphires have been subjected to it or not.

I told the dealer I was going to Mandalay and Mogok, and asked if he had any tips to pass on. He paused to think. Then he said, 'Remember, the closer to a gem mine you are, the more traffic-lights are broken into little pieces and polished. Don't be fooled, be careful.'

On the Road to Mandalay

When Robert Gordon had travelled to Mogok in 1886 it took him three days to cover the five hundred miles from Rangoon to Mandalay – on the new railway as far as the town of Prome, then by boat. Although the railway has long been completed, it still takes around fifteen hours to get to Burma's second city on the 'express' train. I shared my four-berth sleeping compartment with three men who were kind to me and made sure I got all the provisions I needed from the hawkers who parade round every station, selling snacks. The next morning I awoke soon after dawn and, from my eagle position on the upper berth, I saw something curious: an officer's cap, placed on a high shelf and wrapped in a plastic bag to protect it from dust. 'Are you in the army?' I asked, having descended to share my companions' biscuits for breakfast.

'Oh, yes,' they all said. 'We're going back after seeing our families in the south.' I had spent the night, I realised, with the feared Tatmadaw, the force that makes the country's oppressive military government possible.

Apparently in the past, Burmese soldiers carried rubies into war in the belief that the crystals would protect them against bloodshed and give them courage. I asked whether that still happens, and the men laughed. 'No,' one said. 'The Burmese army has guns: much better protection.' In fact it was not just the carrying of rubies in the pockets of one's army uniform that was believed to ward off bullets. Sometimes soldiers would even carry the stones cut into their flesh, to make the charm more effective.

Three Colours

Some people say that Mandalay has three colours: red, green and white. On one level they represent its rich clay soil, its grassy hills and the white Buddhist pagodas that are everywhere in the landscape, but on another they symbolise its chief business interests: rubies, jade and heroin. Rubies, of course, come from Mogok and Mong Hsu; opium poppies are cultivated in the Shan state, near the Chinese border; and jade – or jadeite, as the bright-coloured Burmese stone is called to distinguish it from the paler nephrite jade of China – comes from the far north.

I had a day to explore Mandalay, so I hailed a taxi outside my hotel and asked to go to the jade market, a surprisingly pale, white place, full of dust from cutting. The jade was poor quality and the only solid green I saw was the baize of pool tables as the workers took a break from polishing. I had a strange feeling I was being followed: I saw the same two characters everywhere, drinking tea, looking at goods, and watching me while I picked up offcuts from the ground. So, when I left the market I did so spontaneously and precariously, perched on the back of a man's bicycle. I rode ten blocks, then discreetly took a cycle rickshaw. My next stop was on the tourist itinerary, but since it involved meeting men who had recently been imprisoned for so-called 'political crimes', it seemed wise to be cautious before I visited Mogok the next day with the army's agent.

The Moustache Brothers are the most famous comedy troupe in Burma, although they are less famous for their witty phrases than for their jail sentences. In 1995 they made a joke about how only one hat in Burma was big enough to protect the country from the monsoon rains. It was a typically Burmese pun, which played on the democracy movement's symbol of a conical hat – but two of the three brothers discovered the hard way that the government did not share their sense of humour.

They were arrested and sentenced to seven years' hard labour; thanks to pressure from international comedians, they were released eighteen months early.

I found U Lu Maw – the English-speaking brother who had led the campaign to free the other two – smoking a cheroot and surrounded by puppets. I asked him whether he had any knowledge of the ruby industry. 'Oh, yes,' he said. 'When my brothers were in prison I was looking for a way to make money quick. And I found something red and shining on the ground. So I was very happy, and I took it to a merchant and I said, "How much will you give me for this ruby?" He knew I was a comedian and he began to laugh and wouldn't give me a price. So then I took it to another merchant and I asked him the same thing. And *he* knew I was a comedian and he began to laugh as well. So I took it to another merchant. And he didn't know I was a comedian. And he said, "Are you crazy? Why are you trying to sell me a tomato?"'

It is a surreal joke, but its irony was echoed throughout Burma as I asked about rubies. 'There is something mad about valuing little stones so highly,' said one taxi driver, who spoke excellent English – he had studied it at university. When doctors and teachers earn ten dollars a month – which isn't enough to feed one person in Burma, let alone a family – the market in precious stones seems rather frivolous. 'You can't eat them, you can't read them, you can't shelter under them . . .' the driver said. In fact, in the context of an oppressive government and one of the poorest countries in the world,[30] rubies have less relevance than a second-hand tomato.

Renouncing Jewels

'Did you enjoy the jade market?' asked my guide, Yan Naing, casually when he and the driver collected me to go to the ruby mines. I tried to remember if I had mentioned that I was going there. I thought I hadn't but in any case it reminded me to be wary. He didn't mention the comedians and neither did I. We were driving through the flatlands, the rich rice valleys north-east of Mandalay. All along the road there were thin trees with big leaves that looked yellow and faded, almost as if, even in springtime, for them it would be forever autumn. They were teak. I had not thought that the glory of Burma would look so sad. At the sides of the road women and children were sitting in the shade of banyan trees, busily weaving houses: in that area the walls and roofs of people's homes are made from flat packs of bamboo strips, so even the oldest villages look temporary.

In one village I saw a big building that really was temporary. It was made of bamboo poles from which coloured flags fluttered brightly. It resembled the Cantonese Opera theatres built in Hong Kong for village festivals. Yan Naing asked the driver to stop and we went in. We were greeted by a young boy who – to my astonishment – was dressed like a princess: he was wearing eye-shadow and lipstick, a long white skirt, a flower necklace and glass jewels. Half a dozen other similarly transvestite male children, ranging in age from five to fifteen, were standing behind him. It was a 'novitiation ceremony', I was told, and every Buddhist boy in Burma is expected to go through it before he reaches adulthood.

The first part of the ceremony reflects the story of the Buddha, who was born as Prince Siddhartha and saw only beauty, youth and health from his palace. But that afternoon the boys' lives would change: just as the Buddha had renounced the material world, the boys would exchange satin and jewels for red cloth and prayer beads. Their heads would be shaved and for the next few weeks or months they would live as novices in a nearby monastery, then return to ordinary life. The experience was intended to put everything else – whether pop music, fashion or pretty stones – into perspective. It was a good reminder, on the road to Mogok, that almost every man living in the land

U Lu Maw, one of the Moustache Brothers	*Buddhist novitiate, dressed as a prince*

of rubies has had a ceremonial lesson in the importance of renunciation.

Soon after that we came to a wooden shack labelled 'Immigration'. An armed guard checked my passport and papers. I had paid the army hundreds of dollars to be waved on at this point, rather than turned back. There was a moment of tension as the man frowned and double-checked my internal travel visa. Then he waved us on, and we branched off the highway on to the road to Mogok. Immediately we started to climb and the landscape changed. We passed grapefruit trees and banana plantations, and great slim bamboos that looked like fishing rods casting their hooks over the countryside. This was the area where Robert Gordon's expedition had met bandits, and where the miners' private army had built stockades to hold back the British soldiers and jewellers.

Mogok is surrounded by nine mountains, which means that not only was it easily defended, it was also thought to be lucky.

The people of Burma are Buddhist, but the old animist beliefs still survive, in rural communities in particular, especially the belief in *nats* or guardian angels. Nats are creatures of the trees, the air and, of course, the rocks. Nats protect people, ruby mines and entire states. Nine is a lucky number in Burma: the king was traditionally accompanied by nine umbrellas; the chief nat of the old Shan[31] state, through which we were passing, is called Kyo Myo Shan, meaning 'ruler of nine territories', and the most glorious ruby mines in the world are protected by nine mountains. The only time nine is not lucky is when you are travelling in a group of that size: apparently it annoys the nat of the Shan state. But there was a solution, my guide explained: 'If we are nine people going to Mogok, we pick up a stone and say, "Hello, Mr Rock, would you come on a journey with us?" and the nat thinks we are ten people.' I liked the idea of journeys with Mr Rock and was rather sorry that, with the driver, there were only three of us.

The Land of Rubies

'Welcome to Ruby Land,' announced a huge red archway over the road. And then we were through it and cruising into a decaying town. There were pagoda ruins, covered with creepers, on the hill, a few intriguing alleyways, some sleepy shops. I just had time to scribble in my notebook how picturesquely run-down Mogok was when we were back in countryside again. It hadn't been Mogok at all but its neighbour, Kyatpyin, Ralph Fitch's Caplan. Once upon a time it had been *the* centre of gem discoveries but now it was eclipsed by its neighbour, twelve kilometres away.

By the time we got to the real Mogok it was almost dusk. Which was – philologically, at least – the perfect time to arrive. The town was named by rice farmers who left for their paddies at dawn and did not return until the end of the day: they called it 'Mo-chouk', meaning 'evening-time'.[32] We drove to the largest pagoda, on a hillside, and looked out over the town. Below, a small gang of Nepali boys were playing football. Later they told us they were the grandsons of Gurkha soldiers, who had stayed behind when the British left. Their cries merged with the wuk-wuk-wuk of frogs calling to their mates in the warm twilight.

'Welcome to Ruby Land'

Usually gem towns are small, with only one business and a few streets in which to conduct it. From a 1911 report by the British colonial government, which mentioned a dwindling population of 11,069, I had expected Burma's main ruby town to be compact. But now more than three hundred thousand people live in Mogok, and while the trawl of precious stones is declining the word has not got out – the population keeps growing. Everywhere across the valley I saw red tin roofs, punctuated by the slender stems of white pagodas, and in the middle of it all was a beautiful lake on which people were fishing in small boats.

That evening, in an almost empty Chinese restaurant, I said to Yan Naing that I would like to go to where the miners hung out at night. 'You can't do that,' he said nicely.

'Why not?' I asked.

'Because miners don't hang out. They're not allowed.'

We drove back through empty streets. It seemed that most of Mogok was in bed by nine.

Just Like Home

Breakfast the next morning was in an echoing Communist-style hall. Two bowing men showed me to the head table where papaya, bananas, toast and jam had been laid out for one. The younger waiter looked tired: he had stayed up most of the previous night to watch Manchester City play Leeds United on satellite TV. 'Leeds won,' he said sadly. I felt closer to home in England than I had expected – and I wasn't the first: when George Streeter had reached the town more than a century before, he was amazed at how much it reminded him of home. Just as Europeans were drawn to Burmese stones partly because their origin was remote and exotic, in the same way the rich men of Mogok had invested their wealth in things that were exotic to them. 'In these [people's homes] you meet with an old-fashioned champagne glass or an American clock; or a gold Godama [Buddha] will be seen reclining by an English candle-stick,' Streeter wrote.[33]

As I ate my breakfast in solitary grandeur, I noticed Yan Naing sitting at another table, talking to a man in a bomber jacket, baseball cap and trainers. Later, as we set out to explore the town, the stranger sat in the front seat. 'Who's our friend?' I asked.

'He's from the government,' Yan Naing answered. His name

was Hlaing Win and he would be with us while we were in Mogok. 'It's routine.' It sounded ominous. Mr Win took a small notebook out of his pocket. It had a blue cover on which 'Special Branch' was written in English.

At the marketplace, I took a few photographs of the river that runs beside the stalls to record the ox-blood-red water, thick and polluted with silt from the ruby mines. I asked the stallholder for prices and found that Mogok was as expensive as Rangoon. Mr Win took notes of everything, each name, item and question noted carefully in the Special Branch book. I decided this had to end. When we got back to the car I announced I wanted to change the itinerary. The two men looked worried. 'It's Sunday,' I said. 'I want to go to church.'

The previous day, as we had driven in, I had glimpsed a late-Victorian-style church in the old town and guessed that it was the one that had been built at the turn of the century by the Burma Ruby Mines company. I wanted to see if there were any memorials to the mine personnel or, indeed, anything else connected to the mines' history. I explained this to Mr Win, who obligingly gave instructions to the driver, and a few minutes later we stopped at a modern building proclaiming its evangelism on a big billboard. It was the wrong church, I said.

'But which one do you want?' Mr Win asked. 'There are fifty-four of them!' They all laughed at my expression.

'Also there are several mosques and Hindu temples. And there are Sikh temples, Chinese temples and plenty of pagodas ... This is a big town,' Yan Naing said. It was also a cosmopolitan town. People had come from all over Asia to follow their dream of rubies, and they had brought their priests and mullahs with them.

The church I had seen on the hill turned out to be Catholic. It was probably not the original mining church, but it did date from the time of the Burma Ruby Mines company. Sadly, unlike the Anglicans, Catholics do not usually enshrine their more prominent members with overblown epitaphs on the walls. Those places are reserved for saints. Soon after we arrived, the priest, Father Francis, came out to greet us. He was from the Lisu tribe, one of Burma's poorest ethnic minorities. We stood together to watch his congregation walk to church through the heat in their Sunday best: white shirts, plastic shoes, trousers neatly patched and carefully washed. Few had any connection with the gem trade, Father Francis said. 'These are poor people: they are lucky to find work as road labourers. They don't get much work in the mines.'

'But they came to do that?'

'Oh, yes. Like everyone here, they came dreaming,' he said.

Our conversation was transcribed in Mr Win's blue book. He also made notes during the service, although I've no idea what he thought of it. The women wore crocheted veils; the hymn-singing had the extraordinary mountain sound I had once heard from a Bulgarian women's choir.

On the other side of the valley from the churches was the so-called 'Panthay Mosque'. The Panthays were Muslims who originated from northern China, and were among the greatest ruby traders of the nineteenth century. Although the Chinese are viewed with suspicion throughout Burma because the Chinese government has been a strong supporter of the Burmese military leadership, the Muslim Panthays are in an ambiguous situation. Ever since they rose against the Qing emperor in China in 1855[34] they have often faced persecution in their homeland. Robert Gordon described them as 'perhaps the greatest travellers on the face of the earth'. They carried their gems for thousands of miles, he said, and expressed the hope that the arrival of the steam train might relieve their feet and donkeys. The mosque's ancient guardian told us that the building had been constructed to give thanks to Allah for the success of the ruby business – although, like so many mosques around the world, its architecture was simple, perhaps to emphasise that lasting treasure is not found in material things but in the uncluttered presence of God. As we prepared to leave, the guardian motioned us through one last door. I found myself in a blue-painted school-room in front of twenty-five startled teenage boys, who had been daydreaming during their Qur'an lesson as the sun streamed in, making stripes on their desks. I asked their teacher, Soe Win, whether the Qur'an said anything about rubies.

'Yes,' he said. 'It teaches that rubies were created by Allah, and if you value Allah, then you will value even a single stone. I tell the children that they must remember the difference be-tween a ruby and an educated person. Because a ruby has an exact price, but as an educated person they can be priceless.'

When we returned to the car, the tension between minder and minded had gone. Although Mr Win still wrote down all my questions, from then on we all got on so well that he even helped me bargain for a few cheap gemstones, and allowed me to ride occasionally on the back of his motorbike, to the astonishment of the people in the streets who watched us drive by without helmets.

The Pink Umbrella Market

It is a curious quality of natural light that the world often looks better when seen from beneath a pink umbrella, and the gem market in Mogok takes place every morning beneath dozens of them. This is deliberate: the light filtering through pink canvas makes rubies appear brighter than they are – a reminder of how important it is, when buying gems, to check them under as many different light conditions as possible. Burmese rubies are at their best between ten in the morning and four in the after-noon.[35] They also look better under brilliant tropical sunlight than subdued northern skies, which is one of the reasons they have always been even more prized in the East.[36] The best are fluorescent in natural sunlight. It is a quality they share with only a few other gemstones, including some rare diamonds, and buyers who are aware of it will take the trouble to study the stones in sunlight and shade.[37]

Fluorescence is such a mysterious quality that mythologies have built up around it. The early-sixteenth-century Italian explorer Luigi Barthema reported that the King of Pegu had a ruby 'of so great a magnitude and splendour that by the clear light of it he might in a dark place be seen, even as if the room or place had been illustrated by the sunne beams'.[38] And Burmese puppeteers still tell the story of an eleventh-century Shan princess, who was sent as a bride to King Anawrahta. As part of her dowry she was given a pair of exquisite ear tubes made of rubies that fluoresced in all lights. Ear tubes must be some of the oddest jewellery items ever devised. From the side they look like toilet plungers: a tube goes horizontally through the earlobe, fronted by a circular trumpet-shaped piece of metal. In eleventh-century Burma they were considered to be extraordinarily attractive and the king loved both his new wife and her jewellery. But the courtiers were jealous: they used the quality of her rubies to accuse the young princess of witchcraft. She was banished to her homeland, and on the way back she took out the ear tubes so that she could bathe in the river without losing them. Suddenly she saw what everyone else had seen, that the light danced inside the gems like magical spirits. She became afraid, and decided to build a pagoda in which they would be buried and their unearthly powers contained.[39]

Mogok rubies tend to fluoresce more than any others. This quality is particularly clear in the pigeon's blood rubies, which give out a slightly purplish glow. Their name comes from the ancient Burmese tradition of making animal sacrifices to the nats: they are said to be the precise colour of the drops of blood that burst from a pigeon's beak in the moments after it is strangled. Such an image is not the high point in a sales pitch to most Westerners planning to buy a good ruby. After pigeon's blood, in decreasing order of value, come 'ox blood', 'rabbit blood' and, finally, 'pink like a flower'. Ancient Indian writers had more varied descriptions. In 1879 the Bengali scholar S. M. Tagore compiled a more extensive list of ruby colours from the *Purana* sacred texts: 'like the China rose, like blood, like the seeds of the pomegranate, like red lead, like the red lotus, like saffron, like the resin of certain trees, like the eyes of the Greek partridge or the Indian crane . . . and like the interior of the half-blown red water lily'.[40] With so many gorgeous descriptive possibilities it is curious that in English the two ancient names for rubies have come to sound incredibly ugly. In Shakespeare's time people referred to them as 'carbuncles', from the same Latin root as 'carbon', because they contained the sense of being on fire. Today that metaphor has been extended to boils. The Greeks called them 'anthrax', which also means 'coal', and for a while the English adopted the term. Yet when we hear that word today we mostly think of a white powder posted by terrorists, which can cause deadly red marks all over your skin.

The Morning Gem Market

Mogok is not only a centre for rubies. As soon as we sat down in the central square we were surrounded by a friendly mob holding out little white packets containing all sorts of stones. There were sapphires like milky blue pebbles, moonstones filled with mist, yellow topazes, green peridots and glassy quartz cubes cut as if pagodas were locked inside them. Then there were the red stones: red spinels, red garnets, red glass, red rubies.[41] 'Stop!' I begged. 'How can you tell the difference between rubies and spinel?'

In answer, a young woman wearing a large sun-hat put two mineral specimens into my hand. They were still partly encased in their matrix of white rock and were of a similar crimson colour. But there was an immediate difference: the Burmese term for one variety of spinel is *anyan nat twe*, meaning 'nat-polished spinel', and this sample was almost perfectly 'cut' by natural forces. It looked as if, millions of years ago, the nat spirits had been playing dice games, and a little red cube had fallen on to liquid white marble and stuck there, its corner in the matrix. The ruby was more like a piece of pink bubblegum stuck haphazardly on to the rock by a careless nat-child and forgotten.[42]

And there was another difference. Spinels tend to be the same colour all the way through, while rubies have a quality called dichroism, meaning two-coloured. It happens because of how the light passes through the ruby crystal. Imagine a pencil made of glass: different things happen to the light depending on whether it is travelling along the length of the pencil, or whether it is effectively cutting it in half. Looking along the long 'optic' axis of a ruby the stone is crimson-pink; the other way (imagine cutting across the pencil) it is quite orange. 'Like nun's clothes,' I said, pointing to two Buddhist nuns crossing the edge of the market. They were dressed in the standard costume of bright orange robes topped with pale pink. The gem-dealer laughed. 'Yes, just like that.' Some sapphires have dichroism too: if you look carefully, you will see that they are blue along three angles, but violet along the fourth. Make sure you check all four directions: if you check just two or three you might not see the one that is different.

The Mines

There is something almost classically heart-rending about men having to carry stones up a steep hill in harsh sunlight. But most of the men at the Than Htike Lu ruby mine were young and strong, and as they hauled their rocks there seemed nothing tragic about their plight. After all, as some of them would tell me, they had a dream to keep them going.

Like most gem mines in Burma, the Than Htike Lu is a

Chinese–Burmese joint venture.[43] Its workings are hidden securely behind a high wooden stockade that looks like an Iron Age fortified village. We parked inside the enclosure and were met by one of the managers, who led us up a steep pathway. It was a curious sight: the slope was awash with white unwanted stones. The marble in which Mogok's stones are found is very pale, and from a distance its debris is almost like snow. Indeed, from afar, the workers looked almost like skiers descending well-worn paths, and the effect was compounded by the mechanical workings scattered like lifts over the hill. 'Mogok is like Switzerland,' several of its inhabitants had told me proudly the previous day. Now I could see what they meant. It wasn't just the little wooden chalet houses or the nine hills or the cooler air: Mogok really did have its own interpretation of snow.

I was so intent on looking up that I had not noticed what was below me. Then I heard what sounded like loud applause. Lower down, twenty men were sitting in a small open-sided shed. The 'clapping' came from their energetic tapping of white rocks with dark hammers. This was the first processing point of the ruby gravel after it comes out of the ground. Before the rocks go anywhere near machinery, they are cracked manually so that the best rubies are not ruined. From a distance it looked like hellish work but I tried it later, and when you hit them at the right angle, the white rocks split like coconut ice. It was rather easy.

Half-way up the hill we went into what seemed like a small shed. We found ourselves in a huge tunnel that smelt damp, like a flooded cellar – which, in a way, it was. The first few metres of the tunnel were horizontal, but further in was a deep cavern that led down to the gem-bearing rocks below. The cave descended for 160 metres, belching up dank, cool air. You couldn't see to the bottom, where men were loading baskets with white stones, but you could just see the baskets, swinging up on taut wires like tiny cable cars. Unlike in the Sri Lankan sapphire mines, the miners here used precarious but properly formed ladders. I asked if I could descend, but my police escort said no. I don't think he realised I was serious.

After the rocks had been cracked by hand, the discarded fragments were carried in buckets to a 'cracking machine', which pounded them, then spat them on to a covered platform, on which a dozen men and women were sifting for gems, watched by a young woman in a red sarong whose only job was to make sure no one stole anything. When a piece was found, it was put straight into a little red padlocked box suspended above the workers' heads on a piece of wire.

After this final search, the reject rocks were pushed down the slope where more people were waiting to sift through them for the third time. These were freelancers and whatever they found they could keep. Little had changed since Robert Gordon and his colleagues had gone to Mogok in the 1880s. At that time women had the automatic right to search for precious stones in the piles of discarded gravel. It was one of the few jobs open to them and although the rule has been changed to a more sexually equal one, they outnumber the men by four to one.

I stopped a miner at random. Tan Tomphei was twenty-eight and had worked there for eight years. His father was dead and he had to support his mother and an unmarried aunt. His first job had been as a potter, making things. Now he is a stone-cracker, breaking things. But while before he had no chance of leaving the poverty cycle, at the mine there is always the fantasy that tomorrow a Nga Mauk-like ruby might emerge, whole and flawless, from the powdered marble and he and his colleagues will be rich. Like most of the miners, he does not get a fixed salary, but receives board, lodging and a percentage of profits. He confirmed that the miners were allowed to leave the compound only twice a month, and before they went out they were searched thoroughly – saying this, he raised his eyebrows, which seemed to suggest a level of thoroughness that none of us wanted to contemplate. At least the rule meant that they saved some of their earnings, he said, then added that in eight years he had sent home about a hundred dollars. It sounded a small amount, but he seemed pleased with it. In any case, he would rather do this than any other job, he said, picking up his buckets of rocks again and carrying them up the hill for washing.

We followed and watched him tip the rocks into the machine, and then a few minutes later saw them come out the other end as gravel. Yan Naing looked down at the pile. 'Is this one?' he asked, picking up a red crystal of around five carats.

'Yes,' said the man in charge, who looked annoyed that an outsider had spotted the gem before he had.

Later we saw what looked like a three-storey barn made of rattan. As we passed, the shutters on several windows sprang open like an Advent calendar, and men stuck out their heads to watch us. These were the living quarters, and later I managed to see inside one such building, although it was not on the itinerary. It happened when I climbed a staircase to take a photograph. When I turned round I found myself standing at the open door of a dormitory. It stank of boys and feet, much as I imagine the living area of an eighteenth-century warship to have smelt; and to increase the impression, the haphazard collection of clothes hanging on lines that criss-crossed the room looked rather like hammocks.

I wasn't going to peer any further, but then Tan Tomphei appeared, as if by chance, and invited me in. The room slept two hundred men in about twenty partitions like animal pens. Because it was the end of the working day some of the men were asleep already, lolling peacefully on the floor. Tan Tomphei proudly pointed out his own space: his home was a stretch of bare floor with two folded blankets. There were two Buddha images on the wall above his section – a contrast to his neighbour's, which was decorated with a poster of a Thai film star. There were no pin-ups anywhere of naked women, as there surely would have been if this place had a European equivalent. The company's strictness clearly went far beyond limiting the miners' days out.

From the Mouths of Babes

Once upon a time in Mogok, according to contemporary legend, amethysts were as common as blackberries, rubies were like mulberries, sapphires were like drops of water, and any hard-working miner could come to the mines and do well. But that is not the case today. There are many men like Tan Tomphei, who work hard for years and yet save little because none of the six hundred or so mines are producing much. Some say it is because the gems are almost finished, but the more superstitious have another theory. In the past, they say, miners used to wear white clothes and pray to the nats; they never swore or committed adultery. Now standards have relaxed, and perhaps the nats are displeased.

The miners do their best to counteract this. When later we visited a different mine on the other side of the township there were nat shrines on almost every piece of unexcavated ground. They looked like bird-tables – little wooden boxes balanced on single legs. I looked inside one and was surprised to see nothing in it but a single fresh flower. 'Of course there are no statues of nats,' Yan Naing said, laughing. 'They are invisible.'

The mine it was guarding was a large pit of alluvial gravel, as deep as a ten-storey building and wider than a football pitch. In the late 1890s Edwin Streeter had commented that the one hope for the ruby mines' productivity was electrical machinery, which – once it had been manoeuvred over the mountains – would make the work more efficient. 'It has been said that, after all, pumping is the real crux of Ruby mining,' he wrote. Today this dream of the future is a noisy and noisome reality: the earth and rocks were being sucked up from the bottom of the pit into

Cracking white rocks to look for rubies

A miner climbing down one of the many gem pits at Mogok

Stones in her mouth: the little girl in orange

sorting machines at the top – it was impossible to hear anybody speak, and the whole place stank of dust and diesel. Then everything was sorted in great sieving machines, the rejected material washed out into muddy red streams, populated by dozens of children panning through the mud with round sieves. They shook these strainers vigorously until the gem material – having a greater density than normal gravel – had sunk to the bottom, then emptied them on to a mud bank, where women checked through what was now the top layer for tiny jewels. The corundum waste looked like black poppy seeds on top of pebble-dashed sandcastles, but just occasionally there was a sparkle of colour.

Most of the children were covered with silt from their hair to their toes. But in the middle of it all was a child in a bright orange dress. She marched confidently through the dirt and somehow remained immaculate. She was eight and – she said – she and the other children were on their school holidays. I had heard there was child labour in Mogok, but these children did not look forced to work. When I asked if she had found anything she performed a little conjuring trick as a reply. She waved her right hand in front of her face and suddenly a little piece of pink sand, the size of an unrefined sugar crystal, was between her fingers. Where had she kept it? I asked.

'In her mouth,' Yan Naing said. 'All the children keep their stones like that. That way nobody will steal them.' If I had held that tiny piece in my own mouth I would have swallowed it, I mimed, and some of the other children laughed and stuck out their tongues to show me their own finds. This knack of using your mouth as a safe is traditional practice in Mogok, but it also has echoes in the traditional way of telling whether a 'gem' is genuine or not.

The habit of trying to pass off glass as rubies or other precious stones goes far beyond the practice of vandalising traffic-lights, of which the Thai dealer had warned me. It has probably gone on since the invention of glass in around the fourth millennium BC – certainly by Ancient Egyptian times it was a common enough scam to be mentioned in papyrus documents. One way of seeing the difference between gems and coloured glass is by looking at them through a magnifying-glass: glass 'gems' usually contain little bubbles. But another way is to put the stone into your mouth. When a ruby or sapphire touches your tongue it often feels like ice because of its high thermal conductivity, which enables it to draw heat from your body. Glass – being warmer, or less thermally conductive – rarely has this effect, especially not in the heat of Burma.[44]

Dying for Rubies

The last item on the itinerary I had been given by my military hosts was 'Visit to Kyauk Pyathet Rock Pavilion Pagoda'. When I asked Yan Naing what the point of the visit was, he explained that it was just a pretty Buddhist temple in the countryside. 'Nothing to do with rubies,' he said, 'but tourists really like it.' I almost asked him to strike it off the list, and arrange something more gemstone-based, but he seemed so disappointed at the idea that I decided to go ahead. And I'm glad I did, because it turned out to be one of the most significant places on my journey.

From a distance the Rock Pavilion Pagoda looks like one of King Ludwig's fairytale nineteenth-century Bavarian castles. Its slim fantasy pinnacles are built on an outcrop that looks like an enormous version of the gnarled scholars' rocks that Daoists in China prized for meditation. We parked at the bottom, walked past two huge stone lions, then climbed the 161 steps that spiralled like a helter-skelter around the outcrop. It struck me, as we made the steep ascent, that the natural walls of the pinnacle were made of white marble and that they looked similar to the rocks we had seen being bashed into fragments by the men at the ruby mine the previous day.

At the penultimate staircase there was a simple meditation room. Four men were sitting inside, chatting and drinking the green tea that can be found in thermos flasks all over Burma. The real treasure was a very old Buddha statue, and it was just above us, they said. But as I moved towards the final flight of steps they stopped me. Women weren't allowed to go into the shrine, they said. For a moment I felt cross, but then I decided not to be and to have a cup of tea instead. I was lucky, because the conversation changed my perception of the Valley of Rubies.

Remembering the marble walls of the rock beneath us, I asked whether the place had any connection with rubies. The men nodded and started to talk very quickly, as Yan Naing translated. 'They say the rock beneath us is full of rubies,' he said. 'It has the best ones in the whole of Mogok and it is one of the most precious places in the world, some people say.' However, as a curious echo of the holy mountain in Sri Lanka being the original source of sapphires, this ruby hill is a sacred place where no one is allowed to mine. 'The British tried to dig here once,' said Il Poe Thaung, the president of the Buddhist trustees of the pagoda. When I apologised for my countrymen's insensitivity he laughed. 'It's all right. They had to leave Mogok very soon afterwards . . . The Buddha looks after the sacred rock.'

Sometimes, Il Poe Thaung said, the rubies appear almost magically in the rock overnight. This probably had something to do with the rain eroding the marble, he said, although the erosion can have a human cause. The steps we had just climbed had been built in the 1930s and the workmen had found rubies and spinels embedded in the walls in places as they dug. The monks usually took them out so that pilgrims would not be tempted to steal them, but further up they had left some in place. Just outside the meditation room, Il Poe Thaung showed me a rough rockface, as big as a house. At first I could see nothing but white. Then: 'There it is!' said Yan Naing, always the first to spot a stone. About three metres or so above the ground there it was, a little bright ruby poking out of the rock.

When we went back into the room, the men poured more tea and told a story that animated them all. Yan Naing enjoyed it so much that at times he forgot to translate. They were saying how, just six months earlier, something terrible had happened at the Rock Pavilion Pagoda. Local miners stole in at night and started doing illegal excavations. The first the monks knew of it was the sound of a tunnel collapsing, and when they went to investigate they realised that all the men were dead. No one knew if they had found anything or even how many of them had been killed. The police decided not to open the tunnel, but to leave the bodies there. 'They said it was so their spirits could become the guardian nats of the pagoda,' Mr Thaung added, among much laughter from his listeners. In Islam there is a tradition that God appointed an angel called Atlas to carry the world on his shoulders. The story tells that he was given a rock of bright ruby to stand on, but it emphasises that ultimately, beneath the ruby rock, there is darkness.[45] Now, whenever I think of rubies, I also think of the darkness beneath Atlas's pretty rock and of the skeletons lying in silence below the rubies of the Rock Pavilion Pagoda.

Later Mr Thaung said he wanted to show me something. We walked barefoot across the meditation room, and stood on tip-toe in the corner to peer through the upper window. It was the Buddha statue, seen from below. As the clouds cleared in the sky above, a shaft of sunshine shone like a spotlight on the face of an exquisite golden figure sitting cross-legged above us. Seen through cobwebs and dust, the great treasure of the pagoda seemed all the more precious. But the ancient Buddha wasn't the only thing he wanted to show me. There was another secret of the pagoda, he said, pointing through the same window. Outside there was a little *stupa*, or Buddhist reliquary, about as big as a human head. It was covered with whitewash, like almost every other stupa outside every other pagoda in Burma. But, like the land around us, its treasure was hidden beneath the surface. 'This stupa is ancient and, if you look beneath, it is decorated with rubies and sapphires and topazes and amethysts,' he said. 'But we covered it up. We were afraid people would steal the jewels.' As with all good religious symbols, stupas convey a multitude of meanings, but for the men in that room they symbolised the mind of the Buddha and the one at the pagoda presents an image of a mind searching for enlightenment. On the surface it looks plain but underneath it glistens with gems.

Outside the meditation room there was a balcony from which we could see the whole of Mogok stretching into the distance, and everywhere great orange gashes that testified to the search for buried treasure over many centuries. To the east were the trade routes leading to China. For many hundreds of years the stones had travelled that way on mules, in exchange for porcelain and other luxury goods. Burmese sapphires were made into blue buttons for mandarin officials while the rubies tended to go into imperial headdresses[46] and the pockets of corrupt officials.[47] Today the same roads east of Mogok are major smuggling routes through the disputed Shan state, where money is laundered and gems are exchanged for heroin and opium.

To the west of the pagoda was the road that we would depart on the next day. It was the same winding track along which precious stones had been carried to India and beyond for thousands of years. India had its own ruby mines and its rulers also imported stones from Sri Lanka and from Afghanistan's Oxus valley. But no mines ever produced such fine red gems as Burma's, which were always the most highly prized. Some time later, I found a report sent to the Burma Ruby Mine company shareholders in 1905. It referred to the Rock Pavilion Pagoda as 'Pingutaung', or 'the Hill of Spiders', and identified it as a place that 'native tradition pointed to being the real home of the pigeon blood ruby'. According to the report, the British had found the hill to be such a strange plug-like shape that they wondered if it might contain a volcanic pipe of rubies, like those at Kimberley, in South Africa, which contain diamonds. They attacked it from all sides as well as underneath, spending ruinous amounts of their capital on the excavations. The irony was that on the first day, in a cave high up in the hillside, they found one of the most beautiful pigeon's blood rubies anyone had ever seen. It sold in London for seven thousand pounds. It was the only good stone they found there, 'but what hopes were raised!'[48]

Stones of the First Water

One thing bothered me. I had seen signs of the colonial legacy – the English-style church, the jail buildings, the stories of greed that the lay Buddhists had told at the Rock Pavilion Pagoda – but I kept wondering what had happened to the original Burma Ruby Mine; the one for which the British investors had fought each other in St Swithin's Lane, and of which the Streeters had been so proud. I had understood from old records that the workings had been in the centre of Mogok but in several days of exploring I hadn't seen them. When I asked Yan Naing he laughed, and pointed to the lake covered with half-blown red water-lilies that I had admired every morning from my hotel window. 'That is the Burma Ruby Mine,' he said.

By the 1920s the mine was already running into trouble. Great rubies were no longer being found; even good ones were rare. And for ordinary rubies the price had dropped, ever since Verneuil started marketing his cheap synthetics. Then, in 1925, the drainage tunnel in the main mine flooded. The workers were evacuated and mining stopped. As more and more water came into the great pit all the mine's owners could do was stand on the edge and watch. For a while they hoped to drain it, but as the water became deeper they saw it was impossible and allowed it to become a lake, used by local people for recreation and said to have been a gift from the nats.

Financially speaking, it was the beginning of the end for Burma Ruby Mines Ltd. The company's accounts are still held in the Oriental and India Office Collection, the stacks of papers arriving from the vaults in great leatherbound books held together with the original threads. They reveal, in sepia hand-writing, that in the years immediately following 1925 the com-pany struggled on for a while, trying to exploit smaller mines in the hills, like the one I had seen. However, even in the wealthy, heady era of the late 1920s the company was reporting losses of between five and sixteen thousand pounds a year. Yet the directors were reluctant to stop mining because, under the terms of the lease, Mogok would return automatically to government ownership, and they would have no chance of finding a buyer and cutting their losses. In April 1929 it was decided that business was so disastrous they would have to cease operations but, as the chief accountant reported, a few months later 'at the very moment that the telegram was being drafted . . . a cable was received from Burma announcing the discovery of a sapphire of exceptional size'. It weighed 629.5 carats and when it was first valued at £8333 the company directors celebrated. But this was 1929: the Jazz Age was over; Europe and America were swiftly entering a recession. Over the next months, the excep-tional sapphire was reduced in price to five thousand pounds, but no purchaser came forward. In fact, it was badly flawed and worth no more than five hundred.

No more huge stones were found, and in 1931 the British syndicate disbanded and the government took back the Burma Ruby Mines. Some said it had failed because local miners were smuggling the good stones out of the country to sell privately. Others said it was simply because the seams were mined out, while some devout local people muttered that the *nats* were taking revenge on the British for mining their sacred hill. Others, including the head of the Geological Survey of India, Mr J. Coggin Brown, thought there was a more sinister reason for the ultimate failure of Burma Ruby Mines Ltd.

Coggin Brown was suspicious of one of the more prominent members of the board. 'I cannot refrain from writing an opinion which I have already expressed verbally, that the influence of the De Beers diamond concern has had more to do with the present position of mining for coloured gems in Burma than appears on the surface,' he wrote, in a confidential report in 1927. 'The reasons for this are obvious, and it is significant that there has always been a powerful representative of the Great South African concern on the Board of the Burma Ruby Mines, Ltd.'[49] Diamond companies like De Beers were well aware that, during most of the time that the Burma Ruby Mines had been operating, rubies were seen as the most romantic stones of all, being the symbolic colour of hearts and life and warmth. Coggin Brown's theory was that it was therefore the powerful diamond lobby that had sabotaged Burma Ruby Mines Ltd. The subsequent history of the diamond trade has divided opinion ever since.

9

Diamond

Cloakroom attendant: 'Goodness! What beautiful diamonds.'
MAE WEST: 'Goodness had nothing to do with it!'
Night after Night[1]

'Selling utterly useless yet quite exquisite things is hard enough
for anybody and the odds are stacked against us all.'
GEOFFREY MUNN,[2] *gem-dealer*

'A real tragedy was visited upon [Americans on September 11
2001]. They had been immune to that sort of thing before.
This has caused a push to traditional values in life and,
obviously, diamonds are very much part of that ethos.'
NICKY OPPENHEIMER, *chairman of De Beers*[3]

It was opening time at the Smithsonian Museum in Washington
DC. A small crowd, mostly of schoolchildren, had gathered
outside the Natural History building and as the guards opened
the gates they all rushed in. In any other of the great galleries
that make up this national museum everyone would have scattered to pursue their own individual fascinations, but not in the
Harry Winston Gallery. In what seemed hardly any time at all,
the crowd had re-formed, this time round a glass case in a
small room on the second floor. And each person was staring,
mesmerised, as a clear, steel-blue stone as big as a walnut went
round and round on a mechanical wheel.

'Is that the diamond that has evil in it?' a teenager, with
braces on his teeth, asked the security guard.

333

The man smiled. 'It *is* the Hope diamond,' he confirmed cheerfully, 'but for the museum it's brought only good luck.'

The boy returned to the case to stare for a little longer. He was not alone: every year some four million visitors stand in the same place, paying homage to a stone named after a nine-teenth-century Dutch merchant banker who, had he not owned a fabulous jewel collection, would otherwise have been forgot-ten. But what were we all looking at, as we gazed into the cold heart of one of the most popular museum exhibits in America? Or perhaps the better question is: What were we all looking *for*?

Diamonds are the hardest substance known in the universe: their name comes from the word 'adamantine', or unconquer-able. Nothing can cut them except other diamonds. They score a perfect ten on Mohs' scale of hardness, and on more discerning industrial scales[4] they have been shown to be at least four times harder than rubies or sapphires – yet so often they are used to symbolise one of the softest things in the universe: love. Today they are said to be 'a girl's best friend' because if a man fails her then at least she can sell her diamonds – yet there is almost no second-hand market for diamonds. In a pack of cards dia-monds represent the merchant classes,[5] while in a pack of people they represent the moneyed classes. They are the language of apology and of ostentation, of kings and queens and, increas-ingly, commoners.

Diamonds are at once the most precious of the four 'precious stones' – the others being sapphires, rubies and emeralds – and the least rare. They are often bought by men at exactly the point that they can least afford them. They have been believed both to be poisonous and to protect from poison. Some are said to be cursed. They are pretty and fun, and they twinkle in the pockets of international terrorists. They are the only gemstone that is also a shape. No wonder we look carefully at a famous, named example like the Hope: there is so much in it to try to understand.

The Legend of the Hope

The legend of the Hope includes curses, daring thefts, unusual deaths, bitter divorces, alcoholism, public executions and numerous other misfortunes. It is therefore one of the best and the worst of all gem stories. The saga began hundreds of years ago – no one knows quite when – in the Deccan area of southern India when a dark stone was found, probably by a team of peasants. Diamonds are unlike almost all other stones in that they do not form in the earth's crust or at its surface, but much deeper underground in the layer of volcanic magma called the mantle, where temperatures reach 1000 degrees centigrade and pressures are as high as fifty kilobars. To put this in perspective, the pressure you would feel if you dived down to the deepest point in the ocean – which no one has yet managed – would be just one kilobar, a fiftieth of what is found in the mantle.

Because of the tremendous volume of the earth's mantle, there are probably billions of carats of diamonds below our feet, but the only ones that reach the surface arrive by chance, carried by an almighty underground explosion, which fires magma to the earth's surface at supersonic speed in what is called a 'kimberlite pipe': it is similar to a normal volcano but comes from much deeper. It is an entirely random event and, as Bill Bryson points out in *A Short History of Nearly Everything*,[6] one might be exploding in your back garden as you read this. (If it did, you would never reach the end of the paragraph.) In themselves, kimberlite pipes are nothing to do with diamond formation: they are the lift shafts that carry the gemstones to the surface, the earliest diamond-delivery mechanism.

Like sapphires and rubies, diamonds are almost always alluvial, found in rivers, on plains or in seas long after the pipes that brought them have worn away by erosion. So, perhaps this blue one was just scooped out of the river, like a sapphire in Sri Lanka – but many of the old diamond riverbeds in southern

Jewels: A Secret History

India have been dry for centuries, and just as likely its finders would have spent their days in shallow pits digging the alluvial gravel until they found something special. We can only imagine their reaction on the day they uncovered a large, dark, glassy object, a little smaller than a hen's egg and weighing (it would later be established) some 110 carats, or twenty-two grams. It would probably have been viewed with some perplexity, as nothing quite like it had ever been found in India – before or since. In its rough state the stone would have been much darker than anyone was used to in a diamond, and there would probably have been speculation as to whether it was worth anything at all. Was it a diamond, or was it some less valuable mineral, like obsidian? The local way to check was to study it under a tree or at night[7] where, in the mottled light of the shadows, its status as a true diamond could most easily have been discerned. It would have shone more brightly and more steadily than it would in ordinary sunlight. Even today would-be buyers of fine diamonds must take into account the lighting used in jewellery shops: the lamps of less scrupulous dealers often have a bluish tinge, making diamonds seem more scintillating than they ever would be in the light of day.

If the blue stone had been smaller it would have made its way to a city called Golconda where merchants sat in the shadow of an ancient fort, trading little stones for large fortunes. There were once many diamond areas in India – Karnul, Kollur, Ramallakota and Partiyalah, ranging over five provinces in the Deccan area of central India – but the most famous is Golconda. Until the early eighteenth century, when India's diamonds ran out and Brazil obliged by replacing it as the chief source, almost all of the world's diamonds[8] passed through this place. Like London, New York and Tel Aviv today, it was the diamond capital of the world, even if no gems were found in the ground there. And in the beginning most diamonds found in India stayed there. Until the sixteenth century at least, diamonds were

336

Brazilian slaves washing for diamonds

so rare outside India that they became the subjects of exotic legends. One of the most popular medieval stories about Alexander the Great, for example, told how the young hero once visited an Indian valley where diamonds were found. It was so steep and full of serpents that no one dared descend. But Alexander got his men to throw pieces of raw meat down, which stuck to the stones. Eagles swooped to pick up the flesh, and by following them the soldiers were able to retrieve the precious stones from their nests. The curious thing about this story — which was also told by Marco Polo and appeared in a slightly different version in the Sinbad sagas — is that it contains a grain of truth. If you throw a piece of mutton on to diamonds it picks

Men looking for diamonds   *Eagles carrying diamonds*

them up, while leaving pieces of glass or topaz behind. Diamonds are what are called 'lipophilic', which means they are attracted to fat while most gemstones are not. So this exciting fable could actually have been a mnemonic to remind its listeners of how to test if a 'diamond' they were being sold was real or fake.

By the end of the seventeenth century many of Golconda's diamonds were being traded internationally, often sent to Indonesia in exchange for camphor, pepper and brimstone,[9] then carried on by the Dutch to Europe, or the Chinese to China. However, the blue diamond was not destined to leave its homeland yet. Well above the magic ten carats in weight, it was automatically the property of the kings of Golconda, who kept most of the best finds in their realm to decorate their elephants, robes or thrones, or to trade favours with other royal dignitaries.

From the early 1500s the main diamond areas were ruled by the Muslim Qutb Shahi sultans. But before that, most of the Deccan was Hindu, ruled by the Kakatiya kings. It is said that if one of those Hindu kings was feeling in particular need of spiritual support, he would improve his karma by donating a stone to the temple. Perhaps he would have been happy to part with the blue diamond, as it was ambiguous in its symbolism. Clear, transparent gems were the most prized, and only the Brahmins, members of the priestly caste, were allowed to wear them. Blue diamonds, however, were uncomfortably close, chromatically, to the darkish stones allotted to the Kshatriya or warrior caste.[10] Blue diamonds were the colour of storms, and although, in a country that lives and dies by the monsoon, this could be a beautiful colour, stones were sometimes thought to be too close to the sky, and jealously guarded by the gods.

Gods and Diamonds

Whatever the reason, the next part of the Hope legend tells us that it was set in the eye of a Hindu god. The god's identity is not part of the story although any of the principal manifestations of God in the Hindu pantheon would have fitted. Perhaps it was the inner eye of Vishnu, the Preserver, so-called because if he were to stop breathing for even an instant the whole world and its riches would disappear. Or perhaps it was set into Brahma the Creator, whose energy is present in all things, including diamonds. Or maybe, given the tragedies that became part of the stone's later story, it was Shiva the Destroyer, dancing up a whirlwind to represent the death of material desires, who carried the diamond in his forehead. But whichever manifestation the stone might once have been allied with, for it to have ended up in the Smithsonian performing its own strange turning dance, it must at one time have been removed from its statue. And one version of the story suggests that this was done, discreetly and by a thief, on the orders of the seventeenth-century French celebrity jeweller, Jean-Baptiste Tavernier.

Tavernier made six journeys to Asia between 1631 and 1668, each time returning with such vivid descriptions of his travels and such stunning jewels that he captured the attention of the

The Golden Fleece, created for Louis XIV

young 'Sun King', Louis XIV. Louis would not normally have entertained a man like Tavernier. Not just because he was a merchant but because he was a Huguenot, or Protestant, and was therefore despised in Catholic France. However, although Louis detested Huguenots he loved diamonds more – their shine supported his personification as the Sun King – and he became Tavernier's greatest customer.

Tavernier published the accounts of his journeys at length, going into so many details about the size, weight, name and provenance of the stones and thrones he saw that he is still regarded as one of the most important authorities on historic Indian diamonds. The best stones, he wrote, are 'of the finest water', and this description has captivated jewellers ever since. Gem-dealer Richard Wise has recently[11] urged a return to grad-

ing diamonds not only in terms of carat, colour, cut and clarity
– the four Cs – but also to take account of its 'water' or crystal
nature. 'I first had the idea when I was looking at two stones,'
he wrote. 'The problem I was having was that the two stones
were exactly the same grade – but ... one was more beautiful.
It was diaphanous.' He cites an expert from Christie's, who
described the limpid transparency of the best Golconda-traded
diamonds, like the Hope, as 'a quality in which light appears to
pass through the stone as if it were totally unimpeded, almost
as if light were passing through a vacuum'.[12] It was, she wrote,
a quality possessed by no other diamonds in the world today,
although the same sense of liveliness and 'fine water' is also
seen in Kashmir sapphires and the very best rubies from Burma.

From Tavernier the French court learned how to grade stones
in the Indian way and about the peculiar way in which buyers
and sellers in Golconda traded diamonds. They would sit in
silence, facing each other 'like two tailors', and touching each
other's hands beneath the cloth of their waistbands like lovers
with a secret language. 'When the seller takes the whole hand
of the buyer that means 1000, and as many times as he presses
it so many thousands of [rupees]. When he takes only five fingers
it means 500, and when he takes only one it means 100,'[13]
Tavernier wrote. This is possibly how he negotiated for the blue
diamond, but curiously he does not mention it in his journals,
although he did commission an artist to make a drawing of it.
The blue diamond is one of twenty stones depicted in the book
of the jeweller's last Asian voyage, and it is labelled simply 'A'.
It is from a paper, in the *Philosophical Transactions*,[14] written
at around the same time, that we learn about a clean, rough
stone of *'un beau violet'* (a beautiful violet colour), weighing
just over 110 metric carats, and part of a parcel sold to Louis XIV
for 220,000 livres, or around £16,500. For gem historians
Tavernier's omission of the stone is strange, and may suggest
that it was bought under shameful circumstances.

It is with Tavernier that the curse of the Hope first appears to manifest itself. In 1685 Louis XIV revoked the Edict of Nantes, which had – nominally – protected for nearly a century the Huguenots' freedom to worship as they chose. The king's jeweller had to escape from France, with at least two hundred thousand other Protestants. They left in a hurry, their churches burning behind them. Since early medieval times Paris had been the principal European centre for jewellery, a luxury shopping mall for aristocratic families throughout the continent, and few could afford to disregard its taste and fashion.[15] But with the banishment of the Huguenots in the late seventeenth century, the famous gem-cutting tradition almost disappeared from France. The greatest cutters and designers moved to the largely Protestant lowlands of northern Europe – to Amsterdam, Bruges and Antwerp – where their skills and workshops remain to this day. Indeed, so many goldsmiths and jewellers left Paris at that time that the Duchesse d'Orléans declared in 1706 that it was no longer true that nothing pretty could be found outside France, and no one had the heart to contradict her.[16]

Tavernier settled in Switzerland, lost his money and was said to have died in Moscow, his throat pulled apart by wild dogs. Meanwhile, the Sun King had the blue diamond cut down to sixty-seven carats and set as the central stone of the Order of the Golden Fleece. He longed to revive the age of chivalry, and wore the Order on many occasions. In 1715, a few months before his death, he welcomed the Persian ambassador to Versailles in a black suit embroidered with twelve million pounds' worth of diamonds, and round his neck, suspended from a light blue ribbon, a single dark blue diamond.[17] It was said that he once lent the stone to his finance minister, Nicolas Fouquet, to wear at a grand ball. The next day Fouquet was arrested, and he was later executed. Louis XIV's own death was said to have been slow and painful.

The blue diamond's last confirmed owner was the Sun King's

great-great-great-grandson, Louis XVI, who was guillotined in the Revolution with his queen, Marie Antoinette. Meanwhile, everyone else who was rumoured ever to have worn it, including the queen's lady-in-waiting, Princesse de Lamballe, who was torn apart by a mob, suffered immeasurable ill-fortune. After Louis's death the stone was confiscated and, with the rest of the Versailles treasures, was sent to a museum storage building in Paris called the Garde-meuble. In September 1792 it was among the items stolen by a team of drunken and incompetent thieves, who gained so much confidence during three nights of unde-tected robbery that on the fourth evening fifty turned up with food and wine. The next morning, when the National Guard discovered the robberies, they found some of the perpetrators still lying in an alcoholic stupor on the floor.[18] But while almost every other jewel caught up in that comedy of errors was recov-ered, the French blue diamond was never seen again.

A Mysterious Arrival

About twenty years later a slightly different diamond appeared in London. It was the second-largest fancy blue that had ever been recorded up until then, the largest being the missing French diamond. Diamonds of such rarity never appear on the world market without provenance, but this one had no story at all. All that was known was that it was clean, weighed forty-five carats or so and, as one observer commented admiringly, was the colour of 'indignant indigo'.[19] It was perhaps not '*un beau violet*' but its shape at least was consistent with it having been recut from Tavernier's stone, and several independent experts over the past hundred and fifty years have conceded that this was probably what had happened.[20] Around 1823 the Dutch banker Henry Philip Hope bought it, gave it his name and, being a bachelor, lent it to his sister-in-law to wear at parties. He was later said to have suffered various scandals, and in 1910, his spendthrift descendant, Lord Francis, sold it to pay off his debts. After that it finally landed in the prestigious rue de la Paix offices of the Cartier brothers – Louis, Alfred and Pierre – who hawked it for a while among India's maharajahs, Europe's aristocrats and America's heiresses, before eventually selling it to Evalyn Walsh McLean, daughter of a Colorado gold baron.

Evalyn revelled in the stone, loving its reputation and the awed looks it earned her, and was known to wear it on all kinds of social occasions, especially inappropriate ones. When she was bored she would dress her dog in it, and watch how visitors gawped. Like others of her set, she enjoyed being both reckless and artlessly nonchalant with her possessions. When someone asked her why she wore so much jewellery, she shrugged and said, 'If I take out one or two pieces to put on when I dress up I might as well put it all on and then I know where it is.'[21] She and her husband Ned lived at the height of the Jazz Age, and they lived it to the full. They held wild weekend parties where, as the Hope's biographer, Marian Fowler, writes, 'young men with patent leather hair and too much gin inside them fell into the shrubbery and young women with newly shingled hair and armloads of jade and ivory bangles pulled them out again'.[22] At one infamous New Year's party at the Walsh mansion in Washington DC, Evalyn appeared like a slim sprite on the top step of the grand central staircase. She peeped down at her arriving guests, then darted out of sight. As they told their friends afterwards, she had been wearing the Hope diamond. And nothing else at all.[23]

It was at Evalyn that the stone's malicious eye seemed to wink most energetically. In May 1919 her eldest son died, aged nine, in a car accident. She was away at the Kentucky races, the Hope diamond at her throat like an amulet. Her husband Ned responded to the double tragedy of losing a son and having too much money by becoming an alcoholic – once, infamously, urinating on the leg of the Belgian ambassador during a function at the White House. In 1933, by then divorced, he was committed to an asylum and died, leaving massive debts. Their only daughter, Lizzie, committed suicide, although their two other sons survived into old age, and Evalyn herself spent her adult life addicted to opiates and other drugs. She died at sixty of a combination of cocaine and pneumonia. For five years before that, she had penned a society column in the *Times Herald* and once wrote about her famous diamond: 'If you put it directly under any light and keep it there, you can see it change, sometimes getting darker and sometimes getting a greenish colour … I personally am not afraid of the Hope diamond, but I always warn my friends not to touch it. It is a strange and fearful thing how many people who have touched it have had unnatural and a great many times horrible deaths soon afterwards.' After her own, unhorrible death in 1947, the diamond was bought by the New York jeweller Harry Winston,[24] the son of a Ukrainian immigrant who had built up his business from nothing, and who, in his later years, was said to have a jewellery collection second only to that of the British Royal Family.

Through the previous decades Winston had watched the Hope. He had seen it scintillating at diplomatic soirées, being photographed outside the divorce courts and shining dolefully at funerals. The combination of the curse and of Evalyn Walsh McLean's poor-little-rich-girl life story had already made it one of the most famous stones in the world, so when it came up for sale he bought it. But it seemed that the stone's curse touched him too. Although his client base ranged from movie stars to kings to glamorous Asian princesses, he could not find a buyer for it. He had it recut, which slightly improved its symmetry, but the rich people who believed the Hope's astonishing history would not risk its curse, and those who did not could not see the point of owning it. Instead Winston came up with a strategy as brilliant as his diamond.

He presented the Hope like a celebrity in its own right. He

showed it off, sent it round the world, let it twinkle in the company of famous people at parties, and told its private story in the media – never hesitating to recut and polish the Hope's history when necessary. Sometimes, for a touch of well-publicised bathos, he posted it in the US mail, usually omitting to mention that it was extremely well insured. In 1958 he did something that many people found surprising. He donated it – with its facets glittering in the light of assorted camera flashes – to the Smithsonian. He said it was an act of generosity to the American people, to encourage others to donate their best jewels to the nation. When the Internal Revenue Service queried the substantial sum he wrote off against it, he challenged them to 'find me another like it to compare the price'.[25] They could not.

The diamond was placed where it is today, in solitary grandeur in the Harry Winston Gallery, surrounded during opening hours by large crowds of modern-day pilgrims staring into its godless eye and meditating on what secrets and curses it might hold. It is a compelling reminder not only that money cannot buy happiness, but that it can do much worse: it can buy unhappiness. There is only one problem. Most of the story is simply not true.

Creating a Legend

When Pierre Cartier bought the Hope in the summer of 1910 he, like Harry Winston nearly half a century later, made a small error of judgement. He thought he could easily sell it on. But the stone was slightly lopsided and rather dark, not at all the shade that was in fashion. It was the time of Sergei Diaghilev's Ballets Russes, of Nijinsky, of Van Gogh's yellows, of the Fauves' bright naïve canvases and of Kandinsky. All of Paris was bursting with colour and vibrancy. This dark, rather serious banker's stone simply would not do at all.

Pierre was the second son of Alfred Cartier who, with his

father Louis François, had built an ordinary jewellery company into an extraordinary one, with the assistance of three unexpected circumstances: the discovery of diamonds in a riverbed in South Africa in 1866, the invention of an efficient method to create a new type of metal, and the Franco-Prussian War.

Before 1870, Paris had been in what seemed to be a permanent state of celebration. A contemporary wrote that Parisians 'have no homes; their interest lies elsewhere, in the streets, the museums, the salons, the theatres, the private circles; all this immense social life which breathes day and night, draws you in, excites you, steals your time, your spirit, your soul and devours everything'.[26] In a city where appearance was everything, jewels were its expression. The Cartiers had been struggling to fulfil all the orders coming in for classical-style tiaras, Renaissance-style necklaces, and long earrings to shimmer under the streetlights. Diamonds were particularly prized in those years: the Brazilian mines were running out, the Indian mines had long ceased commercial production, and they were seen as extremely rare and precious.

But in the summer of 1870 France fought and lost a war, and that winter Paris was under siege. The centre of the city was bombarded; twenty thousand people died and almost everyone was unable to find food. After 1875, as the city was rebuilt, the jewellers were surprised to find themselves among the first groups outside the construction industry to thrive once more. During their brief period of poverty people had learned that, of all other possessions, diamonds had held their value best. The image of Parisians swapping tiaras for baguettes has been part of the stones' myth ever since. If you own diamonds, the story goes, you can survive. For women especially, a healthy jewel collection had additional importance: in most European countries in the nineteenth century – and, indeed, in France until the 1930s – married women were not allowed to own property. Their jewels were often their only assets.

From the late 1870s onwards, as Parisian women made every effort to replenish their jewel boxes as a glittering insurance against future disturbances, they demanded new, quite different styles. The brash ostentation of the previous decades was largely gone: they wanted a greater subtlety. And, thanks to the innovative use of a metal called 'platinum', the goldsmiths could oblige.[27] Diamonds, being mostly clear, looked better with silver than gold – white gold had not yet been invented – yet silver was heavy, relatively weak and tarnished easily. The new metal was lighter and stronger than silver – and it allowed for diamonds to be set in open mounts. Nowadays that is almost the only way we see them, but at the time it caused a sensation. For the first time the inner fire of the stones was permitted to flash, unimpeded, into rainbows.

Also, platinum had good marketing people: it quickly became known as the Metal of Heaven. Stylish women ordered their diamonds to be reset in platinum in the shape of brambles, flower baskets or butterflies: natural patterns to celebrate the natural exuberance of the natural minerals. By the 1910s, the maharajahs of India were looking to faraway Europe for inspiration, while Europeans and Americans began to look the other way in their search for the exotic: towards India. The East was all the rage, so if the blue diamond's colour could not sell it for Cartier, perhaps a deliciously scandalous exotic Oriental story could.

Pierre Cartier was not the brilliant jeweller his father had been, but he was a genius at selling. He realised that in the marketing of a precious stone the most terrible curse can be the greatest blessing. So, with the help of a spoof article that had appeared in the *New York Times*[28] in 1909, he simply made it all up. Inspired by his company's own decorative brooches, he wove thorny brambles and elaborate rose garlands of fiction round a skeleton of truth. And Evalyn Walsh bought it.

The Truth about the Hope

Here is the truth. There was probably never an idol so there was never a daring theft from a temple. Louis XIV died naturally of gangrene; his finance minister was arrested seven years before Louis bought the diamond. Although Marie Antoinette was, of course, guillotined, she had probably never worn it, and neither had the Princesse de Lamballe. Despite all rumours to the contrary, most of the Hopes died, as most people do, in their beds with scarcely a hint of a scandal. Even Lord Francis survived his bankruptcy and lived until the age of seventy-five. As for Jean-Baptiste Tavernier, all we know for sure is that he was buried in a Protestant cemetery near Moscow, having died at the admirable age of eighty-four. He had lost part of his fortune, thanks to a corrupt nephew, but there are no documents, rumours or even suggestions that date from before Cartier took over the narrative that wild dogs might have been involved in his demise.[29]

Only one person seemed to suffer from the curse of the Hope and that was its last society owner, Evalyn Walsh McLean, the only person to wear it while believing it contained an unholy influence. Much of her comic, tragic, ridiculous life was certainly more to do with her addictions to both drugs and attention than with any malevolent glow emanating from her jewellery box. But the death of her son was certainly a terrible accident. What could that mother have thought that night as she rushed back from the Kentucky races to find the boy had already stopped breathing? Did she curse the day on which Cartier had shown her the diamond, and her own confidence that its ill-fortune would not touch her? Did she want to throw it far away to where it could do no harm? Perhaps. Yet Evalyn did the opposite. After her son died she wore the Hope so often and so ostentatiously that it came to define her, and in the end her ownership of the diamond became her obituary.[30] Sometimes the mind is cruel: it tells us we are worth no more than our possessions, and that without them we would be nothing. And when we believe it, perhaps it is true.

The Many Eyes of Idols

Pierre Cartier's story of an idol was invented, but it was not original. By 1910 several diamonds in Europe and America were said to have been stolen from Indian statues, so it was hardly surprising that he thought the public would accept another. One of the other stones, the 194-carat Orloff diamond, had been given to Catherine II of Russia by her former lover Prince Orloff, who hoped to win back her favour. He was unsuccessful, although she gave him a nice marble palace in St Petersburg for his trouble. In 1783 a Huguenot clergyman called Louis Dutens[31] wrote of how the Orloff had been ripped from a statue of Brahma in the 'Temple of Sheringham' by a deserter from the French garrison in India. The soldier had pretended to convert to Hinduism and had ingratiated himself into the inner sanctum of the temple, then stolen 'one of the eyes', which he sold in Madras for a cool two thousand pounds. In 1868 the English novelist Wilkie Collins picked up the adventure and used it explicitly as inspiration for his bestselling stolen-diamond thriller *The Moonstone*, *The Da Vinci Code* of its decade, bought by most of the British reading public. Collins was writing for a mass market, whose staple reading was the hugely popular missionary magazines, heavily subsidised and therefore cheap. They were full of graphic illustrations of the exotic 'heathen' Orient and supplemented by tales of Protestant derring-do in a land of idol-worshippers. Like Dutens' book, which had emerged from stories of Protestants forced out of France by statue-worshipping Catholics, Collins's book came from a tradition that wanted idols to be robbed of their power but liked the idea of curses surrounding them.

Almost certainly this story provided the 'provenance' of another diamond, a blue-white stone of some seventy carats called the Idol's Eye. According to a Christie's catalogue in 1865, it was supposed to have been found in 1600 in Golconda, bought by a wealthy Muslim and 'set as an eye in an idol in the sacred temple of Benghazi'.[32] Never mind that Muslims do not have idols or that Benghazi is in Libya, it made a wonderful story and ensured that the stone had a steady progression of keen American owners throughout the twentieth century.

It is unlikely that any jewels were removed from the eyes of Hindu deities because this is not the traditional way in which statues were decorated. There *is* an ancient Hindu temple in Sri Rangam, near Mysore, which would fit Dutens' 'Temple of Sheringham', but it does not contain a statue with a jewel – or even a scar in its forehead where a big diamond might once have lodged. Neither is there a tradition that a European ever stole a sacred jewel from there. The stories of the Hope, the Orloff and the Idol's Eye probably did not start with a European or any other thief: they were much more likely to have been a misreading of an ancient Hindu myth about a lost diamond, that originated in India thousands of years ago.

The story[33] tells of a king who worships the sun faithfully, and in return is given a jewel called the *syamantaka*. When he walks into a room he glitters so much that his people think he is the sun itself, and in the presence of the gem, misfortune, snakes and sadness disappear. But one day the king's brother loses the stone in the forest and the king accuses Krishna, one of the manifestations of the god Vishnu, of having stolen it. To prove his innocence Krishna goes on a quest to find it, and the story ends in an epic battle between the Hindu deity and a monstrous bear called Jambvat, with both wanting to possess the gem. Finally the exhausted beast realises it is fighting Nature itself: 'I know you! You are the air itself,' he exclaims, and gladly renounces the jewel. And this is what jewels have symbolised in

Hindu temples ever since: the dangers of greed, pride and blindness to the truth.

Some say the *syamantaka* was a ruby because it glowed like a coal, but others say it was a diamond because it had eight facets and eight magical qualities. Its radiance was said to light up the darkness, to keep its owner cool, to cause rain to fall, to bring to fruition everything its holder desired, to prevent floods, to emit coloured lights, to cure disease and prevent untimely death.[34] Diamonds must be one of the best metaphors for the concept of cutting through illusion: not only do they embody the delusion of material desires, but they also make the world's finest cutting blades.[35]

Usually the gem appears as a symbol, carved into an icon or painted on to temple walls. But sometimes – and perhaps this is where our European legends of theft and idols spring from – it is represented by a real jewel. One of the most dramatic is a diamond crown kept in the government treasury of Mandya in southern India, not far from Sri Rangam. Once a year more than a hundred thousand visitors gather in the area. The crown is removed from its safe and, to the accompaniment of drums, trumpets and the car horns of the assembled police escort, it is carried high on a ceremonial cushion to the temple at Melkote twenty-five kilometres away. The priests stop at each village and the people run out to watch the procession. The most curious thing about the ceremony is that no one sees the crown, which is kept wrapped in a blue velvet bag; all anyone can make out is its approximate shape. Tradition dictates that no human should ever look upon the diamonds so even the chief priest wears a blindfold as he takes it out of its wrappings and places it on the head of the statue of Cheluvanarayana, the manifestation of wisdom. That night, as the crowned statue sits in darkness behind a screen, the people have a party that lasts until dawn, celebrating a diamond crown they cannot see and whose existence they have to take on trust.

The event has a curious parallel in another aspect of the international diamond story. Every fifth week almost a hundred representatives of major diamond-cutting companies from India, New York, Tel Aviv and elsewhere fly to London for an extraordinary ritual. It is called a 'sight', and it involves the 'sight holder' being escorted to a small room deep in a secure building in Charterhouse Street near Hatton Garden.[36] It is effectively a gathering of the world's most exclusive club of 'diamantaires', or diamond dealers.[37] Each is left alone with a number of boxes,[38] which contain several million dollars' worth of uncut stones. They will have discussed the contents of the boxes at great length with their hosts over the previous four weeks, but this is their first sight of what they are about to buy. They may open the boxes and look, but some observers suggest that they rarely need to do so. Like the priest of Melkote, they might as well have been presented with their diamonds, unseen, in a closed blue bag, because the rules of the ceremonial transaction are simple. According to Edward Epstein in *The Diamond Invention*, until at least the 1980s either the sight holders took the boxes at the price at which they were offered – no haggling, no negotiation – or they lived with the possibility of being struck off the list of those allowed to buy rough diamonds in this way. Once they had taken the box back to their own headquarters they had to accept further rules: allowing accountants to appear without warning to audit their accounts and, most importantly, agreeing never to sell on the rough diamonds, except as faceted stones.[39]

The system sounds as if it might have been thought up by a dictatorship, but instead it was designed by one company. Its uncut-diamond-sales arm is called the Diamond Trading Company (DTC), but it is better known as De Beers. In his book *Diamond*, journalist Matthew Hart quotes former DTC executive Richard Wade-Walker as saying that they used to call Sight Week 'feeding the ducks ... The ducks come paddling over and you throw them the bread and they eat what you throw.'[40] If any of the sight holders had questions about their box, they were made to wait, sometimes 'for hours and hours', until someone was available to see them. Sometimes, Wade-Walker remembered, they waited so long they missed their return flights. Today the situation is different. According to the DTC: 'The emphasis of Sight Week has changed. The DTC now provides, through its Intention to Offer Service, a six-month plan of what supply a sight holder will receive in the period.' Because of this, 'it is rare that a box is rejected as the contents usually meet the sight holder's expectations.'[41] However, until the late 1990s De Beers, with its numerous parent, sibling and associated companies, had control over virtually all the rough diamonds in the world.[42]

The Biggest Diamond Company in the World

The history of how one company cornered the market in diamonds dates back more than a hundred and thirty years and, like the story of the Hope, is as much about stories and mythologies as about diamonds. It begins in South Africa in 1866, with a brownish stone scooped out of the Orange river by a boy called Erasmus Jacobs. This find was quickly followed with better ones, and by 1872 a million carats were being pulled each year from the southern African earth – five times as much as came from Brazil in any one year. By then the Kimberley Mine, one of four mines in Griqualand West, now the Northern Cape province,[43] was being described as one of the wonders of the industrial world. The mine had started off as a flat seven-acre area, but had quickly been divided into some three thousand claims, each thirty-one feet square. By the late 1870s the field had become a canyon – but an uneven one, like a modern city full of buildings standing at dramatically different heights. The strange landscape was caused by some concession-holders digging deep into their squares while others had scarcely touched their claims. To get the men in and the diamond earth out, there was a chaotic mesh of pulleys and wires, along which little tubs travelled up and down like tiny cable cars holding either a man or a bucket of diamond earth. One visitor described it as 'something of the appearance of a flight of birds, darting their ways to and fro in the great abyss'.[44]

Out of this great abyss emerged two of the best entrepreneurial minds of the nineteenth century. Barney Barnato was born to a Jewish family in an East London slum and arrived in Kimberley in 1873 at the age of twenty-one with almost no money in his pocket and forty boxes of fake Havana cigars in his bag. Cecil Rhodes was exactly a year younger, and came from a very different background. He had been born with a weak heart in a Hertfordshire vicarage, and when he was seventeen he was sent for his health to South Africa to join his older brother, Herbert. The family[45] fondly believed that Herbert was farming cotton quietly and would provide a refuge for his brother. When Cecil arrived, in 1871, he found that his brother was upcountry, mining for diamonds, and a year later – having won prizes for his cotton – he joined him. He bought a claim, and was delighted to discover that the dry air of the veldt was good for his health. Later he completed a degree at Oxford, but returned to Africa in the long vacations to buy up claims, rent pumps to miners whose claims were flooded, and read the classics in the shade while his workers did the digging. He set up a diamond company, which he called De Beers Mining Company Ltd. The name was ironic: the Afrikaner De Beers brothers had once owned the farm on which some of the greatest mines were found, but they had sold the land early on and missed out on its profits. Perhaps the choice of name was a small memo to self not to do the same.

By the time he was twenty-eight Rhodes had a degree, a fortune and a hatred of Barney Barnato, who had sold his cigars, run a boxing ring, dealt in illegal diamonds, bought some claims and started a rival company called the Barnato Mining Company, which later merged with the powerful Kimberley Central. The men were both ruthless in business but Rhodes, perhaps, had the edge. In 1884 he negotiated with the Cape government for permission to use convict labour.[46] The first experiments with two hundred men worked so well that the De Beers company offered to build a convict station for four hundred men or more, which would take the convicts 'completely off the hands of the government'.[47] According to Cambridge anthropologist Robert Vicat Turrell, the company had almost absolute control of these men's lives. Convicts went naked to their cells every night 'and when their term was over they were put in solitary confinement, naked and with large leather gloves on their hands to make sure they had not swallowed any to sell later'.[48] If attention to human rights was low, attention to safety was lower. The Kimberley mines had the worst record of any in South Africa: each year, out of every hundred workers, between six and eleven would die in landslips, sickness, fights over diamonds and, on one occasion, from an underground fire, which killed 202 men. According to a witness, the last thing the rescue party heard was the sound of hymns being sung underground as the labourers realised they were trapped and prepared for death.[49]

Over the years, Rhodes and Barnato circled each other as they amassed astonishing riches and power. In 1887 they locked horns and two years later, having secretly bought up the stock of smaller partners, Rhodes gained control of most of the mines in Kimberley. Barnato was content to walk away with a lot of money and a huge block of stock in Rhodes's company.[50] For the first time since the reign of the kings of Golconda almost the entire world supply of diamonds was in the hands of one man. It was the beginning of the diamond cartel.

Diamond prices had quivered since 1873 when the markets realised how many stones had been found in the African earth.

The first to come out had been fairly brown and 'Cape diamonds' earned themselves such a bad name that the better ones were sent abroad and sold as Brazilian. In 1877 the market collapsed again,[51] and again in 1882. By 1889 Rhodes had grasped that if diamonds were no longer rare, he had to promote the illusion that they were.

He slashed production from three million carats a year to two[52] – and the price started to stabilise. When further mines were found, he did his best to control them too. However, when he died in 1902, three more big mines had been discovered, including the lucrative Premier mine, near Johannesburg, found by Thomas Cullinan, a former bricklayer.[53] Apparently when Sir Alfred Beit of De Beers first saw the Premier mine he fainted: its surface was three times larger than that of anything at Kimberley. His reaction was perhaps justified: the De Beers company was in trouble, and by 1908 its share price was falling. 'How far will it go?'[54] wondered the Parisian banker Georges Aubert, in a report for would-be diamond-sector investors. Diamonds, he reminded his clients, were not a necessary commodity, like copper, sugar or cotton: their value was simply a convention – even an invention. 'One buys diamonds because they are luxuries that not everyone can have. If diamonds fall to a quarter of their current value then rich people won't buy diamonds any more but will use their taste to buy other precious stones or luxury items.' Another big find, he warned, might start a panic.

Worse was to come. Just as Aubert was writing his gloomy analysis, another big find was being uncovered in the sea just off the German colony of South West Africa, now Namibia. Millions of years ago, the diamonds had worked their way loose from the kimberlite soil and made their way slowly downstream to the sea. The Namibian diamonds are the ones that actually made it. Once people started to look carefully, more diamonds were found in the desert and on the beaches, and in 1908 the German government declared a *Sperrgebeit*, or 'forbidden zone', that stretched along the coast for 360 kilometres north of the Orange river. It is still forbidden to go there without a permit and a police certificate stating that you do not have a criminal record.

The colonial government employed thousands of African railway labourers to crawl over the beaches with circular sorting pans and brushes, painstakingly sweeping up the white sand to see what was hidden within it. They wore gags so that they could not swallow any diamonds, and when they found anything it was dropped into a tin carried by the guards.[55] Anyone caught stealing was severely punished. Afterwards great dykes were built some two hundred metres out to sea with twenty-metre-thick walls holding back the waves, while the men on the newly created beaches kept brushing, in their enforced silence. They brushed first under the Germans, then, during the First World War, under the Cape government, and finally under De Beers, which was part of a consortium that took over the Namibian mines in 1919 after the Allies had won the war. This odd coastal place is a good metaphor for De Beers, which made its fortune by building barricades against the ocean of diamonds that constantly threatened to wash away the market.

The Cullinan

In 1908 it was as clear in South Africa as it was in Paris that new barricades had to be built. And this was done, partly, with a gift. Three years before, an enormous glassy stone had been found in the Premier mine. It weighed 3106 carats and was the biggest known rough diamond in the world. It was a South African national treasure – and the newly independent Transvaal government gave it away. After the disasters of the Boer War it had been made a crown colony of the British Empire. By 1907 it had been granted self-government but still needed to establish better relations with the British. So in 1908 the premier, Louis

Botha, presented the diamond to King Edward VII, hoping that stories of a new royal diamond might encourage the ordinary population to aspire to the same. The king was not sure whether he should accept it, but in the end he agreed.[56] When the stone arrived at Windsor Castle he was disappointed by its ordinariness: 'I would have kicked it,' he remarked, 'had I seen it in the road.' The diamond, now called the Cullinan, was sent to Amsterdam to be cut into nine large stones. The biggest weighs 530.2 carats and is set into the British royal sceptre. Some of the other Cullinan stones, weighing more than a hundred carats each, were later worn set into a brooch by the king's daughter-in-law, who became Queen Mary; Queen Elizabeth II jokingly calls them 'Granny's chips'.

In 1914, as the world prepared for war, the diamond companies were digging trenches too. That year De Beers met with the owners of the Premier and other South African mines. They agreed that, whatever happened, they would join together to stockpile diamonds, and make sure prices did not fall. This price-fixing arrangement, or 'cartel', worked like the single-company monopoly it was planned to imitate, and prices stayed roughly stable. The cartel propped up the industry even in the mid-1920s when there were two more major South African finds, near Lichtenburg in the North West Province. The first was in 1924 when a farmer, whose cattle were dying of an unidentified illness, decided to dig a dip for them. A worker saw something sparkling in the water, and his son showed it to his science teacher, to see if he knew what it was. So many men turned up to peg claims that the government staged organised 'rushes'. One morning in March 1927, outside a small town called Grasfontein, twenty thousand men queued behind a series of starting ropes, like runners preparing for a marathon. These were mostly wild-looking men with hats and bare feet, pegs in their hands and hunger in their eyes. At exactly ten o'clock, with fifty thousand spectators watching, a Union Jack was dropped 'and the rush began in a cloud of fiery yellow dust'.[57] It was perhaps a little like those early De Beers sight holdings in Charterhouse Street: the strongest ones and those with good contacts got the best concessions; the weaker ones were mostly left with the edges.

Diamond prices dipped, with almost everything else, in the depression years, but by the mid-1930s the stones were one of the few luxury commodities in Europe whose price was rising. As Adolf Hitler's influence grew, so did the value of diamonds. It was not just the industrial diamonds – *booart*, from the Afrikaner word that means 'bastard' – that both sides were amassing. Ordinary people knew that paper currency would be worthless in wartime so, like the Parisians before the Franco-Prussian War, they chose to buy diamonds. However, they had not understood the effect of plentiful supply on a market: ten years later, millions of refugees found that the jewels they had hidden and carried so carefully were worth almost nothing. The US market was sated, and the British forbade imports.

As the refugees queued up outside pawn shops, to be turned away again and again, it was the unofficial end of any second-hand market in ordinary diamonds. Today they lose their value soon after purchase. 'Let us not be too particular. It is better to have old, second-hand diamonds than none at all,' Mark Twain quipped,[58] but it seems that most people do not agree with him: they are superstitious about jewels and don't want any that have been worn by a stranger. The moment you drive a new car out of a showroom it will have lost up to twenty per cent of its value; when you take a new diamond ring out of the jeweller's, it has probably lost at least sixty per cent.[59] Today the best way to invest seriously in gems is probably to become a trader, and perhaps this is why in Manchester, in northern England, the 'curry mile' of Rusholme is also the 'golden mile'. In the 1970s tens of thousands of ethnic Indian refugees were thrown out of Uganda and settled in the UK. They had been given seventy-five days to leave and could carry with them only gold and dia-monds, which they hid about their bodies. On arrival, they set up shops in which to sell and buy them. Perhaps it is the fear that this might happen again that has kept these shops open into the 2000s.

By 1945 De Beers had to reconsider its strategy. The royal courts of Europe had virtually gone, and with them the demand for crowns and tiaras had diminished. De Beers saw that it would have to perform a feat similar to what Mikimoto was achieving with his cultured pearls. Like him, they had to appeal to a mass market while appearing to remain exclusive and, also like him, they decided to concentrate on one type of jewellery. For Mikimoto it had been pearl necklaces, but for De Beers it would be something more personal: diamond betrothal rings.

There were precedents. The first recorded diamond engage-ment ring was given in the late fifteenth century soon after a new way to facet diamonds had been invented in Bruges. In 1477 the eighteen-year-old Archduke Maximilian (later Holy Roman Emperor) proposed marriage to the twenty-year-old Mary of Burgundy, who would bring with her as dowry the Low Coun-tries, including much of today's Belgium and the Netherlands. A few months before the ceremony one of Maximilian's advisers wrote to him: 'At the betrothal your Grace must have a ring set with a diamond and also a gold ring. Moreover, in the morning, your Grace must bestow upon the bride some costly jewels.'[60] De Beers refers to this in its marketing literature as an example of how long diamonds have been associated with love, but in truth it probably had little to do with affection. Mary was the daughter of Charles the Bold, Duke of Burgundy, who was known to have had three of his best stones already sent for reshaping in the new style.[61] To present the young bride with a newfangled cut diamond from Bruges was a clever way for Maximilian to impress the man who would give him as dowry the region in which Bruges was situated.

Sometimes, of course, diamonds did represent love and romance: when Mary Queen of Scots and the Duke of Norfolk were engaged they gave diamonds to each other, and Mary wrote to him that she wore his diamonds concealed under the bosom of her dress.[62] Her cousin Queen Elizabeth I liked to use her diamond rings in flirting, using them as 'scribbling rings' to inscribe love messages to suitors on the windows of her palaces.[63] But in those days every flower, stone and animal was symbolic of something, and for a long time diamonds were perceived as dangerous. Some early lapidaries said they were poisonous, although this idea might have originated as a rumour in the Indian diamond mines, put about to discourage workers from swallowing them. For many years they symbolised state-craft and war. A huge and extraordinary Renaissance medal,[64] struck for Henry II of France when he set out to invade Flanders in 1554, included in the design a diamond ring encircling a map of the world, with a palm branch, for rejoicing and pilgrimage, and an olive branch, for peace after victory. At the time the diamond represented an unbroken and unconquered soul. Per-haps it was no wonder they didn't catch on as sentimental love tokens. As late as 1855 Charles Edwards, a jewellery historian, published *A History of Rings* without mentioning diamond betrothal rings. For him, one of the 'prettiest tokens of friend-ship and affection' was a 'gimmal' ring: a French idea, consisting of twin hoops carefully constructed so that when they are brought together they unite as one.

 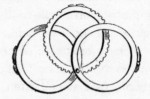

Gimmal rings

In around 1946, De Beers commissioned a survey of more than five thousand young American adults, and learned that its target market did not appear to associate diamonds with engagement at all. Instead the post-war generation wanted to buy all the things they had missed out on during the war: cars, fur coats, machines and holidays. If they bought engagement rings they wanted exotic, colourful stones fixed to them, like rubies, sapphires or turquoises. Not diamonds, which were seen as colourless, like the war years.

Diamonds Are Forever

To get round the problem, the company employed the New York advertising agency N. W. Ayer, who created a series of advertisements based on French paintings of romantic locations, accompanied by fluffy prose along the lines of 'How fair has been each precious moment of their plans come true ... their silent meeting at the altar steps, their first waltz ... Each memory in turn is treasured in the lovely, lighted depths of her engagement diamond, to be an endless source of happy inspiration.' The campaign did only reasonably well until one April evening in 1947[65] when a copywriter, Frances Gerety, was working late into the night. She was exhausted by writing doggerel to deadline and was longing to go home. But the client was expecting a strap-line – something to pull it all together. 'Dog tired, I put my head down and said, "Please God, send me a line."' Then she sat up and wrote: 'A Diamond is Forever.'

It was a masterful slogan. The four words played prettily around the concept of immortality, as well as suggesting that a diamond was something to keep – slicing through any notion of a second-hand market. De Beers wanted the price never to crash again. And so far, astonishingly, it has not. Diamonds have held their appeal although they have become even more plentiful in recent years. In the 1970s kimberlite pipes were found in Australia, at a town called Kimberley. In the 1980s more diamonds were found in Siberia: De Beers struck a deal with the Russians and ran campaigns to promote the quarter- and half-carat diamonds that came in vast quantities from those mines. It led to a craze for 'eternity' rings, made with several small stones.[66] Most recently, in the 1990s, there was a rush to the wastelands of northern Canada. So many diamonds have been found, in fact, that of the estimated 3.6 billion diamond carats mined from 400 BC to date, some forty per cent were discovered between 1991 and 2003.[67]

It could have been a crisis for De Beers, and indeed in 1998 the company was advised by a management-consulting firm to abandon the role of 'market custodian' and sell its stockpile. However, even though there are nearly twice as many diamonds in the world today as there were fifteen years ago, and even though in the past seven years De Beers has disposed of a

Subway poster advertising diamonds

diamond mountain worth some four billion dollars (Matthew Hart described the process as 'shovelling its stockpile out of Charterhouse Street as if it were clearing the driveway of snow'[68]) the market has, amazingly, expanded to embrace the new supply.

Frances Gerety's phrase has been translated into more than thirty languages, most recently Chinese, and today some eighty per cent of engagements in Europe, America and Japan are celebrated with a diamond. Even in China, where the campaign has only been running since 1993, an astonishing fifty-one-per-cent of urban couples are ditching the traditional green jade to mark their betrothal with the hardest stone in the world.

This is only the beginning. Diamonds are now, officially, not just for engaged women: they are for every 'independent' woman. De Beers is promoting a new feminist-sounding campaign to encourage women to wear 'right-hand rings' to show their 'self-expression'. It is tagged 'Women of the World Raise Your Right Hands', and its slogans are full of calls to battle: 'Your left hand rocks the cradle, your right hand rules the world'; 'Your left hand says "we", your right hand says "me"'; 'Your left hand is your heart, your right hand is your voice.' Meanwhile, men have been targeted with a trend for 'bling-bling jewellery' and even long-married couples are not exempt from the machinations of the marketeers. In the past decade diamantaires have pressured people to adopt a new list of anniversary gifts. Previously women had to wait sixty years before they received a diamond but the new list, promoted as 'the modern anniversary gift list',[69] suggests the tenth, thirtieth and sixtieth anniversaries as diamond-jewellery years. Diamonds really are 'forever'.

The Mystery of the Vanishing Diamonds

Although it might have worked a commercial miracle, 'a diamond is forever' is only a catchphrase: it is not actually true. Diamonds might have formed at astonishing temperatures and pressures and they might also be the hardest substance in the universe. But in truth diamonds are only 'forever' if you treat them as if they are not. Like all the other gemstones in the jewel box, and despite their name 'adamantine', diamonds too need to be looked after.

The question of the actual indomitability of diamonds has taxed jewellers and scientists throughout the ages. In the 1690s Grand Duke Cosimo III persuaded the Academy of Cimento in Florence 'to fix a Diamond in the focus of a large burning glass',[70] but as he and his fellow experimenters watched, the stone cracked, coruscated and disappeared 'without leaving any appreciable ash behind'. It seemed like magic – a valuable gemstone had disappeared into thin air – and questions were asked. Had it exploded? Imploded? Was it invisible? Had one of the academicians pulled a conjuring trick? Had the grand duke? The gentlemen of Europe discussed such questions over their Wonder Cabinets for decades. It was many years, though, before anyone came up with a rational explanation.

The first clue to the mystery was uncovered in two experiments of the 1770s. In the first, Monsieur Le Blanc, a well-known Parisian jeweller, formally declared the diamond to be 'indestructible in the furnace'. When he was challenged he put a package of good Brazilian diamonds into his crucible. It was nothing new for him, he shrugged: he often subjected them to intense heat to rid them of blemishes – heat is as useful a treatment for diamonds as it is for sapphires and rubies. However, to the delight of his competitors, when a perplexed Le Blanc opened the oven three hours later it was empty. Just as in the Academy experiment in Florence, the gemstones had completely disappeared.

The problem was taken up by the French scientist Antoine-Laurent Lavoisier. He had missed the first miraculously-disappearing-diamond show, but he made sure he was at the next, when another Parisian jeweller offered to provide three

Combustion of diamond

diamonds for a similar experiment, stipulating only that he should be able to carry out the test in his own way. The jeweller packed his gems tightly in powdered charcoal, placed them in an earthen pipe bowl, and submitted them to whatever heat Lavoisier could coax out of the fire. Three hours later he removed the bowl, and when they opened it they found three diamonds as good as, or better, than those they had started with. It was a puzzle: why should one experiment fail, and the other succeed? Lavoisier came closer than anyone else to understanding it; concluding that when a diamond was burned with a free supply of oxygen it was completely converted into carbon dioxide. He was never certain why this happened, and it was the British scientist Smithson Tennant who, in 1796, put the last piece into the jigsaw, when he placed a weighed diamond in a golden tube with saltpetre, and by looking at what remained after heating it, proved that one of the most precious objects in the world was made of the same element as coal. Diamond, he had demonstrated, was nothing more than graphite on a good day: a rare, transparent form of pure carbon.

As for the shatterability of diamonds, these gemstones are very hard, but not very tough. In the playground there is not much difference between the two concepts but in gems there is. A piece of nephrite jade is one of the toughest stones in the world, rich with fibrous layers like a well-rooted soil: it can scarcely be destroyed with a hammer, even though it is only 6.5 on Mohs' scale. Yet if you attack diamonds in the same way, the crystals will shatter into shards. The eighteenth-century adventurer John Mawe described miners in Brazil coming in from their claims with big diamonds, only for the prospective purchaser to 'test' them with a hammer. When the stones were smashed to smithereens, the buyer would shrug and say that it couldn't be diamond, but he would buy the splinters for a nominal sum as a goodwill gesture.

The myth that real diamonds didn't break was destructive, and not only for the gems. In the early sixteenth century, the conquistador Francisco Pizarro and his companions smashed many of the Incas' finest emeralds, assuming that they were only genuine if they showed the adamantine property of diamond.[71] Fifteen hundred years earlier, in Pliny's time, it was believed that only the blood of a newly sacrificed kid, or lamb, could shatter a diamond. Pliny[72] wondered – as many did until the seventeenth century when this 'fact' was still being quoted as a gemmological curiosity – how anyone could have thought to experiment with such a thing: 'To what spirit of research, or to what accident, are we indebted for this discovery? Or what conjecture can it have been that first led people to experiment upon a thing of such extraordinary value as this?' He did not realise that the story was probably a metaphor, perhaps with the same root as the Christian symbol of the Lamb of God. A diamond is the hardest substance; a sacrificed lamb or goat the most innocent. The only way to overcome harshness and brutality, the imagery suggests, is with love.

The Gem-cutter's Story

The places where diamonds, the most internally ordered gem-stones, are cut and sold are often chaotic, dark and cramped. This is as true of parts of the old diamond quarter of Antwerp, in Belgium, as it is of the famed 47th Street diamond district of New York and the diamond polishing centres of Surat in western India. They are labyrinths of alleyways or corridors, lined with workshops and buildings, apparently modelled more on the randomness of natural diamond formation than on the stones themselves.

To reach Gabi Tolkowsky's office in Antwerp's Diamond Club, you must leave the wide thoroughfares of the nineteenth-century area of the town and dip into a pedestrian alleyway, whose entrance is controlled by armed police. On entering the Diamond Club building, you must wait in a queue to present your passport to armed guards behind bulletproof glass, then pass through metal detectors and step into a lift that bristles with CCTV cameras. My instructions had been detailed and involved going up in one lift, then walking along a corridor, into another lift and down another long corridor. I took several wrong turnings before I found Tolkowsky sitting at a large desk in his office before a fawn-coloured safe. He was on the phone, talking to the guards, who were concerned that I had not yet turned up. 'If you'd been much longer they would have sent an armed search-party out,' he joked.

Gabi Tolkowsky is one of the world's greatest diamond-cutters. His great-uncle was Marcel Tolkowsky who, in 1919, aged nineteen, wrote the first book ever published about the cutting of round brilliant diamonds. It was a risky move: cutting diamonds in this way had been an almost secret business in the close-knit, mainly Jewish communities who carried it out, and although many people knew about it, nobody had written down all the angles and ideal proportions for anyone else to read.

Perhaps if he had been older he would not have dared to publish such a book. But he was a young man, studying engineering at the University of London just after the First World War, and he took the risk. The exact parameters he established in 1919 for round brilliants are still used around the world today.

His great-nephew's daring is of a different nature. He takes some of the biggest and most valuable stones in the world, walks their landscapes, maps their contours, notices their hazards, and then, when he knows them better, perhaps, than one might know a lover, he dares to invent a new shape for them. The words of his trade are like those of butchery: there is cleaving (which involves splitting the stone in two with a sharp tap – it takes courage); bruting, which is rubbing one diamond against another to establish the shape; and sawing. Yet the words of Tolkowsky are those of a lover, or even a cosmetic surgeon. 'Whenever I first see a diamond I ask it, "What do you want to become?" And it says, "I want to be the most beautiful,"' he said.

That was the question he asked before he fashioned the Golden Jubilee[73] in 1997, which, at 545.67 carats, eclipsed the Cullinan as the largest faceted diamond in the world. And when he had listened to its answer, it became a cushion-shaped diamond, which refracts light into gold and looks like flowers and warmth and sparkle. Before that it was simply known as the 'Unknown Brown'. He asked the same question of the Centenary, at 599 carats one of the largest colourless rough diamonds ever found. It took him three years to hear its answer, most of which he and his family spent as guests of De Beers, whose centenary the stone was to celebrate. 'You cannot go quickly: if you polish a wrong facet you can never put it back.' The Centenary yielded a 273.85 carat, colourless, flawless beauty.

'The public cannot imagine what it is to cut a diamond. They think you chop off pieces and make something,' he said. But for him it is perhaps more like an astonishing three-dimensional

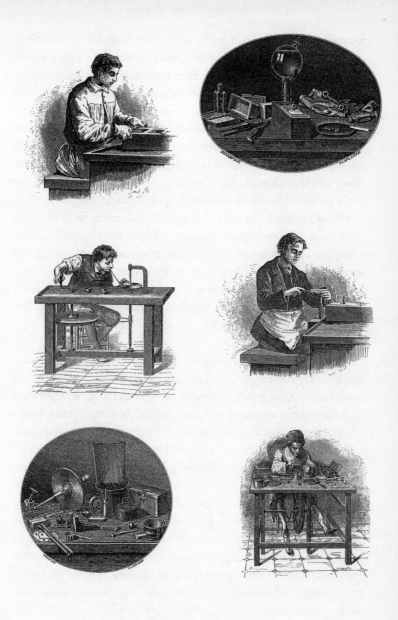

Diamond cutting

strategy game in which everything that happens has an effect on everything else, however far away it may be. And the diamond-cutter, gazing through the microscope, can get lost in a stone's depths, learning it. But eventually he has to step inside it, and make decisions. 'You sit in front of a mountain of problems. There are so many elements involved: colour, shape, clarity, facets. It's everything that you could only imagine. You are so absorbed by the work that you could say you are hypnotised. You must do something very different at the end of the day, like walk or be with family. Otherwise you become a slave.'

Other crystals, like rubies, emeralds and opals, form in stable rock over time, growing like salt. But diamonds form on the move and, for Tolkowsky, this origin gives them their own special sense of life. He describes the way the colours move inside them as a 'journey' of light. 'It is going through a transparent body and on the way it creates scintillation, like light on water. You can imagine whales swimming in it, because it does look as if there is something moving.'

He talks of diamonds as a teacher might of his pupils – they are gifted, problematic, challenging. And, most of all, they are individuals. Like other members of his family he learned as a teenager to cut standard brilliant diamonds in the family workshop; later he became fascinated by the more difficult pupils: 'They were grey-green, brown, bottle-green, grey-yellow, yellow-khaki, all sorts.' When stones like this were cut at the parameters prescribed in his great-uncle's book they 'did not vibrate' so he had to invent something special for them. He had just one example with him, which he wore as a ring. The trade would probably describe it as a '1.2 carat marigold-cut brown' but to me it looked like patina, tobacco, tea, bergamot, smoke, a winter's morning in a continental European city. 'These are stones that people didn't want, and yet now they are beautiful,' he said.

Tolkowsky thinks a lot about beauty, and how each person

perceives it differently. 'If you had diamonds together in a parcel the reaction of most people is "It's yellow," but there will be one that catches your attention. Or if there is a designer who makes a hundred identical dresses and lays them out for you to choose, then there might still be one you like best.' He has his own theory of this, which concerns the way in which we see. Each eye creates a separate 'half' image that the brain processes into one. 'But the final image is slightly empty in the centre, and what do you think fills that?' he asked, then answered himself: 'It is your fantasy that is filling in the centre. And that is why people love diamond: because it is real, and yet it lets your imagination be free.'

It is an appeal that people of many cultures understand, he said, and indeed the diamond industry is one of the oldest globalised trades in the world. 'In five minutes you can speak five languages, to people in Japan, Kamchatka [in the Russian Far East], North Africa, South Africa and round the corner.' And whatever language they speak, there is one word they all know: '*mazal*', the Hebrew word for 'good luck', is binding. 'And when you say it, you can't go back on your word. The deal is done!'

The restaurants in the gem district beyond Tolkowsky's office are testament to the diversity of the community he was talking about: as well as Belgian snack-bars and chocolate shops, there are kosher Jewish, Muslim halal and vegetarian Indian eating-houses. The latter are for the Jains, who over the past hundred years or more have become some of the most powerful traders in the international gem market: their religion precludes any trade involved in killing, so they may not work in farming, leather or any business that might mean taking even the tiniest life. Gems, oil and charging interest are deemed safe, although history has not always borne that out.

The Size of Brillant Diamonds.

Number	Weight	Number	Weight	Number	Weight
1	1	13	$3\frac{3}{4}$	22	7
2	$1\frac{1}{8}$	14	4	23	$7\frac{1}{2}$
3	$1\frac{1}{4}$	15	$4\frac{1}{4}$	24	8
4	$1\frac{1}{2}$	16	$4\frac{1}{2}$	25	9
5	$1\frac{3}{4}$	17	$4\frac{3}{4}$	26	10
6	2	18	5	27	11
7	$2\frac{1}{4}$	19	$5\frac{1}{4}$	28	$12\frac{1}{2}$
8	$2\frac{1}{2}$	20	6		
9	$2\frac{3}{4}$	21	$6\frac{1}{2}$		
10	3				
11	$3\frac{1}{4}$				
12	$3\frac{1}{2}$				

Chart showing how to judge the sizes of diamonds

Amputation Is Forever

The diamond marketeers know that when they tell their stories of famous gemstones – like the Hope or the Orloff – what most listeners want to hear about is a neat little curse that happened long ago in another country. They do not want true curses from which people are still suffering,[74] although that is what the diamond industry is faced with today. US journalist Greg Campbell begins *Blood Diamonds*[75] with the story of Ismael Dalramy, who lost both hands in July 1996 'with two quick blows of the axe'. Ismael had not asked for mercy: instead he quietly removed a small metal ring made by his son from one of the fingers on his left hand and put it into his pocket, 'one of the last acts his hands performed for him'. His crime? He had lived too close to some muddy diamond pits in the jungle of eastern Sierra Leone, and his mutilators were rebel forces from the Revolutionary United Front (RUF), who wanted to take control of the mining. The drug-crazed teenage soldiers lined up the villagers and systematically removed hands, lips, legs, breasts and ears, which ensured that the entire diamond-producing area was empty within hours. The only people who didn't leave Ismael's village that day were those left on the floor, bleeding.

Campbell estimated that the RUF made between $25 million and $125 million every year by selling rough diamonds,[76] and uses the money to buy drugs, food and weapons. These illicit gems constitute an estimated three per cent of the world market and some will have also gone through the pockets of Al-Qa'eda terrorists as part of an elaborate system of money-laundering for arms and funding.[77] Many such diamonds will have been bought as engagement gifts, a symbol of love, and others will have been bought as 'right-hand rings' to celebrate women's independence, their freedom and future. The wearers will never know how much their stones really cost. They should have been a blessing but instead they are a curse, says Sierra Leone film director Sorious Samura, who has produced several documentaries about the social wreckage of his country.[78] 'Diamonds, which should have made Sierra Leone a country fit to compete with Western countries, have us all killing, raping and maiming each other. This senseless war is about diamonds. No two ways to put it.'

With almost any other gemstone it is possible to devise tests to identify where they have come from: the product of each location is discretely and minutely different. But diamonds, of course, did not form where they were found: they were created below the crust and carried to the surface in an explosive moment of release. While some stayed *in situ*, most were carried for, perhaps, thousands of miles along rivers. Indeed, in India and Brazil no kimberlite pipes have been found, which suggests that the diamonds might have exploded on to the earth's surface when the land was the one great continent of Gondwanaland, and that the diamonds came from similar sources to the South African stones.[79] So, unless all stones are certified when they are found, we cannot be certain if our engagement rings were mined in Sierra Leone, Botswana or Russia. We cannot know if they ever paid for the Twin Towers mission or whether they were mined ethically by well-paid workers in Canada, Australia or elsewhere. As the US General Accounting Office pointed out in 2002, diamonds have no natural signature at all.

For a while it looked as if Pliny's speculation might be true and that perhaps the only thing that would shatter the indomitable diamond industry was the blood of innocents. Certainly the concept of 'blood diamonds', commuted by the industry to 'conflict diamonds', has threatened to damage business. According to an article in Amnesty International's US magazine,[80] 'one diamond company executive is rumored to have had nightmares in which the tag line at the end of De Beers' television commercials read, 'Amputation Is Forever.'

It is not that De Beers itself has been involved with blood

diamonds: since 1999 the company has only sold diamonds from its own mines; it stopped dealing with Sierra Leone in 1985; and it has been working in close collaboration with the United Nations and others to stop the illegitimate trade. It is simply that anything that hurts the diamond industry hurts its biggest player by implication.

In an attempt to salvage its reputation the industry introduced 'The Kimberley Process'. It is a dual initiative. On one side, the human-rights groups want to end the trade in war diamonds; on the other, the diamond companies want to end the damage to their profits. The diamond-sellers do not want us to look at our engagement rings and ask whether they might have cost an arm, a leg, a lip or a homeland. But if we ask the question, they want us to feel confident that the stones we buy from a jeweller today were not responsible for someone's injury yesterday. They do not want us to stop buying.

The process has had mixed results. Although in 2003 the US Senate passed a law forbidding the sale of conflict diamonds, the following year an independent survey[81] discovered that 93 per cent of diamond buyers in America had never even heard of the Kimberley Process Certification Scheme. Indeed, only 30 per cent had even heard of conflict diamonds, of whom half were fairly uncertain of what the term meant, and nearly three-quarters of those who had bought diamonds in the previous year said the jewels did not come with any documentation to say they were conflict-free, and neither had they asked for it. It seems from this and other feedback that the diamond industry has, so far, avoided being greatly cursed by these terrible stories. However, it is curious that if it had not been able to keep the price of diamonds artificially high, Ismael Dalramy might still have his hands. A diamond mine would not have been worth fighting for.

Hope and Charity

Sometimes a diamond does not have a story. Some stones did not form a billion years ago as an astonishing natural phenomenon, but were made last Friday, in a piece of machinery of about the size and shape of a washing-machine.

Imagine that there are two coloured, or 'fancy' diamonds lying on a table in front of you. Let us call them Hope and Charity. Both weigh exactly one carat. They were both cut last month by excellent craftsmen. They are the most identical of twins. Not only can the expert eye not see the difference between them, but the only way anyone can tell them apart is with a machine that costs thousands of dollars, with Charity producing one pattern of luminescence and Hope a slightly different one. Yet there are other differences you cannot detect. There is a three or four per cent chance that Hope has come from a conflict area; Charity has no such baggage. Hope has probably been responsible for great gashes across the landscape; Charity has not. And Hope costs at least twice as much as Charity, perhaps much more. If you had to choose one, which would you buy? Remember, they look identical, and your friends would only know if you told them. Logically it would make most sense to buy Charity. Yet buying jewellery is rarely about logic or sense. Most people, given the choice – which they are – still tend to go for Hope.

People had dreamed of making diamonds from graphite ever since Smithson Tennant had confirmed in 1796 that the two were of the same material. However, it was not until a surprising discovery was made in a remote canyon in Arizona that scientists had the clue they needed. The Canyon Diablo crater is a huge hole more than a kilometre wide. It was created when a massive meteorite exploded into it some fifty thousand years ago, like a cannonball into concrete. The impact was so huge that most of the meteorite turned to powder, but fragments of up to ten kilograms have been found, and some contain tiny diamonds. In the mid-nineteenth century, the area was populated by prospectors looking for gold and silver, who were not interested in this dull, heavy metal. But then came engineers building bridges, and surveyors building nations, and some of them picked up the meteorite pieces, and started to look at them more closely. By the 1890s there was quite a trade in Canyon Diablo souvenirs. One was sent to a Nobel Prize-winning scientist, Ferdinand Frédéric Henri Moissan, who thought the tiny diamonds in it might provide him with a clue about how all diamonds were made.

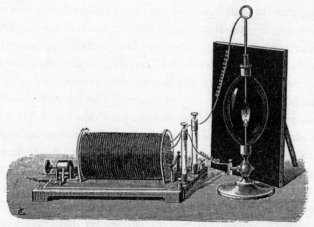

The early, unsuccessful attempt to synthesise diamonds

He concluded that the diamonds might have formed because of the astonishing heat and pressure of the impact, and decided that the iron, which formed around them, might be the key he was looking for. One day in 1904, after many experiments, he pulled out of his crucible some tiny, hard crystals that shone like diamonds and appeared to have the same cutting power. Until the day he died, three years later, he believed he had succeeded in creating diamonds. However, what he had discovered, or invented, was another material. It is almost as hard as diamond (9.3 on Mohs' scale), sparkles even more refractively, can now be created in gemstone size, and is a compound made of silicon and carbon. Today it is called moissanite, and it is one of the prettiest substitutes for diamonds.

Fifty years later, a team of scientists at General Electric in the United States, frustrated after years of trying unsuccessfully to make synthetic diamonds, looked again at the Diablo meteorite. This time they picked up a different clue: as well as iron, it had embedded in it a rarer metal called troilite, which is a compound of iron and sulphur. They hoped that if they heated this to a liquid state it would act as a solvent to break down the carbon atoms in graphite, and that when they reached a high enough temperature and pressure they would crystallise as diamond. 'It was a wintry day,' remembered Tracy Hall, one of the scientists. 'It was cold but the sun was shining through the window, and I had put some troilite in this graphite tube. I turned up my heating system and I put the pressure on.'[82] The pressure reached 100,000 atmospheres – imagine the Eiffel Tower balancing, upside down, on a small dinner plate – and the temperature reached 1600 degrees centigrade. When the machine could take it no longer, he switched it off. Just as he had done so many times in the previous years, Hall broke open the capsule. 'My eyes caught the gleam of the sun shining on these things and I ... twiddled it around a little bit and saw the sparkles and at that instant I knew that man had finally turned graphite into diamond,' Hall said. 'My knees weakened. I had to sit down. I was overwhelmed.'

By 1957 General Electric was marketing 'Manmade Diamonds' as an alternative to De Beers' natural industrial diamonds, while at the same time subsidising its research team, who were experimenting with making diamond crystals from other carbon-rich materials. Scientist Bob Wentorf tried everything he could think of: roofing tar, maple wood, even his favourite brand of peanut butter were transformed into the hardest substance on earth. 'The peanut butter turned into tiny green diamond crystals,' he told journalist after journalist, as they interviewed him over the following years. 'The green was because of all the nitrogen.'[83]

It was not until the Soviet Union collapsed in 1991, leaving some of its best minds bored and virtually unemployed, that the technology was adjusted to make gem-quality diamonds. In just over ten years the industry was facing one of its most severe challenges: near flawless diamonds of up to five carats have been made and look – to the naked eye, at least – just like natural ones.

One of the many contenders in the race to sell synthetic diamonds is Tom Chatham. Although his father, Carroll, was the first person to create gem-quality emeralds, his earliest dream had been to make diamonds. Sixty years later his son achieved it. He was inspired by a trip he made in 1993 to Novosibirsk, Siberia, where he heard that research was being undertaken into synthetic gemstones. Nothing could have prepared him for what he found. 'There were literally thousands of scientists without any projects to do, all sitting around in their offices becoming entrepreneurs. You would go down one hallway and open the first door and you'd be introduced to "Boris whose speciality is high-pressure carbon", and he'd show you all the diamond presses in his office. The next guy would be making emeralds, and the next guy something else. And they would all be working with free materials and no overheads, smuggling the gems into Bangkok and selling them for pennies.' That year he showed one of the Russian diamonds to a man called Willie Goldberg who, until he died in 2003, ranked with Gabi Tolkowsky as one of the top cutters in the world. After he had looked carefully at the diamond, Goldberg did not respond immediately. Instead he pulled another, similar stone out of his pocket. 'He said, "I don't know what to do, Tom. Yesterday this was worth a million dollars." And I said if it was worth a million dollars in his mind then it was worth a million dollars. But, after all, it's just a rock.'

As soon as gem-quality synthetic diamonds became a real possibility, De Beers and the Diamond Trading Company sprang into action. First they had to reassess their slogan. In a subtle semantic shift, their clever catchphrase had to embrace the past as well as the future: diamonds now had to have *been* forever as well as being bought for forever. Then they adopted the philosophy that if you can't beat them, join them . . . and then beat them: so they set up their own laboratories for making synthetic stones. Today the company is one of the world's biggest synthetic industrial-diamond manufacturers – operating out of a relatively secret location on the Isle of Man. The third strand to their strategy was making sure that created diamonds would be detectable. They set up the Gem Defensive Programme in Maidenhead outside London and spent millions of pounds devising a series of tests that would identify whether a stone was or was not natural. So far they have succeeded: the ocean is still being kept out by the barricades, and expensive gem-testing machines are being sent out free of charge to all major laboratories. However, it is the dream of almost every synthetic gem-maker to produce a stone that cannot be detected. With hundreds of top scientific brains working on the challenge – like hackers on a new computer programme – it can be only a matter of time before the barriers implode. The question is, is the sea outside that much of a danger?

The real impact of synthetic stones has still to be tested.[84] In the future, when they realise they have a choice, will most people choose Hope or Charity? In the 1990s I conducted a series of interviews with socialites in Hong Kong, who admitted that many of their handbags and 'designer' accessories were fakes from mainland China. 'They look the same, they last the season, and I'm so rich that nobody would imagine I hadn't bought it real,' one woman told me. 'But I paid a twentieth of the price, and that makes me very happy.' In Hong Kong it was often the middle classes who felt the pressure to prove they were rich enough to buy the genuine article, and perhaps the same thing will happen with diamonds in the rest of the world. If you are a millionaire nobody will suspect you of wearing synthetic crystals, so you may as well do so, and spin the web of illusion that is part of the business of appearing wealthy.

If they are going to make a serious dent in the market for natural diamonds, the sellers of synthetics will have to employ the same skills that the diamond industry has used from its inception: clever marketing. One of the most creative ideas of this kind was conceived one night in 1998, when two sets of brothers[85] were chatting over beer in a Chicago bar and one had an arresting idea. If diamonds can be made of peanut butter, surely they can be made of anything organic? If ashes return to ashes, could human dust become diamonds? Three years later a company was born. It called itself LifeGem, but its real business is with death.

LifeGem works by transforming cremated human remains into diamonds. It is effectively a marketing company and it employs outside laboratories like Lucent, which manufactures in Russia, to perform its alchemy. 'It's very expensive to make a life gem,' Alex Grizenko of Lucent said. 'I sometimes wonder why we agreed to do it.'[86] The problem is that the economies of scale that you work with in normal synthetic diamonds don't apply: each batch has to be kept separately. 'And people expect certain sizes and clarities – if the diamond isn't right we have to do it all over again.'

The process involves ashes being converted into what Grizenko described as 'carbon soup', which goes through a 'graphitisation process'; the resulting slices of graphite are used to make diamonds. Most people reading this – adults of average height and bone structure – could become up to six hundred carats of diamonds.[87] Weight does not affect anyone's diamond potential: all the fat is burned away in the crematorium.

Like a Rock

The first geologist to be made into a rock was an Englishman called Brian Tandy. Had he known it, he would have revelled in the joke. He died in April 2003. He had spent a happy last evening at the cinema, laughing through a comedy, and later that night his heart gave out in his sleep. He was fifty-six. 'We had no warning at all,' said his widow, Lin. 'I felt so angry that he had just left us. We hadn't even said goodbye.' With their two adult daughters, Gayle and Claire, they had been a joyful family, but after Brian had gone, 'For a while we were like three single figures walking around each other, not touching.' Then they heard that it was possible to turn human remains into diamonds. Although it seemed a bizarre idea, it also made sense. 'Brian had been fascinated by the mineral world, so we thought he would love this.' They commissioned two small diamonds, one for each daughter. 'I didn't need one,' Lin said. 'Brian is in my thoughts every day. But the girls wanted something to remember him by, something beautiful that could always be with them.' They knew that the gems had virtually no sell-on value, so their use as heirlooms was strictly sentimental. 'Who'd want a diamond made of somebody else's dad?' said Gayle.

The toughest moment had been spooning out the two hundred or so grams of ashes that had to be sent to America – no one could bring themselves to do it, so the managing director for LifeGem UK stepped in. Six months later the diamonds arrived, personally delivered, in a presentation box. Reactions from the people around them were mixed. 'A couple of my friends said, "That's disgusting,"' said Gayle. 'But I just said to them that until they had walked a mile in my shoes they couldn't understand, and afterwards one of them apologised.'

An older friend of the family had a more extreme reaction. 'I don't want to see Brian's face in it,' she said, and refused even to look. I asked if I could see one of the stones, and Gayle took off a ring from her right hand, and passed it to me. It was large: more than a carat in weight. 'We only asked for a quarter of a carat, but the crystal just grew and grew,' she said, 'so they sent it anyway. It's not as if they could sell the extra.' It was a deep orange-yellow, the colour of lions and sunshine and happiness, quite unlike the jet mourning jewellery that the Victorians loved. And perhaps for the first time, looking into a diamond, I felt I knew exactly what I was looking at.

Human life is fragile: we live in the space between one breath and the next. We often try to maintain an illusion of permanence, through what we do, say, wear and buy, how we enjoy ourselves and who and how we love. Yet it is an illusion that is constantly being undermined by change and death. We can use diamonds in whatever way we like. They are empty things, pretty as water, yet within them – if we want to see it – there is blood, dust, love, curses and suffering. There is desire to make someone happy, there is admiration, there is ostentation . . . and there is a company's profit curve. The diamond I was holding was about illusion and about slicing through illusion. It was about forever and never, and it was about nothing at all.

I remembered one of the last things the diamond-cutter Gabi Tolkowsky had said in Antwerp. I had asked him what he saw when he looked at a polished diamond, away from his cutting wheel. 'I see what everyone else sees, even if they don't know it,' he said. 'I see myself inside the diamond, refracted into tiny, tiny, pieces.'

Postscript

Some time after I had been given my mosaic engagement ring I went to the Hagia Sophia in Istanbul, to see the place from which the stones had been removed. I wanted to see where a child standing in the women's gallery might have prised off a few little tesserae without being noticed during prayers. The place is no longer a church, or even a mosque. Since the 1930s the Hagia Sofia has been a museum: a dark, mysterious place that seems to hold within it the memories of both the prayers and the violence in its long and difficult history.

I went up the stairs to the gallery and found myself alone. I soon identified one place at child-level where a significant number of stones were missing. In fact, so many had gone that the area was covered with Perspex and a photocopied diagram showed how that area of the mosaic might once have been. As I looked more closely at the drawing I realised something unexpected.

My three 'stones' had launched me on this quest not because they were inherently valuable but because they were not. They had suggested to me that the desire for, and sometimes veneration of, pretty stones is simply a matter of human storytelling, complex as that has been. Yet by a sweet coincidence my mosaic pieces turned out to be closer to jewels than I could have guessed.

One day in the thirteenth century a skilled mosaic-maker would have stood in that place, looking for the last time at the design that had been sketched roughly on the wall.[1] Then, when he was sure that this was the right placing, he would have picked up the little tiles his assistant had set out in neat piles on the floor behind him. Among them were three pieces, one dark red, one bottle green and one the colour of apples, that were later taken by a boy who became a priest, and later still became my ring. For a long time I had thought of these fragments as simply random parts of ancient mosaics, but now I could see that the missing pieces did not come from any ordinary picture: instead they came from the section of the mosaic that depicted the glittering gems on the throne of heaven, as Christ returned to fulfil the promise he had made to humanity. And although it was made of stone and glass, the mosaic was intended to represent peridots, sapphires, emeralds and amethysts. The ring had sent me off on all these journeys because it was made of stories not of gems – but in fact it was set with 'jewels' after all.

A Miscellany of Jewels

BIRTHSTONES

January – garnet
February – amethyst
March – aquamarine
April – diamond
May – emerald
June – pearl or moonstone

July – ruby
August – peridot
September – sapphire
October – opal or tourmaline
November – topaz or citrine
December – turquoise/blue topaz

This list was drawn up by the American National Association of Jewellers at a meeting in Kansas City in 1912. These were the stones that jewellers in America most wanted to sell. One of the greatest mysteries about the birthstone system is how widely it was accepted, even if it had no provenance beyond a Missouri boardroom. Until the end of the 1960s 94 per cent of couples in Japan used the bride's birthstone for their engagement ring. Even today people throughout the world choose gems according to an arbitrary decision made by businesspeople nearly a century ago. There is a move to make tanzanite – discovered in 1967 – an alternative December gemstone.

ANNIVERSARY GEMSTONES

OLD LIST: 30th – pearl. 35th – coral or jade. 40th – ruby. 45th – sapphire. 55th – emerald. 60th – diamond. 75th – diamond again.

MODERN LIST: 10th – diamond. 12th – pearls and coloured gems. 30th – diamond. 33rd – amethyst. 34th – opal. 35th – jade. 38th – beryl or tourmaline. 40th – ruby. 45th – sapphire. 55th – emerald. 60th – diamond.

The 'old list' of anniversary stones was drawn up and promoted by the American etiquette writer Emily Post in 1927 and then later, in this revision, in 1957. The 'modern list' was designed by jewellers, who did not want to wait sixty years before selling married couples a diamond.

AN ALPHABET OF JEWELS

A   is for amethyst and aquamarine
B   is for brilliant diamond, balas ruby and beryl
C   is for chrysolite, carnelian, citrine and chrysoprase
D   is for diamond
E   is for emerald and essonite garnet
F   is for flint, fire opal and fluorite
G   is for garnet
H   is for heliotrope and haematite
I   is for iris, iolite and idocrase
J   is for jasper and jade
K   is for kyanite
L   is for lapis lazuli and labradorite
M   is for malachite
N   is for nephrite
O   is for onyx and opal
P   is for pearl, peridot and purpurine
Q   is for quartz
R   is for ruby, rose quartz and rubellite tourmaline
S   is for sapphire and sardonyx
T   is for turquoise and topaz
U   is for uvarovite green garnet
V   is for volcanic glass
W   is for wood stone and water agate
Z   is for zircon and zoisite

Brooches and necklaces in eighteenth- and nineteenth-century England and France were often set with stones so that the first letters expressed a sentiment. For example, you might give a necklace set with Diamond, Emerald, Amethyst, Ruby, Emerald, Sapphire and Topaz to the person you hold DEAREST.

George Frederick Kunz, *Natal Stones*; Frank B. Wade, *A Text-Book of Precious Stones for Jewelers and the Gem-loving Public*; Charles Edwards, *The History and Poetry of Finger Rings*.

——— MOHS' SCALE OF RELATIVE HARDNESS ———

1. Talc
2. Gypsum
3. Calcite
4. Fluorite
5. Apatite

6. Feldspar
7. Quartz
8. Emerald
9. Sapphire and Ruby
10. Diamond

'First we try, with a corner of the given mineral, to scratch the members of the scale, beginning from above in order that we may not waste unnecessarily the specimens representing lower members ... It is necessary also that the force applied in this experiment be always the least possible.' Friedrich Mohs, *Treatise on Mineralogy*, 1825, p.301.

——————— JEWELS THAT ARE ... ———————

Named after a place:
agate from the river Achates in Sicily; jet after Gagates in Turkey; labradorite from Labrador; tanzanite from Tanzania; tsavorite from Tsavo National Park

Named after a person:
morganite after banker J. P. Morgan; kunzite after jeweller Frederick Kunz; alexandrite after the Tsarovich Alexander; uvarovite after nineteenth century Russian finance minister, Count Sergei Uvarov.

Found naturally in the United Kingdom:
Derbyshire Blue John; agate; river pearl; sapphire; jet; amber.

AMERICAN STATE GEMSTONES

Alabama: star blue quartz
Alaska: jade
Arizona: turquoise
Arkansas: diamond
California: benitoite
Colorado: aquamarine
Connecticut: garnet
Florida: moonstone (after the 1969 moon landings)
Georgia: quartz
Hawaii: black coral
Idaho: star garnet
Kentucky: 'fortification' agate
Louisiana: agate
Maine: tourmaline
Massachusetts: rhodonite
Michigan: chlorastrolite or 'greenstone'
Minnesota: Lake Superior agate
Mississippi: petrified wood
Montana: Yogo sapphire
Nebraska: blue agate
Nevada: peridot and Virgin Valley black fire opal
New Hampshire: smoky quartz
New Mexico: turquoise
New York: garnet, black button tourmaline, moonstone
North Carolina: emerald
Oregon: sunstone
South Carolina: amethyst
South Dakota: rose quartz
Tennessee: Tennessee pearl
Texas and Utah: topaz
Washington: petrified wood
West Virginia: lithostrotionella (fossilised coral)
Wisconsin: ruby
Wyoming: jade

— GEM NAMES USED IN FONT SIZES —

3 ½ point – brilliant	5 point – pearl	9 point – 2-line diamond
4 point – gem	5 ½ point – ruby, agate	10 point – 2-line pearl
4 ½ point – diamond	6 ½ point – emerald	11 point – 2-line agate

Source: *Elsevier's Encyclopaedic Dictionary of Meanings*, 1998, and *Webster*, 1913.

Before the publishing industry became computerised, printers used names like pica, bourgeois and brilliant to refer to font sizes. Gem terms were used for the smaller, more jewel-like letters. Agates are still commonly used to measure column depth in newspaper classified advertisements. There are fourteen agates to an inch.

✧ ✧ ✧

————————————— DIAMONDS —————————————

Ten Famous Diamonds in Brief

Braganza: 1680 carats rough. Brazil *circa* 1800. Found by convicts; owned by Portuguese kings; at the time said to have been the largest rough ever found. Lost now; might have been a topaz anyway.

Cullinan I, II, III, IV, V, VI, VII, VIII and IX: 3106 carats rough – 'the size of half a brick'. Found in South Africa's Premier mine, 1905. Given to King Edward VII and sent to England in an unregistered parcel. Split into nine major gems and ninety-six smaller brilliants. Largest is Cullinan I, 530 carats and set into the sceptre of the British regalia. Kept in the Tower of London.

Dresden Green: green fancy, 49.21 carats, pear cut. Possibly Brazil, 1720s. The largest green diamond known. Taken to Moscow after the Second World War. Now back in Dresden's Green Vault.

Golden Jubilee: yellow fancy, 545.67 carats cut. South Africa, 1990s. The world's largest faceted diamond. Cut by Gabi Tolkowsky in Antwerp and given to King Bhumibol Adulyadej of Thailand for his golden jubilee in 1996. Previously known as the 'Unknown Brown'.

Great Mogul: 280 carats cut. India *circa* 1600. The biggest diamond found in India, recorded by J. B. Tavernier on India trip. Now lost. Perhaps became the Koh-i-Noor.

Hope: Blue fancy, 44.5 carats cut. India, seventeenth century or before. Owned mostly by kings, bankers and heiresses. Said to be cursed.

Koh-i-Noor: 108.93 carats cut. India, *circa* seventeenth century. Probably involved more scheming and torture than any other diamond. Name means 'mountain of light' in Persian. Said to be unlucky if worn by a man, but in England it has only been worn by women: Queen Victoria, Queen Mary and Queen Elizabeth II. All long-lived.

Sancy: 55 carats, double-rose cut. Worn in a turban by King Henry III of France after he went bald at twenty-six. Lucky hatpin for King James I of England. Turbulent history; high body count. In the Louvre.

Star of the South: 128-carat 'rose tint' brilliant. Brazil, eighteenth century. Found by a slave who was given her freedom. Owned by the Gaekwar of Baroda, in a Cartier setting. By 2004 Cartier owned it again.

Regent: 410 carats rough. Also known as 'The Pitt', after Thomas Pitt, president of Fort Madras. Pitt accused of stealing the diamond from poor Indian; Alexander Pope wrote a poem about it. Sold to France and stolen in 1792 with French Crown Jewels. Later discovered in a Paris garret. Once represented two-thirds of the value of France's Crown Jewels; now in the Louvre.

Colour Scale Terms for Colourless and
Near-Colourless Diamonds

GIA	D	E	F	G	H	I	J	K	L	M	N	O	P	Q	R	S	T	U	V	W	X	Y	Z
Colour Grading Scale	colourless			near colourless				faint yellow			very light yellow					light yellow							

Colour Scale Terms for Distinct Colours of Diamonds

Faint, Very Light, Light, Fancy Light, Fancy, Fancy Intense, Fancy Vivid

Terms for the Clarity of Diamonds

FL: FLAWLESS
IF: INTERNALLY FLAWLESS
VVS1 and VVS2: VERY VERY SMALL INCLUSIONS
VS1 and VS2: VERY SMALL INCLUSIONS
SI1 and SI2: SLIGHT INCLUSIONS
I1 and I2: IMPERFECT WITH EYE-VISIBLE INCLUSIONS
I3: IMPERFECT WITH HUGE INCLUSIONS

The Hope diamond is a VS1.

——— NAMES FOR CUTS OF GEMS ———

Round brilliant	Emerald	Heart
Indian	Step	Pear/Pendeloque
Cushion	Marquise	Baguette
Princess	Lozenge	Teardrop

——— POPULAR AND MINERAL ———
NAMES FOR GEMSTONES

POPULAR NAME	MINERAL NAME
accabar	black coral
almandine	natural purple spinel
Amazon jade	green microcline feldspar
Arkansas diamond	rock crystal
Balas ruby	red spinel
bishop's stone	amethyst
black amber	jet
canary diamond	yellow diamond

POPULAR NAME	MINERAL NAME
Cape emerald	prehnite
Cape ruby	pyrope garnet
cinnamon stone	hessonite garnet
girasol	fire opal or moonstone
Iceland agate	obsidian
Indian topaz	yellow sapphire
jacinth	red zircon or hessonite garnet
jet stone	black tourmaline
Maori pounamu	nephrite
Oriental amethyst	violet sapphire
Oriental cat's eye	chrysoberyl cat's eye
Oriental emerald	green sapphire
Oriental topaz	yellow sapphire
paste	glass imitation
Red Sea pearls	coral beads
rhinestones	cut glass, quartz
rose kunzite	synthetic pink sapphire
tsavorite	green grossular garnet
Viking compass stone	iolite
volcanic glass	obsidian
zebra stone	layered jasper
raspberry garnet	rhodolite
tashmarine	diopside
unripe ruby	red zircon

THREE TRANSLATIONS OF THE STONES
—— ON THE JEWISH HIGH PRIEST'S ——
BREASTPLATE: EXODUS 28.16–20

1. Jerusalem Bible Translation

'You will make the breastplate of judgement . . . In it you will set four rows of stones: a sard, a topaz, and emerald for the first row; for the second row, a garnet, sapphire and diamond; for the third row a hyacinth, a ruby and an amethyst, and for the fourth row a beryl, carnelian and a jasper.'

2. *King James Bible Translation*

The first row shall be a sardius, a topaz, and a carbuncle: this shall be the first row. And the second row shall be an emerald, a sapphire, and a diamond. And the third row a ligure, an agate, and an amethyst. And the fourth row a beryl, and an onyx, and a jasper.

3. *Mineralogist's Translation*

Odem: carnelian or red jasper

Nophek: turquoise

Leshem: yellow jasper or Amazon stone

Tharshish: green jasper or citrine

Pitadah: garnet or peridot

Sappir: lapis lazuli

Shebo: black and white agate

Shoham: Amazon stone or green turquoise

Bereketh: amethyst or emerald

Yahalom: blue chalcedony or beryl

Achlamath: onyx or amethyst

Yashpeh: green chalcedony

Source: Nevil Story-Maskelyne, *Metals and Minerals of the Bible*, 1888. The meanings of the old Hebrew have been lost, hence the problems of translation.

────── *THE DIAMOND SUTRA* ──────

*The Buddha then asked his disciple Subhuti whether it was possible that the Buddha may be clearly perceived by means of his physical body. And Subhuti replied saying: 'No, that is not possible, because what you referred to as a physical body is not actually just a physical body.' And the Buddha agreed, and said: 'Every form or quality of phenomena is transient and illusive. It is only when the mind realises that the phenomena of life are not real that the Buddha may be clearly perceived.' . . .

*The Buddha then asked Subhuti whether he thought that if a generous person gave away to the poor enough gold, silver, pearls, coral, carnelian, glass and crystal to fill the universe, that person would accrue considerable merit. Subhuti replied that the person would indeed accrue merit. But then the Buddha said, 'Yes, but if a disciple adhered to just one verse of this teaching, then that disciple would gain more merit than the generous person who gave away so much treasure. Because all the Buddhas – and the law by which they have attained their wisdom – owe their inception to the truth of this teaching . . .

*Then Subhuti asked the Buddha what this teaching was called, and the Buddha said: 'It shall be known as 'The Diamond Sutra:' . . . And in years to come, if disciples who hear this lesson truly understand the ephemeral nature of things, then their merit will be intrinsic and wonderful.

Extracted and adapted from *The Diamond Sutra*, translated by William Gemmell, 1912.

PORTABLE INSTRUMENTS FOR JEWELLERS INCLUDE:

*Loupe or magnifying glass *Torch *Colour or 'Chelsea' filter *Spectroscope *Oil to test for stars

CHECKLIST FOR ROCK HOUNDS IN ARIZONA INCLUDES:

*Car in good condition *Spare tyres *First aid kit *Snake-bite kit (although only in summer when the rattlesnakes emerge from hibernation) *High leather boots *Canteen *Strong bag and cotton for wadding *Loupe or magnifying glass *Prospector's hammer (with one end square and tapered and the other pointed or tempered) *Folding army shovel *Set of 10 Mohs hardness minerals *Torch *Binoculars *Water to see what specimens will look like when polished, though spittle will do just as well *An eye for beauty and a love of the outdoors

Source: Jay Ellis Ransom, *Arizona Gem Trails*, 1955, pp. 8ff.

Akoya pearl: a pearl from the salt-water *akoya-gai* oyster *Pinctada martensii*. The most common Japanese pearl; almost always cultured.

Alexandrite: a stone with the strange ability to change colour so that in daylight it is green and at night, under artificial lights, it is red. Discovered in Tokovaya, Ekaterinburg, in April 1830 and named after Tsarevitch Alexander, who was twelve that month and had therefore come of age. Red and green were Russia's national military colours. When synthetic alexandrite was invented it was bought in great quantities by Chinese nationalist leader Chiang Kai-shek.

Alluvial mining: mining of gems that have been left as *secondary deposits* by rivers, seas or glaciers. Alluvial gems are either found in the rivers or seas, or in gravel or clay layers beneath the present land-surface.

Alumina: aluminium oxide (Al_2O_3). A major constituent of *corundum*, including rubies and sapphires.

Ammonite: (*L. cornu Ammonis*) Fossil molluscs with spiralled shells, often found at the Mesozoic levels. Named after the Roman god Jupiter Ammon, whose statues were often shown with ram horns. Also called serpent stones.

Anaerobic: a chemical reaction that takes place without free oxygen. Jet forms anaerobically; coal forms aerobically.

Assembled stone: a stone made up of layers of different material glued or cemented together into *doublets* or *triplets*. Buyers should suspect any stone of being assembled. Check under magnification and if possible in water, looking for rings or layers. Most common are garnet and glass doublets, sapphire and synthetic sapphire doublets, synthetic spinel triplets, and opal doublets and triplets.

Asterism: a star effect produced by light reflecting on small, needle-like inclusions, often made of rutile. It is the cause of star sapphires and rubies. Many stones displaying asterism are now synthetic.

Azurite: copper-based blue pigment. Used by artists since Roman times, now rare. Related to malachite, and often found beside it.

Birthstone: a stone supposedly linked to the month of its wearer's birth. Said to have ancient precedents although the current list of birthstones was drawn up by jewellers in America in 1912, in order to sell more gems.

Brilliant: a cut which creates fifty-eight or fifty-seven facets. It is also a general word for referring to a cut diamond.

Four 'C's: cut, clarity, colour and carat: the four main areas in which the quality of a gemstone is analysed. Other Cs include: 'certificate', to validate where it has come from and what treatments it has had; 'crystal', to assess its diaphanous qualities; 'celebrity', to consider whether or not it has provenance; and 'confidence'.

Cabochon/en cabochon: a curved, convex way of cutting and polishing a gem. The word comes from the French for 'little head'.

Cameo: a gem carved from a material that has formed in stripes of colours – so the carving is raised above the surface of the underlying colour.

Carat: an archaic measurement for weighing gemstones, still used today. One metric carat is 0.2 grams; before the twentieth century a carat could weigh anything from 0.190–0.210 grams, meaning that sometimes the weights of historical stones vary in the telling. Often confused with *karat*.

Conflict diamonds: diamonds found and traded in war zones, and used to profit guerrilla or invading army activities. Also called blood diamonds.

Copal: hardened resin. Formed less than a million years ago. Related to amber, although by definition younger.

Corundum: aluminium oxide (Al_2O_3) and a very hard substance. Mohs' scale 9, capable of scratching almost everything but diamond. When it is gem quality it is called ruby or sapphire; when lower quality it is used as abrasives and bearings.

Crown: the top part of a cut gemstone; the portion above the *girdle*.

Culet: the lowest part of a faceted gemstone; the portion at the bottom of the *pavilion*.

Diamantaire: the diamond trade's term for a dealer.

Dichroism: the characteristic of some gems, to display a second colour or hue, when viewed from a different angle. Used by gemmologists to distinguish between stones, for example rubies show dichroism, and garnets do not. Rubies and sapphires are often cut with the dichroic colours along the *girdle*, which can sometimes disguise the effect.

Diffraction: the modification of white light as it breaks up into colours. Present in opals.

Doublet: two pieces of gem material fused together by heat or colourless cement. Common are garnet and glass doublets, with garnet at the top and glass at the bottom, or opal doublets, with black chalcedony, glass or *potch* backing. Check all stones under magnification.

Drusy/druse: small quartz crystals growing on the surface of a *geode*.

Essonite: reddish-yellow *garnet*, usually from Sri Lanka. Also called cinnamon-stone or *hessonite*.

Eye: the best gemstone in a parcel

Facet: a cut and polished flat surface of a gemstone. Brilliant-cut stones have fifty-eight facets, or fifty-seven if the *culet* ends in a sharp point.

Foil: a thin layer of metal placed under a transparent gemstone to increase its brilliance or colour. Sometimes used under glass, to fake a gemstone. Common since antiquity.

Garnet: a mixed group of gems, all with cubic crystals and containing SiO_4 but with very different chemical formulae. Red garnets include: almandine (brownish), pyrope (cherry red), spessartine (red-orange), mandarin (orange, from Namibia and Pakistan) and rhodolite (pinkish and sometimes called 'raspberry garnets'). Green garnets include *tsavorite*, demantoid and uvarorvite. Very popular in the Dark Ages; many Anglo-Saxon and Viking graves have been found with Indian garnets. From Latin *granatum* because of the similarity between pomegranate seeds and red garnets.

Geode: a hollow rock cavity, usually containing gems, and often lined with *drusy*. Amethysts, citrines and peridots are often found in geodes.

Girdle: the widest point of a gemstone, around its circumference. Where gemstones are sometimes inscribed with details of their provenance.

Grain: unit of measurement for the weight of pearls. There are four grains to the *carat*, and twenty grains to the gram.

Grossular garnet: a yellow-green gem found in Sri Lanka, Pakistan, Russia and parts of Africa. Transparent grossular garnet is known as 'Transvaal jade' and resembles *jadeite*.

Heft: the apparent weight of a gemstone when lifted up in the hand. A useful informal way of distinguishing between precious stones and glass, which is lighter.

Hessonite garnet: see *essonite*.

Idar-Oberstein: two villages in the Hunsrück Mountains in south-west Germany near Luxembourg. Idar was traditionally the gem-cutting centre and Oberstein the jewellery-manufacturing centre. Although they merged in 1933 they have retained their specialities – and rivalry. Thought to have been a gem centre even in Roman times, the villages have certainly been cutting gems since the late fourteenth century when miners found agates and amethysts nearby.

Inclusion: any foreign body or crack in a gemstone. A stone that contains inclusions is described as 'included'. This is not always a negative thing. Sometimes inclusions can enhance a stone – as with asterism for example, or insect inclusions in amber, or, the priceless and fictitious pink diamond featured in the *Pink Panther* films, which had an inclusion shaped like a panther.

Jadeite: intensely-coloured Burmese stone, found at Myitkina in the northern mountains. Usually green but can also be lavender. Highly prized in nineteenth-century Imperial China, when it was first discovered, and even today has many Chinese collectors. Often confused with *nephrite*.

Karat: indication of the proportion of gold in any metal. 24-karat gold is pure gold, 9-karat gold has nine parts gold, and fifteen parts other metal alloys. Often confused with *carat*.

Kimberlite pipe: a type of extinct volcano filled with crumbly rock called kimberlite and named after Kimberley in South Africa where it was first identified. Comes from an eruption in the upper mantle (most volcanoes start much nearer the surface) involving a stream of gaseous rock moving upwards, bringing some of the mantle (and the mantle's diamonds) with it.

Labradorite: according to Inuit legend the northern lights were once trapped in the rocks of Labrador. They were freed by a warrior's spear but some remained in this glinting blue mineral, related to feldspar. First found by Europeans in 1770 on the Labrador peninsula.

Lapidary: name given both to a person who cuts stones and to a book about stones.

Loupe: a jeweller's small hand-held magnifying glass. A stone that is 'loupe clean' is flawless under ten times magnification.

Magma: the super-heated sea of molten rock found in the earth's mantle.

Metamorphic rock: created when igneous or sedimentary rocks were transformed into something else. Metamorphism does not just melt existing rock – it changes it into something denser and more compact.

Mohs' scale: developed by German mineralogist Friedrich Mohs in the early nineteenth century to compare the hardness of minerals. Talc is one, diamond is ten. Everything else comes somewhere in the middle.

Moissanite: synthetic stone invented by Ferdinand Frederick Henri Moissan in 1904. Looks like diamond, measures 9.3 on *Mohs' scale*, and is made of silicon and carbon.

Mullock: a refuse tip of worthless rock from opal (or gold) mining. Australian term.

Nacre: substance secreted by oysters or mussels, surrounding a foreign body and forming the shining layers of pearls, or the inner part of a shell, also called mother-of-pearl.

Nanometre: one thousand-millionth of a metre, or a factor of 10^{-9}. Used to measure visible light, which appears in the range of 380 to 750 nanometres.

Nephrite jade: a green stone, less luminous than the Burmese jade or *jadeite* which is mineralogically no relation. Named by Nicholas Mondardes of Seville, a sixteenth-century doctor, who used it to treat kidney problems, and named it '*piedras de hijades*', or 'flank stone'. Believed in Ancient China to confer immortality, and still treasured there. A prestige stone in Maori and ancient American cultures. Found in western China near Khotan, as well as all around the Pacific Rim, including Japan, New Zealand, California and Peru. One of the toughest, least breakable stones, because of its fibrous structure. Often faked and dyed.

Noodle: to search an opal dump for opals. Australian expression.

Optic axis: a line through a doubly-refracting crystal such as ruby or sapphire, so that a ray of light passing through it does not suffer double refraction.

Organic gemstone: jewellery that comes from animal or plant life, including amber, *copal*, coral, ivory, jet, pearl and tortoiseshell.

Pavilion: the portion of a faceted gemstone that lies below the *girdle*.

Pegmatite: a coarse-grained form of granite rock, containing very large crystals.

Potch: common, non-precious opal that shows no play of colour. Often looks like grey, opaque, glass.

Precious stone: in the nineteenth century only diamonds, sapphires, rubies and emeralds were thought to be precious. Now seen as an old-fashioned distinction. See *semi-precious*.

Pyrite: (FeS_2) heavy, shiny, yellow mineral. Also called fool's gold.

Ratter: a person who steals opal from someone else's mine. Australian slang.

Refraction: the bending of light as it enters the gemstone, and slows down.

Refractive index: one of the keys to identifying gems. Measures the angle that light is bent as it enters the gemstone.

Resin: a hard, sticky and often aromatic substance secreted by trees or plants. When fossilised can become amber.

Rock hound: someone who collects rocks and minerals from their natural environment as a hobby.

Rouge, or jeweller's rouge: a finely ground preparation of ferric oxide, used as a polish for gemstones or metals. When used with gold, it gives it a warm, sunny glow.

Rough: a natural crystal form or irregular shape. A description of a gemstone before it is polished.

Rubellite: pink *tourmaline*. Some of the finest is found in Siberia and Burma. In 1903 two Basque prospectors found the Queen's

Tourmaline Mine in southern California. Most of the rubellite from there was bought by Chinese dealers: it was the favourite stone of Cixi, the Dowager empress.

Scribbling ring: a ring set with a sharp diamond, often used by sixteenth century lovers for scratching romantic graffiti on to glass. Elizabeth I was a famous scribbler, as was Mary Queen of Scots.

Sedimentary rock: formed when many pieces of different rocks, soils and organisms are pushed together under pressure.

Semi-precious: first used in the nineteenth century, to separate the so-called '*precious stones*' from the rest. Today the distinction is not popular among jewellers.

Silk: a silky lustre, usually in sapphires and rubies, deriving from the presence of microscopic inclusions. Usually a defect.

Specific gravity: the weight of a gem compared to that of an equal volume of water.

Spinel: an oxide of magnesium, iron or zinc, with aluminium. Often red or blue and often confused with rubies and sapphires.

Succinite: amber from the Baltic region.

Tailings: the opal dirt, after it has been sorted.

Tanzanite: a purple-blue stone from the zoisite family. Found in 1967 in Tanzania and now one of the most popular gems in the United States. When it comes out of the ground it looks so unpromising that in 1969 a Nairobi gem-cutter turned away a Masai warrior offering a ten-thousand carat tanzanite rough for $50, because he thought it was glass. All tanzanites on sale today are heat-treated. Tanzanites are just 6.5 on *Mohs' scale*, and are therefore not very suitable for rings.

Tourmaline: coloured stone with the property of attracting and rejecting light objects placed near it. Eighteenth-century Dutch sailors, who bought it in Sri Lanka when it was a Dutch colony, called it *aschentrekker*, or 'ash-attractor', and used it to clean their pipes. When two small samples went to Paris in the 1750s they caused a sensation. Today the most expensive tourmaline is from one hill near Paraiba in northern Brazil. It is the intense turquoise colour of swimming pools, and can cost $40,000 per carat. The original supply has already run out. Paraiba tourmaline is heat-treated.

Triplet: an *assembled stone* of three parts, with a protective top layer, a clear or coloured bottom layer, and a thinly sliced gem in the middle. Used for opals and garnets in particular. Check by looking at the gem from the side, and seeing if it is striped.

Troilite: rare compound of iron and sulphur, found in meteorites and an important clue in synthesising diamond.

Tsavorite: green garnet, found in – and named after – Tsavo National Park in Kenya. Matches emerald for colour and, almost, for hardness, but at time of publication is one-sixth of the price, largely for lack of name-recognition. Discovered by British adventurers Campbell and Judy Bridges.

Tumbler: a revolving barrel or container, used in smoothing and sorting rough gems.

Turner: a person who turns wood on a lathe.

Vermeil: form of gilded metal named after the colour 'vermilion'. Can also refer to orange-red garnet.

Vulcanite: An early plastic developed in the mid nineteenth-century and made by subjecting india rubber and sulphur to intense heat. Used as a substitute for jet.

Acknowledgements

There was once a mandarin in China who was very proud of
appearing with jewels on every part of his robe. One day an
old man stopped him in the street, and thanked him for his
jewels. 'What do you mean, my friend?' asked the bewildered
civil servant. 'I never gave you any jewels.' 'No', said the old
man. 'But you have let me look at them and that is all the use
you can make of them yourself. There is no difference between
us, except that you have the trouble of guarding them.'

from JONES, *Credulities Past and Present*

When I set out on these travels through the jewel box I imagined that
I would find out a great deal about the strange lives of gem-miners,
adventurers, collectors and even a few thieves. I was pretty sure that I
would discover obsession and greed aplenty. And I did. But what I did
not guess was that I would also find so much generosity. So, in addition
to all those people who have paraded marvellous jewels throughout
history, and so provided wonderful stories for the rest of us who have
not had the trouble of guarding them, I should like to thank a few of
the people who helped me on my way.

For the Amber chapter, thanks to: Olga Solovjeva for gamely playing
history detectives in the Russian Federation; Marina at Baltma Tours
for rescuing me when I was in Kaliningrad without a map or a clue
and her friend Ivan and his family for their bortsch, hospitality and
so much vodka that I really thought I could speak Russian for the
evening; Professor Ryszard Mazurowscy from the University of Warsaw for letting me dig for Stone Age amber, Alicia at the Amber
Association and Eva Rachon of the Amberif trade fair in Gdansk for
all her information and hospitality. Thanks to: Mariusz Drapikowsky;

Gabriela Gierłowska and her son Krystof for taking me to the Teutonic Knights' castle at Marienburg (Malbork) and Elżbieta Sontag at the Museum of Amber Inclusions who brought a 40-million-year-old world to life. Also thanks to Professor Raif Milki in Beirut for teaching me about the world's oldest amber; Bob Smart at the Cheddar Gorge Museum; Roger Jacobi at the British Museum. And everyone on the Ambericawest newsgroup for their heated and fascinating discussions about all things amber-related; I eavesdropped for many months.

For Jet, my thanks to: Pete Wilson for first introducing me to Skeleton 952; Marjorie Stokes for her vivid reminiscences about growing up in a fishing family in 1930s Whitby; Eileen Bennett and Gill Swales at the Whitby Archives; Hal Redvers-Jones at the Whitby Jet Heritage Centre; Tommy Roe for daring to open the door and Kevin Dixon of One O Five Church Street in Whitby for being so generous with his knowledge of where to find jet and other fossils on the beaches of northern Yorkshire.

For Pearl, thanks to: Timothy Neat for guiding me to the last pearl-fishers of Scotland and Alec John Wilkinson, Angus Wilkinson and Eddie Davis for telling Highlands pearl stories and ghost stories late into the winter evening; John Lochtie at Cairncross in Perth; Michael Shackleton for translating in Toba – and for lending me money when no banks would accept either foreign credit cards or English pounds; Kiyoo Matsuzuki at the Mikimoto Pearl Museum, and Mr Yamamura, the 'living treasure' whose family have worked with pearls for three generations. Also to Jeff Place and Atesh Sonneborn at Smithsonian Folkways, and John and Gina Latendresse at the American Pearl Company in Tennessee for showing me one of the best collections of natural pearls in the world.

For the Opal chapter I should like to thank: Caro Llewellyn at the Sydney Books Festival for inviting me to Australia in 2003, thus making my research so much easier; Dawn Swane; Dawn Jones; Peter Butler; Tony Wong; Harris Au; Ed Radeka for taking me on a church and eccentrics tour of Coober Pedy. In Lightning Ridge, thanks to: Barbara Moritz at the Lightning Ridge Historical Society for one of the best town tours I have ever had; Draco; Peter and Lisa Carroll for their hospitality, help, and for binding my finger when I sliced it like a tomato; Peter Allan and Mick James; Katie Dowell at ANU for her research on carbon-dating opals; Len Cram for his insights. And of course Uwe and Ricardo Barfuss for sharing their stories of the Angel of Yowah.

For Peridot I should like to thank Rabbi Daniel Sperber for his encouragement and stories of luminous pearls; Bill Morrow in Globe for showing me the treasures of a lifetime of rock-hounding; June Stratton – 'the turquoise lady'. And thanks to all at San Carlos Apache Reservation – Frank, Franklyn, Pansy Cassavetes, Kathy Kitchayan and others.

For my Emerald adventures thanks to Tom, Dianna and Barbara Chatham for all their stories and hospitality in California; Ian Shaw at Liverpool University for his help in unravelling the story of Cleopatra's mines; Steven Sidebotham at the University of Delaware; Thomas Krakhover and all the team from Red Sea Desert Adventures – who not only took me to the emerald mines, but showed me the stars as well. Thanks to David and Sally Nicholson-Cole for advice on photographing Theodora at Ravenna. Also to Matt Robins and Nigel Atkins of the Derbyshire Caving Association, for giving me the courage to negotiate ancient disused mines, despite the scorpions.

For Sapphire I should like to thank my father, Patrick Finlay, for buying a small sapphire in Colombo in the late 1950s, and my mother, Jeannie Finlay, for giving it to me, set in a ring, many years later. Also Watadeniya Jayarathna and Lasantha Sudarshana for an extraordinary week of lapidary lessons; all the miners I met at both the river and the illam pits. And Archbishop Rowan Williams and Jane Williams for their help with the question of bishops' rings.

For Ruby a big thank you to Richard Hughes who not only helped me find a way to the remote mines of Mogok when I never thought I'd be able to get there but later fact-checked my corundum chapters, although all mistakes are of course my own; S. K. Samuels and Juleen Eichinger Samuels for their help and advice in Rangoon; Yan Naing and Hlaing Win who made my personal experience of having Burmese army and police guides an unexpectedly pleasant one; the Moustache Brothers Par Par Lay, U Lu Maw and U Lu Zaw and the many other Burmese people, some of whom I cannot name, who helped on my journey to and from Mogok.

For Diamond thanks to: Kirsty Norman; Michel Aliaga, Brigitte Chabert and Veronique Saccaro at Cartier in Paris for showing me the Star of the South; Antoinette Matlins for her invitation to an extraordinary conference on synthetic diamonds in Tucson in February 2004; Gabi Tolkowsky for offering to meet me in Antwerp, even during a major Jewish holiday; Robert Beer for information about the symbolism of the *syamantaka* jewel; Ranchor Prime for his thoughts about diamonds and deities; Daniel White at the Diamond Trading Company for telling me about the system of sights; and Lin, Gayle and Claire Tandy for inviting me to their house to talk about their father/husband Brian, and how he would have smiled at the idea of becoming a diamond.

Also thanks to: William and John Twining for speaking to me about their father, Baron Twining, and particularly for sharing his unpublished manuscript; Alan Brook-Turner and David Beattie for a lively conversation about regalia; Liz James at Sussex University for her invaluable information about Byzantine mosaics; Aidan Hart – formerly Brother Aidan – for his thoughts on jewels in Orthodox icons; Ric Taylor at GIA in California, for running a fascinating course in recognising coloured stones; Edward Johnson at GIA in London; Bryan Ambrose of Rose Narrow Boats for information about *Little Gem*; Brad Bohnert at HSN in Florida; Gary Bowersox; Campbell and Judy Bridges for telling me about their search for stones in Africa's wildernesses; Niamh Collier of the World Bank for pointing me to gem legislation meetings; Peter Tandy; Floyd Mann in the US for explaining why someone would keep looking for buried treasure for thirty-four years ('because I can't wait to get up every morning and get going') despite finding so little; Tim Colman at the British Geological Survey; Ted Katsargiris for his advice on Greek; Craig Finch of Finch & Co. for insights into the contemporary Wonder Cabinet collections; Kirsten Dwight and Amanda Hancox; Jeannie Dunn; Paola Triolo; Joanne Robinson; John Smith; Stephen Midgeley; Cecilie Palmer for being enthusiastic when I read the introduction to her in the hospice on the day she died; AGTA for inviting me to Tucson; Garry Wykes, Jewel House Warden at the Tower of London. Also thanks to Dino Mahoney, Simon Wu, Genevieve Fox, Richard McClure, Chris

Groocock, Alison Nadel, Nick Finlay and Fiona Finlay for all their hospitality on my numerous research trips. And Lizzie Palmer for her addictive DVDs when I needed a break.

Thanks to Rhodes House in Oxford, which houses the Twining papers; Emma Marigliano for climbing the ladders for me at Manchester's wonderful Portico Library; Glossop Library in Derbyshire; Manchester Central Library; the Library of Congress in Washington DC; and of course the British Library in London, one of my favourite places in the world.

Thanks to Simon Trewin, Clare Gill and Sophie Laurimore at pfd for seeing the book's potential; Helen Garnons-Williams at Sceptre for buying it; Richard Atkinson for adopting it; and Nicola Doherty for revealing her admirable lapidary skills as she helped cut and polish (and occasionally cleave) the rough text to make it better and clearer. This book has been a joint effort.

But most of all, thank you to Martin Palmer who has walked and talked every page of this book with me. He always says he had no idea, when he gave me three little mosaic stones to set into a ring, that it could possibly lead to this.

Credits

The quotation from *Blood Diamonds* by Greg Campbell, 2002 on page 374 is by kind permission of Perseus Books. The quotation from *Hope* by Marian Fowler on page 344 is by kind permission of Ballantine, New York; the quotations from Matthew Hart's *Diamond, a Journey to the Heart of an Obsession* on pages 353 and 354 are by kind permission of, and ©, Bloomsbury USA/Walker & Co. The quotation by Richard Hughes on page 341 is by his kind permission. The two quotations by Geoffrey Munn, on pages 128 and 333 are by his kind permission. The extract from Ann Petry's The Narrows 1953 on p. 53 is by kind permission of Russell & Volkening. The quotation by Kurt Vonnegut, from *Slaughterhouse Five,* 1970, is by kind permission of, and ©, Random House. The quotation from Rowan Williams, Archbishop of Canterbury on page 259 is by kind permission of the Archbishop.

Picture Acknowledgements

Author's collection: 1 top, 2 bottom, 4 centre and bottom, 5, 6 top and bottom, 7, 8. © Uwe Barfuss: 4 top, reproduced by kind permission. © The British Museum: 6 centre. © Mariusz Drapikowski: 2 top left, reproduced by kind permission of the artist. © John Smith, ARC: 1 bottom. © Dr Elżbieta Sontag, Curator, Museum of Inclusions, University of Gdansk: 2 top right (insects in amber).
© Victoria and Albert Museum: 3.

Every reasonable effort has been made to contact the copyright holders, but if there are any errors or omissions, Hodder & Stoughton will be pleased to insert the appropriate acknowledgement in any subsequent printing of this publication.

Bibliography

Abeyaratne, Malcolm (ed.), *Ratnapura the District as seen by Government Agents*, Colombo, Department of Government Printing, 1981.

Aeschylus, *Agamemnon*, trans. Gilbert Murray, worldwide, Project Gutenberg, www.gutenberg.org.

Agatharchides of Cnidus, *On the Erythraean Sea*, trans. Stanley Burstein, London, Hakluyt Society, 1989.

Albury, W. R., and Peter Oldroyd, 'From Renaissance Mineral Studies to Historical Geology in the Light of Michel Foucault's *The Order of Things*', *British Journal for the History of Science* vol. 10, 1977, pp. 187–215.

Anderson, William, *Green Man*, London, HarperCollins, 1990.

Andrews, Henry, *Ancient Plants and the World They Lived In*, Ithaca, New York, Comstock Publishing Associates, 1947.

Anon., *Tales from the Thousand and One Nights*, trans. N. J. Dawood, London, Penguin Classics, 1973.

Anon, *Treasury of the National Jewels*, Tehran, Central Bank of the Islamic Republic of Iran, 2001.

Appadurai, Arjun (ed.), *The Social Life of Things: Commodities in Cultural Perspective*, Cambridge, Cambridge University Press, 1986.

Arendt, Hannah, *Eichmann in Jerusalem: The Banality of Evil*, New York, The Viking Press, 1963.

Atlay, Frank, and Arthur H. Morgan, *The Burma Ruby Mines Ltd: note for shareholders*, London, The Burma Ruby Mines, June 1905.

Attar, Farid ud-Din, *The Conference of the Birds*, trans. Afkham Darbandi and Dick Davis, London, Penguin, 1984.

Aubert, Georges, *La Crise des Diamants et la De Beers*, Paris, Georges Aubert, 1908.

Audsley, W. and G., *Handbook of Christian Symbolism*, London, Day & Son, 1865.

Aveni, Anthony, *Behind the Crystal Ball: Magic, Science and the Occult from Antiquity through the New Age*, London, Newleaf, Random House, 1996.

Bahler, Ingrid, and Katherine Gyékényesi Gatto (eds), *The Lapidary of King Alfonso X The Learned*, New Orleans, University Press of the South, 1997.

Bancroft, Peter, *Gem and Crystal Treasures*, Fallbrook, California, Western Enterprises, 1984.

Bapst, Constant Germain, *Histoire des Joyaux de la Couronne de France*, Paris, 1889.

Bard, Kathryn (ed.), *Encyclopaedia of the Archaeology of Ancient Egypt*, London and New York, Routledge, 1999.

Baring, Anne, and Jules Cashford, *The Myth of the Goddess: Evolution of an Image*, London, Arkana/Penguin Books, 1991.

Batchelor, S., *The Cabinet of Gems or vocabulary of Precious Stones with a description of the largest known diamonds and coloured gems in the world arranged according to their comparative Value*, Knaresborough, G. Wilson, 1829.

Batman, Stephen, *Upon Bartholome His Book De Proprietatibus Rerum*, London; Thomas East, 1582.

Beavan, Colin, *Fingerprints: Murder and the Race to Uncover the Science of Identity*, London, Fourth Estate, 2002.

Beer, Robert, *The Encyclopedia of Tibetan Symbols and Motifs*, London, Serindia Publications, 1999.

Bennett, David, and Daniela Mascetti, *Understanding Jewellery*, Woodbridge, Suffolk, Antique Collectors Club, 1989.

Blom, Philip, *To Have and to Hold: An intimate history of collectors and collecting*, London, Allen Lane, 2002.

Bowen, Rusty, *Miners' Tales from the Black Opal Country*, Candelo, New South Wales, Rusty Brown, 1997.

Bowersox, Gary, *Gemstones of Afghanistan*, Tucson, Geoscience Press, 1995.

Boyle, Robert, *An Essay about the Origine & Virtues of Gems*, London, William Godbid, 1672.

Breasted, James Henry, *Ancient Records of Egypt*, Chicago, University of Chicago Press, 1927.

Browne, Thomas, *Nature's Cabinet Unlock'd: Wherein is Discovered the natural causes of Metals, Stones, precious Earths, Juyces, Humours and Spirits*, Twickenham, Edward Farnham, 1657.

Bruton, Eric, *Legendary Gems, or Gems that Made History*, Ipswich, NAG Press, 1986.

Bryson, Bill, *A Short History of Nearly Everything*, London, Doubleday, 2003.

Bunge, Friedrich Georg von, *Liv-, esth- und curländisches Urkundenbuch nebst Regesten*, vol. 1, Riga, Reval, 1840.

Byatt, A. S., *Possession, a Romance*, London, Chatto & Windus, 1990.

Caesar, Julius, *The Conquest of Gaul*, trans. S. A. Handford, London, Penguin Classics, 1951.

Cahn, J. P. 'The Man Who Grows Emeralds', *True: the Man's Magazine*, October 1957.

Cailliaud, Frédéric, *Travels in the Oasis of Thebes and in the Deserts Situated East and West of the Thebaid in the years 1815, 16, 17 and 18*, trans. M. Jomard, London, Sir Richard Philips & Co., 1822.

Caley, Earle, and John Richards, *Theophrastus on Stones*, Columbus, Ohio, Ohio State University, 1956.

Cameron, Kenneth, *English Place Names*, London, B. T. Batsford, 2001.

Campbell, Greg, *Blood Diamonds*, Boulder, Colorado, Westview Press, 2002.

Canfield, Cass, *Outrageous Fortunes: The Story of the Medici, the Rothschilds, and J. Pierpont Morgan*, New York, Harcourt Brace, Jovanovich, 1981.

Carrington Bolton, Henry, *The Follies of Science at the Court of Rudolph II, 1576–1612*, Milwaukee, Pharmaceutical Review Publishing Company, 1904.

Carvalho, David, *Forty Centuries of Ink*, New York, Bank Law Publishing, 1904.

Cassiodorus, Flavius Magnus Aurelius, *The Letters of Cassiodorus*, London, Henry Frowde, 1886.

Castellani, Augusto, *Gems: Notes and Extracts*, trans. Mrs John Brogden, London, Bell & Daldy, 1871.

Catullus, *The Complete Poems*, trans. Jack Lindsay, London, Sylvan Press, 1945.

Chambers, Robert (publisher), *The Book of Days; a Miscellany of Popular Antiquities, in connection with the calendar*, London & Edinburgh, W. R. Chambers, 1863.

Chazal, Gilles, *The Art of Cartier*, Paris, Paris-Musées, 1989.

Chilvers, Hedley, *The Story of De Beers with a Foreword by Sir Ernest Oppenheimer*, London, Cassell, 1939.

Chua, Amy, *World on Fire*, New York, William Heinemann, 2003.

Churchill, Randolph, *Men, Mines and Animals in South Africa*, London, Sampson Low, Marston & Co., 1892.

Clark, Carol, *Seeing Red: A View from Inside the Ruby Trade*, Bangkok, White Lotus Press, 1999.

Clark, Grahame, *Symbols of excellence: precious materials as expressions of status*, Cambridge, Cambridge University Press, 1986.

Colgrave, Bertram, and R. A. B. Mynors (eds), *Bede's Ecclesiastical History of the English People*, Oxford, Clarendon Press, 1969.

Constable, Archibald, *Memoirs of George Heriot, Jeweller to King James VI*, Edinburgh, Archibald Constable, 1822.

Content, Derek (ed.), *The Pearl and the Dragon: a study of Vietnamese Pearls and a History of the Oriental Pearl Trade*, Houlton, Maine, Outset Services, 1999.

Conway, D. J., *Crystal Enchantments: a complete guide to stones and their magical properties*, California, Crossing Press, 1999.

Cook, John, *The Natural History of Lac, Amber and Myrrh with a Plain Account of the many excellent Virtues these three Medicinal Substances are naturally possessed of, and well adapted for the Cure of various Diseases incident to the Human Body*, Essex, John Cook, 1770.

Cram, Len, *Beautiful Queensland Opals: Lightning Ridge*, Buranda, Robert Brown, 1991.

Crawfurd, John, *Journal of an Embassy from the Governor General of India to the Court of Ava*, London, Henry Colburn, 1834.

Cunliffe, Barry, *The Extraordinary Voyage of Pytheas the Greek*, London, Penguin, 2002.

Davey, Richard, *A History of Mourning*, London, Jay's, Regent Street, 1889.

Dennis, Daniel J. Jr, *Gems: a lively guide for the casual collector*, New York, Harry N. Abrams, 1999.

Desanges, Jehan (ed.), *Pline l'Ancien: Histoire Naturelle, Livre V*, Paris, Budé, 1980.

Dieulafait, Louis, *Diamonds and Precious Stones*, London, Blackie & Son, 1874.

Donkin, R. A., *Beyond Price: Pearls and Pearl Fishers from Origins to the Age of Discoveries*, Philadelphia, American Philosophical Society, 1998.

Douglas, Mary, *The World of Goods*, London, Penguin, 1980.

Dutens, Louis, *Des pierres précieuses et des pierres fines, avec les moyens de les connoitre et de les évaluer*, Paris, 1776.

Eckert, Allan W., *The World of Opals*, New York, John Wiley, 1997.

Edwardes, Michael, *Ralph Fitch: Elizabethan in the Indies*, London, Faber & Faber, 1973.

Edwards, Charles, *The History and Poetry of Finger Rings*, New York, Redfield, 1855.

Edwards, I. E. S., *Tutankhamun's Jewelry*, New York, Metropolitan Museum of Art, 1976.

Emanuel, Harry, *Diamonds and Precious Stones*, London, John Camden Hotten, 1865.

Epstein, Edward Jay, *The Diamond Invention*, London, Hutchinson, 1982.

Eunson, Robert, *The Pearl King: The story of the fabulous Mikimoto*, London, Angus & Robertson, 1956.

Evans, Joan, and Mary Serjeantson, *English Mediaeval Lapidaries*, London, Early English Text Society, 1933.

Falk, Fritz, 'The Cutting and Setting of Gems in the 15th Century', in A. Somers-Cocks (ed.), *Princely Magnificence*, London, Debretts Peerage & Victoria and Albert Museum, 1980.

Farish, Thomas Edwin, *History of Arizona*, vols II and VIII, Phoenix, Arizona, privately published, 1918.

Bibliography

Field, Leslie, *The Queen's Jewels: the Personal Collection of Elizabeth II*, New York, Abradale Press, Harry N. Abrams, 2002.

Finlay, Victoria, *Colour: Travels through the Paintbox*, London, Hodder & Stoughton, 2002.

Forte, Elizabeth Williams, *Ancient Near-Eastern Seals*, New York, Metropolitan Museum of Art, 1976.

Fowler, Marian, *Hope: Adventures of a Diamond*, London, Simon & Schuster, 2002.

Frazer, James George, *The Magic Art and the Evolution of Kings: The Golden Bough*, Part 1, Volume 1, London, Macmillan, 1911.

Gautier, Théophile, *Voyage en Russie*, Paris, Charpentier, 1866.

George, E. C. S., *Burma Gazetteer: Ruby Mines District* (reprint), Rangoon, Superintendent Government Printing and Stationery, Union of Burma, 1961.

Ghosh, Amitav, *The Glass Palace*, London, HarperCollins, 2000.

Gibb, H. A. R., and J. H. Kramers, *Shorter Encyclopaedia of Islam, Edited on Behalf of the Royal Netherlands Academy*, Leiden, E. J. Brill, 1974.

Gienger, Michael, *Crystal Power, Crystal Healing: the complete handbook*, trans. Astrid Mick, London, Blandford, 1998.

Gierłowska, Gabriela, *The Beauty of Amber*, Gdansk, Bursztynowa Hossa Publishing House, 2004.

Gierłowska, Gabriela, 'The Varieties and Modification of Baltic Amber', *Amberif*, Gdansk, 2002.

Gierłowski, Wiesław, 'Succinite – the Stone of Life', *Amberif*, Gdansk, 2002.

Gierłowski, Wiesław, 'The Reconstruction of the Amber Chamber', Gdansk, *Amberif*, 2003.

Global Witness, 'For a Few Dollars More, How Al Qaeda Moved into the Diamond Trade', April 2003, www.globalwitness.org.

Gordon, Robert, *On the Ruby Mines near Mogok, Burma. Read at the Evening Meeting February 27th, 1888*, London, Proceedings of the Royal Geographical Society, May 1888.

Graf, Bernhard, *Gems: The World's Greatest Treasures and their Stories*, Munich, Prestel, 2001.

Graillot, Henri, *Le Culte de Cybèle, Mère des Dieux*, Paris, Fontemoing et Cie, 1912.

Grimm, Jacob, *Teutonic Mythology*, trans. J. Stallybrass, London, George Bell, 1883.

Gübelin, E., *Internal World of Gemstones: documents from Space and Time*, London, Newnes-Butterworth, 1979.

Haggard, Henry Rider, *King Solomon's Mines*, London, Penguin Popular Classics, 1994.

Hakluyt, Richard, *The Second Volume of the Principal Navigations, Voyages, Traffiques and Discoueries of the English Nation made by Sea or ouer-land, to the South and South-east parts of the World, at any time within the compasse of these 1600 yeres*, London, George Bishop, Ralph Newbery and Robert Barker, 1599.

Harrison, Charles, and Paul Wood (eds.), *Art in Theory 1900–2000: An Anthology of Changing Ideas*, Oxford, Blackwell, 2002.

Hart, Matthew, *Diamond*, New York, Walker & Company, 1999.

Hartmann, Philipp Jacob, *Succini Prussici, physica et civilis historia*, Frankfurt, 1677.

Hasselquist, Frederick, *Voyages and Travels in the Levant in the Years 1749, 50, 51, 52. Containing Observations in Natural History, Physick, Agriculture and Commerce*, London, Royal Society, 1766.

Hazen, Robert, *The Diamond Makers*, Cambridge, Cambridge University Press, 1999.

Healey, John F. (ed.), *Pliny the Elder, A Natural History*, London, Penguin, 1991.

Heckewelder, John, 'Indian Tradition of the First Arrival of the Dutch at Manhattan Island', in *Collections of the New York Historical Society*, New York, 1841, I, pp. 71–4.

Hiuen Tsiang, *Buddhist Records of the Western World (AD 629)*, trans. Samuel Beal, Delhi, DK Publishers, 1995.

Horne, Charles F., *The Sacred Books and early Literature of the East*, New York, Parke, Austin & Lipscomb, 1917.

Hughes, Richard, *Ruby & Sapphire*, Boulder, Colorado, R. W. H. Publishing, 1997.

Irwin, D. J., 'The Exploration of Gough's Cave and its Development as a Show Cave', in *Proceedings of the University of Bristol Spelaeological Society*, vol.17, no. 2, 1985.

Jervis, W. P., *The Minerals and Metals Mentioned in the Old Testament: their paramount influence on the social and religious history of the nations of antiquity, being a Paper Read before the Victoria Institute*, London, Victoria Institute Transactions, 22 May 1905.

Jones, William, *The Treasures of the Earth, or Mines, Minerals and Metals*, London, Frederick Warne & Co., 1868.

Jones, William, *Credulities Past and Present*, London, Chatto & Windus, 1880.

Joret, Charles, *Jean-Baptiste Tavernier, Ecuyer, Baron d'Aubonne Chambellan du Grand Electeur*, Paris, E. Plon, Nourrit et Cie, 1886.

Joyce, Kristin, and Shellei Addison, *Pearls: Ornament and Obsession*, New York, Simon & Schuster, 1993.

Kamen, Henry, *Spain's Road to Empire*, London, Penguin, 2002.

Kaye, Eugene Walter Whittenbury, *The Romance and Adventures of the notorious Colonel Blood, who attempted to steal the Crown Jewels*, Manchester, John Heywood, Ridgefield, 1903.

Keller, Peter, *Gemstones and their Origins*, New York, Van Nostrand Reinhold, 1990.

Kendall, Hugh, *The Story of Whitby Jet: its workers from earliest times*, Whitby, Whitby Literary and Philosophical Society, 1936 (reprinted 1988).

Kenseth, Joy (ed.), *The Age of the Marvelous*, Hanover, New Hampshire, Hodd Museum of Art, Dartmouth College, 1991.

Khalidi, Omar, *Romance of the Golconda Diamonds*, Middletown, New Jersey, Grantha Corporation, 1999.

Kharin, Gennadij S. Kharin, 'Gas inclusions in Baltic Amber', in Barbara Kosmowska-Ceranowicz and Henryk Paner (eds), *Investigations into Amber*, Gdansk, Archaeological Museum, 1999.

King, C. W., *The Natural History, Ancient and Modern, of Precious Stones and Gems*, London, Bell & Daldy, 1865.

Kloetzli, Randy, *Buddhist Cosmology*, Delhi, Motilal Banarsidass, 1983.

Kornitzer, Louis, *The Jewelled Trail*, London, G. Bles, 1940.

Kosmowska-Ceranowicz, Barbara, and Henryk Paner (eds), *Investigations into Amber*, Gdansk, Archaeological Museum, 1999.

Kunz, George Frederick, *Precious Stones*, Philadelphia, reprinted from the Journal of the Franklin Institute, September and October 1890.

Kunz, George Frederick, *Natal Stones: Sentiment and Superstition connected with Precious Stones*, New York, Tiffany & Co., 1903.

Kunz, George Frederick, *The Magic of Jewels and Charms*, first published 1915, New York, Dover Publications, 1997.

Kunz, George Frederick, *Shakespeare and Precious Stones*, Philadelphia and London, J. B. Lippincott Co., 1916.

Kunz, George Frederick, *Rings for the Finger*, first published 1917, New York, Dover Publications, 1973.

Kunz, George Frederick, and Charles Hugh Stevenson, *The Book of the Pearl: the History, Art, Science and Industry of the Queen of Gems*, first published 1905, New York, Dover Publications, 1993.

Labarge, Margaret Wade, *Medieval Travellers: the Rich and the Restless*, London, Orion Books, 1982.

Landers, John Michael, *An Old Chum Remembers: the story of Lightning Ridge 1906–1921*, ed. Barbara Moritz, Lightning Ridge, Lightning Ridge Historical Society, 2002.

Landman, Neil, Paula Mikkelsen, Rüdiger Bieler and Bennet Bronson, *Pearls: A Natural History*, New York, American Museum of Natural History and the Field Museum, 2001.

Lang, Andrew, *The Book of Dreams and Ghosts*, London, Longmans, Green & Co., 1897.

Lang, Andrew, *Portraits and Jewels of Mary Stuart*, Glasgow, James MacLehose & Sons, 1906.

Lanllier, Jan, and Marie-Anne Pini, *Five Centuries of Jewelry in the West*, New York, Arch Cape Press, 1983.

Laufer, Berthold, *The Diamond*, Chicago, Field Museum, 1915.

Lennon, Jessie, *I'm the One That Know this Country! The story of Jessie Lennon and Coober Pedy*, ed. Michele Madigan, Canberra, Aboriginal Studies Press, 2000.

Leonardus, Camillus, *The Mirror of Stones In Which The Nature, Genera-*

tion, Properties, Virtues and various Species of more than 200 different Jewels, precious and rare Stones, are distinctly described, London, J. Freeman in Fleet, 1750.

Levi, Karen, *The Power of Love: Six centuries of diamond betrothal rings*, London, Diamond Information Centre, and Christie's, 1988.

Levy, Adrian, and Cathy Scott-Clark, *The Stone of Heaven: the Secret History of Imperial Green Jade*, London, Phoenix Books, 2001.

Leyland, Ralph Watts, *A Holiday in South Africa*, London, Sampson Low, Marston, Searle & Rivington, 1882.

Lucanus, Marcus Annaeus, *The Civil War*, trans. J. D. Duff, Cambridge, Harvard University Press, 1958.

Mackintosh-Smith, Tim (ed.), *The Travels of Ibn Battutah*, London, Picador, 2002.

Majumdar, R. C., *The Classical Accounts of India*, Calcutta, K. L. Mukhopadhyay, 1960.

Mallet, Victor (ed.), *Life with Queen Victoria: Marie Mallet's letters from Court 1887–1901*, London, John Murray, 1968.

Manley, Deborah, and Sahar Abdel-Hakim (eds), *Travelling through Egypt*, Cairo, American University in Cairo, 2004.

Marbodus of Rennes (1034–1123), *De lapidus considered as a medical treatise with text, commentary and CW King's translation*, ed. John M. Riddle. Wiesbaden, Franz Steiner, 1977.

Marcus, P. W., *The Story of the Sapphire and the Ruby: Being the fifth of a series of little books which are issued from time to time, and which have to do with the legends, histories, occurrence and fashion of precious stones*, New York, P. W. Marcus & Co., 1938.

Marcus, P. W., *The Story of the Star Stones*, New York, P. W. Marcus & Co., 1935.

Mawe, John, *A Treatise on Diamonds and Precious Stones including their History – natural and commercial*, London, Longman, Hurst, Rees, Orme & Brown, 1823.

Mawe, John, *Travels in the Interior of Brazil, particularly in the Gold and Diamond districts of that country*, London, Longman, Hurst, Rees, Orme & Brown, 1812.

McMillan, Mabel, *Whitby Jet Through the Years*, Whitby, Mabel McMillan, 1992.

Menkes, Suzy, *The Royal Jewels*, London, Grafton, 1988.

Menzhausen, Joachim, *The Green Vault. An introduction*, trans. Hartmut Angermueller, Dresden, Staatliche Kunstsammlungen Dresden, 1977.

Michael, Prince, of Greece, *Crown Jewels*, New York, Crescent Books, 1983.

Mierzwińska, Elżbieta, and Marek Żak, *The Great Book of Amber*, Malbork, Malbork Castle Museum.

Mohs, Frederick, *Treatise on Mineralogy*, trans. William Haidinger, Edinburgh, Archibald Constable & Co., 1825.

Moreland, William Harrison (ed.), *Relations of Golconda in the Early Seventeenth Century*, London, Hakluyt Society, 1931.

Müller, Andy, *Cultured Pearls: the first 100 years*, Lausanne, Golay Buchel, 1997.

Muller, Helen, *Jet Jewellery and Ornaments*, Princes Risborough, Shire Publications, 1998.

Müller, M., *Lettre à M. le Chevalier de Born sur La Tourmaline du Tirol*, Brussels, J. Vanden Berghen, 1779.

Mumme, I. A., *The Emerald. Its Occurrence, Discrimination and Valuation*, Port Hacking, New South Wales, Mumme Publications, 1982.

Mustoe, Anne, *Amber, Furs and Cockle Shells: Bike Rides with Pilgrims and Merchants*, London, Virgin Books, 2005.

Nassau, Kurt, *Gem Made by Man*, Radnor, Pennsylvania, Chiltern, 1980.

Neat, Timothy, *The Summer Walkers, Travelling People and Pearl-Fishers in the Highlands of Scotland*, Edinburgh, Canongate Books, 1996.

Nicholson, Helen, *Love, War and the Grail*, Leiden, Boston, Cologne, Brill, 2001.

Nicols, Thomas, *A Lapidary or The History of Pretious Stones with cautions for the undeceiving of all those that deal with Pretious Stones*, Cambridge, Thomas Buck, 1652.

Noya Carafa, *Lettre du Duc de Noya Carafa sur la Tourmaline à Monsigneur de Buffon*, Paris, Duke de Noya, 1759.

Bibliography

O'Donoghue, Michael, *The Literature of Gemstones*, London, Science Reference and Information Service, 1986.

Oldroyd, David, *Sciences of the Earth: Studies in the History of Mineralogy and Geology*, Aldershot, Ashgate, 1998.

Olins, Peter, *The Teutonic Knights in Latvia*, Riga, B. Lamey, 1928.

Olivier, Jane, 'The Queen's Jewels' in *Housewife*, March and April 1961.

Oppenheimer, H. F., 'A chance discovery that changed the future of the country', *Optima*, June 1966, pp. 88–9.

Osborne, Roger, *The Floating Egg*, London, Pimlico, 1998.

Petry, Ann, *The Narrows*, New York, Houghton Mifflin, 1953.

Phillips, Clare, *Jewelry: From Antiquity to the Present*, London, Thames & Hudson, 1996.

Pliny the Elder, *Natural History. Translated with copious notes by the late John Bostock and H. T. Riley*, London, Henry G. Bohn, 1855.

Plutarch, *Makers of Rome*, trans. Ian Scott-Kilvert, London, Penguin Books, 1965.

Poinar, George, Jr, and Roberta Poinar, *The Amber Forest: A Reconstruction of a Vanished World*, Princeton, New Jersey, Princeton University Press, 1999.

Pointon, Marcia, 'Wearing Memory: Mourning, Jewellery and the Body', in Gisele Ecker (ed.), *Trauer Tragen – Trauer Zeigen. Inszenierungen der Geschlechter*, Munich, Fink Verlag, 1999, pp. 65–81.

Polo, Marco, and Rustichello of Pisa, *The Travels of Marco Polo: the Complete Yule-Cordier edition*, trans. Henry Yule 1903, revised Henri Cordier, London, John Murray, 1920.

Post, Emily, *Etiquette in Society, in Business, in Politics and at Home*, New York, Funk & Wagnalls Co., 1922.

Propertius, *Elegies: Book I*, ed. W. A. Camps, Cambridge, Cambridge University Press, 1977.

Purchas, Samuel, Parson of St Martin's By Ludgat, *Purchas His Pilgrimage*, London, William Stansby, 1626.

Pybus, John, Diary and Reports from a Secret Expedition to Ceylon, unpublished manuscript held in the India Office Library, British Library.

Rainier, Peter, *Green Fire*, London, John Murray, 1943.

Ransom, Jay Ellis, *Arizona Gem Trails and the Colorado Desert of California. A field guide for the gem hunter*, Oregon, Mineralogist Publishing Co., 1955.

Reifenberg, A., *Ancient Hebrew Seals*, London, East and West Library, 1950.

Ribeiro, João, *History of Ceylon*, trans. George Lee, Colombo, Government Press, 1847.

Roach, Michael, *The Diamond Cutter*, New York, Doubleday, 2000.

Rocheblave, Samuel, *Essai sur le Comte de Caylus*, Paris, Librairie Hachette, 1889.

Rogers, J. M., *The Topkapi Saray Museum* (a translation and expansion of the work in Turkish by Cengiz Köseoğlu), London, Thames & Hudson, 1987.

Romer, John, and Elizabeth Romer, *The Seven Wonders of the World, A History of the Modern Imagination*, London, Seven Dials, 1995.

Russell, E. W., *Soil Conditions and Plant Growth*, London, Longmans, 1961.

Ryley, J. Horton, *Ralph Fitch, With His Remarkable Narrative told in his own Words*, London, T. Fisher Unwin, 1899.

Samuels, S. K., *Burma Ruby: A history of Mogok's rubies from antiquity to the present*, Tucson, Arizona, SKS Enterprises, 2002.

Scarisbrick, Diana, *Jewellery*, London, B. T. Batsford, 1984.

Scarisbrick, Diana, *Tudor and Jacobean Jewellery*, London, Tate Publishing, 1994.

Scarisbrick, Diana, Martin Henig, and James Fenton, *Finger Rings: from ancient to modern*, Oxford, Ashmolean Museum, 2003.

Schumann, Walter, *Gemstones of the World*, trans. Evelyne Stern, New York, Sterling Publishing, 1977.

Scott, Walter, *Anne of Geierstein*, Edinburgh, A. & C. Black, 1860.

Scott-Clark, Catherine, and Adrian Levy, *The Amber Room: the untold story of the greatest hoax of the twentieth century*, London, Atlantic Books, 2004.

Seward, A. C., *Catalogue of the Mesozoic Plants in the Department of Geology, British Museum*, London, British Museum, 1904.

Shackford, Martha Hale (ed.), *Legends and Satires from Medieval Literature*, Boston, Massachusetts, Ginn & Co., 1913.

Shaw, Ian, 'Life on the Edge: Gemstones, Politics and Stress in the Deserts of Egypt and Nubia', in Renee Friedman (ed.), *Egypt and Nubia: Gifts of the Desert*, London, British Museum Press, 2002.

Shaw, Ian (ed.), *The Oxford History of Ancient Egypt*, Oxford, Oxford University Press, 2000.

Shirai, Shohei, *The Story of Pearls*, Tokyo, Japan Publications, 1970.

Schoener, R., *Un Portrait de Cléopatre*, Paris, Jules Delorme, 1889.

Sidebotham, Steven E., 'Preliminary Report on archaeological fieldwork at Sikait and environs, 2002–3,' *Sahara* 15/2004, pp. 7–30.

Sinclair, Andrew, *Corsair: The Life of J. Pierpoint Morgan*, London, Weidenfeld & Nicolson, 1981.

Sinkankas, John, *Beryl*, London, Butterworths Gem Books, 1986.

Skeen, William, *Adam's Peak: Legendary, Traditional and Historic Notices of the Samanala and Sri-Pada*, Ceylon, W. L. H. Skeen & Co., 1870.

Smith, Herbert, *Gemstones and Their Distinctive Characters*, London, Methuen, 1912.

Solzhenitsyn, Alexander, *A Day in the Life of Ivan Denisovich*, trans. Gillon Aitken, London, Sphere, 1974.

Somers-Cocks, A. (ed.), *Princely Magnificence: Court Jewels of the Renaissance, 1500–1630*, London, Debretts Peerage and the Victoria and Albert Museum, 1980.

Staples, Ariadne, *From Good Goddess to Vestal Virgins*, London, Routledge, 1998.

Steinem Patch, Susanne, *Blue Mystery: The Story of the Hope Diamond*, New York, Harry Abrams, 1999.

Stoker, Bram, *Dracula*, London, A. Constable & Co., 1897.

Stokowski, Marek, *St Mary's Castle: The World of the Teutonic Order*, Hamburg, Hotspot.

Stopford, Francis, *The Romance of the Jewel*, London, private circulation, 1920.

Story-Maskelyne, Nevil, *Metals and Minerals of the Bible*, London, private circulation, 1888.

Streeter, Edwin, *Precious Stones and Gems*, London, George Bell & Sons. All references come from the fourth edition (1884) except those referring to Burma rubies, which were taken from the fifth (1892) or sixth (1898) edition.

Streeter, Edwin, *The Great Diamonds of the World*, London, George Bell & Sons, 1888.

Streeter, George, 'Burma's Ruby Mines', in *Murray's Magazine*, May 1887, pp. 679–88.

Streeter, Patrick, *Streeter of Bond Street*, Harlow, The Matching Press, 1993.

Stuart, John McDouall, *Explorations in Australia. The Journals of John McDouall Stuart During the Years 1858, 1859, 1860, 1861 and 1862, when he fixed the centre of the Continent and Successfully Crossed it from Sea to Sea*, ed., William Hardman, London, Saunders, Otley & Co., 1864.

Studer, Paul, and Joan Evans, *Anglo-Norman Lapidaries*, Paris, Librairie Ancienne Edouard Champion, 1934.

Suetonius, Gaius Tranquillus, *The Twelve Caesars*, trans. Robert Graves, London, Penguin Books, 1953.

Tagore, Saurīndramohana Thākura, *Mani Málá, a treatise on Gems etc.*, Calcutta, I. C. Bose, 1879.

Tavernier, Jean-Baptiste, *Travels in India*, Delhi, DK Fine Art Print, 2000.

Taylor, Elizabeth, *My Love Affair with Jewelry*, London, Thames & Hudson, 2003.

Taylor, Gerald, and Diane Scarisbrick, *Finger Rings from Ancient Egypt to the Present Day*, Oxford, Ashmolean Museum, 1978.

Tebbs, Barry (ed.), *Trees of the British Isles*, London, Orbis, 1984.

Thirkell White Collection, British Library, MSS Eur. E.254/11, 'Papers relating to Edward Moylan's allegations of maladministration', 1886–92.

Thomas, Keith, *Religion and the Decline of Magic*, London, Penguin Books, 1991.

Tolkowsky, Marcel, *Diamond Design: A study of the reflection and refraction of light in a diamond*, London, E. & F. N. Spon, 1919.

Townsend, George Fyler, *The Arabian Nights Entertainments*, London, Frederick Warne & Co., 1887.

Treitschke, Heinrich von, *Treitschke's Origins of Prussianism (the Teutonic Knights)*, trans. Eden and Cedar Paul, London, George Allen & Unwin, 1942.

Tugny, Anne de, *Pierres de Rêve*, Paris, Flammarion, 1987.

Turrell, Robert Vicat, *Capital and Labour on the Kimberley Diamond Fields 1871 to 1890*, Cambridge, Cambridge University Press, 1987.

Twain, Mark, *Following the Equator*, New York, Hartford Doubleday, 1897.

Twining, Lord, *A History of the Crown Jewels of Europe*, London, B. T. Batsford, 1960.

Twining, Edward Francis, Baron, *European Regalia*, London, B. T. Batsford, 1967.

Twining, Edwin Francis, Baron, In Quest of Stones, unpublished manuscript.

Twitchell, James B., *Twenty Ads that Shook the World*, New York, Random House, 2000.

Urban, William, *The Teutonic Kings: A Military History*, London, Greenhill Books, 2003.

Varthema, Ludovico, *Itinerary of Ludovico di Varthema of Bologna from 1502–1508*, ed. R. C. Temple, London; Argonaut Press, 1928.

Verkhovski, C. C., and C. F. Akhmetov, *The Tears of the Heliads*, Moscow, Planeta, 1991.

Vermaseren, Maarten Jozef, *Cybele and Attis*, trans. A. M. H. Lemmers, London, Thames & Hudson, 1977.

Voillot, Patrick, *Diamonds and Precious Stones*, London, Thames & Hudson, 1998.

Vonnegut, Kurt, *Slaughterhouse Five*, London, Jonathan Cape, 1970.

Wade, Frank B., *A Text-book of Precious Stones for Jewelers and the Gem-loving Public*, London, G. P. Putnam's Sons, 1924.

Walters, Raymond J. L., *The Healing Power of Gemstones*, London, Carlton Books, 1996.

Walton, Stephen, 'Theophrastus on Lyngurium', in *Annals of Science*, 58 (2001), pp. 357–79.

Ward, Fred, *Diamonds*, Bethesda, Maryland, Gem Book Publishers, 1998.

Wilkinson, Gerald, *A History of Britain's Trees*, London, Hutchinson, 1981.

Wise, Richard, *Secrets of the Gem Trade: the Connoisseur's Guide to Precious Gemstones*, Lennox, Massachusetts, Brunswick House Press, 2003.

Wollaston, D. P. T., *Tullie Cornthwaite Wollaston 1863–1931*, Adelaide, privately published, 1994.

Wollaston, Tullie, *Opal: The Gem of the Never Never*, London, Thomas Murby, 1924.

Yogev, Gedalia, *Diamonds and Coral. Anglo-Dutch Jews and Eighteenth Century Trade*, Leicester, Leicester University Press, 1978.

Younghusband, Sir George, and Cyril Davenport, *The Crown Jewels of England*, London, Cassell & Co. Ltd, 1919.

Yule, Henry, *A Narrative of the Mission sent by the Governor-General of India to the Court of Ava in 1855*, London, Smith Elder, 1858.

Zettersten, Arne, *A Middle English Lapidary*, Lund, C. W. K. Gleerup, 1968.

Zucker, Benjamin, *Gems and Jewels: A Connoisseur's Guide*, New York, Overlook Press, 2003.

Notes

Beginning the Search

1. Richard Hughes, 'Romancing the Stone', Gem Key magazine 1999, Vol. 1, No. 5.
2. Interview with icon artist, Aidan Hart, April 2005
3. There is a famous account of how, in 987 AD, Vladimir of Kiev was considering whether to become Christian or Muslim and how in the midst of his indecision he received a letter from his envoys describing their experiences at the Hagia Sophia. They said that as the light filtered through the windows, the priests chanted their prayers and the mosaics shone in the candlelight, 'we knew not whether we stood on earth or in heaven' and on that testimonial he, and all Russia, converted to Orthodoxy. It is a story that many Russian icon painters, in placing their jewels of heaven upon their earthly icons, have reminded us of ever since.
4. Private correspondence. Bryan Ambrose, Rose Narrow Boats, Warwickshire.

Amber

1. C. C. Verkhovski and C. F. Akhmetov, *The Tears of the Heliads*, p. 40.
2. Conversation with Bob Smart, curator of the Cheddar George Museum.
3. The oldest amber artefacts, as opposed to traded but unworked pieces like the Gough's Cave discovery, were found in Late Upper Palaeolithic sites in the Ukraine. An anthropomorphic figurine was found at Dobranichevka in the Dnieper river basin in the early 1970s. Barbara Kosmowska-Ceranowicz and Henryk Paner (eds), *Investigations into Amber*, p. 99.

4. Amber from the Isle of Wight is 120 million years old and not related to Baltic amber.

5. Curt Beck, 'The Origin of the Amber found at Gough's Cave, Cheddar, Somerset', Proceedings of the University of Bristol Speleogical Society, vol. 10, no. 3, 1965.

6. Baltic amber is usually dated as being between thirty and fifty million years old. In this chapter I take the average of forty million years.

7. Conversation with Roger Jacoby, British Museum.

8. The Vistula delta has almost 80 per cent of the total known succinite in the world.

9. Homer, *Odyssey*, Book 4. Telemachus looks with wonder at the palace of Menelaus, remarking on how 'the gleam of bronze and gold – of amber, ivory, and silver . . . is so splendid that it is like seeing the palace of Olympian Jove'. Yet the wise king reminds him that nothing, not even an amber-lined palace, can compete with the immortality of Jove.

10. Cunliffe, *The Extraordinary Voyage of Pytheas the Greek*, p. 74.

11. At one time many Europeans believed that amber was closely related to a legendary precious stone that was also transparent, hard and yellow, with the quality of attracting straws to it. It was known as 'lyngourion' or 'lynx-urine stone', and was said to be notoriously hard to find, mostly because wild cats were in the habit of burying it in earth. The legend of lyngourion dates back to the earliest known lapidary, written by the third century BC philosopher Theophrastus, and it was told until the seventeenth century. Over the years many scholars puzzled over the reference. Did this stone exist, and if not, could a man as intelligent as Theophrastus have believed in wild cats pissing gemstones? There is, perhaps, a clue in the lapidary, which states, wrongly, that amber comes from Liguria, in north-western Italy one of the side arms of the Amber Road leading south from the Baltic during Greek times. It is a place-name that in Greek sounds remarkably like 'lynx urine' and perhaps this ridiculous gemstone was just a pun, intended to entertain students fidgeting in the Athenian heat – rather like a college lecturer today making a joke about the red-brown mineral Cummingtonite named after Cummington in

Massachusetts. The Greeks made a habit of jokily taking words from other languages to make them sound Greek, so it is also possible that they interpreted a purple stone called 'achlamath' in Hebrew to sound like a-methystos, meaning 'without-alcohol'. Today it is usually taken literally, as if the Greeks really thought amethysts would prevent a hangover. Earle Caley and John Richards, *Theophrastus on Stones*, p. 2ff. Lyngourian (urine of lynx) is Αυγγουριον: Liguria is Αιγυστικην.

12. In 2004 Volkswagen introduced a new luxury car called the Phaeton, presumably named after the eighteenth-century racing buggy that was itself named after the myth. In their publicity material VW referred briefly to the Greek myth but instead of mentioning the fatal accident simply noted that 'Only Zeus personally managed to bring the young man in the Sun carriage to a stop.' For them, the legend was 'a symbol for the human desire to tread new paths'. It is, however, a curious marketing decision in any era to name a product after a vehicle renowned for spinning out of control.

13. The Kaliningrad Amber Museum has a piece of 4.28 kilos. C. C. Verkhovski and C. F. Akhmetov, *The Tears of the Heliads*, p. 84. Pliny told of a piece weighing 4.5 kilos brought back by an expedition sent by Nero to bring exotica to his gladiatorial games.

14. Pytheas is recorded as going to *ultima Thule* 'near the congealed sea', which many scholars believe to be Iceland, although others argue that he did not have time to travel so far. Cunliffe, *The Extraordinary Voyage of Pytheas the Greek*, pp. 116–33.

15. Pliny, *Natural History* Book 11, chapter 37. None of the copies of Pytheas' book *Peri Tou Okeanou* have survived the years: he lives only in the history and footnotes of other writers, including Pliny, Polybius and Strabo.

16. 'Long-Haired Lover From Liverpool' was a British number-one single in 1972, sung by Jimmy Osmond.

17. Information from the Yantarny Museum of History.

18. Peter Olins, *The Teutonic Knights in Latvia*, p. 5.

19. Ibid., p. 34.

20. William Urban, *The Teutonic Knights*, pp. 14–15.

21. Marek Stokowski, *St Mary's Castle*, p. 50.

22. F. G. L. Bunge Friedrich Bunge, *Liv-, esth- und curländisches Urkundenbuch nebst Regesten*, p. 180.

23. Other Amber Roads led south from Jutland.

24. Ezekiel 1:4. Jerusalem Bible translation.

25. Published as an appendix to Philipp Jacob Hartmann, *Succini Prussici*, 1677.

26. Luther always wore a nugget of amber round his waist, believing it to protect him from kidney stones. Anne Mustoe, *Amber, Furs and Cockle Shells*, p. 33.

27. The Teutonic Knights continued in western Europe, where they did not accept Albrecht's decision to secularise. They survived Napoleon's abolition of the Order in 1809 and Nazi abolition in 1938. Today the Teutonic Order is made up mostly of Catholic friars and nuns from Austria, Germany, Italy, the Czech Republic, Slovakia and Slovenia. They are true to their beginnings as a hospital order and run mainly charity and medical activities.

28. Eva Rachon, head of the Amberif amber trade fair in Gdansk. It started in 1993 to counter some of the problems of fake amber: it invites only the most reputable suppliers to exhibit and sell amber in both raw and finished form.

29. George Poinar Jr and Roberta Poinar, *The Amber Forest*, p. 5.

30. The Eocene era lasted from 55 to 35 million years ago. The beginning of that period was warm, with tropical evergreen forests extending as far as 60° latitude in the northern hemisphere; crocodiles lived as far north as Arctic Canada. By the end there was ice in Antarctica and fewer tropical forests around the world. The time of the dinosaur was long since over. The Jurassic period dates from 144 to 213 million years ago, the Cretaceous period from 65 to 144.

31. *Discovering the Lost World of the Amber Forests*, 13 July 2004, BBC Radio 4. Gennadij S. Kharin, 'Gas inclusions in Baltic Amber,' in Kosmowska-Ceranowicz and Henryk Paner, (eds) *Investigations into Amber*, pp. 215–19.

32. 'Piltdown Man' was a famous scientific hoax, in which the fragments of so-called early human bones were uncovered in 1912 near Piltdown in England. Half a century later they were revealed to be a combination of ape bones and modern human remains.

33. It is sometimes difficult to tell pressed amber from natural material even when using the best infrared spectral-analysis methods available. However, there is a monotony to pressed amber that isn't evident in the real thing. Wiesłav Gierłowski, 'The Reconstruction of the Amber Chamber' in *Amberif*, 2003, p. 42.

34. Conversation with amber expert Gabriela Gierłowska, Gdansk.

35. Kalinin was chairman of the Central Executive Committee of the All-Russian Congress of Soviets from 1919 to 1922, when he became president of the USSR.

36. Yantarny has an average amber yield of five kilos per cubic metre of earth, in comparison to one-tenth of that in the Ukrainian amber mines.

37. Trade Environment database, http://www.american.edu/TED/hp 1. htm.

38. Pliny, *Natural History*, Book 37, chapter 11.

39. Succinic acid is found in many food ingredients. However, even unripe gooseberries and rhubarb, which contain the richest amounts of succinite, offer a thousand times less than Baltic amber. Gierłowska, 'The Varieties and Modification of Baltic Amber', *Amberif*, 2002, p. 10.

40. Wiesłav Gierłowski, 'Succinite – the Stone of Life', *Amberif*, March 2002, p. 2.

41. Hannah Arendt, *Eichmann in Jerusalem*. Originally published as a series of articles in the *New Yorker*.

42. *A Day in the Life of Ivan Denisovich* was written by former maths teacher, later Nobel Prize winner, Alexander Solzhenitsyn about his years in captivity in a gulag in Kazakhstan. It described the inhumanity of the system in appalling detail.

43. In *Slaughterhouse Five* Kurt Vonnegut deals with the dual evils of totalitarianism and war in a story about aliens. 'Have you ever seen bugs trapped in amber?' the creatures asked their hostage Billy Pilgrim.

'Well, here we are, Mr Pilgrim, trapped in the amber of this moment. There is no why.'

44. From the letters of Theodoric's secretary, Cassiodorus, *Variae*, 5.2.15.

45. The Goths were originally from the Baltic area, but by the third century AD when they split into two factions they were living further south. The Ostrogoths lived in the area east of the Dnestr river, now the Ukraine and Belarus, while the Visigoths were based to the south-west of the Dnestr, now including Romania and Hungary.

46. Elżbieta Mierzwińska and Marek Żak, *The Great Book of Amber*, p. 22.

47. C. C. Verkhovski and C. F. Akmetov, *The Tears of the Heliads*, p. 106.

48. Théophile Gautier, *Voyage en Russie*, in Catherine Scott-Clark and Adrian Levy, *The Amber Room*, p. 56.

49. Ibid., p. 212.

50. In 2003 the governor of St Petersburg, Valentina Matviyenko, answered German newspaper requests for the art taken after the Second World War to be returned. She said, 'It was immoral to steal the Amber Room, besiege Leningrad, destroy thousands of Soviet cities and kill millions of Russians ... We have every right to make terms on the returns [of the art].' Catherine Scott-Clark and Adrian Levy, 'The Amber Façade', *Guardian*, 22 May 2004. pp. 15ff.

51. Parts of the Amber Room were already in a fairly bad condition when it disappeared, i.e. Wiesłav Gierłowski, 'The Reconstruction of the Amber Chamber,' in *Amberif* 2003. The report states that as early as 1913 the Russian authorities had backed out of a conservation contract for the Amber Room with the Moritz Stumpf Company of Gdansk. 'This contract called for rescue conservation,' he said.

52. Customs Service of the Republic of Poland, http://www.mf.gov.pl/sluzba_celna/dokument.php?typ=news&dzial=532&id=41980.

53. In 1949 Pope Pius XII excommunicated all Communists.

54. *Our Lady of Częstochowa* was painted by Franciszek Znaniecki.

55. Conversation with Father Henryk Jankowski, St Bridget's Church, Gdansk, July 2004.

56. Ultramarine paint was made of the blue gemstone lapis lazuli. It came

from just one set of mines, in Badakhshan, Afghanistan. Victoria Finlay, *Colour*, pp. 309–45.

Jet

1. Bertram Colgrave and R. A. B. Mynors (eds), *Bede's Ecclesiastical History of the English People*, chapter 1.
2. Ann Petry, *The Narrows*.
3. Shale is rather like a hard version of coal. It is a sedimentary layer of mud and clay.
4. Coral and petrified wood were also alive. Also, as shown in the pearl chapter, some natural pearls are formed around parasites.
5. Barry Tebbs *Trees of the British Isles*, p. 68.
6. Helen Muller, *Jet Jewellery and ornaments*, p. 10.
7. Bram Stoker, *Dracula*, chapter 6, p. 67.
8. When Bede stated that 'jet, when heated, drives away serpents', he was basing his information on the Roman writings of Caius Julius Solinus, five hundred years earlier. These qualities were repeated (or copied) by the writer of the lapidary of King Alphonsus. He knew this stone as *zequeth*, and said that 'Reptiles will flee from the smoke of this stone when it is being burnt.' Ingrid Bahler and Katherine Gyékényesi Gatto, (eds), *The Lapidary of King Alphonso X*, p. 165.
9. The current abbey of Whitby was rebuilt over the site of Hilda's seventh-century monastery in the twelfth and thirteenth centuries.
10. Bram Stoker, *Dracula*, chapter 6, p. 67.
11. In Ancient Rome there were no burials in the cities, only outside the city walls. The Appian Way is still lined with ancient burial places, and it was one of the most prestigious areas in which to end up.
12. Mabel McMillan, *Whitby Jet Through the Years*, p. 12.
13. Ibid., p. 210.
14. Hugh Kendall, *The Story of Whitby Jet*, p. 13.
15. Richard Davey, *A History of Mourning*, p. 86. Prince Albert was later reinterred in a mausoleum at Frogmore House in Windsor, where Queen Victoria is also buried.

16. NPG 429, *Mary Queen of Scots*, after Nicholas Hilliard.

17. Women on Ancient Greek painted pottery tend to have white skin while men tend to have black. Black and white were metaphors for the division between female and male, inside and outside, and when a woman wore black in widowhood it was perceived that she moved into an asexual ritual category – in other words, that she was more male than female, and therefore not available. Fitzwilliam Museum.

18. Vermeil is gilded metal. It was particularly popular in the eighteenth century as a means of dressing up cheaper metals to look like gold, whether in necklaces or antique objects. In the nineteenth century it was banned because it was discovered that the mercury used in the process sometimes caused the craftsman to go blind. Today it is produced by a safe electrolytic process. The White House in Washington, DC has a Vermeil Room full of gilded objects that were donated in the 1950s by a collector and presidential supporter.

19. Essonite, better known as 'cinnamon stone' because of its reddish-yellow colour, is a form of garnet. It comes mostly from Sri Lanka, and are sometimes confused with zircon. Rubellite is a pinkish or reddish form of tourmaline.

20. George Frederick Kunz, *Natal Stones*, p. 14.

21. Hugh Kendall, *The Story of Whitby Jet*, p. 16.

22. The ichthyosaurus was found at Hawsker village. It was twenty-five feet long and eight feet wide across the paddles, when they were extended out.

23. Frank Sutcliffe, the late curator of the Whitby Museum, wrote that 'the size of the new building was determined by the length of this fossil reptile. Then, when the beast had been cut up into four parts, he was too big to be removed whole through the windows of the old place; and, when ready for fixing up on one of the new walls, it was found that he was longer than the wall. Either he had stretched a foot or so; or the wall had shrunk on drying; or – tell it not in Gath – the tape measure used in taking his measurement had lost some inches, or had shrunk in washing.' Cited in Roger Osborne, *The Floating Egg*, p. 265.

24. In 1904 A. C. Seward, in *Catalogue of the Mesozoic Plants in the Department of Geology, British Museum*, p. 65, wrote: 'The result of an examination of several sections of Whitby jet in the British Museum collection leads me to express the opinion that jet has been formed by the alteration of wood: the masses of wood with the form and structure of that material probably represent portions of trees, the tissues of which underwent certain chemical changes resulting in the partial or complete obliteration of the vegetable structure and in the substitution of jet for wood.'

25. McMillan, *Whitby Jet Through the Years*, p. 35.

26. Interview with Tommy Roe, July 2003.

27. Suzy Menkes, *The Royal Jewels*, p. 16.

28. Victor Mallet (ed.), *Life with Queen Victoria*, p. 32.

29. Hugh Kendall, *The Story of Whitby Jet*, p. 10.

30. The Jet Stone and Silversmith Association in Santiago de Compostela had two hundred members in 2000, half of whom were working exclusively in jet. The raw material comes from the nearby Asturias region, where miners work in narrow pits some five metres deep and fifty metres long. Susan Zimmerman, 'Jet Set', *Lapidary Journal*, September 2000, p. 46.

31. English Cheddar originally came from the area of Somerset around Cheddar Gorge, for which the closest port is Bristol.

32. Coal is similar to jet, but instead of being made of a single type of tree it comes from a random heaping of plants. While jet fossilised airlessly beneath a blanket of sticky clay, leaving it with almost no bubbles, coal had plenty of air and plenty of bubbles. Coal can sometimes be made into jewellery but it is softer and rougher than jet and it never gets a good sheen.

33. Hugh Kendall, *The Story of Whitby Jet*, p. 36.

34. William Anderson, *Green Man*, p. 23.

35. Anne Baring and Jules Cashford, *The Myth of the Goddess*, pp. 393–4.

36. This appears to be a natural extension of eunuch-anxieties across cultures. Court eunuchs in China kept their testicles in glass jars, in the hope that they would arrive complete into the next world.

37. The *gallus* in the Capitoline Museum relief has a torque-like collar with lions and a pendant of Cybele, above which is a three-row string of beads or pearls.

38. Bacchus was also associated with black and, for a while, the English Heritage team considered whether Skeleton 952 might have been associated with the Roman god of wine. But the corpse's cross-dressing ultimately suggested Cybele.

39. Although the Victorians appeared not to know that jet was related to pine, it would not be surprising if the early Anatolians guessed because of the wood-like striations that can sometimes be found in it.

40. The Ka'bah was originally a pagan site. The Prophet rebuilt it after a fire, then ordered that true followers of Allah should pray towards this place rather than to Jerusalem as they had before

41. The information on the Ka'bah comes from H. A. R. Gibb and J. H. (eds), *Shorter Encyclopaedia of Islam*, pp. 192–7.

42. Henri Graillot, *Le Culte de Cybèle*, pp. 329–30. It has been suggested that the Black Stone of Cybele was a meteorite but, according to Graillot, this was a later legend.

43. Ariadne Staples, *From Good Goddess to Vestal Virgins*, p. 118.

44. Ibid.

45. The Roman poet Catullus wrote a poem in which he imagined what might cause a man to castrate himself for a cult. Today the poem is often included in miscellanies of transgender writings, because it describes Attis cutting off his testicles, and from then on portrays him as female. Catullus, *The Complete Poems*, No. 63.

Pearl

1. Haiku written by the author on a remarkably wet day in Toba, Japan, in May 2003.

2. Caesar, *The Conquest of Gaul*, pp. 119–27.

3. Gaius Tranquillus Suetonius, *The Twelve Caesars*, pp. 33–7.

4. Ibid, p. 33.

5. Some natural pearls are still to be found in Welsh and Cornish rivers, a few more in Cumbria; some rare gems also occur in the Nure, Barrow and Suir estuaries in Ireland.

6. The word 'onions' has the same Latin derivation as 'unions', perhaps because the vegetable is pale and translucent, but also because it forms slowly in thin layers, like pearls.

7. Pearls get bigger the longer they stay in the shell; if you cut a natural pearl open you can count the growth rings inside it.

8. There are four grains in a carat, and twenty in a gram.

9. In the seventeenth century Saxon rivers were famous for pearls, and they, too, were protected by strict laws: anyone caught removing mussels from the rivers would be hanged.

10. Joan Evans and Mary Serjeantson: *English Mediaeval Lapidaries*, pp. 107–8: 'Margarita is chef of al stons that ben wyght and preciose, as Ised seyth. And it hathe the name margarita for it is founde in shellis which ben cokelis or in mosclys and in schellfyssh of the see.'

11. Kristin Joyce and Shellei Addison, *Pearls*, p. 20.

12. Ibid, p. 22.

13. 'La plus belle perle n'est donc, en definitive, que le brilliant sarcophagi d'un ver.' Dubois, 'Comptes Rendus de l'Académie des Sciences', vol. 133, 14 October 1901, pp. 603–5. Cited in George Frederick Kunz and Charles Hugh Stevenson, *The Book of the Pearl*, p. 43.

14. Dr John MacInnes, formerly of the School of Scottish Studies, Edinburgh University, private correspondence.

15. The Abernathy pearl was the subject of a complicated legal action during the sale of Cairncross in 1988. However, the new owner won the right to keep it.

16. Andy Müller, 'Black Pearls of French Polynesia', *National Geographic*, June 1997.

17. Shohei Shirai, *The Story of Pearls*, p. 26.

18. George Frederick Kunz and Charles Hugh Stevenson, *The Book of the Pearl*, p. 285.

19. The problem came when Linnaeus wanted to make money from his invention. He offered his secret to the State Council of Sweden for

12,000 dalars (about £55,000) but later sold his method to a merchant called Peter Bagge for half of that. Bagge did nothing with it. *Linnean*, vol. 4, no. 20, October 2004.

20. From a speech by HRH the Prince of Wales at the 150th Anniversary of the Royal Institute of British Architects at Hampton Court Palace, 30 May 1984.

21. Charles Harrison and Paul Wood (eds), *Art in Theory 1900–2000*, p. 382.

22. All details about Julius Caesar in this section are from Gaius Tranquillus Suetonius, *The Twelve Caesars*, pp. 13–53.

23. After paying the ransom money, Caesar raised a fleet, chased the pirates, caught and crucified them. But the gift of the pearl did him few favours. He not only lost the attentions of the woman, Servilia, but, according to some accounts, she had a baby soon afterwards that many assumed was Caesar's. Years later the boy, along with several other conspirators, murdered Julius Caesar at the Senate House. His name was Marcus Brutus. Suetonius had the dying Caesar looking at Servilia's son and asking sadly, 'You too, my child?'

24. This historic bet generated a series of copycat pearl swallowing: Pliny says that 'Clodius, son of Aesopus the tragic actor, having been left a small fortune decided to eat a pearl, not for a wager but, by way of glorification to his palate, to find out what was the taste of pearls. As he found it to be wonderfully pleasing, that he might not be the only one to know it, he had a pearl set before each of his guests for him to swallow.' Pliny, *Natural History* Book 9, chapter 59. There was also a story that when Sir Thomas Gresham opened England's first Royal Exchange he invited Queen Elizabeth I to the opening and drank down a pearl. However, Robert Chambers, in *The Book of Days*, suggested this was poetic licence by contemporary playwright Thomas Heywood.

25. Converted from ten million sesterces by Neil Landman et al, *Pearls: A Natural History.*

26. Cleopatra was going to do the same to the other earring but a friend called Lucius Plancus, who was umpiring the wager, stopped her,

saying that Antony had already been defeated ('an omen that was to be fulfilled,' Pliny noted, with some satisfaction). Instead the pearl was cut in half and sent to decorate the ears of a statue in the Pantheon depicting Venus, who was often shown emerging from shells, so seemed a natural recipient for good pearls. John Healey, *Pliny the Elder, Natural History*, p. 137.

27. Ibid., p. 137.

28. I used a large natural pearl, about a centimetre in diameter, greatly flawed and purchased for ten dollars from the American Pearl Company, Tennessee.

29. Robert Eunson, *The Pearl King*, p. 18.

30. João Ribeiro, *History of Ceylon*, pp. 74–7.

31. *Wall Street Journal*, 14 May 1996. According to this article, the main reason that *nihâms* went blind was not because of the song but because of the searing sun of the Gulf, which can cause cataracts in the eyes of those who are exposed to it for too long.

32. Neil Landman et al, *Pearls: A Natural History*, pp. 13–15.

33. Kunz, *The Book of the Pearl*, p. 226.

34. *Lettera Rarissima*, 7 July 1503; cited in R. A. Donkin, *Beyond Price*, p. 314.

35. Elizabeth Taylor, *My Love Affair with Jewelry*, pp. 90–91.

36. *Proceedings of the Royal Society*, 1 March 1888, p. 463.

37. 'And the twelve gates were twelve pearls; each individual gate was of one pearl; and the street of the city was pure gold, like transparent glass.' Revelation 21:21.

38. Ever since Johann Hieronymus Chemnitz published a paper in Denmark in 1791 pearl researchers had known that the gems were created as part of the defence mechanism of oysters, but they knew little more. Indeed, some people in Japan believed that pearls originated from cancerous growths in the oysters.

39. R. A. Donkin, *Beyond Price*, pp. 6–9.

40. Information about pearl's origins came from the Toba Museum.

41. Mr Kiyoo Matsuzuki, curator of the Toba Pearl Museum.

42. Louis Kornitzer, *The Jewelled Trail*, pp. 62–3.

43. Clerks in the late 1920s earned around £250 a year. In London today their equivalents usually earn at least £20,000. Details of the pearl crash, Benjamin Zucker, *Gems and Jewels*, p. 116.

44. Perhaps the culmination of Mikimoto's model-making career was organising a nationwide USA tour of a dress, handbag and jewellery made of 100,000 cultured pearls. Kristin Joyce and Shellei Addison, *Pearls*, p. 5.

45. The tradition of Mikimoto Ltd giving away showy pearl-encrusted items has continued. In 2002 Mikimoto designed a Miss Universe Crown, to be worn by the winner, and valued at around $200,000 with 500 diamonds and 120 pearls. 'There is a huge market in Japan for tiara sales and rentals for special occasions,' said Kevin Lane, vice president of US Retail for Mikimoto. Press release, Miss Universe Organisation, March 2002.

46. John Latendresse, American Pearl Company, interview February 2004. John is the son of John Latendresse, who started the company in the 1940s.

47. The interest in Mikimoto's pearls extended to the highest levels. On 13 April 1946, Supreme Commander General Douglas MacArthur wrote a memo stipulating the precise quantities of pearls to be supplied weekly to the Army Exchange Service. Andy Müller, *Cultured Pearls*, p. 38.

48. Richard Wise, *Secrets of the Gem Trade*, p. 145.

49. Ibid., p. 151.

Opal

1. Tullie Wollaston, *Opal: The Gem of the Never Never*, p. 24.

2. Mark Twain, *Following the Equator*, chapter 16.

3. Pliny, *Natural History*, Book 37, Chapter 21.

4. There are important opal sources in Mexico and Nevada as well. These tend to be orange and are called 'fire opals' because of the fiery sparks in them. However, production is far less than it is in Australia.

5. Geoffrey Munn, *Art Newspaper*, 1 January 2000.

6. 'The Indians said they saw a ship approaching the island, and they dressed up believing it to be their great spirit Mannitto. When the Dutch landed, they drank with the Indians and gave them, "beads, axes, hoes, stockings etc." and said that they would return in a year and "should then want a little land of them to sow some seeds in order to raise herbs to put in their broth".' John Heckewelder, 'Indian Tradition of the First Arrival of the Dutch,' in *Collections of the New York Historical Society*, pp. 71–4. The tradition that Manhattan was sold in exchange for beads is now disputed. But as this account shows, beads were certainly traded in early contact between the Dutch and Native Americans.

7. Roy Spencer, son of Harry and Emily, was the person who found the famous Black Sapphire of Queensland, on a mullock heap, when he was twelve years old.

8. Different accounts give the Queen of Eulo's surname as, variously, Robinson, Robertson, Richardson or MacIntosh.

9. Len Cram, *Beautiful Queensland Opals*, pp. 18–19.

10. H. H. Batchelor, 'The Eulo Queen', *The Gemmologist*, July 1948.

11. Some of these first opals were sold to Andrew Grima, jeweller to Queen Elizabeth II. 'I went to see him in London and before I opened up my box he told me he already had a Yowah nut, set into a gold chain. But when I saw it I didn't want to embarrass him by showing him my collection,' Uwe Barfuss said. 'What he had was what we used to throw away in those days.'

12. The word 'Jehovah' in English comes from a mistransliteration of YHWH in Hebrew, which was the name for God and too sacred to pronounce.

13. Alan W. Eckert, *The World of Opals*, p. 16.

14. Ibid, pp. 3–5.

15. P. I. Daragh, A. J. Gaskin, and J. V. Sanders, 'Opals', in *Scientific American*, vol. 234, (1976), pp. 84–95. Also J. V. Sanders and P. J. Darragh, 'The Microstructure of Precious Opal', in *Mineralogic Record*, vol. 2 (1971), pp. 261–6.

16. A nanometer is 0.000000001 metres or a millionth of a millimetre.

Visible light contains wavelengths from roughly 380 to 750 nm or 0.00038 to 0.00075 mm.

17. Allan W. Eckert, *The World of Opals*.

18. The population of Alice Springs is around 28,000.

19. Coober Pedy also relies on water supplies from a sub-artesian bore well, twenty-six kilometres away.

20. http://www.business.nsw.gov.au/factsReports.asp?cid=34&subCid=148.

21. John McDouall Stuart, *Explorations in Australia*, Preface.

22. *Register*, Adelaide, 14 May 1921, p. 7.

23. In 1924 Tullie Wollaston wrote of the Coober Pedy miner, 'The equipment he needs is simple and inexpensive – gad and bar and pick and shovel, axe and rope and calico tent, windlass and green hide buckets which he can himself construct, and finally a bike, a brumby and a water bag – and opal snips. He is free and can work when he feels inclined and can spare time to make his dug-out camp reasonably comfortable which, however, he seldom does.' Tullie Wollaston, *Opal: The Gem of the Never Never*, p. 113.

24. Another explanation of the name Orphanus is tied up in the knotted association of opals with pupils (referring, in Teutonic mythology, to both eyes and children). Jacob Grimm, *Teutonic Mythology*, chapter 2.

25. New Year's Day was a traditional day of gifts in Elizabethan England. It was felt that waiting a few days after celebrating Christ's birth was symbolic of the arrival of the Magi, with their presents of gold, frankincense and myrrh.

26. *Royal Insight*, December 2003. www.royal.gov.uk/output/page2821.asp.

27. The technique of doublets and triplets can be used for almost any coloured gemstones including garnets, rubies and sapphires. The method for checking them is the same as for opals: look at them carefully from the side for a striping effect. It is, however, hard for an amateur gemmologist to recognise them when they are set in a clasp.

28. Jessie Lennon, *I'm The One That Know This Country*, pp. 48–9.

29. Allan W. Eckert, *The World of Opals*, p. 60.

30. Edwin Streeter, *Precious Stones and Gems*, p. 192.

31. Ibid., p. 193.

32. Queen Alexandra's tiara is now known as the Indian tiara, because rubies from the Indian subcontinent are set within it.

33. Tullie Wollaston took some samples of black opal to America in 1916, and even though it was wartime, he found some buyers. Two years later, at the end of the war, the market was booming and he sold £50,000 worth to just one buyer in Paris.

34. Tullie Wollaston, *Opal: The Gem of the Never Never*, p. 104.

35. Campbell Bridges, private conversation.

36. Eric the Pliosaur was saved from being sold overseas by a national appeal in 1993, which raised $450,000. It was named by the original finder after a sketch by British comedy team Monty Python, about Eric the fish who, after an accident, was only 'half a fish or half a bee'.

37. Feldspar is a group of minerals occurring in many igneous and metamorphic rocks. It is made up of aluminosilicates of potassium, sodium, calcium, or occasionally barium. It can come in the form of gemstones including amazon stone (containing potassium) and moonstone, labradorite and sunstone (all containing varying degrees of calcium and sodium).

38. Radiocarbon dating of black opal constrained their formation between 1740 and 7790 years, within the Holocene Epoch of the Quaternary period. Katie Quilpie and J. A. Maytogenes, *The Mystery of Lightning Ridge's Black Opal* (abstract). Research School of Earth Sciences, Australian National University. Personal correspondence, Katie Quilpie.

39. The information in this section is not enough to solve the puzzle of the origin of opals.

40. Aeschylus, *Agamemnon*, www.gutenberg.org/files/14417/14417.txt.

41. Plutarch, *Makers of Rome*, p. 293.

Peridot

1. Zabargad is fifty-four kilometres south-east of the tip of the Ras Banas peninsula and fifty kilometres east of the port of Berenice. It is triangular, and about five square kilometres in area.

2. Agatharchides of Cnidus, *On the Erythraean Sea*, p. 137 ff.

3. In 1980 Swiss gem expert Edward Gübelin and American dealer Peter Bancroft led an exhibition to Zabargad to assess its viability as a mining venture. The journey took seven hours from the mainland by traditional felucca. They set up camp in the old mining office and went to look for peridot. They found almost nothing: the only crystals near the surface were smaller than one centimetre long. Peter Bancroft, *Gem and Crystal Treasures*, cited on www.palagems.com/peridot_buyers_guide.htm#peridot_buying_guide.

4. Topaz was once celebrated for its similarity to gold. The Ancient Greeks used to put topazes on divining wands to try to locate caches of precious metal.

5. Juba, reported by Pliny and cited in Jehan Desanges (ed.), *Pline l'Ancien: Histoire Naturelle*, p. 283.

6. Zabargad means 'peridot' in Arabic; indeed, there is a theory that the Arabic name for peridot comes from the name of the island.

7. Peridot rock is called a xenolith because it is a stranger rock in magma – not part of the magma, just there for the ride.

8. Information from Smithsonian Museum, Washington DC.

9. NASA scientists were particularly excited at the peridot find in the Nili Fossae region of Mars because it gave them clues about the history of the planet. Olivine weathers easily as it is so soft. This sample was found near to an impact basin that was probably made by a comet some 3.6 billion years ago. If the samples were formed shortly after that time, they indicate that the surface of Mars was dry and cold for more than three billion years. If they were more recent than that, it would allow for the theory that Mars was once more like Earth, with running water and a thicker atmosphere. *Daily Telegraph*, 24 October 2003.

10. The Camp Grant massacre took place in the Aravipa Canyon, fifty kilometres south-west of the current San Carlos reservation.

11. Thomas Edwin Farish, *History of Arizona*, vol. II, p. 269ff. Manuscript is held by the Arizona Historical Society.

12. In the Book of Revelation Christ is described as breaking the seven seals on the scroll of revelation, as a sign that only God has the right to open what God has sealed. Revelation 5:5.

13. Translation by Edwin Streeter, *Precious Stones and Gems*, p. 286.

14. Genesis 41:42.

15. Charles Edwards, *The History and Poetry of Finger Rings*, p. 52.

16. Diana Scarisbrick, Martin Henig and James Fenton, *Finger Rings*, Preface.

17. Sard and sardonyx are both forms of chalcedony, which is an opaque and fibrous form of quartz. Sard is the name given to brown chalcedony (orange chalcedony is called carnelian). Onyx is derived from the Greek word for 'nail' or 'claw', and is the generic word given to striped chalcedony. 'Sardonyx', therefore, is striped brown chalcedony.

18. Agatharchides of Cnidus, *On the Erythraean Sea*, Book 5, p. 137ff.

19. It is possible that Agatharchides might have confused peridot with a stone called cancrinite, mined by the Ptolemies under the name iris, a silicate of sodium, magnesium and calcium, which forms large hexagonal crystals and was noted for spectacular visual effects when seen in the dark. Ibid., p. 137: translator's note.

20. Peridot's chemical structure is written as $(Mg, Fe)_2[SiO_4]$ to show that it can range from Mg_2SiO_4 (fayalite) to Fe_2SiO_4 (forsterite) depending on its iron content.

21. Kenneth Cameron, *English Place Names*, p. 37.

22. Pliny, *Natural History*, Book 37, chapter 32.

23. J. M. Rogers, *The Topkapi Saray Museum*, p. 87. Egypt had been held by the Ottomans since 1518.

24. The Natural History Museum in London owns a nearly flawless peridot crystal from Zabargad, some six centimetres long and five centimetres wide. It is said to be the largest peridot crystal in the world. It

was found in the 1930s by the Red Sea Mining Company, which took over operations in 1922 when the rule of the Ottomans in Egypt finally ended.

25. It is easy to confuse gem carats with gold karats. The latter describes the proportion of gold to other substances in the metal, so while 24-karat gold is gold, 14-karat gold is only fourteen twenty-fourths gold, and when a metal is nine-karat it scarcely deserves to be called gold at all as so much else is melted into it.

26. Diana Scarisbrick, *Tudor and Jacobean Jewellery*, p. 52.

Emerald

1. William Jones, *Credulities Past and Present*, p. 33.

2. Robert Webster, 'The Identification of Gemstones by Color'. *The Gemmologist*, 1948, pp. 39–44.

3. Edwin Streeter, *Precious Stones and Gems*, p. 176.

4. Frederick H. Pough, 'The Emerald Makers', in *Science Illustrated*, July 1948.

5. J. P. Cahn, 'The Man Who Grows Emeralds', *True: the Man's Magazine*, October 1957, pp. 58ff.

6. Barbara and Tom Chatham, private conversation, California, October 2003.

7. Marcus Annaeus Lucanus, *The Civil War*, Book 10, pp. 110–25.

8. Edwin Streeter, *Precious Stones and Gems*.

9. The latest technology used in emerald improvement is a polymer called opticon, which is hard to detect. Some unscrupulous dealers also introduce green dye into the polymer, which may enhance the stone's colour and clarity even more. Buyers should insist on full, written disclosure, backed up by an expert laboratory analysis, before buying an emerald. Richard Wise, *Secrets of the Gem Trade*.

10. http://www.newadvent.org/cathen/12400b.htm. Catholic Encyclopaedia.

11. Pliny, *Natural History*, Book 37, chapter 16. Some scholars have suggested that he might have been referring to aquamarine instead, as emerald is usually too dark to see through.

12. Pliny, *Natural History*, Book 37, chapter 17.

13. Personal research, journey to Bamiyan, April 2000.

14. The word 'smaragdus' comes from the Greek generic word for 'green stones'. The Persian equivalent is *zabarjad* and there is speculation about whether this word comes from the emerald mine of Zubara or the peridot island of Zabargad. Probably they all come from the same root.

15. *Geography XVII I:45* cited in *Encyclopaedia of the Archaeology of Ancient Egypt*, ed. Kathryn A. Bard, p. 732.

16. Charles F. Horne, *The Sacred Books and Early Literature of the East*, vol. II: Egypt, pp. 62–78.

17. Cited in the Inscription of Harurre, James Henry Breasted, *Ancient Records of Egypt*, Part One, p. 736.

18. The Ababdeh called themselves after the prophet Abbad, who was praying one day in the desert when a man started shooting at him. He would not break his prayers, even to avoid the arrows. He survived the wounds and from then on was said to be blessed.

19. The original message, inscribed on the rock, was: 'Ingʳ JL Leonidas a EXPLᶜ CES MINES DEPUIS LE 22 Novᵇʳᵉ 1846 JUSQ'AU 18 JAN 1846' [*sic*].

20. Egyptian Museum, Cairo.

21. John Healey (ed.), *Pliny the Elder, A Natural History*, p. 136.

22. Lampridius, *Maximini Fil. Vita*, cited in C. W. King, *The Natural History, Ancient and Modern, of Precious Stones and Gems*, p. 404.

23. The emerald mines of Austria lie in the valley between the Nasenkogl (2462m) and Graukogl (2834m) mountains, near Salzburg. From them come two emeralds famously used in 1806 by Abbé Hauy to describe their crystal nature; as well as the medieval St Louis emerald in the Holy Crown of France.

24. Kristin Leutwyler, 'Tracking the Emerald Trade', in *Scientific American*, 13 January 2000.

25. Frédéric Cailliaud, *Travels in the Oasis of Thebes and in the Deserts*, p. 50.

26. The Italian tricolor flag was introduced in 1796; some suggest that it is

the French tricolor with green replacing blue because it was Napoleon's favourite colour.

27. Information from Fort Lauderdale Museum of Art.
28. Colin Beavan, *Fingerprints*, p. 27.
29. Frédéric Cailliaud, *Travels in the Oasis of Thebes and in the Deserts*, p. 31.
30. Clare Phillips, *Jewelry: From Antiquity to the Present*, pp. 33–4.
31. Ibid., p. 38.
32. Steven Sidebotham and Ginger Pinholster, 'Research in Egypt shows ancient trade customs', *UpDate*, University of Delaware, vol. 16, no. 10, 7 November 1996.
33. The chemical formula for beryl is $Be_3Al_2[Si_6O_{18}]$.
34. On average there are 2.8g of beryllium per tonne of crystal rock. Most comes from granitic pegmatites. John Sinkankas, *Beryl*, p. 171.
35. Cass Canfield, *Outrageous Fortunes*, p. 89.
36. http://www.research.amnh.org/earthplan/collects/mins.html, American Natural History Museum website.
37. Steven E. Sidebotham, 'Preliminary Report on archaeological fieldwork at Sikait and environs', 2002–3, p. 14.
38. Steven Sidebotham, private conversation, October 2004.
39. 'lateri uestis adusta fuit, et solitum digito beryllon adederat ignis', from 'Cynthia Restored', in Propertius, *Elegies: Book 1* (ed. W. A. Camps), p. 12.
40. Edwin Streeter, *Precious Stones and Gems*, 1892, p. 60.
41. *The Book of the Dead*, cited in Clare Phillips, *Jewelry: From Antiquity to the Present*, p. 12.
42. Information from the Fitzwilliam Museum, Cambridge.
43. Henry Kamen, *Spain's Road to Empire*.
44. Benjamin Zucker, *Gems and Jewels*, p. 53.
45. Ibid., p. 54.
46. Peter Rainier, *Green Fire*, p. 19.
47. Chivor emeralds were deposited 65 million years ago; Muzo is more recent at around 35 million years. Source: Joe Tenhagen, presentation at Tucson Gems Fair, February 2004.

48. Thomas Nicols, *A Lapidary*, p. 30.
49. http://www.melfisher.org/melstory.htm.
50. Joachim Menzhausen, *The Green Vault*, p. 37.
51. Treasury of the Iranian National Jewels, catalogue, p. 4.
52. http://www.cbi.ir/legislation/PDF/BankingLawE.pdf, Article 8, Iran's central banking legislation.
53. Peter Keller, *Gemstones and their Origins*, p. 45.
54. Peter Rainier, *Green Fire*, pp. 32–3.
55. This is the price in 2005 for a created emerald smaller than five carats. Tom Chatham, personal correspondence, July 2005.

Sapphire

1. Martha Hale Shackford (ed.), *Legends and Satires from Medieval Literature*.
2. Arthur Conan Doyle, 'The Adventure of the Blue Carbuncle', (1887).
3. Richard Hughes, *Ruby & Sapphire*, p. 390. Also 2 Chronicles 9:1 and 9:10.
4. Antichthones could also mean the people who lived on the opposite of earth, i.e. heaven.
5. Pliny, *Natural History*, Book 6, chapter 22. It was a place, he wrote, where people lived a hundred years and where the elected king was always an old man, of gentle disposition and without children, so the position never became corrupt or hereditary.
6. The first European ever recorded as visiting Sri Lanka was a freed slave shipwrecked there during Roman times, although the stories that he brought back were scarcely accurate and further contributed to the island entering into the realms of myth. Ibid.
7. Marco Polo and Rustichello of Pisa, *The Travels of Marco Polo*, chapter 14.
8. Ibid., chapter 24.
9. Richard Hughes, *Ruby & Sapphire*, p. 392.
10. The Mandarin word for ruby is *hung pao shi* which translates as 'red treasured stone'.

11. Horace Walpole is said to have coined the word serendipity in a letter in 1754 to Horace Mann, an envoy to King George II. He was describing his delight at unravelling the mysteries of a sixteenth-century portrait of a beauty called Bianca Capello, and of learning quite by chance of how the coronet in the painting probably signified a connection with the Medicis.

12. Anon., *Tales from the Thousand and One Nights*, p. 152.

13. Serendib's capital, as Sinbad later narrates, 'stands at the end of a fine valley, in the middle of the island, encompassed by high mountains . . . Rubies and several sorts of minerals abound.' George Fyler Townsend, *The Arabian Nights Entertainments*, p. 381.

14. Control of Ceylon was transferred, formally, in 1802 as a clause in the Treaty of Amiens, marking a victory of the British against Napoleon and his Batavian puppet state set up in the Netherlands. The British had successfully sent expeditionary forces in 1795, taking over the southern part of the island.

15. India Library Collection, British Library.

16. George Frederick Kunz, *Rings for the Finger*, p. 9.

17. John Pybus, Diary and Reports from a Secret Expedition to Ceylon, p. 343. In the 1330s the Muslim traveller Ibn Battutah had been impressed to see, when he went to visit the Sultan Ayri Shakarwati in Kandy, that the sultan's white elephant wore six sapphires as big as hen's eggs on its head. Moreover, the king owned a ruby dish 'as large as a man's hand' in which he kept oil of aloes-wood. 'When I showed my astonishment, he said, "We have things larger than that".' Tim Mackintosh-Smith (ed.), *The Travels of Ibn Battutah*, p. 246.

18. Information from both C. W. King, *The Natural History, Ancient and Modern, of Precious Stones and Gems*, pp. 399ff and Edward Francis Twining, *A History of the Crown Jewels of Europe*, p. 583. The crown was found by accident in 1858 by some labourers digging a cemetery near Toledo. It is currently held at the Archaeological Museum in Madrid.

19. Buckingham Palace Press Release (royal.gov.org).

20. The notion of 'sapphires' being holy stones predates even the naming

of the stones we know as sapphires. In Ancient Mediterranean history the stone called *sapphirus* was among the most sacred gems: it was said to be what the Ten Commandments had been carved on, and also, by the Greeks, to have been carved into 365 steps leading to a temple in India dedicated to Dionysus. However this *sapphirus* was probably lapis lazuli from Afghanistan and it was only much later that the name was given, exclusively, to the stones we call sapphire today. C. W. King, *The Natural History, Ancient and Modern, of Precious Stones and Gems*, p. 293.

21. Personal conversation, Rowan Williams, 4 May 2005.

22. The best specimen has been cut as the 9.7 carat 'Saltire Sapphire', and can be seen at the Hunterian Museum in Glasgow.

23. Richard Hughes, *Ruby & Sapphire*, p. 351 for Chinese sapphires and p. 455 for Yogo Gulch.

24. The 1932 Sapphire Act of Jammu and Kashmir states that 'No one shall have, keep or retain in his possession or custody any sapphire or ruby within the State territory ... or buy or sell or be otherwise a party to the transfer of any sapphire or ruby ... or transport it or dig, cut or dress it.'

25. Richard Wise, *Secrets of the Gem Trade*, p. 220.

26. Robert Block and Daniel Pearl, 'Much-smuggled gem aids al-Qa'eda', in *The Wall Street Journal*, 16 November 2001. According to this article, some of the tanzanite on sale today has been used by al-Qa'eda as a means of laundering money.

27. Frank B. Wade, *A Text-Book of Precious Stones for Jewelers and the Gem-loving Public*. The seventeenth-century scientist Robert Boyle wrote of bi-coloured sapphires as marvels, and recounted how: 'if my memory do not much deceive me, I saw in a great and curious Prince's Cabinet, among other rarities, a Ring in which was set a Stone of a moderate bigness, whereof only one half, or thereabouts, was well tincted, the other being colourless.' Robert Boyle, *An Essay about the Origine & Virtues of Gems*, pp. 36–7.

28. Richard Hughes, *Ruby & Sapphire*, pp. 487–90.

29. In 1823 English gem-hunter John Mawe described oriental amethysts

as appearing 'to unite the blue of the sapphire with the red of the ruby, so nicely blended as to produce the most perfect violet colour.' John Mawe, *A Treatise on Diamonds and Precious Stones*, p. 92.

30. http://www.agta.org/consumer/gtclab/treatedsapps04.htm. Report by John Emmett and Troy Douthit.

31. P. W. Marcus, *The Story of the Star Stones*, pp. 1–2.

32. Information from Natural History Museum, New York.

33. Richard Hughes, *Ruby & Sapphire*, p. 104.

34. Ibid., pp. 487–9.

35. If you get heat treatment wrong, the stone may disintegrate. An eleventh-century Indian text by Bhojarajah warned, 'Nobody should heat gem stones for testing purposes or for enhancing their qualities because if the right temperature is not known then a gem becomes polluted and the owner, the examiner and the person who sent the stone for testing all become losers.' Ibid., p. 104.

36. The jewels in watch mechanisms today are not valuable. Since around 1905 watch-bearings have been made of synthetic stones, meaning that all the rubies, sapphires or diamonds in the bearings of a watch today cost less than a pound.

37. Marcel Tolkowsky, *Diamond Design: A study of the reflection and refraction of light in a diamond*, Preface.

38. 'Finding the parent rock is interesting to the scientist, but very important economically to the gem industry.' One geologist in 1929 believed that the gem minerals came from the crystalline rocks of the Highland series; in 1972 another argued the gems could come from the gneiss in the south-west. As recently as 1945 geologists were arguing that the Sri Lankan gems including beryl, moonstone, tourmaline and topaz came from pegmatites, but this theory has been discounted. Peter Keller, *Gemstones and their Origins*, p. 9.

39. William Skeen, *Adam's Peak*, pp. 281ff.

40. Ezekiel 28:13–14.

Ruby

1. Edwin Streeter, *Precious Stones and Gems*, 1884, p. 159.

2. Ibid., 1892.

3. The first British visitor to Mogok was, according to legend, a runaway sailor in the employ of King Phagyidoa in 1830. He never returned. *The Times*, 16 February 1889. An Italian missionary called Father Giuseppe d'Amato went there in 1833, followed by a party of French investors in 1881.

4. Exchange rate taken from *The Times*, 23 May 1888, p. 3.

5. Information about Edwin Streeter is taken from: Edwin Streeter, *Precious Stones and Gems*, 1892 and 1898; Patrick Streeter, *Streeter of Bond Street*, pp. 122ff, and Richard Hughes, *Ruby & Sapphire*, pp. 315ff.

6. 'To come to business, Good and I took the diamonds to Streeter's to be valued, as we arranged, and really I am afraid to tell you what they put them at, it seems so enormous. They say that of course it is more or less guesswork, as such stones have never to their knowledge been put on the market in anything like such quantities. It appears that (with the exception of one or two of the largest) they are of the finest water, and equal in every way to the best Brazilian stones. I asked them if they would buy them, but they said that it was beyond their power to do so, and recommended us to sell by degrees, over a period of years indeed, for fear lest we should flood the market. They offer, however, a hundred and eighty thousand for a very small portion of them.' A letter to Allan Quatermain from Henry Curtis, Henry Rider Haggard, *King Solomon's Mines*, p. 296.

7. Michael Edwardes, *Ralph Fitch*, p. 118.

8. Ava, capital of Burma for four hundred years, has now been renamed Inwa. It lies a few kilometres south of Mandalay and is so ruined that it has almost vanished. Where the most fabulous processions of bejewelled elephants and soldiers once paraded through the streets, a few squeaking traps pulled by scraggy ponies now carry tourists to the few buildings that are still recognisable. Everything else was

carried, brick by brick, to the new cities of Amarapura (now also a ruin) and later to Mandalay.

9. Michael Edwardes, *Ralph Fitch*, p. 172.

10. John Crawfurd, *Journal of an Embassy from the Governor General of India to the Court of Ava*, p. 230.

11. Lord Randolph Churchill, The Dufferin Papers, cited Patrick Streeter, *Streeter of Bond Street*, p. 122.

12. Conversion rate from the accounts of Burma Ruby Mines Ltd, Oriental and India Office Library.

13. The first local accounts of Burmese rubies are from the Pyu tribes who came in from Mongolia two thousand years ago. They left stone inscriptions referring to their deep love of Upper Burma's gemstones. S. K. Samuels, *Burma Ruby*, p. 42.

14. Ibid., p. 27.

15. Comment by J. Annan Bryce after Gordon's speech to the Royal Geographical Society, 27 February 1888. Robert Gordon, *On the Ruby Mines near Mogok*, p. 274.

16. Adapted from S. K. Samuels, *Burma Ruby*, pp. 43ff; and Richard Hughes, *Ruby & Sapphire*, p. 313.

17. George Streeter, *Murray's Magazine*, May 1887, pp. 679–88.

18. Edwin Streeter, *Precious Stones and Gems*, 1898, p. 173.

19. The Burma Ruby Mines Ltd., report to shareholders by Lepel Griffin, 1905.

20. Thirkell White Collection, Oriental and India Office library, p.4.

21. Streeter was furious about *The Times* campaign: 'If any undue influence was at work during the negotiations, as insinuated by the Press, *it was most assuredly not on our side* ... And the idea, as suggested in certain papers, of our bribing some of the Indian officials was *absolutely unfounded*. I can say that in not one instance did I give or offer a bribe during the whole time.' Edwin Streeter, *Precious Stones and Gems*, 1898, p. 175.

22. Streeter, his son George, Mr Charles Bill of Stafford, Mr George Baird of Berkeley Square and Mr Reginald Beech of Eaton Square signed the Burma Ruby Mines Ltd. licence on a piece of calf vellum, now

held in the British Library. They agreed to pay 400,000 rupees (£26,666) plus one-sixth of net profit.

23. *Engineering and Mining Journal*, New York, 16 March 1889. This section on the stock sale is from Richard Hughes, *Ruby & Sapphire*, p. 317, and from the Burma Ruby Mine Ltd. accounts held in the British Library.

24. Patrick Streeter, *Streeter of Bond Street*, pp. 126–7.

25. With thanks to Richard Hughes, now at AGTA, for his advice and support.

26. The Burmese government likes new names: in 1989 – the year the charismatic opposition leader Aung San Suu Kyi was placed under house arrest – the country was renamed Myanmar and its capital Rangoon was renamed Yangon. Many democrats oppose the change, and I have followed their example.

27. Thailand does have rubies, but many are heavily treated and few have the quality of Burmese stones.

28. S. K. Samuels, *Burma Ruby*, p. 127.

29. U Tin Hlaing's reports in *Australian Gemmologist*, vol. 17, p. 12; vol. 18, p. 5.

30. In the UN's *Human Poverty Index*, 2004, Burma was ranked 132 of 177 countries.

31. Mogok was officially part of the Shan state until the fifteenth century when it was taken over by the Burmese kings so that they could control the mine. It keeps many cultural links with the Shan.

32. S. K. Samuels, *Burma Ruby*, p. 22.

33. George Streeter, 'Burma's Ruby Mines', *Murray's Magazine*, vol. 1, no. 5, June 1887. pp. 669–78.

34. Adrian Levy and Catherine Scott-Clark, *The Stone of Heaven*, p. 97.

35. S. K. Samuels, *Burma Ruby*. This book has been an important source for this chapter.

36. Benjamin Zucker, *Gems and Jewels*, p. 14.

37. When coloured crystals come into contact with sunlight, their electrons become excited, and jump from one orbit to the next. This is what, in many gemstones, causes the sensation of colour. When the

light disappears or diminishes, the electrons are returned to a lower energy state. And when this happens extremely quickly, the result is fluorescence. In the past, some 20 per cent of rubies had this characteristic; however, it is rarely seen in newly-mined gems in Burma. It is only present in the most deeply-coloured red stones, the result of large amounts of chromium in the crystals. It is rarely ever seen in pinkish- and purplish-coloured rubies. Therefore a red stone with fluorescence commands a premium. S. K. Samuels, *Burma Ruby*, pp. 147ff. and private correspondence, S. K. Samuels, July, 2005.

38. Ludovico Varthema, *Itinerary of Ludovico di Varthema of Bologna from 1502–1508*.

39. S. K. Samuels, *Burma Ruby*, p. 147 and pp. 28–30. The pagoda is near Mamyo, in north-east Burma.

40. Richard Hughes, *Ruby & Sapphire*, pp. 487ff.

41. Not everything called a ruby is actually a ruby. 'Balas ruby' is another word for spinel; 'Bohemian', 'Colorado,' or 'Cape' rubies are actually pyrope garnets; 'Adelaide' rubies are almandine garnets; 'Brazilian' or 'Siberian' rubies are pink tourmalines.

42. This is not a perfect way to tell the difference between these two red gemstones. Many rubies look like spinel when the rhombohedral faces are well developed. Private correspondence, Richard Hughes.

43. According to Amy Chua, *World on Fire*, a Chinese company called Lo Hsing-han jointly owns a hundred gem mines in Burma producing more than two tonnes of rough rubies a year. The industry is dominated by Burmese Chinese, 'from the financiers to the concession operators to the owners of scores of new jewelry shops that sprang up all over Mandalay and Rangoon. Needless to say, SLORC officials are also handsomely paid off at every level.'

44. This is why you can walk across hot coals at 500 degrees centigrade, but would not try it on a piece of more thermally conductive metal at the same temperature. Private correspondence, Richard Hughes.

45. *Arabian Society in the Middle Ages*, ed. Stanley Lane-Poole, London, 1883, p. 106.

46. A 1368 royal headdress found in a burial tomb includes dragons

symbolising the emperor and phoenixes for the empress, made of gold thread, pearls and more than a hundred rubies and sapphires.

47. One of the most corrupt Chinese officials was He Shen. For years he collected bribes without being punished. Then, in 1799, he was found to be in possession of a collection of Burmese rubies better than any the emperor owned. He received a royal decree ordering him to hang himself.

48. Frank Atlay and Arthur H. Morgan. *Burma Ruby Mines Ltd*: note for shareholders 1905, in the British Library collection.

49. J. Coggin Brown, 1927. Gem mining in the Mogok Stone Tract (confidential report), Richard Hughes, *Ruby & Sapphire*, p. 319.

Diamond

1. *Night After Night*, directed by Archie Mayo, 1932

2. Geoffrey Munn, 'Fifty percent is bought by men', *The Art Newspaper*, 1 January 2000.

3. *The Times*, 3 December 2002, T2, p. 4.

4. In 1929 the Vickers laboratory in the UK designed a way to determine hardness using a 'diamond indenter', which works by pressing a diamond point into an object and then measuring how big the resulting mark is. Ten years later a team from National Bureau of Standards in the US designed the 'Knoop' scale (named after the team-leader, F. Knoop), which used a lighter indentation to allow more brittle materials including glass to be tested.

5. Clubs are for soldiers, spades for peasants and courtly hearts are reserved for aristocrats.

6. Bill Bryson, *A Short History of Nearly Everything*, p. 268.

7. Jean-Baptiste Tavernier, *Travels in India*, p. 58.

8. Until the eighteenth century the only diamond mines were in India and Borneo. The latter produced little.

9. William Harrison Moreland (ed.), *Relations of Golconda in the Early Seventeenth Century*, p. 38.

10. Benjamin Zucker, *Gems and Jewels*, pp. 73–4.

11. Richard Wise, *Secrets of the Gem Trade*, p. 40. Also presentation by Richard Wise at Tucson Gem Fair in February 2003.

12. Ibid., p. 41.

13. Jean-Baptiste Tavernier, *Travels in India*, p. 58.

14. *Philosophical Transactions*, 27 April 1674.

15. In 1380 Amadeus, son of Amadeus VI of Savoy, attended the coronation of Charles VI in Reims. His procession made a substantial detour to Paris to stock up on jewellery so that the Savoyards would appear to come from a sophisticated place and not a backwater. Margaret Wade Labarge, *Medieval Travellers: the Rich and the Restless*, p. 73.

16. Diana Scarisbrick, *Jewellery*, p. 7.

17. Susanne Steinem Patch, *Blue Mystery: The Story of the Hope Diamond*, p. 65.

18. German Bapst, *Histoire des Joyaux de la Couronne de France*.

19. Susanne Steinem Patch, *Blue Mystery*, p. 9.

20. Edwin Streeter believed a 13.5-carat blue diamond owned by the Duke of Brunswick was the missing section, although this theory has been cast into doubt by contemporary gemmologists. In 2005 Smithsonian curator Jeffrey Post successfully commissioned cubic zirconium cut in the shape of the French blue diamond to be recut in the shape of the Hope. *Smithsonian Weekly Newsletter*, vol. 3, no. 2, 25 February 2005.

21. Susanne Steinem Patch, *Blue Mystery*, p. 43.

22. Marian Fowler, *Hope*, p. 282. Much of the information in this section on the Hope diamond is sourced from Fowler and Steinem Patch.

23. Ibid., p. 282.

24. When Harry Winston was thirteen he spotted a green stone in a '25 Cent – Take Your Pick' stall and later discovered it was an emerald worth $800. 'Think big' was his motto, and in his time he bought and sold many of the biggest gemstones in the world; he even got to name some of them. He once sold a 62-carat flawless diamond called 'The Winston' to the King of Saudi Arabia, and when he bought it back two years later it was still in its original wrapping.

25. Marian Fowler, *Hope*, p. 316.

26. Gilles Chazal, *The Art of Cartier*, p. 36.

27. Platinum was not new: the Spaniards had found it in the New World and had called it 'little silver' or *platina*, but had thought it almost valueless. It was only in the nineteenth century that people developed efficient ways of extracting and casting it.

28. Marian Fowler, *Hope*, pp. 235–6.

29. Susanne Steinem Patch, *Blue Mystery*, pp. 77–83.

30. Obituary for Evalyn Walsh McLean, *Time*, 5 May 1947.

31. Louis Dutens, *Des pierres précieuses et des pierres fines*.

32. Eric Bruton, *Legendary Gems*, pp. 201–2.

33. The legend of the *syamantaka* comes from the *Bhagavata Mahapurana*. It is retold in Pierre Grimal (ed.), *The Larousse Encyclopaedia of World Mythology*, Hamlyn, 1965, p. 247.

34. Robert Beer, *The Encyclopedia of Tibetan Symbols and Motifs*, p. 162.

35. The oldest dated printed book in the world is an eighth-century copy of the *Diamond Cutter Sutra* translated into Chinese and owned by the British Library. It uses the diamond both as a symbol of emptiness and of the most perfect blade we can find on earth to help us cut through illusion. Meanwhile, Tibetan Buddhism associates the diamond with the *vajra*, or lord of stones, and sees it as the hardest, clearest, most brilliant of stones, symbolising the indestructible, indivisible, infallible and unchangeable nature of the enlightened mind. Ibid., p. 210.

36. Sometimes sights are also held in Johannesburg, South Africa, with sight holders often flying between Johannesburg and London midweek.

37. Information from the Diamond Trading Company, Dan White, personal correspondence, July 2005. Sight holders usually attend with several staff to examine the rough diamonds and to meet with staff from the Diamond Trading Company.

38. The sight holders' boxes are thirty centimetres long, fifteen centimetres wide and six centimetres deep.

39. Edward Jay Epstein, *The Diamond Invention*, chapter 6.

40. Matthew Hart, *Diamond*, p. 133.

41. Personal correspondence, DTC, July 2005.

42. De Beers still controls some two-thirds of the market. Matthew Hart, *Diamond*, pp. 136–7.

43. The Kimberley was one of five mines in the area, and it was the most abundant. Bultfontein was low quality and although Dutoitspan produced some of the most beautiful stones, it had such a poor return that it was initially used as a latrine. Robert Vicat Turrell, *Capital and Labour on the Kimberley Diamond Fields 1871 to 1890*, p. 6. The two other mines were Wesselton and the De Beers mine, although today neither the De Beers nor the Kimberley are being worked.

44. R. W. Leyland, *A Holiday in South Africa*, p. 92.

45. Cecil Rhodes obituary, *The Times of London*, 27 March 1902.

46. Robert Vicat Turrell, *Capital and Labour on the Kimberley Diamond Fields*, p. 55.

47. Cape Parliamentary Papers Commission on Convicts and Gaols, II, xliii.

48. Robert Vicat Turrell, *Capital and Labour on the Kimberley Diamond Fields*, pp. 155ff. This book was the main reference for the section on the early human rights record of South African diamond mines.

49. Today things have improved, and in 2005 the Kimberley mines were awarded the Mines Health and Safety Council 'Millionaire Award' for achieving three million fatality-free shifts. *Creamer Media's Mining Weekly*, 20 July 2005.

50. De Beers, by then called De Beers Consolidated Mines Ltd, was granted an official listing on the Johannesburg Stock Exchange in August 1893.

51. The price collapse of diamonds in 1877 was connected to Russia's decision to declare war on Turkey, which, until then, had been one of the major markets for the new South African stones.

52. Edward Jay Epstein, *The Diamond Invention*, chapter 7.

53. Matthew Hart, *Diamond*, p. 45.

54. Georges Aubert, *La Crise des Diamants et la De Beers*, pp. 1ff.

55. Edward Jay Epstein, *The Diamond Invention*, chapter 8.

56. Information from the Tower of London.

57. Hedley Chilvers, *The Story of De Beers with a Foreword by Sir Ernest Oppenheimer*, p. 233.

58. Mark Twain, *Following the Equator*, chapter 34 (Pudd'nhead Wilson's New Calendar).

59. In 1971 the British consumer magazine *Which?* bought a 1.4-carat diamond from a reputable London dealer for £2595. When it tried to sell it a week later, the maximum offer was £1000. Some years later the Dutch Consumer Association tried to test the price appreciation of diamonds by buying a flawless one-carat diamond in Amsterdam, holding it for eight months, then offering it for sale. Nineteen of the twenty leading Amsterdam dealers they approached refused to buy it, and the twentieth offered only a fraction of the purchase price. Edward Jay Epstein, 'Have you Ever Tried to Sell a Diamond?' in *Atlantic*, February 1982.

60. Letter written 30 July 1477 from Dr Wilhelm Moroltinger in Ghent to Archduke Maximilian. George Frederick Kunz, *Rings for the Finger*, p. 233.

61. One of Charles the Bold's three stones went to the Pope, one to Louis XI, whom he detested, and one he kept for himself.

62. Andrew Lang, *Portraits and Jewels of Mary Stuart*, p. 34.

63. David Carvalho, *Forty Centuries of Ink*, chapter 25.

64. George Frederick Kunz, *Rings for the Finger*, p. 171.

65. James B. Twitchell, *Twenty Ads that Shook the World*, p. 98. This section is indebted to Twitchell's research.

66. Edward Jay Epstein, 'Have You Ever Tried to Sell a Diamond?' in *Atlantic*, February 1982.

67. Fred Ward, *Diamonds*, p. 25.

68. Matthew Hart, *Diamond*, p. 136.

69. Emily Post, *Etiquette in Society, in Business, in Politics and at Home*. See Appendix for the two anniversary lists

70. Edwin Streeter, *Precious Stones and Gems*, 1884, pp. 70ff.

71. Ibid.

72. Pliny, *Natural History*, Book 37, chapter 15.

73. The Golden Jubilee was given to the King of Thailand in 1997 for his fiftieth anniversary, meaning that the biggest cut diamond in the world is owned by a man.

74. In 2002 all the Bushmen in the Central Kalahari Game Reserve in Botswana were evicted from the area that had been given them in 1961. Although Botswana's president, Festus Mogae, said in November 2002 that 'there is neither any actual mining nor any plan for future mining inside the reserve', the human rights group Survival International has obtained two confidential maps of the reserve that appear to contradict this. The first one, from March 2001, shows almost no diamond concessions; the second, dated November 2002, has almost the whole area carved out. Most concessions were allocated to three companies: Australian-based BHP Billiton World Exploration, Canadian-based Motapa Diamonds, and De Beers Prospecting Botswana Ltd. Information from Survival International, www.survival-international.org.

75. Greg Campbell, *Blood Diamonds*, p. xiii.

76. Ibid., p.xxii.

77. Global Witness, 'For a Few Dollars More, How Al Qa'eda Moved into the Diamond Trade', April 2003, www.globalwitness.org.

78. Interview for www.cryfreetown.org.

79. Michael Roach, *The Diamond Cutter*, p. 72.

80. *Amnesty Now*, USA, Fall 2002. De Beers issued a formal statement on 6 November 2001, stating that: it condemns the activities of terrorists; reasserting the fact that it does not buy diamonds on the open market, has not operated in Sierra Leone since 1985, and has been working closely (through the World Diamond Council) with the UN and national governments for more than three years to bring an end to the 'small but significant trade in diamonds – less than three percent of world production – that fund conflict' . . . and calls upon the international community to use the full force of law to bring these criminals to justice.

81. The survey was carried out by the Jewelry Consumer Opinion Council, interviewed 3342 diamond consumers, of whom 83 per cent were

female. *Jewelers' Circular Keystone*, 14 October 2004. Nearly 70 per cent of respondents were 'extremely unfamiliar' with the term 'conflict diamonds', and 50 per cent said that when purchasing a diamond it was 'extremely unlikely' that they would ask if it was conflict-free. About 17 per cent had purchased diamonds or diamond jewellery in the past six months; with nearly 93 per cent of them reporting that the jeweller had not discussed conflict diamonds.

82. Tracy Hall, in *The Diamond Makers*, BBC *Horizon*, 18 August 2002.

83. Robert Hazen, *The Diamond Makers*, p. 147.

84. So far, most synthetic diamonds have been yellows, blues or reds. Colourless diamonds might be among the most common in nature, but ironically they have been the hardest to make in a laboratory.

85. The founders of LifeGem are Dean and Rusty VandenBiesen and Greg and Mark Herro.

86. Private conversation, Tucson, Arizona, February 2004. Because of this, and because of the LifeGem patent, these diamonds are expensive, perhaps four times more than equivalent natural-treated or synthetic diamonds would be. The smallest quarter-carat diamonds cost £2250 while one-carat diamonds cost £11,950.

87. Information from Synthetic Gemstones Conference, Tucson, Arizona, February 2004.

Postscript

1. Thanks to Dr Elizabeth James at the University of Sussex for her help with the depiction of the mosaic maker.

Index

Fitch, Ralph 290, 291, 293
Fitzgerald, Scott 192
Fitzwilliam Museum, Cambridge 83
Flagman Vodka 37
fossils 164
Foul Bay 172
Fouquet, Nicholas 342
Fowler, Marian 344
France 347
Franco-Prussian War 347
Frederick I, King 45
Frederick III, Elector 44, 45
Frederick William I, King 44, 45

gambling 189–91
Garcilaso the Inca 234
Garden of Eden 285–86
garnets 189, 400, 458 n. 41
Gautier, Théophile 46
Gdansk 22, 23, 47, 49, 50, 51
Gemmell, William 397
gems:
　alphabet of 389
　anniversary 388–89
　birthstones 388
　colours 270–71
　curses 345
　doublets 444 n. 27
　facets 400
　font sizes and 392
　geodes 200
　hardness 7
　heat treatment 270–72
　light and 278
　names and 126, 390
　'organic' 7
　placenames and 390
　planetary discovery 173
　supernatural powers 189
　symbolism of 201–2, 221, 291
　synthetic 242–43
　triplets 444 n. 27
　watches 454 n. 36

General Electric 380
geodes 200, 400
geomancy 61–62
Gerety, Frances 363, 365
Germany 15, 20, 62, 357–58
Gandhi, Indira 43
Gierłowska, Gabriela 28
Gilbert, William 13, 49
Gillanders, Arbuthnot & Co. 294, 300
Gilson, Pierre 242
gimmal rings 362
glass:
　beads 220–21
　as fake jewels 325–26
　hardness 7, 193
global warming 13
Globe 183, 184, 195
Golconda 336, 338, 341, 351
Goldberg, Willie 381–82
Golden Jubilee diamond 370, 392
Gondwanaland 376
Gonzaga, Maria 44
Goodyear 70
Gordon, Robert 298–300, 306, 310, 315, 321
Goths 152: 434 n. 45
Gough's Cave 9
grains 401
Granada, New Kingdom of 240
graphite 378, 380
Great Britain:
　coronation ring 257
　Crown Jewels 258
　gems found in 260, 390
　Imperial State Crown 258
　jet 56 *see also under* Whitby
　opals 144
　pearls 86–90
　precious stone found in 260, 390
　royal sceptre 359
　Yorkshire 57
　see also under Burma